Beginning GIMP

From Novice to Professional, Second Edition

Akkana Peck

Apress®

Beginning GIMP: From Novice to Professional, Second Edition

Copyright © 2008 by Akkana Peck

ISBN-13 (pbk): 978-1-4302-1070-2

ISBN-13 (electronic): 978-1-4302-1069-6

Printed and bound in China 9 8 7 6 5 4 3 2 1

Lead Editor: Matt Wade
Technical Reviewer: Guillermo S. Romero
Editorial Board: Clay Andres, Steve Anglin, Ewan Buckingham, Tony Campbell, Gary Cornell, Jonathan Gennick, Matthew Moodie, Joseph Ottinger, Jeffrey Pepper, Frank Pohlmann, Ben Renow-Clarke, Dominic Shakeshaft, Matt Wade, Tom Welsh
Project Manager: Beth Christmas
Copy Editor: Liz Welch
Associate Production Director: Kari Brooks-Copony
Production Editor: Jill Ellis
Compositor: Dina Quan
Proofreaders: April Eddy and Kim Burton
Indexer: Broccoli Information Management
Artist: April Milne
Cover Designer: Kurt Krames
Manufacturing Director: Tom Debolski

Distributed to the book trade worldwide by Springer-Verlag New York, Inc., 233 Spring Street, 6th Floor, New York, NY 10013. Phone 1-800-SPRINGER, fax 201-348-4505, e-mail orders-ny@springer-sbm.com, or visit http://www.springeronline.com.

For information on translations, please contact Apress directly at 2855 Telegraph Avenue, Suite 600, Berkeley, CA 94705. Phone 510-549-5930, fax 510-549-5939, e-mail info@apress.com, or visit http://www.apress.com.

Apress and friends of ED books may be purchased in bulk for academic, corporate, or promotional use. eBook versions and licenses are also available for most titles. For more information, reference our Special Bulk Sales–eBook Licensing web page at http://www.apress.com/info/bulksales.

The source code for this book is available to readers at http://www.apress.com.

To Dave.

Contents at a Glance

Contents

About the Author

AKKANA PECK is a freelance software developer and writer who has been working with open source software for over 20 years, and using GIMP for nearly half that time. Starting with a high school summer job writing image processing and data visualization routines for a cell biology lab, she has worked for a diverse collection of companies, including Netscape, Silicon Graphics, Los Alamos National Lab, and City of Hope. She has written software ranging from GIMP plug-ins to HTML editing, photo viewing to email clients, as well as penning articles and how-tos on Linux, astronomy, and other topics for various publications and websites.

About a decade ago, her longstanding hobby of photography spawned an interest in digital imaging and creating photos for the web. Frustration with the existing Windows tools, combined with a switch to Linux as her primary platform, led to fiddling with the basics of GIMP. After a long period of resistance she was finally persuaded to go beyond basic photo cropping and resizing and try "that layer thing," and the rest is history.

Akkana is a long-time member of the GIMP community and an occasional contributor to GIMP's source code. She enjoys hiking, mountain biking, and astronomy, giving talks about all sorts of topics (especially GIMP), and filling up her hard drive with digital images that she can never bring herself to delete, mostly of scenes from local hiking trails and from travels in the desert southwest. She lives in San Jose, California, with her husband and a motley assortment of old computers.

About the Technical Reviewer

A native of Madrid, Spain, **GUILLERMO S. ROMERO**, while always technically oriented, became interested in art through building and painting scale kits as a child, and that has shaped his life ever since. He graduated from Universidad Politécnica de Madrid, with a degree in Telemática, a specialization of Ingenieria Técnica de Telecomunicaciones. While studying, he began to explore Linux, POV-Ray, GIMP, and Blender, mixing technology and art. This knowledge led to some freelance jobs in the form of articles for magazines and reviews for book publishers.

With a career mixing telecommunications jobs with others more focused in publishing and photography fields, he discovered that drawing with a pen can be learned, step by step, with the right people around providing guidance. His other hobbies are reading, playing in a black and white photography laboratory, walking, and swimming.

Acknowledgments

First of all, thanks to my husband, David North. Not only did he help enormously with formatting, proofreading, finding sample photos, and endless testing of GIMP quirks on multiple platforms, but he also put up with the neuroses of a stressed-out first-time author. And then he was willing to do it all again for a second edition!

Equally important is Guillermo Romero, the book's technical reviewer, without whom this book would not have been possible. He patiently waded through first drafts, flagged my silly errors, asked probing questions, and took the time to teach me a lot about digital art. I'm not an artist yet, but I'm learning.

Thanks to Pat Peck (hi, Mom!) and the members of Linuxchix who were willing to be guinea pigs for the online GIMP course that indirectly led to this book. And to two other Linuxchix: Carla Schroder, for all her encouragement, writing tips, and witty remarks; and Dana Sibera, for laughs, explanations of techniques, and an appreciation of what a real artist can do with (or to) a photo.

Thanks to all the GIMP developers for using their talents and spare time to create such a wonderful program, and for spending even more time explaining details of the program to folks who need help. Some of the most active: Sven Neumann, Michael Natterer, Bill Skaggs, Martin Nordholts, Øyvind Kolås, Kevin Cozens, João S. O. Bueno, Alexia Death, Michael Schumacher, Mukund Sivaraman, Ulf-D. Ehlert, Simon Budig, Tor Lillqvist, Manish Singh, Karine Delvare, David Odin, and Maurits Rijk.

Thanks to Lisa and Evan Avery, for letting me use the photo of their son Ethan; to Cathleen Wang Blythe and Polarbear; to Bill Condrashoff, Benita Asher, and Jackpot; and to Dave Nakamoto and Dragan Stanojević - Nevidljivi for helping out with samples of image stacking (which unfortunately didn't make it into the final version due to space considerations).

Last but not least, many thanks to the folks at Apress for helping me through every step of the process, and for putting up with all my tweaks and revisions. In particular, thanks to open source editor Matt Wade, project manager Beth Christmas, awesome copy editor Liz Welch, production editor Jill Ellis, and proofreader April Eddy.

Introduction

So you want to learn image editing!

Maybe you've been shooting lots of pictures with your digital camera and want to learn how to make them look great, or prepare them for the web.

Maybe you're interested in creating drawings or cartoons. Or you're already editing photos, but you want to do more… even learn some of the theory behind imaging.

In any case, you've been hearing about GIMP—the GNU Image Manipulation Program—and you're ready to learn how to use it and get the most out of it.

This book is ideal for anyone attempting image editing for the first time, but it goes deep enough to satisfy the intermediate GIMPster who knows the basics but needs more. Plus, it contains enough tricks and reference matter to gratify even power users. Anyone with an interest in digital art and a willingness to explore should find lots of useful tips and fun projects throughout the book.

This second edition includes several new projects and tips not in the first edition, and covers some of the new features that went into 2.4 at the last minute (as well as a preview of GIMP 2.6).

Structure of the Book

The first few chapters assume no knowledge at all of GIMP or of any other image-editing program. Later chapters will assume you've picked up these basics, and will build on them.

Chapter 1 introduces GIMP's various windows, menus, and interface conventions. GIMP has a somewhat different user interface from most other programs, so it helps to get an idea of how its windows and dialog boxes work together and how the menus are structured.

Beginning with Chapter 2, you'll dive into practical image-editing tasks. Chapters 2 through 6 each cover a different category of image operations—layers, drawing, selection, touching up—and each one describes a series of different and related techniques.

Chapter 7 takes you on a whirlwind tour of the special effects available in GIMP. Then you'll dive into more advanced topics in Chapters 8 through 10, which cover subjects such as color theory, layer mode effects, shading, perspective, image stacking, and panoramas.

Chapter 11 explores scripts and plug-ins: how they work, how to install existing ones, and how to take one and tweak it to do something slightly different. I hope that even people with no programming experience will at least take a look at the scripting sections—there's a lot you can do with GIMP scripts, even if you've never written a line of code before.

For the exercises throughout most of the book, you will want to have some digital photographs handy. If you don't already have a digital camera or a collection of scanned photos, the section "Additional Resources" in Chapter 12 offers a list of websites where you'll find all sorts of terrific photos you can use in your own projects. The rest of Chapter 12 covers a few topics that don't fit anywhere else in the book, plus web resources for finding more GIMP information.

If you don't already have GIMP installed on your computer, skip straight to Appendix A for an outline of how to install GIMP on the most common platforms it supports—Windows, Mac OS X, and Linux. Appendix B gives tips on installing on older versions of those operating systems. If you ever decide you want to build GIMP from source, Appendix C has tips on how to do just that. Finally, Appendix D gives a look at the upcoming GIMP 2.6.

A Note on GIMP Versions

This book was written based on GIMP 2.4. As it goes to press, the development version, 2.5, is coming along and there's no telling when it will be released as 2.6.

Therefore, I've tried to include enough 2.5 information, where it differs from 2.4, that the book will be useful with 2.6. Appendix D gives an overview of the differences. You can also use the book with an older 2.2 or even 2.0 GIMP version, though you'll miss some of the nice new features introduced with 2.4. When possible, I mention locations of menu items that have moved.

If you're using *Beginning GIMP* with GIMP 2.6, check the book's website, *http://gimpbook.com*, for notes on any features that may have changed after the book went to press.

Downloads and Feedback

When learning image editing, it's always helpful to have lots of examples you can use. Some of the images that appear in the book are available in GIMP's native XCF format on the Apress website, along with any scripts used to create them. You'll also find source code there for the scripts and plug-ins presented in Chapter 11, a collection of the images used in the book, and any (gasp!) errata. Just point your browser to *www.apress.com* and search for this book.

I also maintain a website for the book at *http://gimpbook.com*, with a separate errata page, the images used in the book, and an updated version of the links from Chapter 12.

Please email any feedback or suggestions to *akkana@gimpbook.com*.

I hope you enjoy your introduction to GIMP!

■ ■ ■

## CHAPTER 1

Getting to Know GIMP

Welcome to the GNU Image Manipulation Program—more commonly known as GIMP.

GIMP is the premiere open source image-editing program. It's powerful and fun to use...but it's also easy to get lost in when you're just starting out. This chapter will introduce you to the program, and offer some tips on how to get the most out of GIMP.

You'll become familiar with GIMP's interface—its most important windows, dialogs, and menus, plus some handy tricks and shortcuts. If you've already used GIMP a bit, a lot of the chapter may be review, but you may find some helpful tips you haven't seen before.

Along the way, I'll cover

- What is GIMP?

- A tour of important GIMP windows

- Menu overview

- Some GIMP settings you can customize (and why you might want to)

- A first GIMP project

What Is GIMP?

GIMP, sometimes called *the* GIMP, is the *GNU Image Manipulation Program*.

It's a computer program for creating and editing digital images. In particular, it's designed for editing digital photographs and typical web graphics. You can also use it to make some pretty amazing drawings.

GIMP is a complex program suitable for professional artwork, but it's also just plain fun—a place to play with pretty pictures and let your imagination run wild. As you read this book, please keep that in mind. Make a point of "fooling around" and having fun with your image-editing projects.

GIMP is also free open source software. It's written and maintained by volunteers and distributed without cost. In fact, you're encouraged to make copies of it to share with friends, and you can even contribute to it yourself.

GIMP arose out of a 1995 computer science class project by Spencer Kimball and Peter Mattis. Within a year, it had grown into a popular open source image editor, with users and contributors from around the world. It's been growing and improving ever since.

Today, GIMP is used by countless people worldwide. It runs on most Windows systems, Mac OS X, Linux, and most versions of UNIX, as well as a few more obscure systems. The program is free software in both senses of the word "free": you don't have to pay anything to use it, and GIMP's inner workings ("source code") are available for anyone to examine, contribute to, distribute, or learn from. The latest is always available from *http://www.gimp.org*.

GIMP stands as a shining example of the power of free, open source software. It's written and maintained by volunteers who keep in touch by means of internet relay chat (IRC) and mailing lists, despite time zone and language differences. GIMP users who want to get more involved can participate in the GIMP project's mailing lists, contribute bug fixes or new features, design new brushes or patterns, or write their own plug-ins and scripts to share with the world. Or they can just enter goofy photo contests to show what cool things can be done with GIMP!

A note about terminology: you'll often see GIMP referred to as *the* GIMP. "The GIMP" was the program's official name until the 2.4 release, when the name was officially changed to just "GIMP." You'll still see lots of references to "the GIMP" in tutorials and other articles (and even, sometimes, on the *gimp.org* website). In the second edition of *Beginning GIMP* I'll mostly avoid the "the" and call it just plain GIMP, but I hope you'll bear with me if I slip from time to time.

A Tour of the Most Important GIMP Windows

One of the first things you'll probably notice about GIMP is that it likes to use lots of windows. Instead of having one big window that contains the various images you're using, the GIMP model lets you control your toolbox, layer controls, and each image separately. You can choose which windows are visible at any given time.

The main windows you need to know about are the Toolbox with its Tool Options, image windows (one for each image you have open), and the Layers dialog.

The Toolbox

The Toolbox window (Figure 1-1) is GIMP's main window. It appears when you run GIMP without any images, and closing it exits the GIMP application. It has a menu bar where you can find GIMP functions that aren't tied to any particular image (though in GIMP 2.6, the Toolbox no longer has a menu and these functions will move to the image window menus—see Appendix D for more details). It also has a collection of tool buttons and a couple of helpful controls.

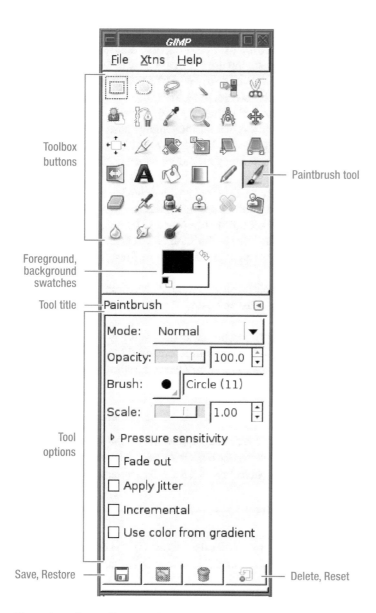

Figure 1-1. *The Toolbox window*

The tool buttons are the heart of the Toolbox window. GIMP has tools for selection (like Rectangular Select, the first tool in the Toolbox), tools for painting (like the Paintbrush, the tool that's active in Figure 1-1), and tools for changing images in a variety of ways. GIMP always has one active tool; if the active tool corresponds to one of the tool buttons, that button will appear "pressed," as with the Paintbrush tool in Figure 1-1.

You can resize the Toolbox to taste, and the tool buttons will adjust their positions. As GIMP comes out with new versions, the tool buttons sometimes change position, so it's best not to rely on a button being in any particular place. Each tool has a tooltip to help you remember its function, which you can see by hovering your mouse over a button and pausing for a second or two.

There are a couple of other ways to activate a GIMP tool besides clicking a Toolbox button. There's the Tools dialog, accessed from the Toolbox as *File* ➤ *Dialogs* ➤ *Tools* or from any image window as *Dialogs* ➤ *Tools*. It lists every tool GIMP has (not all of them are in the Toolbox). You can control which tools show up as buttons in the Toolbox by clicking the "eye" icon next to each tool in the Tools dialog, and you can change their order by dragging tools to a different place within the dialog.

You can also activate tools through the *Tools* top-level menu in every image window. Finally, most tools also have a keyboard shortcut associated with them; these shortcuts are listed in the image window's *Tools* menu.

Below the tool buttons, the Toolbox shows two color "swatches," initially black and white. These represent GIMP's current foreground and background colors, used in all sorts of operations. Clicking on either swatch brings up a color chooser. You'll use the color swatches a lot in Chapters 3 and 4.

Tip GIMP supports drag-and-drop in many places throughout the application. You can open images by dragging them from your desktop or file manager window to the GIMP Toolbox—just drop the image on top of the buttons. (Unfortunately, this doesn't currently work on Mac OS X due to limitations in Apple's X11 package.)

You can configure GIMP to show some other useful selectors next to the color swatches; see the section "A Few GIMP Settings You Can Customize," later in this chapter, to learn which settings you can customize.

Tool Options

Below the color swatches is typically an area called *Tool Options*, which shows settings affecting the operation of the active tool. In Figure 1-1, the active tool is the Paintbrush, so the options showing are the ones for that tool. You can make Tool Options a separate dialog if you like (see the section "The Layers Dialog and Dialog Docking"), but most people prefer to leave it in its standard position, docked underneath the Toolbox. The buttons at the bottom of the dialog let you save or restore settings for the tool, or reset the options to their default values.

Image Windows

A toolbox is fine, but an image-editing program isn't any fun without images! GIMP uses a separate window for each image you open. That way, you can have big windows for big images, and small windows for small ones.

A fun and easy way to create an image window is to run one of the Logo scripts. There are lots of them (you'll see a complete list in Chapter 7), but for now, you just need one. Go to the Toolbox's *Xtns* menu (in GIMP 2.6, look under *File* ➤ *New*) and click *Xtns* ➤ *Logos* ➤ *Cool Metal*. In the dialog that opens, you can change the *Text* to anything you want…or you can leave it at the default, "Cool Metal." Click *OK*, and you have a new image window (Figure 1-2).

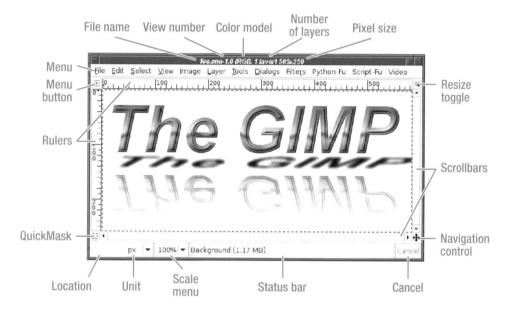

Figure 1-2. *An image window*

Let's start at the top. The image window's title bar gives information about the image: its file name and "view number," whether it's in full color (denoted RGB, for Red, Green, and Blue), the number of layers, and the current size of the image in pixels. You can change the information GIMP shows here; see the "GIMP Preferences" section in Chapter 12.

The window also has a menu bar, which offers a collection of operations for working on the image. You can hide the menu bar to offer more space for the image (Preferences again); in that case, use the menu button at the upper left of the window to show the menu, or right-click on the image to open the context menu.

The rulers at the top and left sides of the image window show the position of your mouse in the image. You can also use the rulers to set up "guides," gridlines on the image to help you draw exactly where you want (you'll meet guides in Chapter 4).

Moving down to the bottom-left corner, the QuickMask button helps with defining selections. See Chapter 5 for details.

The location area below the QuickMask button gives a precise readout of the current mouse position if your mouse is in the window (otherwise it's blank); the menu button next to it lets you display the mouse position in any unit you find most comfortable, such as pixels, inches, or points (most of the time, I recommend sticking with pixels).

The scale menu, or zoom control, shows whether the image is currently being displayed at actual size (100%), shrunk to a smaller size, or magnified to a larger size. There are lots of other ways to zoom, too. You can use the *View ➤ Zoom* menu, or use the + and – keys to zoom in or out. You can activate the Zoom tool (in the Toolbox, click on the tool button that looks like a magnifying glass), then click in the image to zoom in (Ctrl+click to zoom out). If you have a mouse with a scroll wheel, you can also zoom by using the Ctrl key in combination with the mouse wheel. Finally, if you click on the resize toggle in the upper-right corner of the image window, you can resize the image window and the image will automatically zoom to fit the new window size.

The status bar along the bottom of the window shows more information about the image: specifically, which layer is selected and how much memory the image is using. It also shows a progress bar when GIMP is performing a time-consuming operation, with a Cancel button right next to it.

The navigation control at the bottom right lets you "pan" around the image instead of using the scrollbars (click on it to see how it works). For images that are too big to fit on the screen, panning can be quicker than scrolling. You can also pan by dragging anywhere in the image window while holding down the middle mouse button, or by holding down the spacebar while dragging in the image with the left button. (You can configure the spacebar to call up the Move tool rather than panning: see the section "A Few GIMP Settings You Can Customize," later in this chapter).

The Layers Dialog and Dialog Docking

GIMP has a lot of useful dialogs—you can see the whole list from *File ➤ Dialogs* in the Toolbox menu or the image window's top-level *Dialogs* menu—and it lets you configure which dialogs will be grouped together using a mechanism called *docking*.

Each separate dialog window is called a dock, and can hold quite a few dialogs inside it. Aside from the Toolbox, GIMP 2.4 initially makes one dock visible (Figure 1-3).

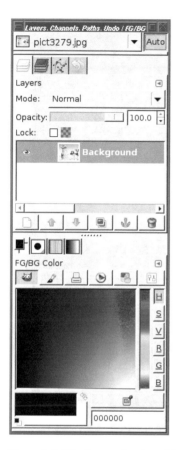

Figure 1-3. *The Layers (top) and Color (bottom) dialogs docked together, along with many other dialogs also docked (see the tabs above "Layers" and above "FG/BG Color")*

Initially you can see two dialogs in this dock: the Layers dialog (the top half) and the FG/BG Color dialog (the bottom). But there are many more dialogs docked here, visible only through tabs. The Layers half of the dock also includes tabs for *Channels*, *Paths*, and *History* (*Undo*), while the Color half includes tabs for the *Brush*, *Patterns*, and *Gradients* dialogs. Select any tab to make that dialog visible.

But you're not stuck with this layout: you can group dialogs together any way you like, using *docking* (Figure 1-4). Press and hold the left mouse button in the *drag handle* area—the title area or tab, highlighted as "Drag from" in Figure 1-4—and drag to where you want the dialog to be. You can drag to the drag handle or tab area of another dock, and the dialog will be added as a new tab; or you can drag to the *docking bar* at the bottom of an existing dock to create a new dialog area below what's already there. Take care to drop exactly where you want the dialog to end up: if you drop between two tabs of an existing dock, that's where the dragged dialog's tab will end up.

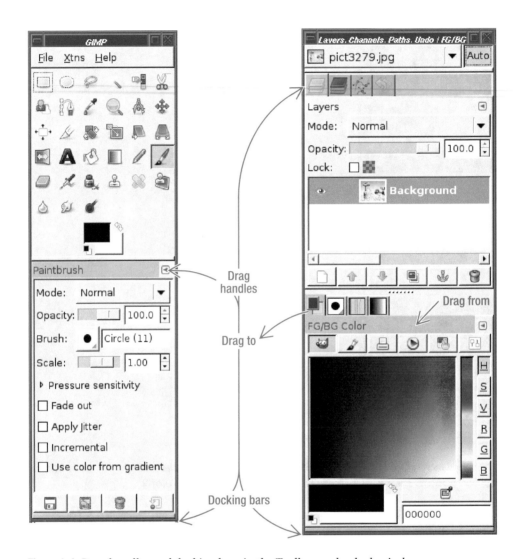

Figure 1-4. *Drag handles and docking bars in the Toolbox and a dock window*

You can also drag a dialog to your desktop, which gives you a new dock window containing only that dialog. Finally, from the Toolbox *File ➤ Dialogs* or the image window *Dialogs* menu, you can choose *Create a New Dock*, which offers a few popular combinations like *Layers, Channels & Paths* (which, confusingly, will also include *Undo*).

■**Caution** When you close a dock containing several dialogs, GIMP 2.4 will forget how they were docked—even if it was just GIMP's default initial configuration. There are two ways to get the default configuration back: you can build them up from the combinations in *File* ➤ *Dialogs* ➤ *Create a New Dock*; or you can exit GIMP, remove your GIMP profile, and start over. GIMP 2.6 will offer a solution: *Windows* ➤ *Recently Closed Docks*.

I'll refer to dialogs by their individual names throughout this book. In particular, you'll be using the Layers dialog quite a lot starting with Chapter 3, and I'll just call it the Layers dialog—it doesn't matter whether you keep it by itself or docked with seven other dialogs.

Menu Overview

You'll learn all about the functions in GIMP's menus as you explore later chapters, but here's a quick tour of which menu does what.

The Toolbox menu bar offers operations that don't apply to a specific image. This includes *File* operations such as *New* and *Open*, the *Dialogs* menu, a *Help* menu for online help, and a menu labeled *Xtns* (short for "Extensions").

Of particular interest is the *Xtns* menu. This menu gives you access to a menagerie of extensions that can create new images. Included are submenus offering a collection of scripts to create various styles of text logos, buttons (for use on web pages), shapes such as a sphere, interesting patterns and brushes, and themes you can use for web pages.

The *Xtns* menu also contains GIMP's Plug-in Browser. Many of GIMP's functions are implemented as plug-ins, and it can sometimes be difficult to find a specific function in the menus. The Plug-in Browser lets you search for plug-ins by name, and then tells you where in the menus you can find them. See Chapter 11 for more details.

■**Note** Don't get too attached to the Toolbox menus. In GIMP 2.6, the Toolbox will no longer have a menu bar, and all those functions will move to image window menus. This will include a new top-level *Windows* menu you can use to access any dialog or any currently open image—it also includes a helpful *Recently Closed Docks* category—and a menu under *File* ➤ *New* that replaces the new image-creation operations in the *Xtns* menu.

The Toolbox menus also offer another very handy feature: *tear-offs*.

Tear-off Menus and Context Menus

GIMP has a lot of features, and exploring can get frustrating when you want to try out lots of different options that are buried in the same deep menu. Tear-offs can help: they let you grab any menu and turn it into a window of its own.

For instance, suppose you want to explore GIMP's long list of Logo scripts, available from the Toolbox's *Xtns* ➤ *Logos* submenu (Figure 1-5). You'd have to keep clicking on *Xtns*, then click or drag to *Logos*, then choose the item you want to try next. But click on the *Logos* tear-off, and the submenu detaches and becomes a new window on your desktop, where you can keep it as long as you like.

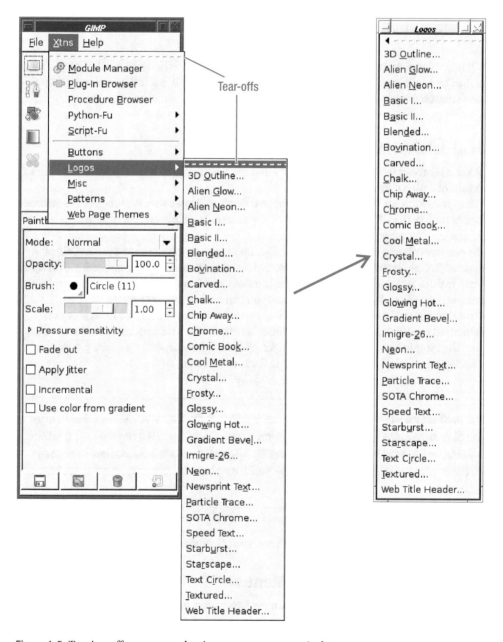

Figure 1-5. *Tearing off a menu makes it appear as a new window.*

Tear-offs can save you a lot of time and frustration. So when you start exploring the image window menus, you might be disappointed not to find them there as well.

GIMP can tear off image window menus, but there's a trick. Every item available through the image window's menu bar is also available as a *context* (right-click) menu. In fact, some GIMP users prefer not to show the image window menu bar at all, and use that extra space to show more of the image they're working on (you can show or hide the menu bar with *View* ➤ *Show Menubar*). If you right-click (Command-click for Mac users with one-button mice) in an image window, you'll see the same menus you see in the menu bar, except that they now have tear-offs.

Context menus are useful even if you don't use tear-offs. Some dialogs, like the Layers dialog, don't have a menu bar at all, so you perform most Layers operations by right-clicking on a layer to get a context menu.

Image Window Menus

The image window's menus, when combined with the tools in the Toolbox, make up the heart of GIMP. Everything you'll need to do to modify an image should be accessible here.

The *File* menu contains familiar file operations: *New, Open, Save, Save As....* Don't neglect the *Open Recent* submenu: you can use it to get back quickly to images you've edited in the past few days.

Edit includes the usual *Cut, Copy,* and *Paste* operations, which you will use frequently to move information between images and layers. Other useful items in this menu are *Clear* (which erases the contents of the current selection) and three variants of *Fill with*. Most of the items in the *Edit* menu have keyboard equivalents. You may find it useful to learn the shortcuts for these items since they're used so often.

The *Select* menu controls actions that modify the current selection. You can select *All* or *None, Invert* the selection (select everything not currently selected, and vice versa), make the selection smaller (*Shrink*) or larger (*Grow*), or make its edges fuzzier (*Feather*) or sharper (*Sharpen*). You'll work with these operations in Chapter 5.

The *View* menu controls how you see the image. Items in this menu don't change what will be saved to disk, merely the way you see it on screen as you edit it. The menu includes a *Zoom* submenu that lets you zoom in or out on the image (this does not make the image any bigger or smaller when you save it; it merely changes your view of it), a *Shrink Wrap* option that fits the window to the image being displayed, and a *Fullscreen* option, as well as toggles to select whether various attributes such as the selection, guides, rulers, layer boundaries, grids, and the menu bar are visible. If you want to change any of those attributes permanently, you can do so in the Preferences for *Image Windows* ➤ *Appearance*, and you can set them separately for full-screen image windows and normal ones.

Tip An easy item to overlook in the *View* menu is the very first one: *New View*. It lets you have more than one view of the same image. For example, you might have one window showing the image zoomed in so you can change individual pixels, and another showing the image at normal size to see what the image will look like when you've finished. They're both still the same image as far as GIMP is concerned: any changes you make in one view will be reflected in the other.

The *Image* menu contains functions that apply to the current image as a whole, while the *Layer* menu contains functions that operate only on the current layer. In some cases they look like copies of each other: for instance, *Transform*, *Scale*, and *Autocrop* appear in both menus. But they're different in whether they affect a single layer or the whole image. This distinction will become much clearer in Chapter 3 when you start to use layers.

The *Colors* menu contains functions related to (you guessed it) the colors of the image. GIMP versions 2.2 and earlier located this menu inside the *Layer* menu.

The *Tools* menu gives you another way to access the stuff in the Toolbox window. Most of the time you'll probably keep the Toolbox open and access tools through Toolbox buttons, but the menu does offer access to tools that aren't showing in the Toolbox.

The *Dialogs* menu gives you access to any dialog, whether or not it's currently visible; it's the same as the *File* ➤ *Dialogs* menu in the Toolbox window.

Filters provides access to the plethora of image filters and plug-ins available in GIMP. Most external plug-ins you install will also show up under *Filters*. (In earlier versions of GIMP, some of these functions appeared in additional menus such as *Script-Fu* and *Python-Fu*.)

A Few GIMP Settings You Can Customize

First: you don't *need* to change any of these preferences. GIMP should work fine out of the box. But there are a few options here that can make a big difference to your GIMP experience. I'll mention some of my favorites; if you want more details on GIMP's preferences, you'll find them in Chapter 12.

You'll find all of these options in the Preferences window, *Edit* ➤ *Preferences* from an image window or *File* ➤ *Preferences* from the Toolbox.

Tool Settings Changes

In the *Toolbox* category, you can choose *Show active brush, pattern & gradient* as well as an option to show the foreground/background color swatches. I recommend enabling both: it doesn't make the Toolbox much larger, and if you have the pattern and gradient in the Toolbox you can drag them into the image, a really easy way to fill areas. You can also choose *Show active image* here, but that's less useful.

Under *Tool Options*, look at *Scaling: Default interpolation* and make sure it's *Cubic* or *Sinc (Lanczos)*. Either of those settings is fine (the difference is subtle). Some GIMP versions defaulted this to *Linear*, which will give you far worse quality, especially if you ever scale images larger.

Default Image lets you set the size for images you create with *File* ➤ *New*. You can override the default to set each new image's size separately, but when you get to Chapter 4 you might want to choose a default image size that you find comfortable.

Window Controls

Image Windows offers *Resize window on zoom* and *Resize window on image size change*. Both of these options are helpful if you get tired of resizing your window every time you zoom or scale.

Window Management is a tricky section. But it nevertheless can make a big difference in usability, with several key choices:

Window Manager Hints for the Toolbox and for other docks controls whether these windows are considered as top-level windows or as transient dialogs. On Windows you may prefer *Utility window* here, since it reduces the number of entries that show up in your taskbar. Linux users may prefer the extra flexibility that goes with *Normal window. Keep above* is a compromise between the two.

Activate the focused image is on by default, but Linux users who use "pointer focus" ("focus follows mouse") will want to disable it. Otherwise the active image—the one reflected in the Layers dialog—will change every time you move the mouse across the screen. If you do disable it and need a way to activate a particular image, move the mouse into the window and press the spacebar or a modifier key like Shift or Ctrl.

Save window positions on exit is something most users will probably want, so GIMP remembers where its toolbox and docked dialogs are.

Of course, GIMP has a lot more preferences. You can explore as much as you want, or take a look at Chapter 12, where they'll be covered in much more detail.

Keyboard Shortcuts

In the *Interface* category, *Use dynamic keyboard shortcuts* is a great feature you won't find in most programs. If there's some GIMP operation you do all the time, you can put it on a key, even if it didn't have a shortcut assigned by the developers.

For instance, let's say you do a lot of screenshots and you find yourself going to the Toolbox *File* ➤ *Acquire* ➤ *Screenshot…* all the time. You decide you'd like to put that on a key. The obvious key is Ctrl+S (S for screen shot), but that does a *File* ➤ *Save*, and you wouldn't want to change that. How about Shift+S? That brings up the *Shear* tool, not something most of us use very often, so it sounds like a good choice to use for screen shots.

Why Shift+S—why not assign it to just S? Single-key shortcuts without any modifier key like Shift or Ctrl can conflict with menu "mnemonics," or "access keys." To assign a bare key to a function, you may need to turn off mnemonics (using the *Preferences* checkbox just above the one for dynamic keyboard shortcuts)—or use *Edit* ➤ *Keyboard Shortcuts.…*

Now navigate through the menus to where *Screenshot* is: click *File* ➤ *Acquire*. Move your mouse over *Screenshot* but don't click on it yet—just hover over it. Then type your intended key binding (Shift+S). The menu item changes to show the new shortcut, and you're set! Now any time you press Shift+S in any GIMP window, you'll get the Screenshot dialog. (You can remove a binding by pressing Backspace while hovering over the item.)

I mentioned the *Edit* ➤ *Keyboard Shortcuts* dialog, available from the image window's *Edit* menu or the Toolbox's *File* menu. It gives you another way to set your own shortcuts, even for some items that don't appear in the menus. The dialog also helpfully warns you when you're about to set a binding that's currently used by something else. The bad news is that the dialog can be confusing: GIMP functions are grouped by type, not according to their place in the menus, so it can be difficult to find the function you're looking for.

A First GIMP Project

Enough exposition. The only way to learn GIMP is to edit images, so let's get started!

Begin with any photo you like. I'll start with a vacation photo: some Anasazi ruins from Chaco Canyon in New Mexico.

You can use an image you already have in a file on your hard disk, and use GIMP's *File* ➤ *Open…* dialog to open it. But you may want to choose an image you're keeping on a website. GIMP makes it especially easy to open images that are on the web: with most browsers, you can drag from the image in the browser window and drop it onto GIMP's Toolbox window. (Make sure you're viewing just the full-sized image in the browser, not a small "thumbnail" with a link over it. If you drag an image with a link over it, GIMP will try to open the link rather than the image. You can ensure that you're viewing just the image in Firefox by right-clicking and choosing *View Image*. In Google image search, click on *See full sized image*.) Drop it anywhere over the tool buttons; it doesn't matter which button is underneath.

■**Tip** What if you don't have any images of your own yet? See "Where to Find Freely Available Images" in Chapter 12, or under "Outside Links" on this book's website, *http://gimpbook.com*.

When you drop the image (release the mouse button) over the Toolbox window, a new image window appears (Figure 1-6). At this point, you don't yet have a copy of the image on disk; that won't happen until you save it and give it a file name.

Figure 1-6. *Image window showing Chaco Canyon ruins*

To jazz up the image, it's time to introduce a new character: Wilber (Figure 1-7). Wilber is GIMP's mascot, drawn by GIMP contributor Tuomas Kuosmanen ("Tigert").

Figure 1-7. *Wilber, the GIMP mascot*

Images of Wilber can be found on GIMP's website, *http://www.gimp.org*, if you hunt around, or on the website for this book under "Photos from the book." Of course, feel free to substitute your own favorite character.

Tip When you're inserting a character like Wilber into another image, you'll usually want the Wilber image to have a transparent background so you don't end up with a white square around the image you inserted. You'll learn more about image formats in Chapter 2, and about ways to separate a foreground object from its background in Chapter 5. For now, look for an image in GIF or PNG format that already has a transparent background. In Google image search, the image format is listed next to the size, for example, "300 x 225 - 92k – png."

Once you've found the image you want, whether online or on your local disk, drag it from the browser window into the GIMP image window you already opened. GIMP will add the image to the current window as a separate layer (Figure 1-8).

Figure 1-8. *Chaco image with Wilber added*

If you have your Layers dialog open, you may notice a new layer has appeared. If not, don't worry about it; you'll learn about layers in Chapter 3. The yellow and black outline around Wilber is the layer boundary: it shows the size of the layer. It's not really part of the image, and will not be visible when you save the image.

Wilber appears in the middle of the image, which probably isn't where you want him. In my Chaco image, I want Wilber's head to appear in the window. To move a layer, click on the Move tool in the Toolbox window (Figure 1-9).

Figure 1-9. *The Move tool*

With the Move tool active, you can drag the layer around with your mouse to position it exactly where you want it. Then save the image: choose *File* ➤ *Save As…* from the image window, and give it a file name, such as *chaco-wilber.jpg*. If GIMP opens a dialog about JPEG not handling transparency or layers, or needing to export, just click *OK*.

Figure 1-10 shows the final image.

Figure 1-10. *Wilber visits Chaco Canyon*

That's all there is to it! Now you can invite Wilber (or any other character you like) along on your next vacation.

Summary

At this point, you should have a basic understanding of GIMP's windows, menus, and preferences. You've seen how to create text logos using the built-in Logo scripts, and how to combine two images in a simple GIMP project. Perhaps you've spent some time playing with some of GIMP's built-in filters and plug-ins and getting comfortable with its interface. Now let's move on to the details of image editing. Chapter 2 will cover photographs: how to work with them, and a collection of ways GIMP can improve a flaky photo.

■■■

## CHAPTER 2

Improving Digital Photos

You have your shiny new digital camera, and it takes great pictures. But straight out of the camera, the photos are huge, and far too big to put on a website or email to friends. Maybe they also have other problems you'd like to correct before you show them to anyone.

This chapter will explore some of the most common ways you can use GIMP to improve your digital photos and share them with the world. It will cover the following:

- Opening files

- Scaling

- Saving files

- Cropping

- Brightening and darkening

- Rotating

- Sharpening

- Fixing red-eye

Opening Files

The first step in editing any image is to open it.

If GIMP isn't running yet, you can start it by dragging one or more images to GIMP's desktop icon (if you have one), or simply run GIMP from the command line: `gimp file1.jpg file2.jpg`…. GIMP will start up and display windows for each image.

But if GIMP is already running, opening images this way will start a second instance of GIMP. You're better off dragging images to GIMP's Toolbox window, as described in Chapter 1, or using the Open dialog (*File* ➤ *Open…*). (Mac users should use *File* ➤ *Open…*, as Apple's version of X11 doesn't support drag and drop.)

Figure 2-1 shows GIMP's Open dialog.

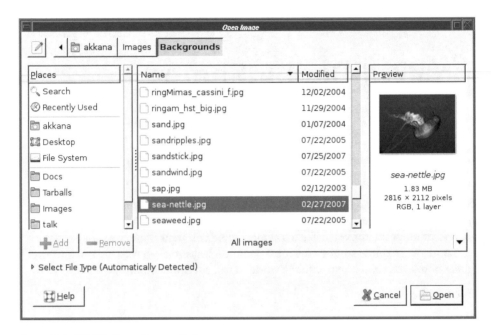

Figure 2-1. *GIMP's Open Image dialog*

GIMP's Open Image dialog lists files and folders in the main frame of the dialog. Above the file area is a sequence of buttons representing the location of the currently chosen folder. Clicking on these buttons can move you up one level, or several.

You can select more than one file at a time in the file list. Click on the first file, and then hold down the Shift key while clicking to highlight a range of files (they may not highlight until you release Shift); or hold the Ctrl key down while clicking individual files to select or deselect them. GIMP will open each file as a separate image.

Try typing the first few letters of an image's name to jump to that image in the file list. Ctrl+L will bring up a text field that allows typing or pasting a file name (another Ctrl+L hides it again). On Linux, typing certain characters (such as a forward slash, /) will cause this dialog to pop up without the need for Ctrl+L.

On the left side of the dialog is a list of *bookmarks*. You can click on a bookmark to jump directly there, or add the current folder to the bookmarks list by clicking the *Add* button.

Underneath the file list is a menu for file type, initialized to *All Images*. You can use this menu to restrict the types of images you see in the dialog.

Below the *Add* and *Remove* buttons is an expander for *Select File Type*. This is different from the file type list right above it: it's for unusual situations where GIMP cannot detect the format of an image file automatically. It is seldom useful: if GIMP can't detect an image file's type on its own, it usually means that the file has been damaged in some way, in which case the selector won't help. However, if you have an image that you think may have the wrong extension, it's worth a try.

Besides the Open dialog, GIMP offers two more Open options in its *File* menu: *Open Location*, which allows you to paste a web URL, and the *Open Recent* menu, which lists images you've edited... well, recently. If the file you're looking for is no longer listed in the *Open Recent* menu, you may still find it in *Document History* at the bottom of the *Open Recent* menu.

Caution When editing a digital camera photo, it's a good idea to make a copy of the image first, and then edit the copy. Although you can use GIMP's *Save As* dialog to save a file to a different name, it's easy to forget to do that and thus overwrite your original image.

Scaling

Modern digital cameras take beautiful photos in high resolution: 6 or 7 megapixels or even more. That's great, but higher resolution makes for larger files of at least half a megabyte each and perhaps much more. If you put images this big on the web, or send them via email, the recipients will not thank you.

The solution is to *scale* the images: make them smaller. Don't confuse this with changing the canvas size: in GIMP, that only changes the size of the work area without changing the contents. To take the image contents and blow them up or shrink them down, Scale is what you want.

The Scale Image dialog (Figure 2-2) is accessed from the *Image* menu in the image window: *Image* ➤ *Scale Image.*

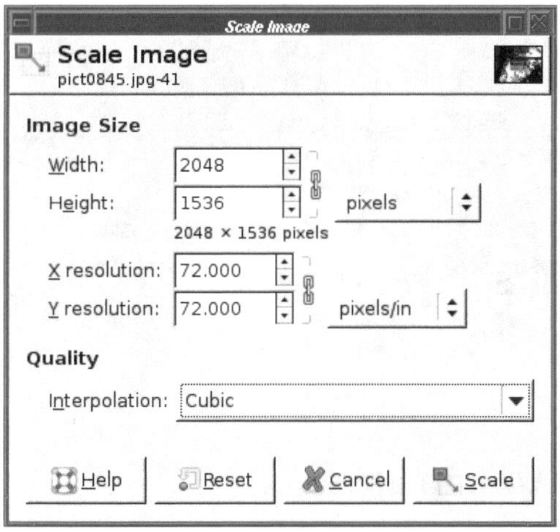

Figure 2-2. *The Scale Image dialog*

The dialog has three sections. The most important section comes first: the new size (width and height) of the image. By default, size is given in pixels. This is a good choice, and you should use it unless you have a firm reason to do otherwise.

The width and height are "chain linked" together. You can type a new number into either the *Width* or *Height* field, then hit the Tab key or click in another field, and the other dimension will automatically update to keep the *aspect ratio*—the ratio of width to height—of the image unchanged. This prevents the contents of your photo from getting taller and skinnier, or shorter and fatter. Very convenient!

If you actually do want to scale the two dimensions independently, clicking the chain link icon breaks the chain and unlinks width and height, so you can change one without changing the other. Welcome to the Hall of Funhouse Mirrors. Clicking on the chain link again will link them back together.

Even if you work in pixel dimensions, you may want to use the units drop-down menu (initially in pixels) in order to scale an image to some multiple or fraction of its current size. With the units menu set to *percent*, you can set the width or height to 200 to make the image twice as large, or to 50 to make it half the size. (You only need to set width or height, not both; if they're chained together, the other will adjust automatically.)

THE UNDO COMMAND: A GIMP USER'S BEST FRIEND

If you're curious about how the chain link icons work, or how the image might look when scaled to a particular size, you can try it without any fear of losing your data. GIMP's Undo command is your friend! Get familiar with it early on. It's very useful to be able to try things while knowing you can always undo your changes and go back to the previous version.

Undo is in the *Edit* menu, along with *Redo* and an item called *Undo History*, which brings up a window showing the history of commands you've used recently. You can also undo the last command by pressing Ctrl+Z. Undo is so frequently useful that it's well worth learning that keyboard command.

GIMP can undo several operations in a row, not just the last single operation. By default, it remembers the last five operations. You can change that number in Preferences (*File* ➤ *Preferences*, under *Environment*). A larger Undo stack takes more memory, so it may be best to stick with the default setting unless your machine has quite a lot of RAM. There's also a preference to limit the amount of memory the Undo system can use, though the preference for the number of Undo operations takes precedence. Therefore, you know you'll always have at least the number of Undo operations you specify in Preferences.

Try Undo now: type something into the Scale dialog, perhaps even with width and height unchained from each other, and click the Scale button. Then undo the Scale operation, using Ctrl+Z or *Edit* ➤ *Undo*, so that you're confident it works.

What Size Should You Choose for Your Images?

For photos intended for web pages, it's usually best to keep the largest dimension of the image at 640 pixels or less (400 × 300 images are free on eBay!). If you have a lot of images, or if many of the people who will view your images have slow network connections, smaller is better.

The *Resolution* section in the Scale Image dialog allows you to specify the number of pixels per inch (or other units, if you choose). This doesn't change the size of the image; it's merely a note that gets added to the image so the image size can later be converted to physical units (such as inches). Most of the time, you won't need to look at these values.

The *Interpolation Quality* controls details of how the image is scaled. *Linear*, which is the default in at least some GIMP versions, does not produce the best quality, but it's fairly fast. Unless you're on a very slow machine, you'll probably want to change this to one of the higher-quality settings, such as *Cubic* or *Lanczos*. These settings will run a little slower, but they'll produce much better-looking images, especially if you ever scale images larger instead of smaller. I recommend changing this value permanently, in the Preferences dialog under *Tool Options*, so you don't have to think about it when you're using the Scale dialog.

Note Which quality setting is considered "Best" can vary with GIMP versions and with the sort of image you're scaling. The difference between *Cubic* and *Lanczos* is fairly subtle.

Usually, when you click *Scale* in the dialog to make a digital photo smaller, and GIMP rescales the image, the window will resize to be tiny (Figure 2-3). Don't be fooled: the image probably isn't as small as GIMP is showing you.

Figure 2-3. *The scaled image now looks too small!*

What happened? Since the original image was too large to fit on the screen, GIMP showed it as "zoomed out"—in the example in Figure 2-3, it is shown at only 33% of actual size. After the image is scaled, GIMP keeps the same zoom setting (it may or may not make the actual window smaller, depending on your setting for *Resize window on zoom* in the *Image Windows* preference category). So now, even though the image could easily fit on the screen, you're still seeing it at 33%. The solution is to zoom after rescaling. Use the *Zoom* menu in the image window, the menu under *View ➤ Zoom*, or the keyboard shortcut +, or type **1**. Typing **1** (the numeral one) in the image window always zooms it to full size (100%). Typing + (plus) zooms in (makes the image appear larger); – (minus or dash) zooms out. When preparing images for the web, you'll probably want the image window at 100% so you can see exactly what your audience will see.

■**Caution** The + and − keys on the numeric keypad may not work. If they don't, use the ones on the regular keyboard. On some earlier GIMP versions, zooming in used = instead of + (on most US keyboards, = is the un-Shifted version of +, and so is easier to type). Remember, you can always change these key bindings, as described in Chapter 1 in the section "Keyboard Shortcuts."

Scaling an image is easy, and it's an important operation when you're sharing images with other people. For many images, scaling may be the only operation you need. But if you plan other operations that may affect image size, such as rotation or cropping, do them first. Scaling should usually be the *last* thing you do when you're editing an image; that way, you have the greatest control over the image's exact final size.

The exception that proves the rule is a very slow machine. If you scale the image first, subsequent operations will go much faster. However, you'll find that this matters only with very slow machines—or *very* large images!

The Scale Tool

Most of the time, *Image* ➤ *Scale* is perfect for rescaling an image. But there's another way of scaling: the Scale tool.

You'll find it in the Toolbox next to the Rotate tool, or through the menu *Tools* ➤ *Transform Tools* ➤ *Scale*. This tool lets you scale interactively: with the tool active, click anywhere in the image to begin, and then drag from any corner of the image into the image. You'll see the image change size as you drag.

The Scale tool is a bit trickier to use than *Image* ➤ *Scale…* for a couple of reasons. First, you have to remember to click in the tool to start the operation. Second, it only scales the current layer, not the whole image, and it doesn't change the image size at the end. (You'll learn more about using layers in Chapter 3.)

Third, by default it doesn't maintain the layer's original aspect ratio. You may end up with a "funhouse mirror" version of your image where everything looks tall and skinny or short and fat. *Keep aspect* in the tool options can fix that (there are also options to keep height while varying width, and vice versa). It also offers Interpolation, Clipping, and Preview options similar to those for the Rotate tool.

For improving digital photos, you probably won't want to use the Scale tool. But keep it in mind for later when you're using lots of layers and doing crazy things to them. It might be just the ticket then, as it does have the advantage of giving a live preview of what the image will look like when scaled. Sometimes that's awfully helpful.

Saving Files

Image editing is just like any other type of document editing: once you've made any significant change to a file, you should save it. It's smart to save your work frequently, in case of a computer crash or other disaster.

GIMP uses Ctrl+S as the keyboard shortcut for *File* ➤ *Save*, just like most word processing programs. If the image already has a file name, that's a quick way to save your work.

If you've edited an original image, modified it, and now want to save to a new file name, use *File ➤ Save As…* (Figure 2-4). You'll also see this dialog the first time you save a new image.

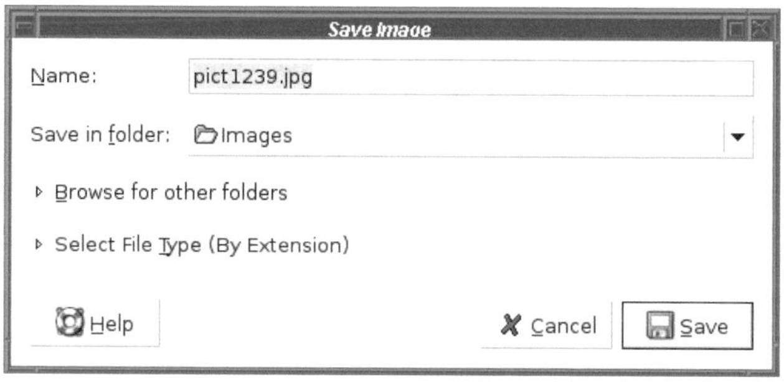

```
┌─────────────────────────────────────────────────────────┐
│                       Save Image                    ▭ ▢ ✕ │
├─────────────────────────────────────────────────────────┤
│  Name:          pict1239.jpg                              │
│                                                           │
│  Save in folder:  📁 Images                          ▼    │
│                                                           │
│   ▹ Browse for other folders                              │
│                                                           │
│   ▹ Select File Type (By Extension)                       │
│                                                           │
│   🕮 Help                         ✖ Cancel      💾 Save    │
└─────────────────────────────────────────────────────────┘
```

Figure 2-4. *The Save dialog*

The *Save in folder* popup offers a list that corresponds to the "bookmarks" you've set up in GIMP's Open dialog. You can get a file selector that gives you more choices by clicking on the expander next to *Browse for other folders.*

The *Select File Type* expander lets you choose an image format. Normally, you don't need it: just type the extension as part of the file name (e.g., *mypicture.jpg* to save in JPEG format) and GIMP will use the appropriate format. The expander is there in case you need to see a list of formats GIMP can handle, or in the rare case that you need to save a file with an extension that doesn't match the file type you need to use—for example, if you want to save a JPEG image but name it "image.jfif" instead of "image.jpg". You'll learn more about file types in the next section, "Image File Types."

Once you *Save As…*, the GIMP considers your entry to be the new name for the image. From then on, you can save and any changes will be saved to the new file name, without over-writing the original file. The file name is visible in the title bar of the image window, so you can check easily to make sure you're saving to the right file name. There's one other save option worth noting: *Save a Copy….* This works like *Save As…* in that you can choose a file name different from the one you're currently using. The difference is that *Save a Copy…* does not change GIMP's notion of the current image file name. After you *Save a Copy…*, subsequent saves will still use the original file name. This is very useful when you're making repeated edits to an image, and you want to save it in a format that preserves all your work, such as XCF, but you want to share the final result on the web in a more efficient format, such as JPEG or GIF.

Image File Types

The choice of file types used to hold images—GIF, JPEG, BMP, PNG, TIFF—is baffling. What do each of these file types mean, and which format should you use?

When choosing a format for the web, or to send images by email, the most important criterion is usually file size. In order to view your image, each user will need to download it. This is especially important if anyone in your intended audience might be connected via a slow modem, or if you're sending images by email and some recipients might have an email account with a disk quota. Also, many email systems will simply refuse to transfer files that are too big.

The other important factor when choosing an image format is image quality. There's typically a trade-off between file size and quality: you can compress an image to a smaller size only by sacrificing some quality. But by choosing the right file type, you can find the best balance of quality and file size.

JPEG

For sharing full-color photographs, the best format to use is usually JPEG. Pronounced "jay-peg," the name comes from the group that defined the format, the *Joint Photographic Experts Group*. Usually, a JPEG file will have an extension of ".jpg", or occasionally ".jpeg". JPEG images are highly compressed and are encoded in full color, so it's a very efficient format for photographs or other images with a wide range of colors.

The drawback to this format is that the compression is *lossy*. That means that every time you read a JPEG file, make a change (however minor), and write the file back to disk, the image quality degrades slightly. Don't use JPEG for images you plan to edit over and over. But as a format for exchanging photographs with other people, JPEG excels. (There's no quality loss when you copy the file from one place to another, only when you edit it and write it back to disk.)

You may be wondering, "My camera stores images as JPEGs. Does that mean I'm losing quality?"

The answer is yes. That's why many cameras provide a non-lossy *raw* format (discussed in the section, "Other Formats") as well as JPEG. However, JPEG files are so efficient that you can store many, many more images than is possible with raw mode on the same memory card. Use raw format if you're worried about making sure you preserve every detail, or if you're bothered by the image quality of a JPEG; but for most people, the slight quality loss caused by using JPEG on a camera, plus editing an image once or twice and saving it *again* in JPEG format, will not be noticed. The space savings are worth it.

GIF

The *Graphics Interchange Format*, pronounced "giff" with a hard "g" as in "graphics," is an *indexed* format. This means that it uses a fixed list of colors instead of encoding every color separately. This is very efficient for images with a small number of colors, like a five-color corporate logo.

GIF can represent up to 256 colors (256 is 2 to the 8th power, so this is also called *8-bit color*). Typical photographs have many more colors than that (typically tens or hundreds of thousands), so saving a photograph in GIF format will usually result in very poor quality. Even worse, with 256 colors, the file will usually be larger than a full-color JPEG version of the same image! The lesson is clear: don't use GIF for photographs; use it only for simple icons and logos.

So what is GIF good for? The GIF format offers two very useful features: transparency and animation. With transparency, you can make an icon with a clear background. If you display it on a web page, or on a button in a program's user interface, whatever's behind the icon (a color, or even another image) will show through. GIF doesn't allow for partial transparency; a pixel is either fully transparent or not transparent at all.

GIF animation allows you to create images that move. Most web browsers support animated GIF images. (Whether this is a good idea is unclear; some users dislike animated images on web pages, and will avoid websites that use them. But animations have their uses.) To learn how to create GIF animation, see "Making Simple GIF Animations" in Chapter 3.

PNG

PNG, pronounced "ping," once stood for "PNG's Not GIF," though it's now sometimes referred to as the Portable Network Graphics format. It's a relatively new format, originally intended as a replacement for GIF because of legal issues regarding the GIF format.

PNG offers two modes: it can be used for full-color images, like JPEG, or for indexed images, like GIF. In full-color mode, it's not nearly as efficient as JPEG: a PNG will be much larger than a JPEG of the same image. However, it's not lossy, so if you read a full-color PNG, make a modification, and write it back out, the quality will be just as good as it was before. This makes full-color PNG a good format for storing original copies of your own images if you might want to edit them later.

Indexed PNG is just as efficient as GIF (sometimes more efficient) for images such as logos and icons with a small number of colors, and it can support more than 256 colors. Nearly all web browsers support basic PNG, so it's safe to use PNG images on web pages. PNG supports transparency, like GIF, and it also supports partial transparency so you can have translucent areas. However, some browsers (such as older versions of Internet Explorer) don't support PNG transparency, so transparent PNG images on a web page may not always display properly.

PNG doesn't support animation. There's a format called MNG that adds animation to PNG images, but no web browsers support it yet. For animated images, GIF is pretty much the only choice.

XCF

This is GIMP's own format. When you're editing an image and you have a lot of layers and paths and other information you want to save, this is the format to use. Otherwise, don't. XCF files are usually quite large and can only be read by GIMP, not by other programs. Since XCF files are so large, you can compress them using the GZIP or BZIP2 formats—save to a file name ending in xcf.gz or xcf.bz2, and GIMP will handle the compression and decompression when it reads or writes the file.

TIFF

Tagged Image File Format (with a file extension of either .tif or .tiff) is another full-color, non-lossy format. Like full-color PNG, it's not very compact (don't use it on web pages—many web browsers can't display it anyway), but it's fine for keeping originals of images you might want to edit again. The reason I recommend using PNG instead of TIFF, aside from web browser compatibility, is that TIFF isn't a single standard, but many different standards with different interpretations. A TIFF written by one program may not always read correctly in another program. GIMP will read most TIFF files, but sometimes it will "have a tiff" about certain types of TIFFs.

One advantage to TIFF over other full-color formats is that it handles a wider range of colors. For the technically minded, it can handle 16 bits per color channel. This is important to some professional artists and graphic designers. However, GIMP doesn't currently handle 16-bit color anyway (that's planned for a future release), so if you're editing in GIMP, you don't get any benefit from using TIFF.

Other Formats

There are more image formats. Lots more. *Too many* more. Here are some of the most common:

- *Raw*: Not actually a format, *raw* is a term encompassing all the various proprietary formats used by camera manufacturers. GIMP supports many of these (usually requiring external plug-ins, such as ufraw). A few raw formats are held as "trade secrets" by the camera manufacturer, and your only option is to use another program to convert the image to a more standard format before editing it.

- *BMP*: This is Microsoft's Windows Bitmap format. BMP files are quite large and don't offer any advantage over PNG or TIFF. Save to BMP if you need to (for example, for writing Windows software), but otherwise it's usually better to choose a different format.

- *PCD*: This is Kodak's proprietary Photo CD format. It includes several resolutions within one file (so files tend to be very large) and is not lossy. GIMP doesn't handle PCD directly, though there's a plug-in available to read it. You're usually better off converting PCD files to something else.

- *PSD*: This is Adobe's proprietary Photoshop format. It saves layers and other information, analogous to XCF in GIMP. PSD is really two formats: GIMP can read the older version, while the newer one is a closed standard that can't be read by GIMP or most other non-Adobe programs.

- *ICO*: This is the Microsoft Windows Icon format. It can contain several resolutions in one file. This format is useful not only for Windows icons, but also to create a *favicon* for your website—those tiny images that show up if someone bookmarks your site—as well as next to the web page address in some browsers. GIMP can read and write ICO files directly.

- *PDF and PostScript*: These are vector graphics formats, not raster (pixel) graphics like the other formats discussed so far. Instead of representing an image as a rectangular collection of pixels, a vector image is a collection of drawing instructions involving points, lines, and curves. GIMP can't edit vector graphics directly (though there are a few plug-ins that give you limited vector image support), but it can import PostScript or PDF through a plug-in that converts the image into a raster image. If you're planning to save your image as PostScript or PDF, you're usually better off using a program intended for editing vector graphics.

- *SVG*: Scalable Vector Graphics is another vector format that is growing in popularity on the web. GIMP can import images from SVG, and in the future it may be able to export them to SVG as well. In addition, you can use the Path tool (which you'll meet in Chapter 5) to make simple vector graphics that you can save as SVG, and you can import paths from SVG.

Experimenting with JPEG and GIF Settings

Some image formats let you adjust settings to trade quality for smaller file size. In some cases (for instance, small buttons on a web page), it may be important to make the file as small as possible, and a slight loss of quality may be worthwhile.

JPEG and GIF both have quality adjustments, but their methods are very different.

JPEG Quality Settings

JPEG's quality adjustments come by varying the amount of image compression. JPEG's compression takes advantage of tricks of human perception; it tries to degrade quality in ways that won't be very noticeable. By experimenting with the *Quality* setting in the *Save as JPEG* dialog (Figure 2-5), which appears after you specify a file name ending in .jpg, you can find a balance that gives you a very small file size but still a pretty good-looking image.

Figure 2-5. *JPEG save options*

Begin by making sure the checkbox for *Show Preview in image window* is checked. This lets you see the effect of changing the Quality setting. The file size will also be shown in the dialog. GIMP's default Quality setting is 85 when saving to new files (when editing existing files, it uses whatever Quality setting is already there). The value 85 is a good choice for photographic images stored locally, but you may find that you can get away with settings as low as 50 with surprisingly little degradation. Figure 2-6 shows an example of how the quality can change with different compression settings, but I encourage you to try this on one of your own images to see the differences in quality and file size.

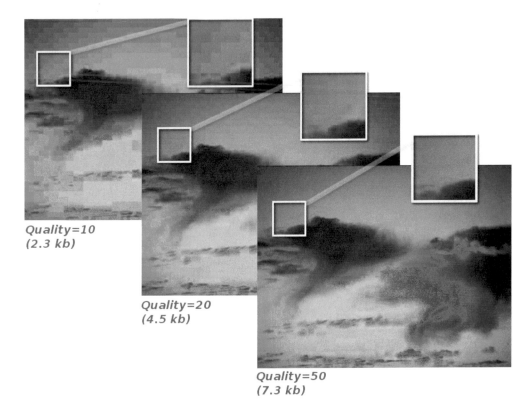

Quality=10
(2.3 kb)

Quality=20
(4.5 kb)

Quality=50
(7.3 kb)

Figure 2-6. *Comparing JPEG quality settings. The original (at Quality=85) was 16kb.*

You may be tempted to move the slider to 100% for images you store locally. Surely that would be best for images you're storing, and would prevent loss of data from JPEG compression?

Alas, even at 100%, JPEG still loses some data every time you save. Using a setting of 100% will produce a file two or three times larger than a setting of 95%, and the quality won't be any better. There's no advantage in using quality settings above 95%. If you want to save without any loss, you're better off using formats such as PNG or TIFF.

Finally, GIMP has some other JPEG settings in the *Advanced* area of the Save as JPEG dialog (Figure 2-7).

Optimize gives you an additional reduction in file size without any further reduction in image quality. It's on by default, and there's no reason to change that.

Progressive is a useful setting for images that will be uploaded to the web. It makes the image load in a different way, so people viewing the image will see a poor-quality version right away, which gradually improves, instead of seeing the image load line by line starting from the top.

Smoothing, Use restart markers, Force baseline JPEG, Subsampling, and *DCT method* control details of the JPEG format. You shouldn't need to change these unless you want very fine control over the way the JPEG file is saved.

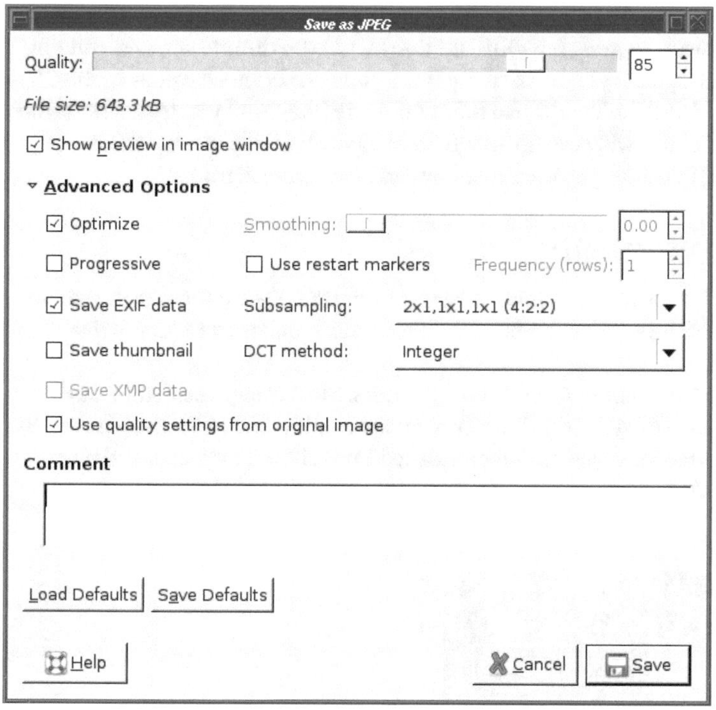

Figure 2-7. *Advanced JPEG settings*

Save EXIF data is a good option to know. JPEG includes a way of holding information (called metadata) about the file using something called *Exchangeable Image File Format*, or EXIF. Most digital cameras add EXIF information about the date the photo was taken, the resolution, and the camera's settings, such as lens focal length and whether a flash was used. GIMP cannot show or edit this EXIF information (that will probably be available in some future release), but it can preserve the information so that you can view it with other programs. If you don't want the EXIF information preserved, deselecting this box will make the file slightly smaller. (You can see exactly how much smaller by watching the *File size* value at the top of the dialog.)

EXIF can embed a thumbnail of the image in the file. Many cameras include this thumbnail, which adds several kilobytes, but most programs don't do anything useful with it. Deselecting *Save thumbnail* prevents saving this extra information, making the resulting file smaller.

XMP data is another metadata format (from Adobe). Some of the same tools that can read EXIF can also handle XMP, but it's not as widely used as EXIF.

Comment is a place to put any text you might want to add to an image. You can use this to include your name, a copyright notice, or details about where the photo was taken or what it portrays.

Load Defaults and *Save Defaults* let you save settings you want to use most of the time. For instance, if you always want to preserve EXIF but don't want the thumbnail, and you find an 83% quality setting is enough for you most of the time, you can set those values in the dialog and click Save Defaults. GIMP still won't use them for every image—if you load a JPEG file that uses different settings, GIMP will use the image's settings unless you change them—but the defaults are helpful for JPEG files you create or convert from other formats.

GIF and Indexed PNG Quality Settings

GIF and indexed PNG quality settings are quite different from JPEG. Since these indexed formats use a fixed number of colors, you can make the files much smaller by reducing the number of colors they use.

To do this, you need to know about GIMP's *image modes*. Most images edited in GIMP are full-color images, denoted as *RGB* in the title bar of the image window (for instance, Figure 2-3). But images that are destined to be saved as GIF or indexed PNG should be converted first using the *Image* ➤ *Mode* ➤ *Indexed...* menu item, which brings up the dialog shown in Figure 2-8.

Figure 2-8. *Convert Image to Indexed Colors dialog*

When converting an RGB image to indexed mode, you first need to choose a *palette*, the set of colors that will be represented in the final image. You can choose a predefined palette, such as a *web-optimized palette*, or one from the custom palette menu; you can choose a black-and-white palette, if you know that the image contains only those two colors; or, the most common case, you can let GIMP create a palette based on the colors actually in the image. You specify the number of colors, up to a maximum of 256, and GIMP will try to approximate any other colors that exist in the image by using combinations of the colors in the palette (Figure 2-9).

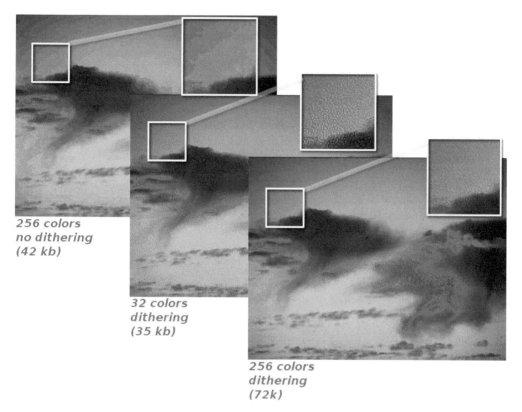

256 colors
no dithering
(42 kb)

32 colors
dithering
(35 kb)

256 colors
dithering
(72k)

Figure 2-9. *Different levels of indexing, showing file sizes when saved as GIF. Note that all the GIF versions of this photo, even the smallest, result in a bigger file than the best JPEG.*

This process of approximation is called *dithering*: it involves combining pixels of several different colors. You can choose from several types of dithering that create different effects, or you can specify no dithering, which may create a smaller file size and a cleaner appearance for images with sharp lines and only a few colors. See Chapter 8 for a detailed discussion of optimizing indexed images.

The Convert Image to Indexed Colors dialog does not include a *Preview* button. So you'll probably need to run it several times: choose some settings, click OK, and then use Undo to go back to RGB mode and try again with different settings. It's worth spending some time on this if you're trying to squeeze an indexed GIF or PNG image as small as possible.

Note GIMP offers a third image mode, *grayscale*, for black-and-white images. Grayscale mode is useful for scans of black-and-white documents or photographs, or simply for converting color photos to black and white.

When saving an RGB image as GIF, if you skip the step of converting it to indexed mode, GIMP will offer to do the indexing for you. In this case, GIMP will choose a palette intended to represent as many of the image's colors as possible. This helps preserve image quality, but it doesn't do much to reduce the file size. You may even end up with a larger, yet poorer quality file than if you'd used JPEG. You're much better off doing your own conversion.

The Save as GIF dialog offers a few additional options:

- *Interlace* is like JPEG's progressive option: it makes images load in a different way, so that someone viewing them in a web browser can see more of the image before it has loaded completely.

- *GIF comment* is like a JPEG comment, a place where you can store copyright information or details about where or how the image was taken. (GIF doesn't include EXIF, so the GIF comment is the only place such information can be recorded.)

- *Animated GIF Options* Controls ways of making an animation, as you'll see in Chapter 3.

Saving an RGB image as PNG will save it as a full-color PNG. If you want indexed PNG, you *must* convert the image to indexed mode before saving it. That said, the Save as PNG dialog offers yet another set of options:

- *Interlacing* is similar to GIF's interlacing or JPEG's progressive options.

- *Save background color* relates to images with transparency. Since not all web browsers handle PNG transparency, those that don't can use the GIMP's current background color instead.

- *Save gamma* stores information about your monitor (see the section on color profiles in Chapter 8). Some viewing programs can compensate for this, and try to adjust the PNG image so that it looks the same on the viewer's monitor as it did on yours. (Most viewing programs probably won't get this right, so for most people, there's no point in choosing this option. It increases file size slightly.)

- *Save layer offset* is only meaningful if you're saving a layer that has been moved relative to the rest of the image (you'll learn about layers in Chapter 3). Most viewers probably won't handle this correctly either.

- *Save resolution* records the current resolution (dots per inch or dpi) of the image, and is only useful if you're trading files with someone whose software cares about dpi.

- *Save creation time* records the time the image was last modified.

- *Save comment* is like the GIF or JPEG comment, but alas, you can't set it in this dialog. Set it on the Comment tab in the Image Properties dialog (*Image* ➤ *Image Properties…*).

- *Save color values from transparent pixels* is similar to *Save background color*, intended mainly for browsers that don't handle transparency properly.

Finally, PNG offers a settable *Compression level*. Unlike JPEG, PNG's compression is not lossy. The only disadvantage to using high compression levels is that it will take slightly longer to save the file. Most of the time difference happens when saving; it doesn't take a viewer much longer to uncompress a highly compressed PNG image. So usually it's best to use the largest amount of compression possible.

Cropping

Fairly often, a photo has more in it than you want. Perhaps you took a picture of something far away, and your zoom wasn't quite enough to get "up close," so the subject only occupies a small part of the center of the photo. Or perhaps there's some unwanted object intruding on part of the frame, such as another person, a garbage bin, or your finger. (Not that you'd ever take a photo with your finger in front of the lens! At least, with GIMP, you don't ever have to admit to doing such a thing.)

The solution to this problem is *cropping*. Click on the *Crop tool* button in the Toolbox to select it; it looks like a scalpel blade (Figure 2-10).

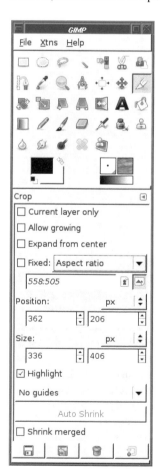

Figure 2-10. *The Crop button in the Toolbox, and its tool options*

To use the Crop tool, press the left mouse button down in the image window at the upper-left point of where you want the cropped image, drag down and to the right to where you want the lower-right point to be, and then release the mouse button. (You can start at any corner, as long as you drag diagonally to the opposite corner of the rectangle you want cropped.) You will see a preview of the cropped image (Figure 2-11) with drag handles outlined on each corner to help you adjust the crop rectangle.

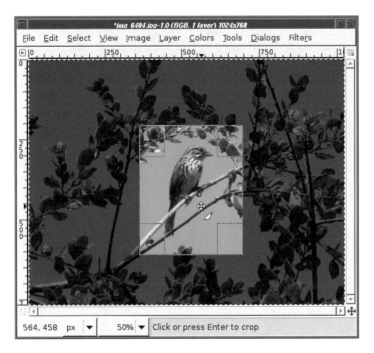

Figure 2-11. *The 2.2 Crop tool in action*

In GIMP 2.4, drag any corner or any edge to resize the rectangle; dragging inside the rectangle lets you move it. (In earlier versions of GIMP, dragging the upper-left or lower-right drag handles let you make the crop rectangle larger or smaller, while dragging the upper-right or lower-left drag handles moved the rectangle without changing its size.) Watch the mouse cursor carefully as you move it over the drag handles. The cursor will change as the mouse covers the handle, and will give you a clue as to what GIMP will do if you begin dragging at that position. Figure 2-11 shows the Crop tool in "move" mode, where the cursor is positioned near the center of the image and not on a drag handle. The cursor itself is a pair of crossed arrows (to indicate "Move"), plus a copy of the Crop tool's "scalpel" symbol. When you move over a handle, the crossed arrows will change to a cursor showing which corner or edge will be resized if you start a drag.

GIMP 2.2 and earlier also popped up a Crop dialog showing information about the location of the upper-left corner, the width and height of the cropped image, and the aspect ratio. In GIMP 2.4, there's no more Crop dialog; the information shows up in tool options in the Toolbox. If you find that the Crop dialog gets in your way in earlier versions, hold the Shift key down when you first drag in the image to start the crop. That will prevent the dialog from coming up. When you have the rectangle adjusted precisely to where you want it, click near the middle of the rectangle or hit Enter to make it final. (In 2.2 and earlier, you can also use the *Crop* button in the dialog.)

CANCELING GIMP OPERATIONS

In GIMP 2.2 it was obvious how to cancel an operation like Crop: press *Cancel* in the dialog. But how do you cancel a Crop operation in 2.4?

There are two ways. First, you can cancel any unfinished operation in a GIMP tool by choosing a different tool in the Toolbox or Tools menu. Second, hit the Esc key. Esc dismisses most dialogs that offer a Cancel button, and it will also cancel out of some operations that don't have a dialog at all, like Crop and some selection tools like Scissors or SIOX.

The Crop tool offers quite a few options (Figure 2-10):

Current Layer Only crops only a single layer (see Chapter 3 for more information about using layers).

Allow growing lets you drag outside the image's boundaries; once you execute the crop, GIMP will make these new areas transparent.

Expand from center takes the point where you start dragging as the center of a rectangle rather than one corner.

Fixed lets you restrict the final image to a specific *Aspect ratio* (the width-to-height proportions of the image; use a colon—for example, 4:3), *Width* or *Height* (to fix only one dimension but let the other vary freely), or *Size* (use x, as in 640x480). This is especially useful if you're creating desktop wallpaper, or creating a set of fixed-size icons for a website. The two buttons next to the *Fixed* field let you specify "portrait" or "landscape" mode.

The *Position* and *Size* fields update to show where the current crop rectangle is. Most of the time you won't use these fields, but they're available if you need to specify exact pixel positions. You can also move the crop rectangle by one pixel at a time using the arrow keys on your keyboard, as long as the mouse is over one of the corner or edge control areas. Add the Shift key to adjust by larger amounts.

Highlight, which is on by default, darkens the area outside the crop (this area will be discarded).

Next is a menu that draws guides to help you visualize the layout of the cropped image. You can choose *No guides* (the default), *Center lines* (showing you the halfway points between top and bottom, left and right), or *Rule of thirds* or *Golden sections* (two guidelines taught in many photography and art books). Guides won't show up when you save the image (you'll use them again in Chapter 4).

Auto Shrink will attempt to shrink the crop rectangle to a hard boundary, but it's not very good at finding boundaries, so you're probably better off using *Image* ➤ *Autocrop Image* for that. On photographs, this usually won't do anything because there are no obvious "edges" to tell GIMP which parts can be removed. *Shrink merged* considers all layers of the image when auto-shrinking, not just the active layer—a useful option *Autocrop Image* doesn't offer.

Tip If you already have an area selected, there's a faster way to crop: use the *Image* ➤ *Crop to Selection* command in the image window menus.

Brightening and Darkening

A common problem with camera images is that they are either too light or too dark. GIMP has three powerful level adjustment tools to correct such problems: Brightness-Contrast, Levels, and Curves. You can find these tools in two different places in the menu system: in the top-level *Colors* menu (*Layer* ➤ *Colors* in earlier versions of GIMP), or in *Tools* ➤ *Color Tools*.

Tip Since Brightness/Contrast, Levels, and Curves are tools, you can also make them available as buttons in the Toolbox. Choose *File* ➤ *Dialogs* ➤ *Tools* in the Toolbox window, and click to the left of the tool you want to add to turn on the "eye" visibility icon.

Brightness-Contrast

The simplest level adjustment tool is Brightness-Contrast (Figure 2-12).

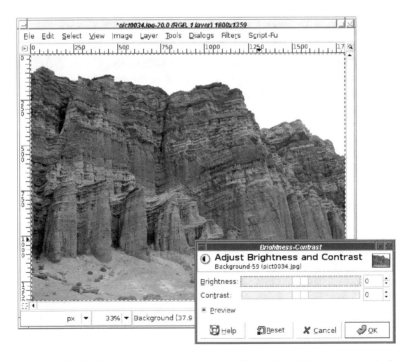

Figure 2-12. *The Brightness-Contrast dialog. The original image is too dark.*

The basic controls in the dialog are simple: two sliders, one for brightness and one for contrast. You can also type in numbers (the values go from –127 to 127, with 0 as the current image), but most of the time you'll probably just drag the sliders until the image looks best.

In addition, the dialog has a checkbox marked *Preview*. With *Preview* on, any changes you make to the sliders will be shown in the image window, so you can see exactly how your changes will look. No actual changes will be made until you click *OK*. Many GIMP dialogs have a *Preview* option; it's a useful feature that you'll want to leave enabled unless you have a very slow machine.

If you get the settings too far off, the *Reset* button at the bottom of the dialog will set them back to zero so you can start over. *Cancel* will dismiss the dialog without making any changes to the image, while *OK* will take the current settings and change the image accordingly.

Figures 2-13, 2-14, and 2-15 show some examples of the changes brightness and contrast can make. Play around with the sliders to get a feel for what they do. You'll probably find that when you make an image brighter, you'll want to increase contrast a bit, or it will look washed out. You may also be surprised at how well a slight contrast increase can bring out brighter colors in an image. Be careful of pushing contrast too far, though, or you can make the image look grainy.

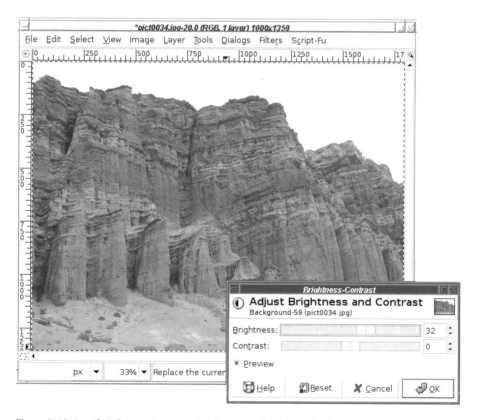

Figure 2-13. *Just brightness increased. The image looks washed out.*

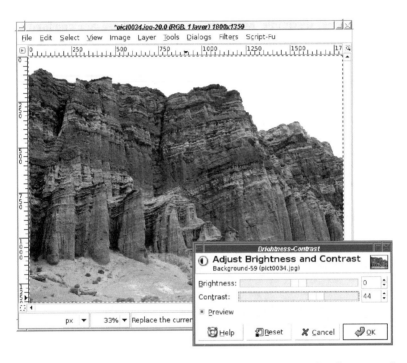

Figure 2-14. *Just contrast increased. Notice how colors seem brighter, even though the image is still too dark.*

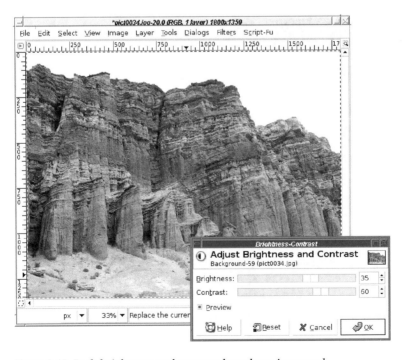

Figure 2-15. *Both brightness and contrast have been increased.*

Levels

The Brightness-Contrast tool is straightforward and useful. But GIMP has two other bright-ness tools that are much more powerful: Levels and Curves. As with Brightness-Contrast, make sure that *Preview* is checked so that you can see the effects as you play with settings.

Levels (Figure 2-16) has two sets of controls: *Input Levels* and *Output Levels*. *Input Levels* shows a histogram representing the current brightness, or *tonal range* of the image: this is a graph where the horizontal axis represents brightness, and the vertical axis represents the number of pixels that have that brightness. If the image is fairly well balanced, the histogram should be spread fairly evenly across the image. Such an image is said to have *full tonal range*. If an image is way under- or overexposed, the histogram is probably bunched up at one end, or shows a spike over to the left or the right. Such an image has a *reduced tonal range*—it is not using all the possible pixel values that can be displayed.

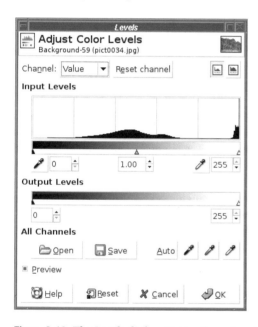

Figure 2-16. *The Levels dialog. Notice the values bunched up at the right (light) end: that's the white sky in Figure 2-12.*

Both input and output have sliders that you can play with to make the image brighter or darker, or give it more or less contrast. The three input sliders are referred to as *shadow*, *midtone*, and *highlight*, representing the darkest points in the image, a midpoint, and the brightest points.

Sometimes you can use the histogram for guidance: drag the left input slider to where it lines up with the left edge of the thick part of the histogram, and line up the right slider with the right side of the histogram (Figure 2-17). Don't neglect to experiment with the middle input level slider, which is also called *gamma value*—you can fine-tune the contrast of the image with it.

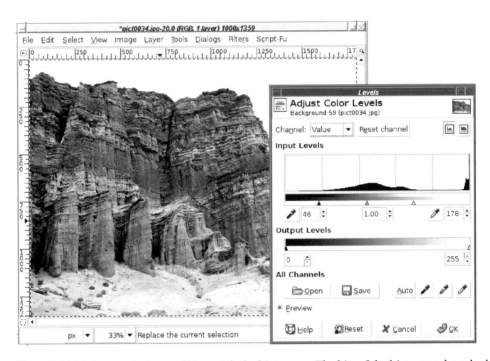

Figure 2-17. *Lining up the input sliders with the histogram. The bits of the histogram bunched at the far right are because of the bright sky.*

You can also use the *eyedropper* buttons under the input levels slider to pick points in your image that should be all black or all white: click on the left eyedropper button, and then click on the darkest point in the image. Then do the same to match the right eyedropper to the lightest point in the image.

At the dialog's upper right are two buttons, *Linear* and *Logarithmic*. These control the way the histogram is drawn. They have no effect on the operation of Levels, but switching to *Logarithmic* can make the histogram easier to see by making it taller.

One common point of confusion is that the sliders on input and output seem to work in opposite directions. If you move the leftmost input slider (at the dark end) to the right, the image gets darker; if you move the leftmost output slider (also at the dark end) to the right, the image gets lighter. What's going on here, and how can you remember which slider does what?

Think about it this way: the input sliders let you expand the tonal range of an image that has a restricted range. The leftmost *shadow* slider controls the black level: anything in the original image that was darker than the position of this slider will be mapped to black. Similarly, anything to the right of (brighter than) the rightmost *highlight* slider will end up entirely white.

Once the image has been remapped according to the positions of the input sliders, the output sliders do the opposite: they let you restrict the tonal range of the final image. Moving the leftmost output slider right means that nothing in the final image will be fully black: anything that would have been black will now be a little bit less dark. Conversely, moving the rightmost output slider to the left means that anything that would have been white will now be a little less bright.

So input expands tonal range; then output restricts it. The leftmost input slider, which represents the blackest pixels in the image, gets mapped to wherever the black output slider is positioned; and likewise the right input slider gets mapped to the right output slider (Figure 2-18).

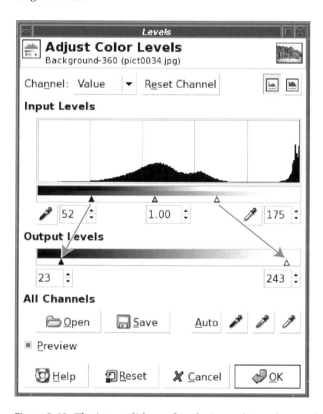

Figure 2-18. *The input sliders, after the image's tonal range has been expanded, map to the output sliders to compress the final tonal range.*

In most cases, full tonal range is a good thing; once you've adjusted the input sliders to expand your image's tonal range, you wouldn't want to restrict it again. Most of the time, you won't need the output sliders at all. They're there for the rare cases when an image needs to have a restricted range, or for images that are legitimately lacking some part of their tonal range (no highlights or no shadows).

HISTOGRAM GAPS

If you open the Levels dialog on an image when you've previously made a brightness, levels, or curves adjustment, you may notice gaps in the new histogram. What do the gaps mean? The following image shows gaps in the histogram after correcting brightness. Logarithmic mode is used to make the histogram easier to see.

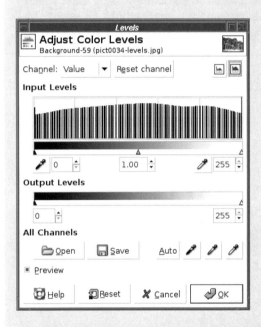

The gaps represent lost information. When GIMP uses the input sliders to expand the tonal range of an image, some of the fine differences between pixels at the extremes of the image (in the very bright or very dark parts) may be lost. "Lost information" sounds bad, but most of the time, it wasn't anything you cared about, or you would have set the sliders differently. But you can see the result in the histogram when you look at the image. This also means that you can sometimes use GIMP as a forensic tool, to tell whether someone else's image has been edited in this way.

Another thing you may notice about the Levels dialog is the *Auto* button. This is theoretically comparable to the Auto Levels in some other photo-editing programs, but in practice, I find that it seldom helps photographs very much. (This may say more about which photos I try it on than it does about GIMP's Auto Levels.) It's always worth a try; you can fine-tune from there if it doesn't quite do the right thing, and you always have the *Reset* and *Cancel* buttons if you don't like the effect.

Color Correction

Finally, at the top of the Levels dialog is a menu allowing you to choose a *channel* (Curves has one, too). Initially this is set to *Value,* which you can think of as meaning "brightness," but you can also choose *Red, Green, Blue,* or *Alpha*. The three color channels allow you to adjust color problems, such as a yellow cast from a photograph taken indoors without a flash. Color correction will be explored later, in the "Correcting Color Balance" section of Chapter 8, but meanwhile, if you have an image that needs color correction, try using this menu in Layers or Curves. *Alpha* is a term meaning "transparency"; you'll work more with transparency in Chapters 3 and 4.

Curves

The Curves dialog (Figure 2-19) adjusts many of the same values as Levels, but in a different way. Some people find it more intuitive than Levels; others less so. You'll probably find that you prefer one or the other; which one you use is purely a matter of preference.

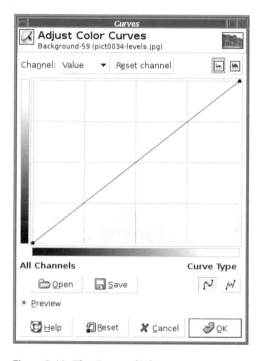

Figure 2-19. *The Curves dialog*

    In the Curves dialog, the horizontal bar at the bottom of the graph represents input values, just like the input graph in the Levels dialog. The vertical bar represents output levels. But you don't need to know that to use Curves. To begin using it, just click on the line and drag it up a little (to make the image brighter) or down a little (to make it darker).

    As soon as you click on the line, GIMP creates a *control point*: a handle you can use to grab the curve and drag it higher (brighter) or lower (darker). You can go back and click again on an existing control point and slide it up or down along the curve, or you can leave existing control points where they are and click somewhere else on the line to create more control points (Figure 2-20). If you need to get rid of a control point you've made, just slide it all the way left or right to another control point or to one of the endpoints of the curve.

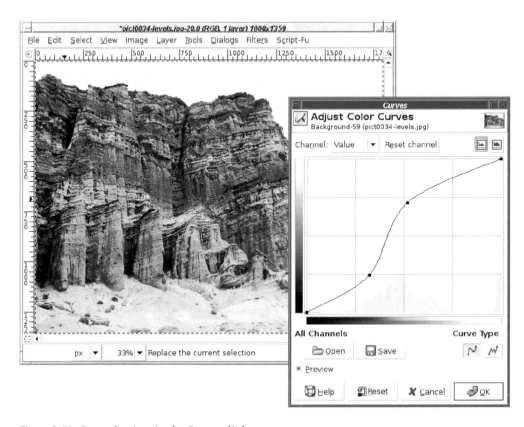

Figure 2-20. *Control points in the Curves dialog*

The advantage of the Curves tool (besides being fun to play around with) is that you can easily control which parts of the image are adjusted. The upper-right part of the curve corresponds to parts of the image that are already bright, while the lower-left part corresponds to darker areas. If most of the image is fine, but there are some bright areas that look blown out and you just want to tone those down, you can make a curve that's straight except at the upper right, where it curves below the original line to make the bright areas darker. Then if the dark parts are too dark, you can grab the lower-left corner and drag it upward to brighten just those parts. You can make as many control points as you wish, and as complicated a curve as you desire, to fine-tune the correction you will make. (The catch is that such complex curves seldom accomplish much more than a single control point moved to the right place on the curve. But try it yourself. Experiment and see what you can do!)

Options in the Curves Dialog

The *Linear* versus *Logarithmic* buttons at the upper right of the dialog control the way the histogram is presented, just as in Levels; they have no effect on the operation of Curves.

At the lower right are two buttons for *Curve Type*. By default, the Curves dialog will make a smooth curve connecting your control points, but if you want finer control than that, click on the *Freehand* button and draw your curve directly.

At the lower-left are buttons enabling you to *Save* a curve, or *Open* one you've previously saved. This may be helpful if you have a large number of images that all have basically the same exposure problems.

Finally, Curves, like Levels, offers a menu that lets you work on color channels individually, in case you need to fine-tune the image's color.

Other Exposure Adjustments

In addition to the three general tools for adjusting exposure, GIMP's *Colors* menu has several other useful tools.

Threshold (Figure 2-21) lets you map an image to black and white, adjusting the threshold point between the two. Like Levels and Curves, Threshold shows a histogram of the image's brightness. The area between the black-and-white sliders, colored blue, represents the range that will be white in the final image. Everything else will be black. You can drag the sliders directly, or mouse down in the histogram area and drag out the area that should be white.

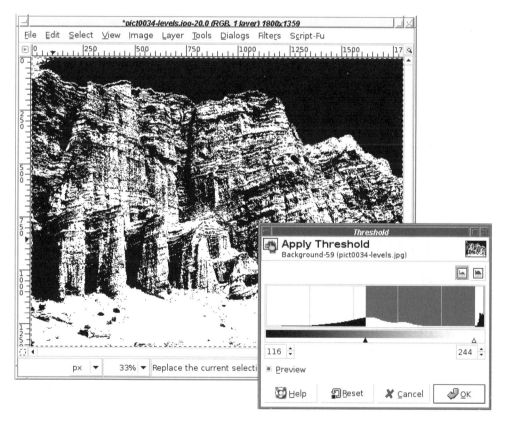

Figure 2-21. *The Threshold dialog. Notice the black sky, corresponding to the white area at the far right of the dialog.*

Tip Threshold is particularly useful for scans of printed text documents and line art (you'll see an example in Chapter 8). If you end up with a few extra speckles of the wrong color, you can clean them up afterward using GIMP's drawing tools (see Chapter 4).

Posterize (Figure 2-22) reduces the number of colors in the image, creating a gaudy display like you might see on an artistic poster. You can achieve a similar effect by converting an RGB image to indexed mode, but posterize is a quick way to achieve this effect, and it still leaves you with an RGB image in case you want to do further editing. The effect is most obvious when you use a small number of colors.

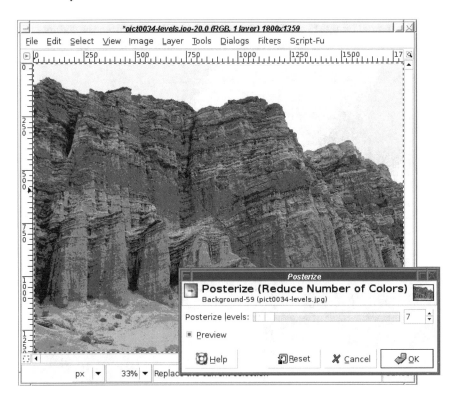

Figure 2-22. *A posterized image*

Desaturate (Figure 2-23) removes the colors from an image, changing it to a grayscale image without requiring you to convert to grayscale mode. The three choices in the dialog let you choose the gray level in three ways, giving subtly different results. (GIMP 2.2 and earlier didn't offer a choice of methods.) Desaturate has no preview, so you'll have to try it and use Undo if you don't like the results.

Figure 2-23. *A desaturated image*

Invert reverses every color in the image, turning it into its own photographic negative. This is most useful with black-and-white images but can have an interesting effect on color images (Figure 2-24).

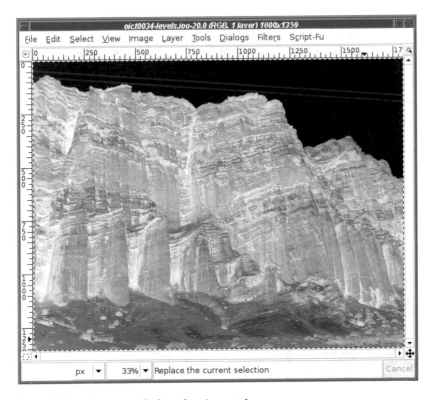

Figure 2-24. *An image with the colors inverted*

The *Auto* menu includes a set of automated functions useful for correcting photographs with poor exposure. They're worth trying if you have a difficult image you're trying to save; if you don't like the effect, there's always Undo.

- *Equalize* tries to spread the image's colors out among a wider range of intensities. Most of the time, you probably won't like the effect, but sometimes it brings out detail you didn't realize was there.

- *White Balance* tries to correct color casts, and often does a decent job. It's worth trying if you have an off-color image.

- *Color Enhance* makes the colors more intense—usually *too* intense, but try it and see.

- *Normalize* helps adjust the exposure on underexposed images. On images that are well balanced except for being too dark, it may help immensely, but if the image's levels are uneven, *Normalize* will probably just make things worse.

- *Stretch Contrast* and *Stretch HSV* are similar to *Normalize* except that they operate on the three color channels independently. Sometimes they can help remove color casts.

Rotating

GIMP offers two types of rotation. One is a quick fix for images shot in *vertical* format, while the other, free rotation, is a more subtle tool that can correct minor errors made while shooting.

Rotating by Multiples of 90 Degrees

I shoot lots of *verticals*: photos where I rotate the camera by 90 degrees to the left or right in order to make an image that's taller than it is wide.

That's fine, but when I put it on a website, or load it into GIMP, everything's sideways! The camera doesn't know that the image should be rotated, so it just saves it in the normal way, wider than it is tall. (Some cameras are smart enough to notice when they're rotated, and save the information in the file. Starting with 2.4, GIMP detects this and asks whether you want the image rotated.)

But fixing a rotated image in GIMP is incredibly easy, using the *Image* ➤ *Transform* menu. You can *Flip Horizontally*, *Flip Vertically*, *Rotate 90 degrees CW* (that's clockwise), *Rotate 90 degrees CCW* (counterclockwise), or *Rotate 180 degrees*. (The *Flips* are different from *Rotate 180 degrees* because *Flip* makes a mirror image, while *Rotate* preserves left and right if you look at the image upside-down.)

The final option in the menu, *Guillotine*, is a different operation (not a rotation) and will be discussed in Chapter 7.

Free Rotation

Do you ever shoot a photo of a landscape, and notice later that you didn't hold the camera perfectly horizontal?

Okay, maybe *you* don't, but I have to confess I make that mistake from time to time. Fortunately, GIMP comes to the rescue with the Rotate tool (Figure 2-25).

Select the Rotate tool in the Toolbox. There are several other tools that look similar, but remember, you can always hold the mouse over a tool (technically: *hover*) and read the tooltip to remind yourself which tool is which. Now look at the tool options—in particular, the *Transform Direction* option. For correcting a photo with a non-level horizon, set *Transform Direction* to *Backward*, and set *Preview* to *Grid*.

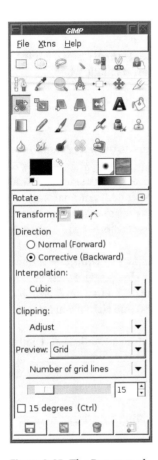

Figure 2-25. *The Rotate tool*

With the Rotate tool selected, click in the image to begin the rotation process. The Rotate dialog appears. You can use it to type in an explicit angle in degrees, or to change the center of rotation. Most of the time, though, you won't need to do that.

If you have *Preview* set to *Grid* , you'll see a grid of lines drawn on the image.

Now drag in the image and watch the grid change. The goal is to line the grid up to where the horizon *should* be in the image (Figure 2-26). When you're happy with how the grid lines up, clicking the *Rotate* button will rotate the image (Figure 2-27). Rotating a large image takes a while: GIMP's progress bar, at the lower right of the image window, gives you an idea of how long the operation is taking (there's a *Cancel* button next to it, if you change your mind).

Figure 2-26. *The Rotate tool in action: lining up the grid lines*

Notice that rotating makes the picture larger: the corners hang off the edges of the image. Behind the image, you see a gray checkerboard pattern. This pattern isn't really part of the image; it's how GIMP represents transparency. Your rotated image is now on a transparent background. If you would prefer the image cropped to its original dimensions, with no transparency added, the checkbox for *Clip Result* in the Rotate tool options will do the crop for you. Alternately, you can increase the image size to show the corners using *Image ➤ Fit Canvas to Layers* or *Image ➤ Canvas Size*.

Figure 2-27. *A rotated image (not clipped)*

The Rotate tool has quite a few options:

- *Transform* lets you apply the rotation to the current layer, just the selection, or the current path. If you use the "chain link" buttons in the Layers dialog to link several layers together, they will all rotate together (you'll see an example of that in Chapter 3).

- *Direction* changes the direction of the rotation, and the *Preview* options work along with it. While *Backward* and *Grid* work perfectly for an image with a tilted horizon, there are other times when you want to rotate an object and see exactly how it will look. In that case, set *Transform Direction* to *Forward*, and *Preview* to *Image* or *Image+Grid*.

- *Interpolation* affects the quality of the rotated image. Unless your machine is very slow, you'll probably want to change this to *Cubic* or *Lanczos*.

- *Clipping* lets you crop the rotated image to the same size as the original, as already noted. (Unfortunately, there's no setting that will clip the result to eliminate the transparent corners entirely.)

- *Preview* (discussed earlier) controls the way GIMP will show the effect of the rotation.

- You can also restrict the rotation to be an even multiple of 15 degrees. If you don't check this option, you can still constrain the rotation by holding down the Ctrl key while rotating.

Sharpening

Alas, photographs aren't always as sharp as we'd like. (Blame it on the camera's autofocus! Yes, that's it!) For instance, the kestrel in Figure 2-28 is a little out of focus.

Figure 2-28. *A blurry kestrel*

GIMP can sharpen it. GIMP can't work miracles, but it can go a long way toward sharpening an image that's a little fuzzy. It offers several sharpening methods. The two most important are Sharpen and Unsharp Mask, both located in the *Filters* ➤ *Enhance* submenu of the image window (Figure 2-29).

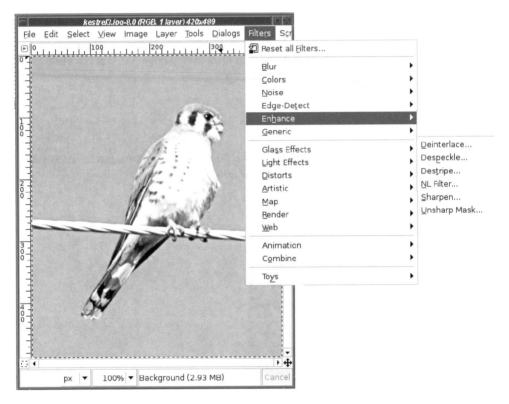

Figure 2-29. *The Enhance submenu*

Sharpen is very simple (Figure 2-30). It has a slider to control the amount of sharpening, and a preview window to show what the effect will look like. Scroll the preview window to the appropriate part of the image, or use Preferences to increase the preview size. (Resizing the dialog also changes the size of the preview area.)

Figure 2-30. *The Sharpen dialog*

Here's what the kestrel looks like when sharpened (Figure 2-31).

Figure 2-31. *The kestrel after sharpening. The effects of Sharpen are usually fairly subtle.*

For more extreme sharpening, use Unsharp Mask (Figure 2-32). Don't be misled by the name, which comes from the details of how it works. Unsharp Mask makes an image much sharper—not less sharp—but it does that by making a blurry copy of the image, and then using that as a mask for the sharpening operation. Like Sharpen, it brings up a window with sliders and a preview area, but it has three parameters you can control, and it's capable of sharpening an image much more than the standard Sharpen.

Fiddle with the three parameters of Unsharp Mask and see what they do. Generally speaking, *Radius* affects the distance over which the sharpening works; make this bigger for large images, or very fuzzy ones. *Amount* controls how strong the effect will be; make this as small as you can so as not to oversharpen and end up with a grainy image, or with halos around the object you're hoping to sharpen. *Threshold* controls the smoothness of the image; if you end up with grainy areas that should look smooth, such as the sky, an adjustment here may help.

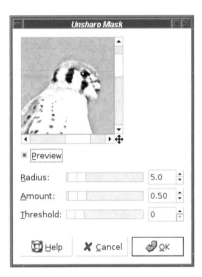

Figure 2-32. *The Unsharp Mask dialog*

Unlike Sharpen, which can only create fairly subtle changes, Unsharp Mask can easily go too far in sharpening an image (for instance, see Figure 2-33). In fact, I find that the default values are usually already too extreme, and I decrease them slightly. Figure 2-33 shows the effect of the default values on the kestrel.

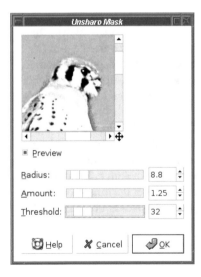

Figure 2-33. *Too much sharpening makes an image look grainy or can give it a halo.*

Figure 2-34. *Kestrel, sharpened with Unsharp Mask*

Figure 2-34 shows what happens if I decrease *Radius* to 4, and increase *Threshold* to prevent the sky from becoming grainy.

Fixing Red-eye

Flash pictures of people, especially children, often exhibit *red-eye*: pupils reflect too much light from the flash, turning the eye a diabolical crimson. This is particularly noticeable in photos of children (Figure 2-35) since their pupils are especially large.

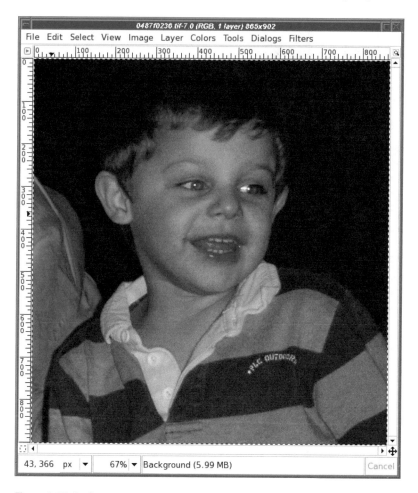

Figure 2-35. *Red-eye can turn a sweet child into a demon.*

Fortunately, the fix is very easy, especially now that GIMP 2.4 has a red-eye filter built in. Just use the Rectangle Select tool to outline a box around the eyes, then choose *Filters* ➤ *Enhance* ➤ *Red Eye Removal* to open the dialog shown in Figure 2-36. Adjust the threshold as needed, and click OK when you're happy with the result.

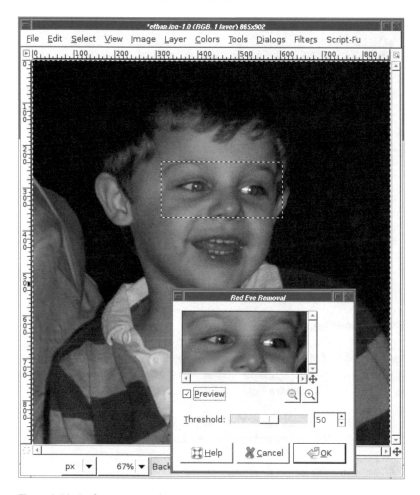

Figure 2-36. *Red-eye removal*

Why do you need to select the area with the eyes? If you're curious, try using the red-eye filter without making a selection first. Figure 2-37 shows what happens to any other parts of the image that just happen to be pink or red.

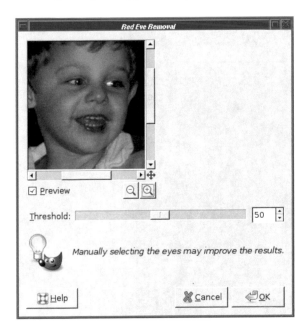

Figure 2-37. *Why you need to select the eyes first*

In GIMP 2.2 and earlier, red-eye removal was a little more complicated—you had to do it by hand, and it can be useful to know the technique in case you ever want to remove green-eye or yellow-eye from animal photos. Here's a quick-and-dirty method that usually works fairly well.

First, zoom in on the image, using the *View ➤ Zoom* menu, the *Zoom* button near the lower-left of the image window, or the + key. Zoom in a lot. Make the pupils nice and big. We'll change one pupil at a time.

Now choose the Ellipse Select tool in the Toolbox (Figure 2-38).

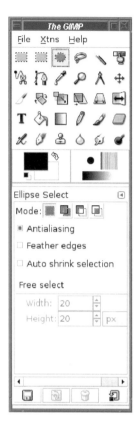

Figure 2-38. *The Ellipse Select tool*

Click slightly above and to the left of the pupil. Imagine a square box around the pupil—you want to hit the corner of where that square box would be. Then drag down and right (just like when you were making a crop rectangle with the Crop tool) until you have a circular selection around the pupil (Figure 2-39).

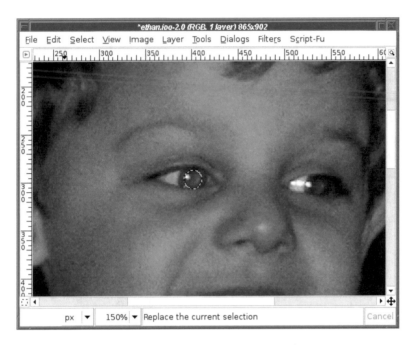

Figure 2-39. *Make a circular selection around one pupil.*

In GIMP 2.4, you can adjust the size and position of the ellipse interactively, though unfortunately earlier GIMP versions didn't allow this. In earlier GIMPs, if your elliptical selection ends up in the wrong place, just undo and try again. It's not critical that it match the pupil exactly; just get it close. Try to err on the side of too large rather than too small (too small may give you a halo). Once you have the pupil selected, go to the *Colors* menu (in GIMP 2.2 and earlier, find it under *Layer* ➤ *Colors* or *Tools* ➤ *Color Tools*) and choose *Hue-Saturation*. Without going too deeply into how colors are represented (see Chapter 8), the goal here will be to remove the red color from the pupil without losing the bright reflection.

First, click on the toggle button under *R*. This will restrict the operation to only the red color. (The eyes of animals sometimes show "red-eye" in colors other than red, so if you're trying to fix a demon bunny or kitty, you may want to leave the setting on *Master*.) Then slide the *Saturation* control all the way to the left. *Desaturating* an image means removing all the color, or making it grayscale, though in this case, we're only removing all of the red.

The hue-saturation operation only applies to what's selected, if there's a selection—otherwise it applies to the whole layer (you can think of it as applying to the whole image, until you begin working with layers in Chapter 3). That's true of most GIMP operations: if a selection is active, then only what's inside the selection will be changed.

With the pupil desaturated, the photo looks much better. The red is gone, and for some photos this may be all you need. But in this case, the pupil looks lighter than it should. I'd like to darken it a little.

If you find the selection boundary distracting, using Ctrl+T toggles the selection outline off temporarily: it's a shortcut for *View* ➤ *Show Selection*. You can do this even when you're in the middle of an operation like hue-saturation. Be sure to press Ctrl+T again right afterward to turn it back on, or you'll end up with a selection you can't see!

The *Lightness* slider makes the image brighter or darker, much as the *Brightness* slider in the Brightness-Contrast dialog did. With *Lightness* adjusted much darker (Figure 2-40), the pupil looks much more natural.

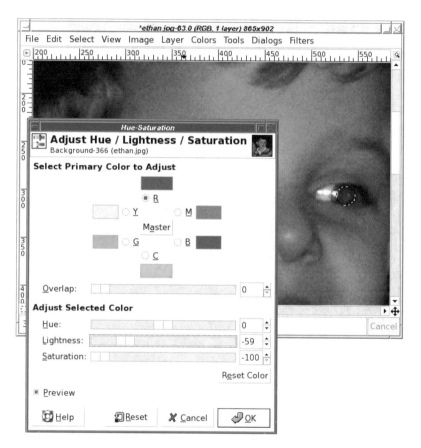

Figure 2-40. *Making the pupil slightly darker*

Now go back to the Ellipse Selection tool, select the other pupil, and apply the same operation. Voilà! No more demon! (See Figure 2-41.)

Figure 2-41. *No longer a demon!*

Summary

Now you know enough to take your photos, fix any minor problems they may have, and share them with anyone in an appropriate size and format. You can crop your photos to preserve the most important parts and get rid of the rest. You can correct problems with brightness and contrast, minor rotation difficulties, and red-eye caused by too much flash. You know when to use GIF, when to use JPEG, and when to use PNG or TIFF. You can even modify photographs that aren't completely in focus. That may be enough to keep you busy for quite a while.

But there's so much more that you can do with an image-editing program! The heart of image editing is learning to use layers. It's a different model from anything you may have used in simpler photo-editing programs, but once you begin to use layers, you'll wonder how you ever lived without them.

So take a deep breath, and prepare to explore layers, the real power of GIMP.

CHAPTER 3

■■■

Introduction to Layers

Layers sound intimidating. When you start to use an image-editing program, your first impulse is to avoid them and just make all your changes directly to the image.

But multiple layers make almost every aspect of image editing easier. If you learn about them now, you'll save an amazing amount of time, and operations that previously would have been impossible become easy. This chapter will cover the following topics:

- What is a layer?

- Using layers to add text

- Using the Move tool

- Changing colors: GIMP's color chooser

- Simple effects using layers

- Linking layers together

- Performing operations on layers

- Using layers for copy and paste

- Aligning layers

- A tour of the Layers dialog

- Bonus project: Making simple GIF animations

What Is a Layer?

Every image in GIMP is made by combining one or more separate images, called layers, laid on top of each other.

As you'll recall from the discussion of file types in Chapter 2, images can include full or partial transparency. So can layers.

In the simplest way of combining layers, *normal mode*, anything completely opaque (not transparent at all) in the top layer is all you see in the final image. If the top layer is a photograph, like the ones you worked with in Chapter 2, then that's all you'll see in the final image, even if there are other layers underneath.

Layers get much more interesting when they include transparency. A transparent layer lets you put part of one image on top of another. Everywhere that the top layer is opaque is what you see in the final image, but where the top layer is transparent, you can see through to the next layer down. If that layer, in turn, has transparency, you can see through to the next layer down, and so forth.

Figure 3-1 illustrates how a layer stack works in an image with several components. The top layer contains text; everything else is transparent. Next down is part of a flower photograph. The edges fade away just outside the flower so anything outside of that is transparent. Under the flower are layers for a picture frame, a shadow cast by the frame, and the background color. When these layers are combined, the image looks like Figure 3-2.

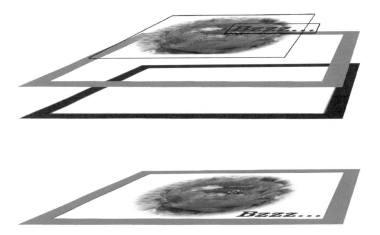

Figure 3-1. *How multiple layers combine to form an image*

Figure 3-2. *The image created by the layers in Figure 3-1*

Why bother with all that? After all, you could just take a photo, put text in it, draw the frame directly on it, and get the same result. Right?

The difference is that with layers you have much more control. If you draw text directly onto an image, you'd better choose the right location for it, and the right font, size, and color. If you later decide the text would look better twice as big and over on the left instead of the right, there's no easy way to make the changes.

With layers, you can edit and revise to your heart's content. Set up a text layer. If you don't like it where it is, move it somewhere else. If you want to make it bigger, or move part of it behind another layer, or turn it off to see what the image looks like without it, you can do that too.

In addition, each layer contains only a specific part of the image. That can help when you apply other effects. A text layer contains only text, which means you can go back and change what it says, or try a different font or color. The frame in Figure 3-1 and Figure 3-2 was in its own layer, which made it easy to generate a drop shadow from it.

Since layers are so powerful, GIMP is designed around them. Most of GIMP's effects (beyond the basic photo-manipulation methods you learned in Chapter 2) either create new layers or assume that you're working from a single layer in an image that has other layers. Therefore, some familiarity with layers is crucial to getting the most out of GIMP.

Using Layers to Add Text

Layers are much easier to understand when you create them yourself. So let's try a couple of basic projects.

The first step is making sure the Layers dialog is visible. It's shown by default when you start GIMP, but if you closed it at some point, bring it back now by using the Toolbox menu *File ➤ Dialogs ➤ Layers*. (Ctrl+L will also show the Layers dialog.) The Layers dialog looks like Figure 3-3 (the layers shown are the ones that correspond with the flower image earlier).

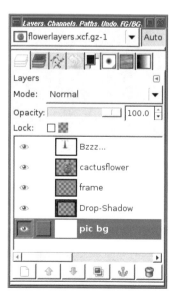

Figure 3-3. *The Layers dialog*

I'll talk about the various parts of the Layers dialog later in the chapter. For now, just make sure it's visible.

Next open an image—any image. I'll use this photo of a rock formation from Goblin Valley, Utah (Figure 3-4).

The Layers dialog now looks like Figure 3-5. The image only has one layer, named "Background".

Figure 3-4. *A rock formation in Goblin Valley*

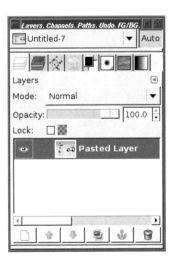

Figure 3-5. *The Layers dialog when the image is a single photo with no additional layers*

Note Remember in the first paragraph when I said you could just make the changes to the image itself instead of using layers? Now you know it's really a layer anyway!

The Text Tool

Now you'll add some text to the image. To do that, select the Text tool in the Toolbox (Figure 3-6).

Figure 3-6. *Activating the Text tool*

I'll talk about the Text tool's options in a moment, but it's easier to see their effect when you have some text to work with. So click anywhere in the image. The Text Editor window pops up (Figure 3-7).

Figure 3-7. *GIMP's Text Editor window, ready for you to type something*

The Text Editor is a very simple dialog:

- *Open* lets you load text from a file.

- *Clear* deletes whatever text you've typed and lets you start over. Of course, normal editing operations also work, like selecting the text and typing something else, or using the Backspace key repeatedly.

- *LTR* and *RTL* stand for "Left To Right" and "Right To Left." Some languages require a right-to-left option, but for English text, you can safely ignore these buttons.

As soon as you type into the Text Editor, your text appears in the window. But something else happens: a new layer appears in the Layers dialog (Figure 3-8). You're now using multiple layers!

Figure 3-8. *The new text layer in the Layers dialog*

I'll type some text in my sample (Figure 3-9). But it's tiny! My font size is much too small for this large image. Now it's time to look at the Text tool options.

Figure 3-9. *The initial font size is much too small.*

Like all Toolbox tools, the Text tool has options shown below the Toolbox (or in the Tool Options dialog, if you've undocked it). You saw those options in Figure 3-6.

Note The title for this area is the name of the tool—in this case, *Text*—but this area, in the same place for all tools, is referred to as *Tool Options*.

You'll probably already be familiar with many of the Text tool options from using word processors. *Font, Size, Color,* and *Justify* all change the appearance of the text in the specified way.

Hinting and *Force auto-hinter* control how text is displayed at small sizes. In image editing, you'll be using fairly large text sizes most of the time, so you shouldn't need to change these settings. But if you're using small text, they're worth trying.

Antialiasing, however, is important to know. When it's on (the default), edges of letters will be smoothed by making jagged edges partially transparent. This is usually a good thing. However, in some cases you may not want this, such as in an indexed image with a limited number of colors, or text in small sizes where you want the letters to look sharp.

The three options *Indent*, *Line spacing*, and *Letter spacing* let you fine-tune the way characters are displayed. Most of the time you shouldn't need to change these, but some fonts may not correctly report their size (and therefore look awful) unless you adjust these numbers. Of course, sometimes you just want to space things out a little more than usual.

Text along path and *Create path from text* are two options that will become very handy once you begin using paths (they're discussed and in the section "Bending Text into Other Shapes" in Chapter 7).

If the text is too small, as in this case, the solution is to adjust *Size*. You can click on the up and down arrow buttons, or type a different number into the text field.

You may also notice that *Size* has a units menu next to it. By default, GIMP uses pixel sizes for fonts, but you can specify a different unit, such as points, inches, or millimeters.

The text will change in the image window as soon as you change any of the Text tool options.

Don't count on the Text tool creating text in exactly the size the units menu leads you to expect. The size at which text is drawn on an image depends on many factors, such as the size of the image, the current resolution setting, and options such as hinting. Choose a text size that looks right in the image, rather than trying to force it to a specific number of points or inches.

With the text size set to 150 pixels, the text looks much better (Figure 3-10).

Figure 3-10. *The font size is much better now.*

SAVE YOUR WORK

To save the results of your hard work when you're gimping an image with multiple layers, use GIMP's native format: XCF.

The XCF format saves everything about the image: all the layers, the current selection, any paths or guides (those will be discussed in later chapters)—in short, all the details you need to continue working on the image later. (There's one exception: *Undo* steps won't be remembered.)

In GIMP's Save As dialog, if you type a file name ending in ".xcf", GIMP will automatically save to the right type. Of course, once you save as XCF, GIMP will continue doing so until you tell it otherwise.

Since XCF files can be quite large, you can use .xcf.gz or .xcf.bz2 to tell GIMP to compress using the gzip or bzip2 compression formats.

The disadvantage of XCF format? Other programs can't read it. You should definitely use XCF to save a copy of the image with all the parts preserved. But once you've finished editing, you'll want to use *File ➤ Save a Copy…* to save another copy of the file in a more standard format, such as JPEG, PNG, or GIF (see Chapter 2).

Save frequently. Get into the habit of pressing Ctrl+S whenever you get to a place where you're satisfied with a set of changes. Then you're protected against unforeseen events such as computer crashes, power losses, or alien invasions.

Using the Move Tool

Since the text is in a different layer, you can move it to different places in the image, and see where you like it best.

For that, you need the Move tool (Figure 3-11). The Move tool's icon is a set of crossed arrows pointing up, down, left, and right. Become familiar with this glyph: you'll see it used to mean "move" in many places throughout GIMP.

Figure 3-11. *The Move tool*

For instance, when the Move tool is active, moving your mouse over the text in the image window changes the cursor from a pointing hand to an arrow with the Move tool's crossed arrows next to it: the Move cursor (Figure 3-12).

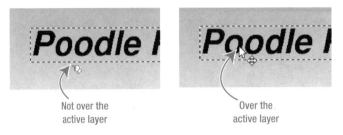

Not over the
active layer

Over the
active layer

Figure 3-12. *At left is the cursor when not pointing at the active layer. At right is the Move cursor when pointing at a nontransparent part of the active layer. The blue arrow points to each cursor's "hot spot."*

Tip Every cursor shown in a computer program has a *hot spot*, the location where the cursor points. In the case of the Move cursor, the tip of the arrow is the important part and the rest is just decoration to let you know which layer will be moved. For the Hand cursor, the tip of the pointing finger is the hot spot.

Why does the cursor change? The answer lies in the Move tool's single option: a choice between *Pick a layer or guide* and *Move the current layer.*

Every image open in GIMP has a currently selected layer, or *active layer*. This is the layer that is highlighted in the Layers dialog (and that's why it's helpful to keep the Layers dialog visible). Back in Figure 3-8, the active layer was the text layer that had just been created.

You can change the active layer at any time by clicking a different line in the Layers dialog (click either on the layer name or the thumbnail preview image).

By default, GIMP's Move tool uses *Pick a layer or guide*. In this mode, if you click somewhere in the image, whichever layer is visible at that location will become the active layer and will move if you drag it. For text layers, this can be tricky, especially at small sizes: if you move the cursor just slightly, it may no longer be over a letter, and dragging would then drag the layer under the text layer. The Move cursor, with the crossed arrows, shows that you're pointing at the active layer. If you click and drag, that's the layer that will move.

If your mouse is not over the current active layer (in this case, that means anywhere that it's not directly over text), the Move tool will switch to a different cursor to warn you that you might not be moving the layer you expect.

Caution *Pick a layer or guide* only makes the chosen layer active while it is being moved. After you release the mouse button, whichever layer was previously active becomes active again. In some earlier versions, the layer stayed active even after you released the mouse button.

Go ahead and experiment (Figure 3-13). Try moving your mouse over the text while watching the cursor. Make sure it shows the crossed arrows indicating "move." Then drag the text layer to a new location. Also, try dragging when you're not over the text layer (no Move cursor showing). Notice that in this case, the background layer—not the text layer—is the one that moves.

Remember, Ctrl+Z or *Edit* ➤ *Undo* will undo any layer movement you don't want to keep.

Figure 3-13. *Find the right spot for your text.*

When moving text (especially tiny stuff), it can sometimes be tricky to get your mouse over the text and keep it there. The cursor has to be exactly over part of a letter, not just near it. It can be even harder when you have partially transparent areas, like antialiased text. In the Move tool's alternate mode, *Move the current layer*, the active layer will always be moved when you drag anywhere in the image. This is safer—you don't have to be as careful where you put your mouse, or watch the cursor carefully to see where it changes. However, it can be inconvenient if you're moving several layers, since you have to go back to the Layers dialog and switch to a new active layer for each move.

Regardless of which Move tool mode you decide to use, you can switch to the other mode temporarily by pressing the Shift key before you click. Try both modes, and see which one you prefer.

When the Move tool is selected in the Toolbox, pressing the arrow keys (up, down, left, and right) will move the active layer one pixel in the indicated direction. Combining the Shift key with one of the arrow keys will move the active layer by 25 pixels instead of just one.

MOVE TOOL SHORTCUT

If you find yourself too frequently switching between the Move tool and other tools, there's a trick that might help: you can set up the spacebar to activate the Move tool temporarily. By default, if you press and hold down the spacebar in GIMP 2.4 (as if it was a modifier key like Shift or Ctrl) and drag in the image, GIMP will "pan" around the image. But you can change its behavior: choose *File* ➤ *Preferences* (from the Toolbox window), click on *Image Windows*, and look for *Space Bar*. If you set it to *Switch to Move Tool*, then as long as you hold down the spacebar, GIMP will keep the Move tool active. Release the spacebar, and GIMP will go back to whatever tool previously was active. (GIMP 2.2 and earlier always tied the spacebar to the Move tool, and didn't offer the panning option.) This is an especially useful shortcut for moving newly created text layers or newly pasted layers.

Changing Colors

Now that the text is the right size, it becomes more obvious that it's boring in plain old black. It's time for another color.

When you created text, it showed up as black because it used GIMP's current foreground color, the foremost of the two color swatches in the Toolbox window (Figure 3-14). It's black in Figure 3-14, meaning black is the current foreground color. Any text you add to the image, or any lines you draw, will be in this color.

Behind the foreground color is another swatch showing the background color. The most common use of the background color swatch is to save a second foreground color. You can swap foreground and background by clicking on the small arrow to the upper right of the two swatches.

The background color does have other uses more consistent with its name. Erasing or clearing uses the background color in images that lack transparency. Some drawing tools have options to use the background color instead of foreground in certain circumstances (you will see an example at the end of this chapter and more details in Chapter 4).

To change either the foreground or background color, click on the appropriate color swatch in the Toolbox.

Sometimes you may have to click twice. If the first click doesn't do anything, click again.

The tiny black-and-white boxes to the lower left of the swatches are a quick way of resetting the colors to black and white.

Figure 3-14 also shows how the Text tool's color may be different from the foreground color in the Toolbox. To change the color of an existing text layer, with the Text Editor window showing, click on the bar next to Color in the Text tool options to bring up the color chooser. Like the color swatches, this changes to mirror the color of the text layer.

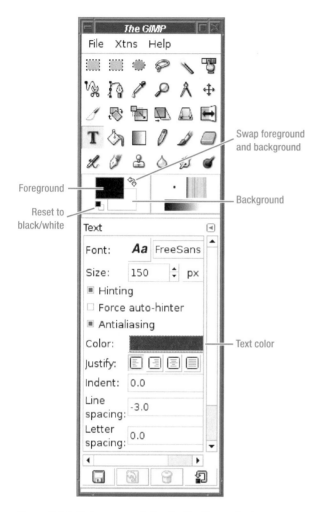

Figure 3-14. *Color controls in the Toolbox window*

If you need to change text, color, or other attributes of an existing text layer that is no longer being edited, you can do that from the Layers dialog. Right-click on the text layer, and choose the first menu item: *Text Tool* (Figure 3-15). This will bring back the Text Editor window. You can also get the Text Editor back by double-clicking on the layer preview (the "T") in the Layers dialog. If you don't need the Text Editor and merely want to change color, font, size, or other tool options, try selecting the layer in the Layers dialog, then clicking on the text in the image window. (A second click on the text will bring back the Text Editor window.)

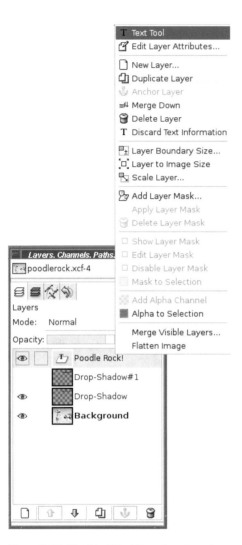

Figure 3-15. *The Text Tool item in a layer's context menu*

How do you know when the tool options are telling you about an existing text layer, instead of just the default settings for a new layer you might create? Watch the tool options to see if they change to the values you expect for that text layer. If it's still hard to tell, check the *Text along path* and *Create path from text* buttons at the bottom of the Text tool options: they're grayed out for new text, but active for existing text. (I'll talk about text along paths in Chapter 7.)

GIMP's Color Chooser

The color swatches in the Toolbox and the Color button in the Text tool options both bring up the GIMP's color chooser (Figure 3-16).

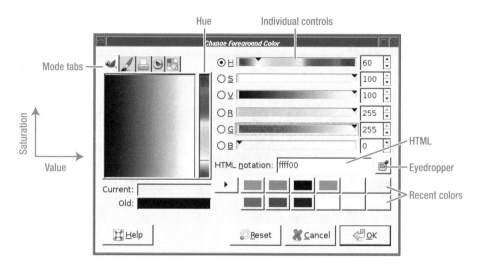

Figure 3-16. *The Color Chooser dialog*

Don't panic! Choosing colors isn't hard, even if the dialog looks complicated.

Let's start with the easiest way to choose a color. First pick a hue, using the rainbow-colored vertical slider. Click near the shade you want. If you "feel lucky" you can just stop there, or you can modify the hue by dragging up or down in the rainbow hue slider area. (Unfortunately, your arrow keys won't help here.) Then, use the square area to the left to adjust the brightness (value) and intensity (saturation) of the color.

Try to click in a place that shows a color close to your goal. Then slide around, watching the Current sample area underneath.

To get a bright color like the ones shown in the hue slider, click in the value-saturation square and drag all the way to the upper right. Dragging all the way to the left will always give black, regardless of the hue; dragging to the lower right will always give white. (For a discussion of HSV versus RGB color, see the first two sections of Chapter 8.)

When you see the color you want in *Current*, stop!

OTHER COLOR ADJUSTMENT MODES

Other ways of adjusting the color in this dialog include dragging the individual controls for Hue, Saturation, and Value (HSV) or for Red, Green, and Blue (RGB), or clicking on one of the recent colors buttons, if one happens to show a color you want. If you have an HTML page that specifies a color by number, like #0276f4, you can match it by typing the number (without the #) into the HTML Notation field. If you then hit a tab, or click in some other field to indicate that you've finished typing, you'll see the new color.

There are lots of other ways to select color in GIMP. You can click on the eyedropper, then anywhere on the screen, to choose any color you can see. Or try clicking on the mode tabs to see some of the other types of color choosers GIMP offers. Chapter 8 will discuss them in much more detail.

The *OK* button finalizes the color and applies it to the appropriate color swatch. Or, if you got to the color chooser by clicking on the Text tool's color button, the new color will be applied to the current text layer.

Figure 3-17 shows the text, now yellow.

Figure 3-17. *The text has been changed to yellow.*

Simple Effects Using Layers

I mentioned earlier that a lot of GIMP's special effects either assume that you're using layers, or they create new layers of their own.

A good example is the *drop shadow*.

Drop Shadows

Text on its own, in a single color, can look flat and boring. Adding a shadow makes it look more three-dimensional, like it's floating above the page. You know your text is on a layer by itself, but a drop shadow makes it look like a separate layer to everyone else!

A drop shadow has another useful property: it adds a dark edge to light-colored text (or vice versa). This helps if you need to show text against a complex background that includes both light and dark colors.

You'll normally use drop shadow for a layer with transparent parts, such as a text layer. Transparency is how GIMP decides where the shadow will be. (You can also generate a drop shadow based on a selection.)

To make a drop shadow for a layer, make sure the right layer is highlighted in the Layers dialog, and then go to the image window's menus and choose *Filters* ➤ *Light and Shadow* ➤ *Drop-Shadow…* (previous versions of GIMP will show it in *Script-Fu* ➤ *Shadow* ➤ *Drop-Shadow…*). This brings up the Drop Shadow dialog (Figure 3-18).

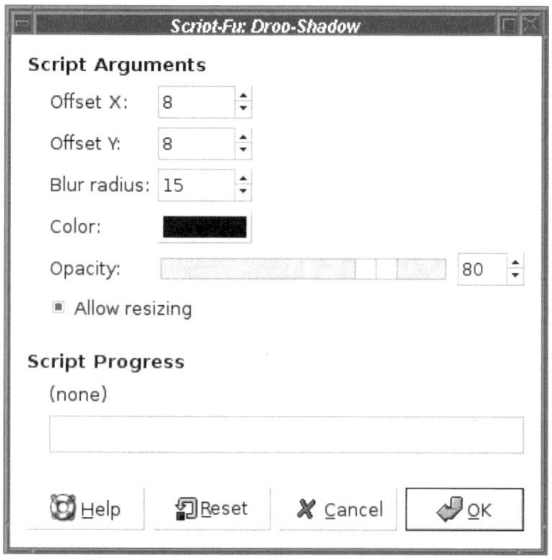

Figure 3-18. *The Drop Shadow dialog*

Offset X and *Y* represent how far (in pixels) the shadow will "drop" from the layer that casts it. Larger offsets make the object appear to be floating higher off the page, but increase the offset too far and the shadow won't look realistic.

If you decide later that you want a larger or smaller offset, you can use the Move tool to drag the shadow layer toward or away from the text layer.

Blur radius controls how blurry the shadow's edges will be. If you increase the offset, the shadow may not look right unless you increase the blur as well.

Hold your hand above a table and observe its shadow. Notice how it gets sharper as you move your hand closer to the table, and blurrier as you move your hand higher. Our brains expect shadows to act this way. If you want a realistic shadow, it's best to try to match this.

Color controls (surprise!) the color of the shadow. Usually you want a black or dark gray shadow, but tinting it slightly (using a very dark blue, for instance) can sometimes add an impression of richness. You can also make drop shadows with bright colors, or with white: they won't look like shadows, but they can help make dark text stand out against a dark background (an effect sometimes called "outer glow").

Opacity controls whether the shadow will be opaque or partially transparent. With a real shadow you can often see the pattern underneath. Less opacity creates a similar effect by letting you see a bit of the layer below. The opacity number is a percentage, from 0 (fully transparent) to 100 (fully opaque).

The *Script Progress* area is where GIMP will show a progress bar while the drop shadow script runs.

Figure 3-19 shows the effect of drop shadow with the default settings. Notice that in the Layers dialog, a new layer named "Drop-Shadow" has been added for the shadow, but the text layer is still the active layer.

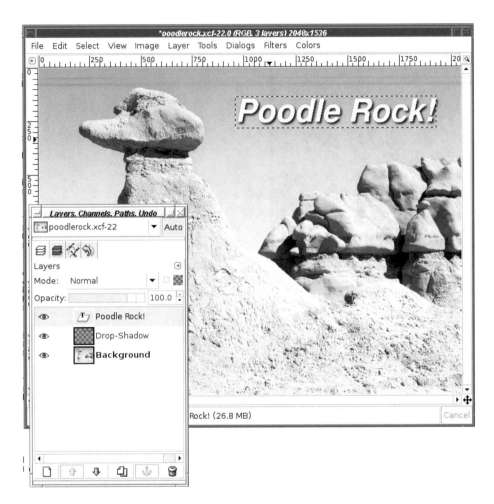

Figure 3-19. *Text with drop shadow added*

The first time you make a drop shadow, I recommend using the default settings. If you decide you need an adjustment, you can always undo and try again with different settings.

■**Tip** This is one of those times when using the tear-off feature of the context menus (discussed in Chapter 1) can really pay. You can keep the *Light and Shadow* menu up and click *Drop-Shadow…* over and over as you adjust parameters.

LAYER VISIBILITY

Wait! Don't undo your first drop shadow just yet. The Layers dialog has another nifty feature: you can turn layers on and off to try alternate versions of the same effect.

Notice the "eyeball" icon next to the left of each layer in the Layers dialog? This is a button controlling visibility of the layer. Click on the eyeball next to the Drop-Shadow layer, and the shadow vanishes. You haven't deleted it from the image; you've just temporarily made it invisible.

When you save as XCF, the invisible layers will also be saved, just like other layers.

If you make another drop shadow with different settings, GIMP will make a new layer, this time named Drop-Shadow#1, as shown in the following image:

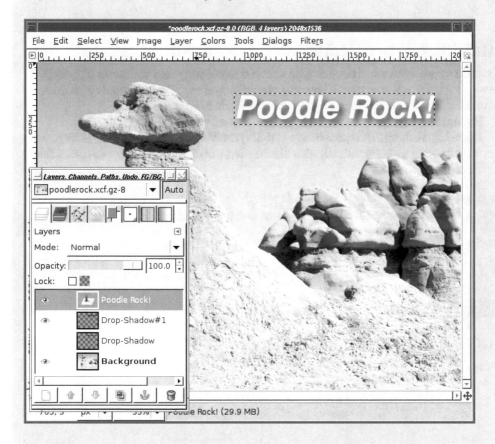

With both drop shadows stored as layers in the image, it's easy to compare them. Make first one, then the other visible. You can even try making them both visible at once, though with drop shadows that usually won't help much.

Beyond drop shadows, you'll find some other interesting effects you can try on text layers in the *Filters* ➤ *Alpha to Logo* submenu (in earlier versions, *Script-Fu* ➤ *Alpha to Logo*). Each one starts with an existing layer (most often they're used for text, but they don't have to be) and transforms it in some whizzy way. Try them all! But beware: some of them don't play nice with other layers in the image, so be ready to Undo. If you want to try out the Logo scripts without affecting an existing image, try the versions in the Toolbox menu: *Xtns* ➤ *Logos*.

Tip Exploring the Logo scripts is another job where using tear-off menus can really help.

Linking Layers Together

Once you've run a text effect or generated a drop shadow, you're left with several layers that have very specific relationships. If you drag your text layer with the Move tool and it leaves the shadow behind, you've lost your carefully calculated shadow offset.

Fortunately, GIMP offers a solution: you can link several layers together.

In the Layers dialog, the space between the "eyeball" visibility icon and the layer preview is a chain link (Figure 3-20). Initially it's a blank space, but clicking in this space makes the *chain link* icon appear.

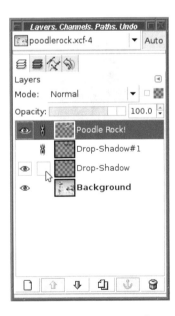

Figure 3-20. *Chain-linking layers together*

When you turn on chain link icons for several layers, they will be linked together. (It doesn't make sense to link just one layer. What's the sound of one hand clapping?) Select any one of the layers and drag with the Move tool, and they will all move together.

Linking works on invisible layers, too. If you have several alternate drop shadows, as in Figure 3-20, go ahead and link them all. They'll move together, and if you later decide to use one of the alternatives, it'll be in the right place.

Other operations are affected by layer chaining as well, as you'll see in a moment.

Performing Operations on Layers

Most GIMP operations work only on the selected layer, not the whole image. The drop shadow is a fine example.

The Rotate tool you used in Chapter 2 actually works on layers, not the whole image. You didn't notice because that image *had* only one layer. But when you have multiple layers, you can use that to your advantage.

For instance, you can rotate just a text layer (Figure 3-21).

Figure 3-21. *Just the text layer rotated*

Whoops! What happened here?

In this case, GIMP rotated the text layer—but the drop shadow layer is still in the same place. That doesn't look good at all.

There are a couple of ways you could solve this.

You could rotate the text layer first, and then create the drop shadow later. That works, but it's not helpful when you've already spent time making a drop shadow that looks just right.

Or you could make a note of the number of degrees you rotated the text, and then apply the same rotation to the drop shadow layer. Ick! Computers are supposed to handle repetitious tasks for us.

Fortunately, if you chain-link several layers together, the Rotate tool will treat them as one. The preview will only show the selected layer, but don't worry: the final rotation will include the whole chain (Figure 3-22).

Figure 3-22. *Text and drop shadow rotated together*

Unfortunately, chaining layers together doesn't work for all GIMP operations. It works for most of the "transform tools," like Rotate, which distort the image in some way. But chaining won't work for most basic operations in the *Layer* or *Colors* menu, such as Brightness-Contrast, Levels, or Curves. Those operations generally work only on the active layer.

A few operations can work either on a layer or on the whole image. Scale and the *Transform* submenu appear in both the *Image* menu and the *Layer* menu. Depending on which menu you use to call them, they will work on either the active layer or the whole image (all layers).

Using Layers for Copy and Paste

Very often, you need to copy all or part of an image and put it into another image.

In the exercise at the end of Chapter 1, you dragged a small image on top of a larger one, creating a new layer. That was straightforward. But sometimes you don't have anything to drag, or you need to copy only part of an image.

For example, I have a nice image of Mars (Figure 3-23) downloaded from NASA's Hubble Space Telescope site. What would the poodle look like with Mars for a nose?

Figure 3-23. *Mars, from NASA's Hubble Space Telescope*

Tip NASA and other US government agencies, such as the National Oceanic and Atmospheric Administration, the National Park Service, and the Fish and Wildlife Service, are excellent sources for beautiful public domain images you can use in your GIMP projects. For more details, see the "Additional Resources" section of Chapter 12.

Select Only the Part You Want to Paste

Pasting the whole Mars image won't work: you need to get rid of the black background first. To do that, use the Ellipse Select tool just as you did in Chapter 2.

In the red-eye project in Chapter 2, it wasn't important that the selection exactly match the pupil of the eye. But in this case, it's critical: it will be very obvious if some of that black background gets pasted into the poodle's face.

Fortunately, GIMP 2.4's Ellipse Select tool lets you modify a selection until it's exactly where you want it. It works a lot like the Crop tool back in Chapter 2: drag from a side or corner to adjust the size, or from near the center to move the whole selection.

In GIMP 2.2, ellipse selection is a bit trickier. If you make a circular selection that doesn't end up in exactly the right place, there are two easy ways to move it. The easiest way to move a selection without moving its contents is by holding the Alt key and dragging.

But on some systems, Alt-drag already has another function, such as moving the whole window. If that case, GIMP never sees your Alt-drag. If that happens to you, try holding the Shift key as well as Alt when you drag.

In addition, the Move tool in both 2.2 and 2.4 has an option to move just selections rather than entire layers. The key is the *Affect:* set of buttons (Figure 3-24). The second tab (with a tooltip of Selection) makes the Move tool move only the selection, not the layer.

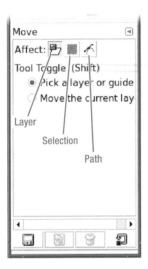

Figure 3-24. *The Affect buttons in the Move tool options*

If you switch Affect tabs in the Move tool to move a selection, I recommend switching back to *Layer* as soon as you're happy with your work. Otherwise, the next time you use the Move tool, it will still be in *Affect Selection* mode and may give you a puzzling surprise.

If you discover after moving the selection that you also made it a bit too large or small, *Select ➤ Shrink* (Figure 3-25) and *Select ➤ Grow* let you make a selection slightly larger or smaller.

Figure 3-25. *Shrink Selection dialog (Grow is similar)*

Shrink from image border only matters if the selection goes all the way to the image edge. If this box is not checked, the part of a selection at the edge will not be shrunk, even when the rest of the selection shrinks. (Of course, with the Ellipse or Rectangular selection tools, you can resize a selection using the tool's grab handles as well.)

Paste into the Image

Now that the selection is made, you can copy in the Mars image: *Edit ➤ Copy*, or just press Ctrl+C. Then paste the selection into the main image: *Edit ➤ Paste*, or Ctrl+V (Figure 3-26).

Figure 3-26. *Immediately after pasting*

A curiosity of pasting is that although the new image does paste as a separate layer, it's a special kind of layer, called a *floating selection*.

What is a floating selection?

Basically, it's a historical artifact that most people agree is not very useful any more. It may look abnormal or fragmented, many layer operations won't work right, and you can't work with any other layers while it's there.

In future versions of GIMP, pasting may create a normal layer, just like drag and drop did in the project at the end of Chapter 1, rather than a floating selection. In the meantime, click the *New Layer* button (at the bottom of the Layers dialog, Figure 3-27) to turn the floating selection into a normal layer.

Figure 3-27. *New Layer and Anchor buttons in the Layers dialog*

If you're quite sure the floating selection doesn't need to be its own separate layer, and it's already in the right place, clicking the Anchor button will merge the newly pasted image into the previously active layer. I strongly recommend doing one or the other: every time you paste into an image, click either New Layer or Anchor afterward.

■**Note** *Float* has another meaning that's slightly different. When you have part of a layer selected, *Select ➤ Float* will cut the selected piece from the layer and paste it as a new floating selection, leaving a "hole" behind. It's like a shortcut for *Cut* then *Paste*, but with one difference: Float doesn't move the selected piece, while *Paste* will center it. Older GIMP versions used to float selections automatically if you dragged from inside an existing selection. Version 2.4 no longer does that, but you can float and drag simultaneously by dragging with the Ctrl and Alt keys held down. That Ctrl+Alt trick, however, doesn't work in a few cases (like if there's a rectangular or elliptical selection that's still in resize mode, with resize handles showing). Because of this confusion, I recommend always using *Select ➤ Float* explicitly rather than depending on Ctrl+Alt-drag.

Scale the Pasted Layer

There's one more problem—the pasted image isn't the right size. Mars is too big to be the poodle's nose!

The Scale tool in the Toolbox might be just the ticket. But if you want to make sure Mars keeps its correct aspect ratio, you might want to use the Scale dialog. You already learned in

Chapter 2 how to scale an image with the dialog. Scaling a layer is just the same, except that you call *Scale* from the *Layer* menu, not the *Image* menu. But how do you figure out how big it needs to be?

For that, you can use GIMP's Measure tool, an icon that looks like a set of calipers (Figure 3-28).

Figure 3-28. *Using the Measure tool to measure the poodle's nose*

Click in the image at one end of what you want to measure, and then drag to the other end. At the bottom of the image window, the Measure tool will report the distance between the two points, the angle, and (in GIMP 2.4) how big a rectangle you'd need to use to cover the diagonal.

The tool says the poodle's nose is about 75 pixels across. So I should scale the Mars layer to 75 pixels if I want it to be about the same size as the current nose. I'll make it slightly bigger, since I want the nose to stand out.

Scale the layer, use the Move tool to move it precisely where you want it—and you're done! Figure 3-29 shows the poodle with Mars for a nose.

Figure 3-29. *The poodle with Mars for a nose*

Aligning Layers

A new addition to GIMP 2.4 is the Align tool (Figure 3-30). This tool helps you position layers precisely, though it's still in development and still needs some polishing. (Earlier GIMP versions used the somewhat more complicated *Image* ➤ *Align Visible Layers...* dialog.)

You can align just one layer, or several at a time. To choose a layer to align, click on it: GIMP should draw dots in the four corners of the layer. To operate on more layers, Shift-click on each additional layer. Or you can choose several layers at once by dragging out a rectangular box big enough to encompass all of your chosen layers.

Once you've picked your layers, choose from the *Relative to:* menu to specify whether to align them relative to the *Image*, *Selection*, or *Active* layer; or you can start with one layer and align several others relative to it (*First Item* in the menu). Eventually it may also be possible to align relative to the active channel or path, but that feature isn't working as of early 2.4 releases.

Under the menu are two sets of buttons. For using the Align tool it's important to understand that each button can move layers either vertically or horizontally, but not both. The first set of buttons is relatively straightforward: you can choose to move layers to the center, or either edge, of whatever you've chosen in *Relative to*.

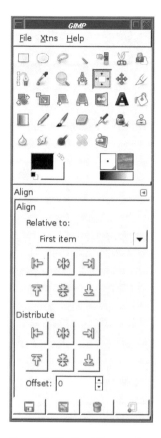

Figure 3-30. *The Align tool*

The second set of buttons, marked *Distribute*, lets you specify an offset. So, for example, you could align a layer so that its left edge falls 5 pixels to the right of another layer's by setting *Offset* to 5 and clicking the left-edge *Distribute* button. But the Distribute buttons don't work very predictably for aligning multiple layers.

What if you just want to center a single layer? Here's a trick that might be easier than either Align method: *Cut* the layer, then *Paste* it (and, of course, click *New Layer* immediately, to unfloat the selection). Cutting and then pasting automatically puts the pasted layer in the center of the currently active layer.

A Tour of the Layers Dialog

You've seen how to do quite a few things with layers. Now it's time to explore the other features of the Layers dialog. It's small, but it packs a lot of information (Figure 3-31).

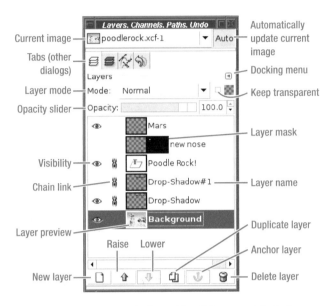

Figure 3-31. *The Layers dialog with all features labeled*

Title Area

At the top of the dialog is the name of the current image, along with a small preview of it. This is a drop-down menu: you can switch to a different image using this menu.

Next to it, on the right, is a toggle for making GIMP automatically update the Layers dialog whenever you switch to another image. (You only have one Layers dialog, so it can only show the layers in one image at a time.) Usually this is what you want, but everyone has different styles of working, and some people may prefer to turn this off.

Some versions of GIMP may not show this title area by default. To turn it on or off, click on the icon for the *Docking* menu (see the next section), and choose *Show Image Selectio*n.

Tabs

Below the current image menu are the tabs for any other dialogs that may be docked in this window (remember "Docking" from Chapter 1?). Typically Channels, Paths, and Undo History are docked in the same window with Layers, though Layers is by far the most commonly used. Other dialogs may be docked there too.

If you don't have any other dialogs docked in the window, the tab area won't be visible.

The *Docking* menu, on the right just below the tabs, lets you close or undock the dialog, or configure the dialog window in other ways. The word "Layers" to the far left of the Docking menu is simply the name of the current tab.

Some versions may also show an x button next to the Docking menu, a shortcut to remove the dialog from the window. If other dialogs are docked in the window, the window itself won't close—just the current tab.

The rest of the dialog applies to whichever layer is currently active.

Layer Mode

First is *Layer mode*.

So far you've only seen layers combined in Normal mode: anything that's opaque in the top layer is visible, while anything transparent lets you see through to lower layers. However, layers can be combined in many other ways, such as Overlay, Multiply, Dodge, or Burn, in which you see the two layers combined according to various mathematical functions. See Chapters 9 and 10 for more information on how to use the other modes.

Opacity

Next is the *Opacity slider*.

In addition to having transparent areas, a layer can be entirely transparent, entirely opaque, or anything in between. You've seen that indirectly when making drop shadows: the transparency entry in the Drop-Shadow dialog sets the opacity for the drop shadow layer.

Select your drop shadow layer in the Layers dialog, look at the Opacity slider, and notice that it's at something less than 100%. Try changing the opacity, and watch the effect it has on the appearance of the shadow.

You can use the opacity slider to create all sorts of useful effects. For example, you can render a text layer translucent and make it float over an image. Or you can create a layer that's entirely white, make it mostly transparent, and lay it over the top of an image to create an impression of haze. That's just the tip of the iceberg.

Keep Transparent

The button labeled *Lock* is more often known as Keep transparent. The checkerboard icon next to it is similar to the checkerboard background the GIMP uses to indicate transparency, and is simply a reminder of the button's meaning.) Its position varies with the GIMP version: it may be to the right of the Layer mode menu or below it, but look for the checkerboard icon.

When Keep transparent is checked, you will not be able to draw anywhere that the current layer is transparent. This is useful for drawing, but is also a common source of confusion. You'll learn more about this option in Chapter 4.

Layers List

Below the opacity slider is the list of layers in the image (with a scrollbar if needed), one layer per line. This is also called the *layer stack*, because the layers are stacked one above the other. You're already familiar with most of the items shown, but there are a few you haven't seen yet.

The Visibility Eye

On the far left is the "eyeball" *Visibility* icon. When it's on, the layer is visible; when it's off, invisible. Clicking on the eye toggles the layer's visibility. Shift-clicking makes only that layer visible; another Shift-click brings all the other layers back.

The Chain Link

Next is the *Chain link* icon. When several layers display this icon, they are linked together. Moving or transforming any one of the layers (via tools such as Rotate) will work on all of them together.

Shift-clicking on the chain link removes any layers that were already linked. This can offer a shortcut if you have a lot of layers linked and want to unlink them. A second Shift-click will select all the layers in the image.

The Layer Preview

The *Layer preview* shows a small thumbnail image of what the layer looks like.

You can't tell the difference between two text layers using the preview, but it can be useful for telling image layers apart. Double-clicking on the preview brings up a dialog that lets you edit the layer attributes (mostly, its name)… unless it's a text layer, in which case double-clicking brings up the text edit window. Clicking on the layer preview is one way to select the layer (make it active). It also ensures that if you draw, you will draw on the layer and not its mask.

Its mask?

Layer Masks

To the right of the layer preview is the *Layer mask preview* (if there is a layer mask).

A mask controls which part of the layer is visible. Most layers don't have masks, but when a mask does exist, wherever it is white, the layer is visible. Where the mask is black, the layer will be invisible (transparent) even if that part of the layer has something in it.

Clicking on the layer mask makes it active: if you draw with the mask selected, you'll be drawing in the mask, not in the layer. On a selected layer, the border of either the layer preview or the layer mask preview will be highlighted to indicate which one is active.

A layer mask is another way of representing transparency. In some cases it's easier to work with a mask than to work with transparency directly. You'll learn how to use layer masks in Chapter 5.

Layer Name

To the right of the layer and mask previews is the name of the layer. Clicking on the layer name selects the layer; double-clicking allows you to edit the layer name (for example, to change "Pasted Layer" to "Mars"). You can change layer names at any time.

Layer Buttons

Finally, at the bottom of the Layers dialog is a row of buttons that can create or delete layers, or change the order of existing ones. You can either click on them (to affect the active layer) or drag a layer on top of them. They all have tooltips, so you can remind yourself which button does what. The buttons each correspond to an action in the image window's *Layer* menu; some of them also have key bindings, which you can learn, or set, using the *Layer* menu.

The New Layer Button

New layer, the leftmost button, creates a (surprise!) new layer. You can choose the layer name, size, and fill color. (You'll create lots of new layers in Chapter 4 when you start making drawings.)

Dragging an existing layer onto the *New layer* button creates a blank new layer with the same size and position.

New layer can also convert a floating selection into a regular layer.

The Raise and Lower Buttons

The Raise and Lower buttons move the current layer up or down in the layer stack. If you want something to appear on top of something else, adjust the orders of the layers with these buttons. (In GIMP prior to 2.4, the bottom Background layer could not be moved up without first adding transparency via the *Add alpha channel* menu item.)

You can also change the order of layers by dragging a layer preview directly to a new place in the layer stack. Not only that, you can drag a layer preview out of the Layers dialog into a new image, to add a copy as a new layer in that image. You can even drag to the Toolbox, to create a new image containing only that layer.

The Duplicate Layer Button

Duplicate layer creates a new layer that is an exact copy of the active layer, or of any layer you drag onto the button. You can then move the layer up or down in the layer stack, or modify it in all kinds of ways. You'll see some ways to use this button when you create an animation, at the end of this chapter.

The Anchor Layer Button

Anchor layer is used to merge a floating selection with whichever layer was previously active.

The Delete Layer Button

Delete layer deletes the active layer. You can also drag a layer to the button to delete it.

Tip If you change your mind about a layer operation and need to undo, and Ctrl+Z in the Layers dialog doesn't undo it, try undoing in the image window.

Layer Context Menus

Right-clicking on any layer line brings up a context menu offering operations on that layer (Figure 3-32).

Caution Right-clicking on a layer line will also make it active. If you're not careful, it's possible to end up working on the wrong layer.

Figure 3-32. *The layer context menu*

The (Sometimes) Text Tool Item

If the layer is a text layer, the top item will be *Text Tool*. Choosing this will display the Text Editor window. It also activates the Text tool options in case you need to make changes to color, font, size, or other text properties.

If the layer is not a text layer, this item won't be there.

A text layer is a special type of layer, indicated by a special icon in place of the normal layer preview. Many changes to text layers, such as drawing on them or rotating them, change the layer to a normal graphics layer. After that, you will no longer be able to edit the text in the Text Editor window nor change the text properties.

Edit Layer Attributes

Edit Layer Attributes… brings up a dialog showing some properties of the layer you can change. Usually all this offers is the layer name. It's easier to change the layer name by double-clicking on the layer's name in the layer stack, so this item isn't very useful. Double-clicking on the layer's preview button is another way to access this dialog (except on text layers).

Layer Controls

New Layer, Duplicate Layer, Anchor Layer, and *Delete Layer* have the same meanings as the corresponding buttons.

Merge Down combines the active layer with the next visible layer below, using the active layer's mode. Any transparency is retained.

Discard Text Information will only appear for a text layer. It changes a text layer to a normal graphic layer. Lots of other operations will also do this as a side effect. However, there's not much reason to do it before you need to.

Layer Boundary Size

Every layer has a size, which may be different from the whole image. For example, text layers are just barely big enough to hold the text they contain. *Layer Boundary Size…* lets you change a layer's size.

Most often you'll use this to make a layer slightly larger—for example, to make room if you want to blur a text layer, make a line longer, or increase the size of a white background area. You'll see an example in Chapter 4.

Layer to Image Size

Layer to Image Size is a special case of Layer Boundary Size: it makes the layer as large as the whole image. You often need to do this after increasing image size.

Scale Layer

You've already seen *Scale Layer…,* which makes a layer and its contents larger or smaller.

Mask Options

Add, Apply, Delete, Show, Edit, Disable Layer Mask, and *Mask to Selection* are all tools for working with layer masks, which you'll learn about in Chapters 5 and 9.

Add Alpha Channel

Alpha is a fancy term graphics people use to mean transparency. *Add Alpha Channel* makes the layer capable of using transparency. It doesn't make anything transparent immediately, but if you use *Edit* ➤ *Clear,* or use tools such as the Eraser, you will create transparent areas instead of white.

If you see an error when you try to raise the bottom layer in the stack, or the arrow to raise the layer is grayed out, it may be because it needs an alpha channel (a common point of confusion in GIMP 2.2; it's fixed in 2.4).

Alpha to Selection

Alpha to Selection selects everything in the current layer that is not transparent. The name is a bit confusing, since it suggests that only the transparent parts would be selected.

Merge or Flatten

Merge Visible Layers… and *Flatten Image* are two different ways of combining multiple layers into one.

Merge retains any invisible layers, and shows a dialog asking what to do about the layer size of the result. If the image has transparency, it will be retained.

Flatten merges all the visible layers, deletes any invisible layers, fills any transparent areas with the current background color, and gives you an image with a single layer and no alpha channel. *Flatten* is sometimes done for you, temporarily, when you save to a format such as JPEG that cannot represent transparency or layers.

Bonus Project: Making Simple GIF Animations

Animations are a fun use of layers.

An animation is just a set of images in which the picture changes slightly from frame to frame. Played one after the other, they make a movie.

GIMP represents each animation frame as a layer. The first frame is the lowest layer; the last frame is the top layer.

Since you know how to create layers, there's not much more you need to know to make an animation. So let's jump right in and try one.

I have a nice photo of a biplane (Figure 3-33). Wouldn't it be a kick to make it land and take off?

Figure 3-33. *A biplane. You can make it fly!*

Create a Base Image

First, you need to create an image big enough for every part of the animation. I'll make mine about ten times the length of the plane, and four times the height—that should allow plenty of room. (Too big is better than too small: you can always crop it later if you don't need that much room.)

Usually you'll want to scale animations fairly small, especially if they'll be put on the web. An animation stores quite a few images in one file, so the file size can be quite large even if the pixel size isn't. If you're animating an image that starts as a high- resolution digital photograph, you'll probably want to scale it down quite a bit. Also, a flat (single-color) background will compress to a smaller file size.

But first, before you create the new image, why not give it a background the color of the sky?

New Image (unless you tell it otherwise) will use GIMP's current background color as the color of the new image. So click on the background color swatch in the Toolbox, and choose a nice light blue similar to the background of the plane.

Better still, use the exact shade of blue used in the biplane image. To match a color such as this plane's blue background, you can use a tool called the *Color Picker* (Figure 3-34). By default it sets the foreground color. In this case, you want it to set the background color, so check that box in the tool options.

In some GIMP versions it also pops up a dialog with information about the color (which you're free to read, ignore, or dismiss).

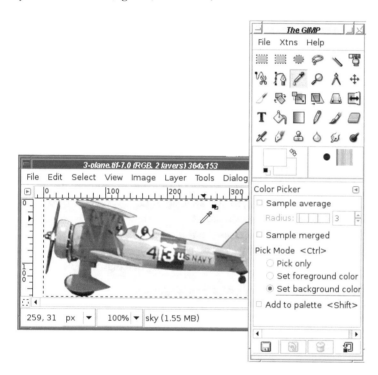

Figure 3-34. *Picking colors from the image. Notice that Set background color has been checked.*

Once the background color has been set, it's time to create the new image, with *File* ➤ *New...*, at whatever size is best for your animation.

Add the Animation Frames

Now comes the time-consuming part: adding each frame of the animation.

Start by copying (*Edit* ➤ *Copy* or Ctrl+C) the biplane image. Paste into the new image, click the *New Layer* button to turn the floating selection into a regular layer, and then use the Move tool to move it to where you want it for the first frame (Figure 3-35).

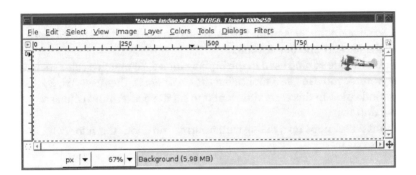

Figure 3-35. *The first frame has been pasted.*

If you've developed good layer management habits, you may be tempted to name each layer—for example, "biplane 1", "biplane 2", and so on. Although that's usually a good idea, it isn't worthwhile at this stage. The layer names will change, perhaps several times, before you're through.

Next, paste the same image again. (You shouldn't need to copy again first.) You might think that the second paste didn't work—there's no visual indication that anything happened. Why not? Because GIMP pasted the second image right on top of the first. You can tell by looking at the Layers dialog that you have a new floating selection in addition to the biplane layer you pasted already. If you drag the new layer (using the Move tool) to its new location, you'll see there's another identical biplane layer right underneath it.

Continue pasting, clicking *New Layer*, and then moving the pasted layer to a new position, until you've made as many animation frames as you want. Take a look at your creation and decide if it looks like you want it. Your image may look something like Figure 3-36.

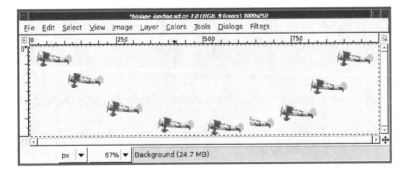

Figure 3-36. *All the planes pasted*

■**Note** You can also use *Duplicate Layer* to make each new layer, rather than successive paste operations.

Save your work (as an XCF) now. There's potential for error in the next step, so make sure you have a copy of what you've already done.

Give Each Frame Its Own Background

The final step is to add in the sky on each frame. The frames depict a biplane on a transparent background. But in the final animation, each frame will replace the previous one, so each frame needs its own copy of the sky.

Start by clicking on the bottom layer, the Background layer. That layer should already have a blue background and a single biplane on it (if you want to make sure of that, click the visibility eye icon next to it and see what disappears). You need to create another blue layer above the bottom layer. So click the *New Layer* button (the same one you've been using to turn a floating selection into a regular layer). Since there's nothing floating now, the New Layer dialog pops up.

You'll explore this dialog in more detail in the next chapter, but for now, just set *Layer fill type* to *Background color* and click *OK*. A new sky blue layer, probably named something like "New Layer", should appear between *Background* and your first *Pasted Layer*.

Right-click on the airplane layer just above the sky you just created and choose *Merge down*. Now you have a second layer consisting of an airplane on a blue sky.

Repeat for each layer. Starting on the layer you just finished, click *New layer*, then run Merge down from the biplane just above it.

At each stage, you can tell which layer is which by looking at the layer thumbnail. The checkerboard pattern GIMP uses to indicate transparency is visible in the thumbnails, as in Figure 3-37.

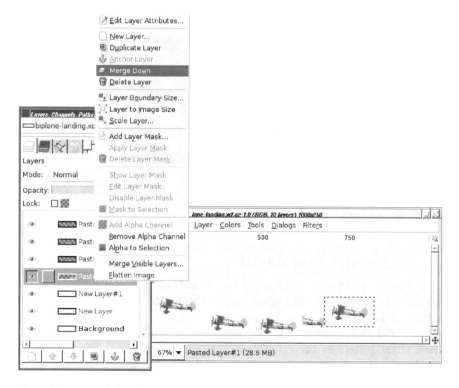

Figure 3-37. *At each level, make a new blue layer, then merge the next biplane (checkerboard) layer down into it.*

You may notice that at each step, one more plane disappears in the image the GIMP is showing you. This is because each time you add the sky background, that layer becomes opaque, so it hides the airplanes in the layers below it. Clicking the visibility eye on a few layers should convince you that your planes are still there.

Test Your Animation

Check your work: the GIMP should show only the last frame, but if you turn visibility off for the top layer, you should see the next frame down; turn off visibility for that layer too, and you'll see the next layer; and so on.

Tip You can also Shift-click on a layer in the Layers dialog to see only that layer, and turn off visibility on all other layers. Another Shift-click brings the other layers back.

Now turn them all back on. It's time to test the animation!

GIMP has a very basic animation player in *Filters* ➤ *Animation* ➤ *Playback…* (Figure 3-38). It has a play/stop button, rewind button, and step button. But that should at least give you an idea of how well your animation is working.

Don't worry if it's too fast. You can control that in the next step.

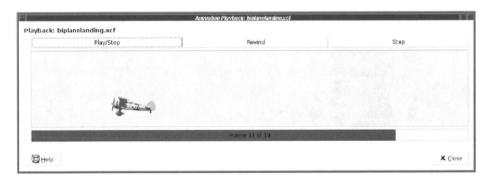

Figure 3-38. *Animation playback*

Animation for the Web: Save As GIF

Now, if you save a copy of the image as a GIF, you get a series of dialogs (Figure 3-39).

First is the normal Save a Copy dialog; type a file name ending in ".gif" here, or use the menu to select the GIF file type.

This leads to the GIF Export dialog. It reminds you there are multiple layers, and asks you whether to merge all the layers into a single still image or create an animation. Merging is the default; you will have to check the box for animation each time you save, unfortunately.

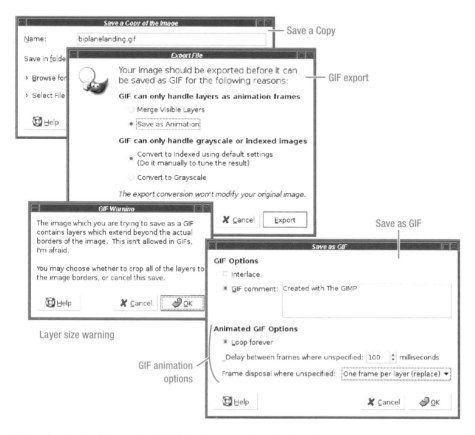

Figure 3-39. *The dialogs involved with saving a GIF animation*

The GIF Export dialog is also the one controlling conversion to indexed mode. You can make your animation file smaller if you convert the image to indexed mode first, as was discussed in Chapter 2.

If you've dragged any of your layers beyond the image borders, you may get a warning like the one shown. It doesn't do any harm; if you see this, just click OK.

Finally you get the important dialog: Save as GIF. This offers several animation options.

Loop forever is on by default. You can make your animation play once and then stop, or loop back to the beginning once it gets to the end.

Delay between frames controls the speed of the animation. The default is 100 milliseconds (1/10 of a second), but you can make the animation run slower or faster if you choose.

Frame disposal can usually be set to I don't care, as long as you've made each frame opaque, as in this example. If you do care, the choices are *Cumulative layers (combine)* and *One frame per layer (replace)*. This option only makes a difference if you create an animation with transparent frames: it lets you control whether previous frames are erased before drawing the next.

TUNING YOUR GIF ANIMATION WITH LAYER NAMES

Remember I suggested not changing the layer names early on? You saw how the layer names got lost when you merged them with copies of the background. But once you've done that, it's safe to change the layer names to something a little clearer.

While you're looking at layer names, though, it's useful to know that layer names can also specify the interval between frames. You can even vary the intervals: have your biplane come in slowly, and then use a smaller interval as it's revving up to take off.

To specify frame rate of a layer, edit the layer name (by double-clicking on the layer name in the Layers dialog) and give the layer a name that ends with a millisecond interval (in parentheses). The name might look something like: "biplane 3 (200ms)."

You can also add (*combine*) or (*replace*) after the layer name to indicate that the current layer should combine with what's in the previous frame without replacing it, or should replace everything. The name now might look like: "biplane 3 (200ms)(replace)."

If you use *File* ➤ *Open* to open the animated GIF you saved, and look at the Layers dialog, you'll find that GIMP will now show the frames with names such as "Frame 8 (200ms)." Rather than edit each frame to insert the interval, it's usually easiest simply to open the GIF, and then change the few layers where you want to use a different interval.

Filters ➤ *Animation* ➤ *Optimize (for GIF)* will also insert intervals in each layer name, but it's hardwired to 100ms, so it's not very helpful if you want most frames to have a different interval.

Now that you know how to make a biplane land and take off again, it's not that much harder to make it loop. You'd need to start with a taller blank image, of course (or use *Image* ➤ *Canvas Size*, which you'll learn about in Chapter 4). Then use the Rotate tool on each layer before you move it to the right place. I'm sure you can think of other fun animation projects as well. If you decide you like making animations, there's a GIMP plug-in called GAP (GIMP Animation Package) that can help. The sky's the limit.

Summary

By now you should be very comfortable with using layers to make new images.

You keep your Layers dialog visible and you know how to use it. You've used layers for newly created text, and for objects pasted or dragged from other images. You know how to link several layers together to move them as a group, and apply transforms or other GIMP operations to a single layer. In addition, you've learned some basic GIMP tools such as the Move tool and the color chooser.

You're ready for anything. With that in mind, it's time to lighten up a bit, take what you've learned about layers, and apply that knowledge to a really fun aspect of GIMP: drawing.

CHAPTER 4

■ ■ ■

Drawing

In this chapter, I'll take a step back from photographs and explore how to use GIMP as a drawing program. I'll cover the following topics:

- Making new images
- Using layers for drawing
- Drawing lines and curves
- Changing colors and brushes
- Erasing
- Drawing rectangles, circles, and other shapes
- Outlining and filling regions
- Filling with patterns and gradients
- Importing brushes or gradients, or making your own
- When GIMP won't draw
- A drawing project

A New Image

Most drawing projects begin with a blank canvas in a new window. Create one using *File* ➤ *New* from either the Toolbox or any image window.

Choose a reasonable size for the image. To practice drawing techniques, use a size that fits easily on your screen and leaves room for the Toolbox and Layers dialog. I often use 800 × 600. For real-world projects, you may want to use a larger canvas, in order to have high resolution for printing or for including fine details. The *Template* drop-down menu at the top of the New Image dialog lets you choose from a list of popular image sizes.

■**Caution** In the Preferences category *Default Image* (called *New Image* in earlier versions of GIMP), you can set an image size. However, the New Image dialog may not always show this size. Sometimes it reflects the dimensions of the last image you created, or of the last region you copied. To go back to the default size you specified in Preferences, click *Reset.*

Expanding the *Advanced Options* tab in the New Image dialog (Figure 4-1) shows some additional choices, such as

- *Resolution* (in pixels per inch—this is just a hint for printing programs, as discussed in the "Scaling" section of Chapter 2)

- *Color space* (RGB versus grayscale)

- *Fill with* (the color to make the new image, or you can make it transparent)

By default, GIMP will fill your new image with the current background color. For starters, you probably want a white background; though later you might want to use other colors for a richer effect. You can change your background color using the color swatch in the Toolbox, or for white, you can simply choose *White* from the *Fill with* menu of the New Layer dialog.

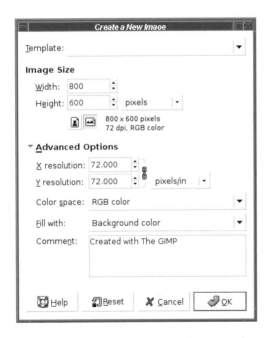

Figure 4-1. *The New Image dialog showing advanced options*

You can also make a new image transparent. This can be useful if you're making an icon for a web page, or an image that will be pasted onto a photograph later. But the gray checker-board pattern GIMP uses for transparency can be distracting. When you're learning drawing techniques, it's easier to draw on layers over a white background, even if you want transparency (you can always turn off the background before you save the file). You'll see how that helps in the drawing project at the end of this chapter.

The New Image dialog offers one more option: a space for a comment, defaulting to "Created with GIMP." You can use this space for your name and copyright information, or information about the image you're creating and what it represents. Or, of course, you can leave it blank.

Note Not all image formats can include a comment, but the most common formats—JPEG, PNG, and GIF—all have it.

Using Layers for Drawing

The first rule of drawing is *use a new layer*.

You just created a new image with a perfectly clean white background. Why should you add yet another layer?

What if you want to change the background color later? Or make the background transparent? What if you decide you want to move part of your image to a different place? What if you want to duplicate a figure you've drawn, so you can have two of them against the same background?

Sure, it's possible to make all these changes with GIMP later; but it's a lot more work than just using layers from the start.

You don't need to make a new layer for every line you draw. But try to think of your drawing in terms of functional units: the background is one layer, grass might be another, trees a third, and the sky a fourth.

So, the first step is to create a new blank layer. To do that, go to the Layers dialog and click the *New Layer* button in the lower-left corner. Up pops the New Layer dialog (Figure 4-2).

The *Layer Name* field lets you choose a memorable name for the layer. You don't have to choose a name; GIMP will assign one for you, something like "New Layer." But a well-chosen layer name can help in the long run. The name shows up in the Layers dialog, so a layer named "red arrow" or "sky" can tell you right away what's in it.

Width and *Height* default to the size of the image. That's usually fine. If you know you don't need a layer quite that big, you might be able to save some memory by specifying a smaller size (or you can crop the layer later).

Layer Fill Type lets you specify whether the layer will start out transparent (much like *Fill with* in the New Image dialog). The default is *Transparency*. Most often, when you add new drawing layers, transparency is just the ticket. But some of the special effects you'll learn in later chapters will use a solid-colored layer.

The *OK* button creates the new layer and adds it to the Layers dialog. If you need to move it up or down in the layer stack, use the up and down arrow buttons at the bottom of the Layers dialog, next to the *New Layer* button; or drag the layer's line to where you want it. The new layer automatically becomes the active layer.

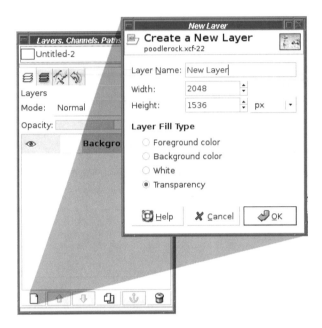

Figure 4-2. *The New Layer dialog*

Note If you're using an earlier GIMP version and you try moving your new layer down in the stack (the only choice available now), you might be surprised to discover that you can't! Remember the note about right-clicking to *Add Alpha Channel* in the Layers dialog's context menu in Chapter 3? By default, the background layer doesn't have transparency, and GIMP versions prior to 2.4 won't let a layer be moved up if it doesn't have transparency.

Drawing Lines and Curves

You're ready to draw! Choose a nice color (using the foreground color swatch), or just leave it black.

GIMP has a collection of four tools for drawing lines and freehand curves. I'll start with the simplest: the Pencil.

Drawing Hard-Edged Lines: The Pencil Tool

The Pencil tool lets you draw sharp-edged lines (Figure 4-3). Select it in the Toolbox, and then try scribbling by dragging on the image to see what it does. The Pencil tool will leave a trail everywhere you go, as long as you have the left mouse button pressed.

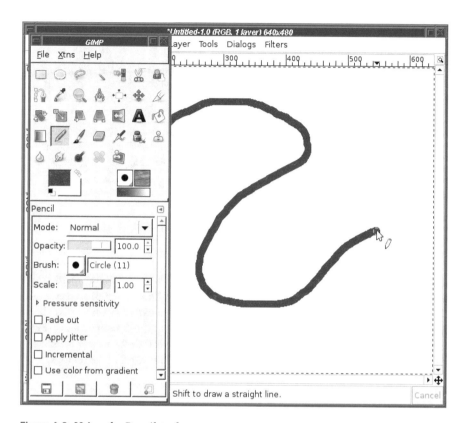

Figure 4-3. *Using the Pencil tool*

■**Tip** It's easy to draw straight lines with any of the line-drawing tools. Click once where you want one end of the line to be (GIMP paints a dot there the size of the brush). Then move (with the mouse button up—you're not dragging) to where you want the other end of the line, hold down the Shift key (GIMP will show a thin line between the mouse position and the last place that you clicked), choose your endpoint, and when you're happy with the line, click the mouse button.

Notice the mouse cursor in Figure 4-3. In addition to the normal arrow and the pencil icon telling you which drawing tool is selected, there's a circle around the arrow's point. This shows the size of the current *brush*.

Okay, a pencil normally has a point, not a brush. But this is a Super GIMP Pencil.

GIMP BRUSH ICON DISPLAY OPTIONS

You can stop GIMP from showing brush size in the cursor by turning off *Show brush outline* under *Preferences* ➤ *Image Windows*. However, the brush size feature is very useful: most people, except on extremely slow machines, will want this enabled. *Show paint tool cursor*, on the same Preferences screen, will turn off the pencil and arrow icons and show *only* the brush outline.

Alternately you can turn off *Show brush outline*, turn on *Show paint tool cursor*, and change the cursor mode from *Tool Icon* to either *Tool icon with crosshair* or *Crosshair only*. This gives you a similar but perhaps more precise result. Your call! You can also choose *Black and White* instead of *Fancy* for *Cursor Rendering*, which may help performance slightly on very slow machines.

Brushes

Changing the brush gives you control over the width and shape of the line you draw with any of GIMP's drawing tools. There are two ways of changing the brush. You can click on the brush icon in Tool Options, which drops down a menu (Figure 4-4). Or you can click on the brush icon in the Toolbox, to the right of the color swatches, which pops up the Brushes dialog (Figure 4-5). Depending on your GIMP version and how you've set up your desktop, the Brushes dialog may be a separate dialog, or it might be a tab shared with Layers and other dialogs.

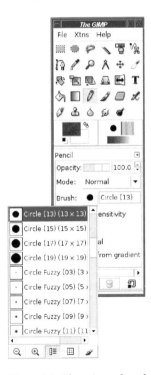

Figure 4-4. *Choosing a brush from the menu*

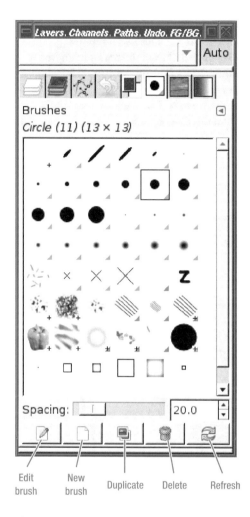

Figure 4-5. *The Brushes dialog (docked with Layers and many other dialogs)*

Clicking on a new brush in either the menu or the dialog changes the active brush immediately. You can try one, draw with it, undo it if you don't like it, and try another brush, all without dismissing the dialog.

Tip You can also get to the Brushes dialog using *File* ➤ *Dialogs* ➤ *Brushes* from the Toolbox, *Dialogs* ➤ *Brushes* from an image window, or from various docking menus, since it's a dockable dialog.

Brushes are like very small images. When you use a paint tool such as the Pencil, it's as though you've dipped the brush image in ink and then dragged it across the screen.

In addition to the normal hard-edged circles, some brushes have fuzzy edges. The Pencil tool will ignore the fuzzy edge; I'll talk about how to use those brushes in a moment.

GIMP 2.4 added a special brush: the Clipboard Brush. Select a small area from an image and copy it. Then look at the brush menu or the Brushes dialog. The first entry will be whatever you just copied, which you can now use like a brush.

Some brushes, such as the diagonal slashes, are asymmetric. They yield different patterns depending on the direction in which you drag. (You can use this effect for calligraphy, as if you were using a classic quill pen.)

A few brushes are actually animated images. Why would you ever want an animated brush? Since it changes as you drag it across the screen, you get a line that's varied or random. A fun example is the Vine brush (Figure 4-6).

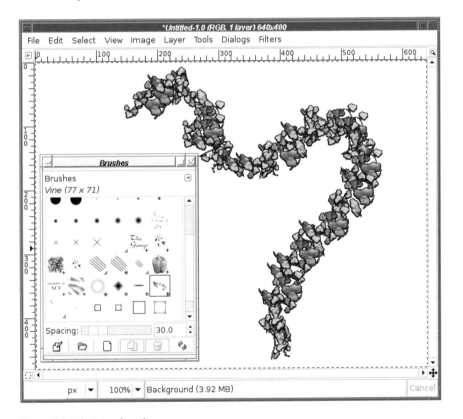

Figure 4-6. *The Vine brush*

■ **Note** Like a few other colored brushes, the Vine brush has another weird property: a fixed color that ignores GIMP's current foreground and background colors.

The Brushes dialog, shown in Figure 4-5, has a few options. *Spacing* can make the brush's patterns look more spread out as you drag across the screen. Try it with the Vine brush to see the effect, but you can use it on non-animated brushes as well.

Most of the buttons at the bottom of the Brushes dialog help with changing brushes or adding new ones:

- *Edit brush* brings up a Brush Editor dialog. On most existing brushes, everything in this dialog will be grayed out because built-in brushes cannot be edited: they're read-only.

- *New brush* opens the Brush Editor dialog and lets you create a *parametric brush* (Figure 4-7). You can specify shape, size, hardness, and related parameters. The button at the lower left lets you save your brush by the name chosen at the top of the Brush Editor. Your new brush will then appear in the Brushes dialog every time you start GIMP, unless you delete it.

Note When you save a parametric brush, the file will appear with a .vbr extension in your GIMP brushes folder.

- *Duplicate brush* makes a copy of a parametric brush. You can edit it and save under a new name.

- *Delete brush* does just what it says. You can't delete any of the built-in brushes this way, only those that you've saved in your personal collection.

- *Refresh brushes* re-reads your brushes directory to see if you installed any new brushes while GIMP was running. Click this button after editing a brush.

If you right-click on a brush, a context menu will offer some additional brush operations. *Open brush as image* (new for GIMP 2.4) is the most useful of these. You can edit the image using normal GIMP operations, and then save it as type *GIMP brush* (with the extension ".gbr") or *GIMP brush (animated)* (".gih") in the Brushes folder of your GIMP profile. In the case of animated brushes, you'll be able to see each frame as a layer, just like the animation you made in Chapter 3. You'll see a more detailed example of making an animated brush in Chapter 9.

Tip Because a brush is just an image, you can create a brush image yourself in GIMP, starting from scratch. You don't have to start by editing an existing brush.

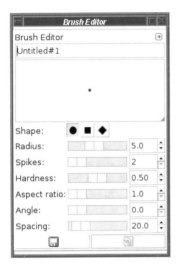

Figure 4-7. *Creating a parametric brush with the Brush Editor*

Parametric Brushes vs. Image Brushes

Most brushes are images. But a brush you create with the Brushes dialog's *Edit* or *New* buttons is a different type, as mentioned previously, called a parametric brush. You can choose from a few simple shapes (round, square, diamond), and then specify the size (*Radius*), *Hardness* (how fuzzy the edge is), *Aspect ratio* (whether it's long and thin or basically square), *Angle* (which rotates it), and *Spacing* (which makes it draw discrete blobs as you drag across the window, instead of placing the images close together so that they appear to be a continuous line).

Since parametric brushes and image brushes are specified differently, you can't change one into the other. You can't do anything useful with *Edit brush* on an image brush, and you can't choose *Open brush as image* on a parametric brush. In the Brushes dialog, each parametric brush shows a blue triangle at its lower-right corner, while animated brushes have a red corner. And a plus symbol means the brush is larger than the preview shown in the dialog.

■**Tip** There are lots of excellent GIMP brushes available for free downloading. Try a web search for *gimp brushes*.

Drawing Tool Options

All the line-drawing tools have similar options. The basics shared by all tools include the following:

- *Mode* offers the same list of modes as the Layers dialog (those modes will be discussed in Chapters 9 and 10), plus a few that are special (see the section, "Special Drawing Tool Modes" later in this chapter).

- *Opacity* makes the tool's line more transparent. It's a percentage, from 0 to 100.

- *Scale* (new for 2.4) lets you make the brush bigger or smaller—very useful!

- *Fade out* makes the line fade out after a specified distance, even if you keep dragging.

- *Jitter* (new for 2.4) adds some randomness to the line. Sometimes that can make a drawing look more natural.

- *Incremental* only makes a difference if *Opacity* is less than 100%. Using a tool with no spacing, or drawing on top of a previous line, will make the line darker (more opaque). Without incremental mode, the line won't get darker.

- *Use color from gradient* uses the gradient (displayed below the current brush in the Toolbox window) instead of the current foreground color. It even works with color brushes like the Vine brush. Click on the gradient in the Toolbox to see some examples; you'll learn more about gradients later.

Tip Some people like to make GIMP 2.4's new brush scaling available as a mouse wheel control. You can do that from the Preferences window in the category *Input Controllers*: click on *Main mouse wheel* under *Active Controllers*, click the button at the bottom of the active controller list (the tooltip says "Configure the selected controller"), choose the action (e.g., Shift-Scroll up) in the dialog that pops up, click *Edit* to get an Action dialog, and then expand the *Tools* category and scroll down to *Increase Brush Scale*. Then do the same for a scroll-down.

In addition to these options, the drawing tools can respond to pressure if you have a drawing tablet.

Special Drawing Tool Modes

In addition to the normal layer modes (which will be discussed in Chapters 9 and 10), the drawing tools offer three modes that are special (Figure 4-8).

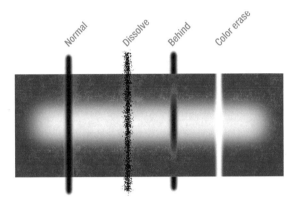

Figure 4-8. *The three special drawing modes*

- *Dissolve* adds randomness to the drawing (similar to the *Jitter* option). Wherever GIMP would have drawn partial transparency, instead it will draw a random pattern of dots. (*Dissolve* is also available as a layer mode, but it's more often useful for drawing.)

- *Behind* draws behind anything that's already drawn in the layer. This only works when drawing onto a layer that has transparency. (On an opaque layer, such as a background layer filled with white, it would make no sense. You wouldn't be able to see something drawn *behind* an opaque background.)

- *Color erase* seeks out the current foreground color and erases it, replacing it with transparency. It doesn't erase any other colors; only the current foreground color, making it very useful for erasing a solid-color background. Of course, like *Behind*, this only works if the layer allows transparency. In Figure 4-8, I changed the foreground color to red before drawing the color-erase sample; if the foreground color were black, there would be no visible effect since it wouldn't match the red box.

Drawing Fuzzy or Smooth Lines: The Paintbrush Tool

The Pencil tool is okay when you're using hard-edged brushes. But what if you want to use one of those fuzzy brushes? Or what if you want a line without those "jaggy" edges that the Pencil tool makes?

In that case, use the Paintbrush tool (Figure 4-9).

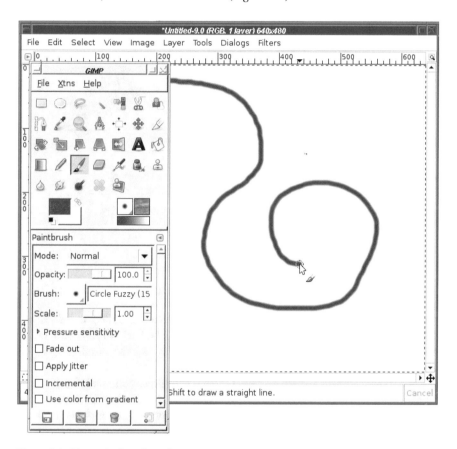

Figure 4-9. *The Paintbrush tool*

The Paintbrush tool differs from the Pencil tool in two important ways. First, it can use fuzzy-edged brushes. Second, it can use the hard-edged brushes too, but it uses them in a different way from the Pencil tool.

Figure 4-10 shows some of the differences. In 4-10A, each tool is used with a large, hard-edged brush. The results look similar until you look closely.

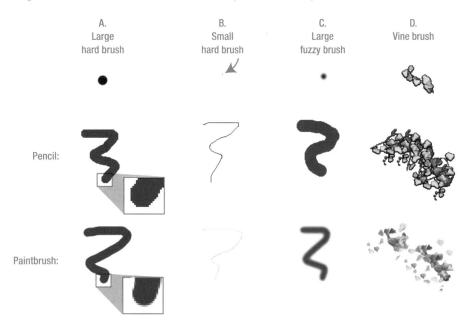

Figure 4-10. *Differences between the Pencil and Paintbrush tools*

The Paintbrush uses a technique known as *antialiasing* on the edges of diagonal lines: pixels along the edges are made semitransparent, or blended into the background color, to fool the eye into seeing a smooth diagonal line. The Pencil tool does not use antialiasing, so the edges look jagged.

Then why would you ever want to use the Pencil tool? 4-10B shows you one reason. Antialiasing on a thin line can make it fade into the background.

The lower Paintbrush line in B was drawn in the same black color as the upper Pencil line. Notice the Pencil line is sharp, black, and distinct as compared to the fuzzy gray Paintbrush line. For small, fine artwork, the Pencil tool is often best.

The other reason is indexed images. It takes more colors to draw an antialiased line. This means that the eventual file size will be larger. It also means the final image might not be usable for processes such as T-shirt or business-card printing that can only handle a small, fixed number of colors.

4-10C shows the tools when used with a fuzzy-edged brush. Obviously, the Paintbrush tool wins here. The Pencil tool ignores any fuzzy edges in the brush, and paints a wide, fat line.

4-10D shows how the choice of tool can make a difference with some of the more elaborate brushes. The Pencil preserves all the details of the vine leaves, while the Paintbrush creates an interesting sponge-art effect.

The Airbrush Tool

GIMP offers two more tools for drawing lines. One of them is the Airbrush tool (Figure 4-11).

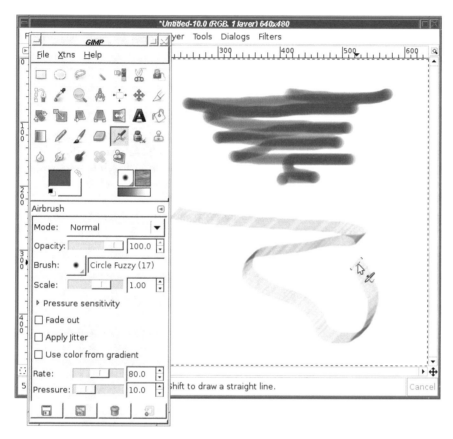

Figure 4-11. *The Airbrush tool, using a large, hard-edged brush (top) and a slanted calligraphic brush (below)*

The Airbrush almost always draws fuzzy edges, even if you use a hard-edged brush. It's also time sensitive. The slower you drag across the page, the darker the line will be, just as if you were using a real airbrush or a can of spray paint. Hover over one spot holding the mouse button down, and the spot will get darker and darker until it's completely opaque. (That means that if you stay in one place with a hard-edged brush, eventually the edges will become sharp. That's the one way the Airbrush can draw nonfuzzy edges.)

Painting with the Airbrush takes some practice and a deft touch… just like a real airbrush! The Airbrush adds two additional options to the normal set:

- *Rate* controls how sensitive the Airbrush tool is to movement, that is, how fast things get darker if you slow down.

- *Pressure* controls the darkness. Think of it as the amount of paint the airbrush is spraying.

> **Tip** If you ever try to draw straight lines with the airbrush, you might hit a snag: since you have to click once to start the line, and then draw a line starting at the same place, your starting point may come out darker than the rest of the line. As usual, there's a trick: click at one end of the line, then undo, and then Shift-click at the other end. The undo removes all the paint from your first endpoint but still remembers to start the line there.

The Ink Pen Tool

The Ink Pen tool (Figure 4-12) is the most complex of the basic drawing tools, but it can be very rewarding. It emulates an old-fashioned fountain pen with replaceable nibs (tips).

Not only can you make nibs of different shapes (analogous to choosing different brushes with the other tools), the Ink Pen reacts to your speed as you draw, creating a line that varies in width like a line from a real ink pen.

Careful: you can create blobs of ink if your penmanship isn't quite right. But unlike a real ink pen, you won't get ink all over your shirt pockets.

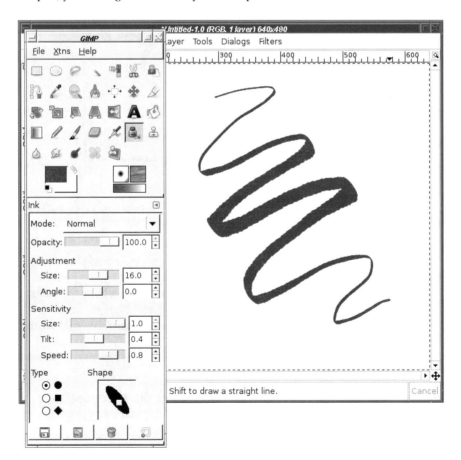

Figure 4-12. *The Ink Pen, showing how changing pressure can vary the line thickness*

The Ink Pen is most useful if you have a drawing tablet rather than a mouse. It will change line thickness in response to pressure or tilt on a tablet. But even with a regular mouse, you can sometimes create nice effects.

The Ink Pen, unlike all the other drawing tools, ignores GIMP's current brush. It has its own notion of a brush, similar to GIMP's parametric brushes, with the following options:

- *Adjustment* controls the width of the pen's nib and its angle (0 is horizontal).

- *Sensitivity* controls how much the Ink Pen will react as you vary your drawing style with your speed or the pressure and tilt on a tablet.

- *Type* controls the shape of the nib. Initially, you choose one of three basic shapes.

- The *Shape* box to the right of the type selector lets you refine the nib. It shows the chosen shape with a small square in the middle of it. Drag the square to change the aspect ratio and tilt of the nib (Figure 4-13).

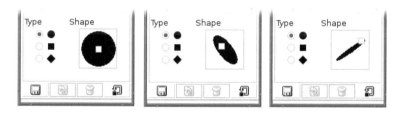

Figure 4-13. *Dragging the box to change the nib's shape*

USING A DRAWING TABLET

Drawing tablets, or graphics tablets, are devices that include a pad, a stylus, and sometimes a mouse or additional buttons. They're available in a variety of sizes from several manufacturers.

Tablets are very popular with professional computer artists for two reasons. First, drawing with a pen-shaped object feels more natural to most people. You have much more control over shapes, and most people find that they can make lines flow more smoothly with a pen on a tablet than with a mouse.

The other reason? Most graphics tablets offer additional controls. They're sensitive to *pressure*: GIMP can vary line width, color, or opacity of the line you draw depending on how hard you press on the tablet. Some tablets are also sensitive to *tilt*: GIMP can detect whether you're holding the pen straight up or tilted over on its side, and can vary the line accordingly.

All of GIMP's drawing tools allow you to specify pressure sensitivity if you have a tablet, and some (like the Ink Pen) are sensitive to tilt as well.

Many tablets use a double-ended stylus: the upper end works as a second tool, usually called the *eraser*. GIMP can assign different tools to the stylus and the eraser, which makes it very convenient to switch tools simply by flipping the stylus over.

There's a catch to all this, though. It's sometimes difficult to get the operating system to see all the drawing-tablet information GIMP needs.

Tablets under Windows usually work, though there may be some problems with particular models. Tablets under Linux sometimes require you to download additional drivers for the kernel and for X. On the Mac, Apple's implementation of the X Window System does not currently support drawing tablets. The X supplied by Mac Ports does offer support, though it may depend on drivers supplied by the manufacturers.

If you have a drawing tablet, you can tell GIMP about it by clicking on *Configure Extended Input Devices* in the *Input Devices* section of the Preferences window. This will pop up the Input dialog:

By default, the tablet's tools will have *Mode: Disabled.* Set this to *Screen* for each tool in turn, then click *Save*, and GIMP should remember the settings next time.

The other *Mode* option besides *Screen* is *Window*, which restricts the tool to work only in the image window. This in theory could give you better control, especially with smaller-sized tablets. However, in practice, it doesn't work very well on most systems, and it makes it impossible to move the stylus back to the Toolbox window to choose a new tool.

Try *Window* if you want, but most people find that setting all tools to *Screen* works best.

GIMP also has a *Device Status* dialog, accessed from the Toolbox via *File* ➤ *Dialogs* ➤ *Device Status*, as shown in the following image. This shows the pointer devices GIMP currently knows about (including tablet devices and the mouse, denoted *Core Pointer*). It also shows each device's assigned tool, foreground and background color, brush, pattern, and gradient. You can drag and drop items in this dialog to change the values there.

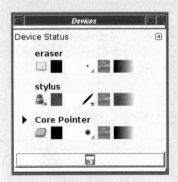

The Eraser Tool

The Eraser (Figure 4-14) erases. Simple, no?

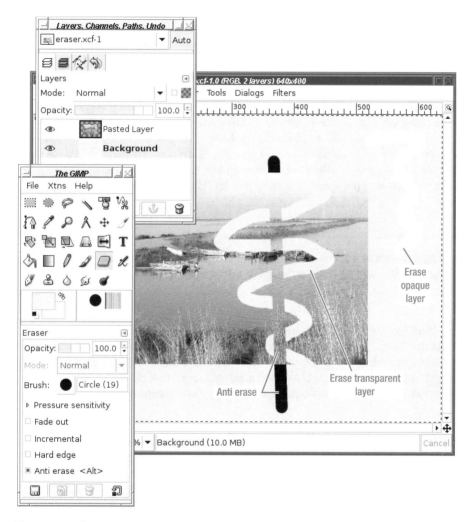

Figure 4-14. *The Eraser tool*

Well, not *quite* that simple. The definition of *erase* depends on the image. If the current layer has an alpha channel, then erasing makes the current layer transparent wherever the eraser touches it.

Remember, *alpha channel* means that a layer or image supports transparency. GIMP uses alpha as a synonym for transparency in quite a few places. Tutorials on the web for GIMP or other image-editing programs use this term quite a bit, so it's good to remember it.

In a layer that does not support transparency, the Eraser just paints the current background color.

The Eraser, like other drawing tools, uses the current brush. Use a large brush for erasing large areas. For erasing smaller areas or single pixels, use a smaller brush. Remember, you can zoom in on an image to magnify it so that you have more control over exactly what gets erased.

Most of the time, there are more precise ways to remove detail than the Eraser. (You'll learn about some of these methods in Chapters 5 and 6.) But the Eraser is useful for quick-and-dirty touch-ups of drawings.

The Eraser adds two new options to the usual drawing tool set. *Hard edge* makes the Eraser ignore any fuzzy edges in the brush. Remember how the Pencil tool made fuzzy-edged tools look large and sharp-edged? The *Hard edge* option will make the Eraser behave like that.

Anti erase is trickier. How is it possible that GIMP could un-erase something?

When you erase in a layer with an alpha channel, you're merely telling GIMP to make that part of the layer transparent. Behind the scenes, though, GIMP knows which colors were there before you made it transparent. With the *Anti erase* option, GIMP removes transparency from the layer wherever you drag the eraser. If there was color there that you erased earlier, you'll see it again.

Caution Using *Anti erase* on a transparent area that has always been transparent will leave a black trail, as though you were drawing with the Pencil or Paintbrush with a black foreground color.

Figure 4-14 shows the difference in how the anti-eraser behaves in various circumstances. The image has two layers: an opaque background layer, and another layer that includes a photograph in the center, with transparency everywhere outside of the area of the photograph.

Selecting the opaque background layer and erasing leaves a trail of white (the current background color). Anti-erase on this layer does nothing, since there's no transparency to remove.

Selecting the pasted photograph layer gives more complex behavior. Erasing over the photograph makes the photograph transparent, so you can see through to the background layer. Notice that where the erased trail moves off the bottom of the photograph into the area that's already transparent, nothing changes: erasing transparency just gives you transparency.

Anti-erase over the photograph does nothing, except in areas that were previously erased. There, it un-erases, removing the transparency and revealing the photograph again. But where anti-erase strays outside of the photograph into purely transparent areas, it erases the transparency and replaces it with black, since there was previously no other color there.

Drawing Rectangles, Circles, and Other Shapes

Now that you're an expert on drawing lines and erasing them, you'd probably like to draw some shapes, too.

Defining Regions

GIMP doesn't have any tools specifically for drawing shapes, which confuses some people coming to it from vector-drawing programs. But GIMP doesn't need shape-drawing tools: the trick is to make a selection, then *fill* or *stroke* the selection.

To try this, first use either the Rectangle or Ellipse Select tool and drag out a selection in the image.

Tip To constrain the Rectangle Select tool to a square, or the Ellipse Select tool to a circle, press the Shift key *after* you start dragging in the image. Pressing Shift first might sometimes work, but often it will give surprising results, which will be explained in Chapter 5. Of course, you can also use *Fixed: Aspect Ratio* in Tool Options with a 1:1 ratio.

Outlining Selections: Stroking

Stroking a selection outlines the boundaries of the selection. It's located in *Edit* ➤ *Stroke Selection…*, and brings up the Stroke Selection dialog (Figure 4-15).

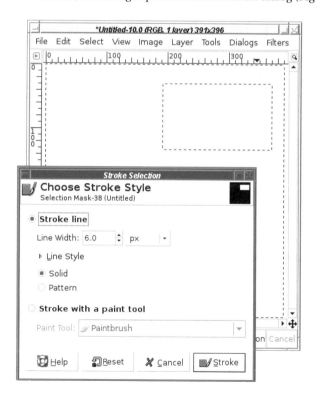

Figure 4-15. *The Stroke Selection dialog, with a rectangular selection active*

Stroke line will draw outlines using the current foreground color. You can specify the *Line Width* in pixels (or, if you choose, in some other unit). The default 6-pixel line is quite wide.

Alternatively, you can stroke with a line-painting tool, such as Pencil or Paintbrush. GIMP will act as though you had run that paint tool around the borders of the selection, using the current color and brush. (You can even make picture frames by stroking with a wide brush, especially if you use one of the more elaborate brushes, such as some of the animated ones.)

Sometimes stroking with a paint tool, especially an antialiased tool like the Paintbrush, works better on curves than specifying a line width. Try it both ways on a circular selection and see.

If you use *Line Width* rather than a paint tool, you can specify the type of line used by clicking the expander next to *Line Style* (Figure 4-16).

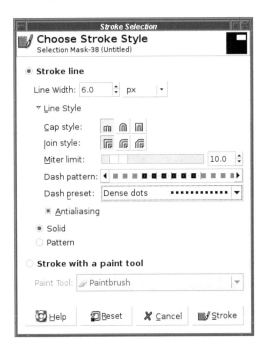

Figure 4-16. *Line styles in Stroke Selection*

Cap style changes the look of the ends of lines (useful when stroking paths, not so useful with selections); *Join style* does the same for places where lines connect to other lines (for instance, at the corners of a rectangle).

Miter limit specifies how sharp or blunt the corners will be. A limit of zero makes the corners more rounded; higher numbers will make them sharper. Cap and join styles and miter limits won't be very noticeable unless your line is quite wide.

Dash pattern lets you make a dashed line and specify exactly how the dashes will appear (drag horizontally in the preview to make different patterns). *Dash preset* lets you choose from a selection of common dashed-line styles.

You've already seen what *Antialiasing* can do, in the section on the Paintbrush tool. It can be helpful on rounded or diagonal lines.

You can also stroke with a pattern, which generally will only be interesting if you use a fairly large line width. I'll talk about patterns in a moment.

Note Both rectangular and elliptical selections offer *antialiasing*, which uses transparency along the edges of the selection to make boundaries smoother. They also let you *feather edges*: you can make the edges of your selection fuzzy rather than sharp. This isn't useful for outlining selections, but it can be useful when you're filling them. There are also some other selection options that you'll learn about in Chapter 5.

Free Select with the Lasso

Another selection tool you'll find useful for drawing is Free Select, also called the Lasso tool, from its Toolbox icon.

The Lasso lets you draw a freehand selection of any shape (Figure 4-17). Just outline your shape in the image, and end somewhere near where you started, and GIMP will make a closed curve. You can treat it just like you would a rectangular or elliptical selection. It offers the same antialiasing and feather options as the other selection tools.

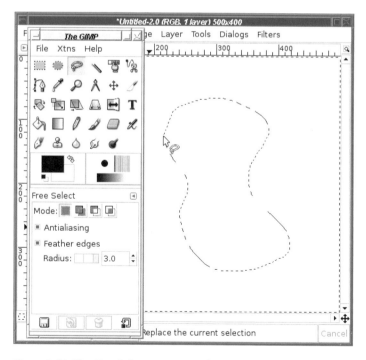

Figure 4-17. *The Free Select (Lasso) tool*

Filling Regions

Filling a selection with a solid color or pattern is even easier than stroking a selection. Just above *Stroke Selection* in the *Edit* menu, *Edit* ➤ *Fill with FG Color* (Figure 4-18) does the obvious: it fills your selection with the current foreground color. *Fill with BG Color* does the same thing but uses the background color, and *Fill with Pattern* fills the selection with the current pattern.

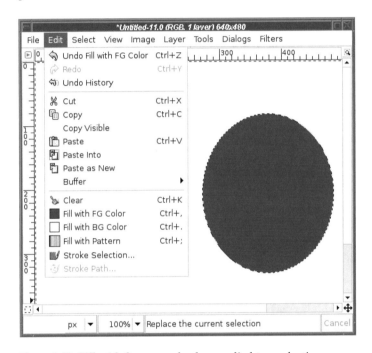

Figure 4-18. *Fill with foreground color, applied to a selection*

Notice that all three of these *Fill with* items show the current color or pattern next to the entry in the menu. This gives you a quick sanity check to make sure you're using the color you expect. Of course, if you decide that you don't like the color, just go to the Toolbox and click on the color swatch to change the color, then *Fill with FG Color* again.

If you don't have a selection, the *Fill with* items will fill the whole layer. This is an easy way to change the color of a background layer.

You can also fill a selection (or the whole layer) by dragging from the Toolbox's foreground, background, or pattern swatches, from the *Current* or *Old* colors in the color chooser dialog, or from any of the patterns in the Patterns dialog, directly into the image.

The Bucket Fill Tool

For more complicated fill-ups, use the Bucket Fill tool (Figure 4-19). Choose it in the Toolbox, then click anywhere inside your selection or layer to fill it with the foreground color.

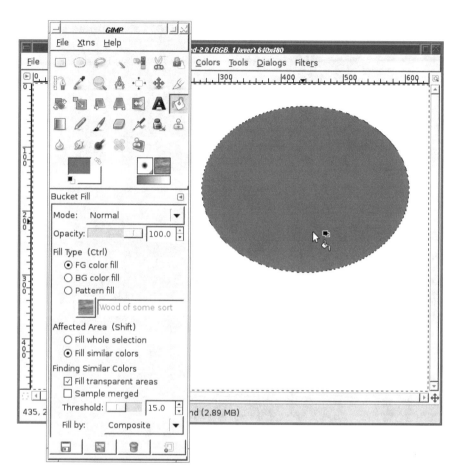

Figure 4-19. *The Bucket Fill tool*

So what does Bucket Fill add, compared to *Fill with FG* or just dragging a color to the image window? The difference is in the tool options. Bucket Fill has lots of options, starting with the *Opacity* and *Mode* selections shared with the line-drawing tools.

Fill Type lets you fill with the foreground color (FG), background color (BG), or a pattern. The *<Ctrl>* next to *Fill Type* tells you that pressing the Ctrl key when you click in the image will choose the opposite of your specified color: if FG is chosen, then Ctrl-click will fill with the background color rather than the foreground, and vice versa.

Affected Area lets you control what area will be filled. *Fill whole selection* is easy: select the area you want to fill, and click in it. But with *Fill similar colors*, when you click somewhere in the image, GIMP will look for adjacent areas that are colored similarly. (If there's a selection, GIMP still won't fill outside it.)

Just *how* similar the color needs to be is controlled by the *Threshold* slider (Figure 4-20).

Figure 4-20. *Fill similar colors*

For example, in a photo like Figure 4-20, you might want to use *Fill similar colors* to replace a cloudy sky with a blue one. Set the foreground color to light blue, then click somewhere in the sky.

With a very low *Threshold*, not much of the sky is likely to have the same color as the point where you click; you end up with color bands and an unnatural look. With the default *Threshold* of 15, a lot of the clouds get replaced, but not all of them; sometimes this looks okay, but other times it looks weird. With just the right *Threshold* (50, for this image), the whole sky is replaced, but nothing else. Go higher, and some of the fill will spill over into other areas, like the cliff face. At very high settings, nearly every color in the image will be replaced, and at the highest setting of 255, the entire image will be blue. The only way to determine the exact *Threshold* setting is by experimenting; it's different for every image.

Fill transparent areas lets you fill similar colors, even if you click on a transparent or nearly transparent area. Normally, clicking on transparency won't fill anything.

Sample merged uses the colors from all layers in the image to determine the color GIMP will try to match, instead of just the color in the currently active layer. This is useful when you're building up an image with a lot of layers stacked on top of one another. Of course, when GIMP fills, it will still put the color only in the current layer.

Fill by lets you specify how GIMP will decide which areas are similar. You can tell GIMP to look only at the red, green, or blue channel: for instance, if you set *Fill by* to *Blue*, then GIMP will consider a bright blue spot to be equivalent to a white one. Or you can set it to *Hue*, *Saturation*, or *Value*: using *Hue* would treat light blue and dark blue areas the same, while using *Saturation* would treat bright blue and bright red similarly, ignoring pale and washed-out colors. In Chapter 8, you'll see examples of how to use color or HSV decomposition to select different parts of an image. For now, you can leave *Fill by* at its default value of *Composite*, meaning all aspects of the pixel values will be considered.

Patterns

What's all this about patterns?

GIMP has a diverse collection of patterns (Figure 4-21). The current pattern is always shown in the Toolbox next to the current brush. It will also be shown next to tools and menu items that use patterns, such as Bucket Fill and *Edit* ➤ *Fill with Pattern*.

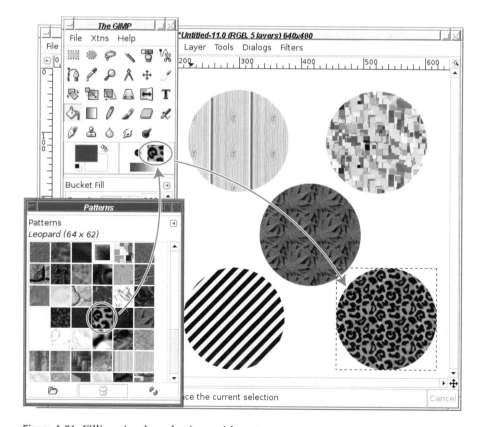

Figure 4-21. *Filling circular selections with patterns*

Clicking on the pattern shown in the Toolbox will bring up the Patterns dialog, where you can select from all the patterns GIMP knows about.

A pattern is just an image. Right-clicking on any square in the Patterns dialog offers *Open Pattern as Image*, from which you can edit the image and save it as a new pattern (usually with a file name ending in .pat, though .png and .tga will also work).

But a pattern is a slightly special type of image: it's usually *tileable*. Imagine the pattern image is a tile and you're flooring a room with it. You'd want the right edge of each tile to match the left edge of the tile next to it, and similarly with the top and bottom of each tile.

If the edges match, then the tile job will be seamless and look like a single huge pattern. If they don't match, then you will be able to see seams between each image. It will be obvious that you used a lot of small images, and the result won't look so good.

Most of the time, the patterns built into GIMP offer whatever you need. If you want more, there are plenty of sites that offer downloadable patterns. But if you crave something really special, GIMP can help you make an image into a tileable pattern. *Filters ➤ Map ➤ Make Seamless* alters the edges of the current image so it can be tiled better. It doesn't always do a great job; if you need something better, there's an external plug-in called Resynthesizer that can do more accurate tiling. Chapter 9 will go into pattern creation in a little more detail.

Gradients: The Blend Tool

The Gradient, or Blend, tool is another way to fill areas (Figure 4-22). It's also useful in all sorts of GIMP effects, as you'll learn in later chapters.

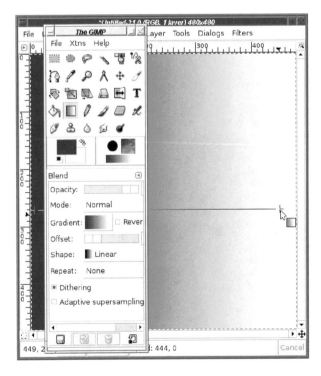

Figure 4-22. *Filling with a gradient*

The typical gradient makes a smooth transition from the foreground color to the background color. (There are also other gradients that display different effects, such as *Golden* for making metallic golden glows, *Neon Cyan* for making neon lights, or the fun *Radial Eyeball* choices for making bloodshot eyes.) With the Gradient tool selected in the Toolbox, mouse down in one place, drag to another place, and release the mouse button to draw a gradient into the current layer (of course, if there's a selection, the tool will only draw inside it).

Tip If you drag even slightly off horizontally or vertically, you'll get a gradient that's noticeably diagonal. If that isn't what you want, try holding down the Ctrl key as you drag. This will constrain your dragged line to a multiple of 15 degrees, which makes it much easier to drag a perfectly horizontal or vertical line. This Ctrl-key constraint works in most drawing tools, and also in the transform tools such as Rotation.

The Gradient Chooser

You may have already noticed that there's a gradient indicator in the Toolbox, below the current brush and pattern. That's because the default gradient, a smooth blend from foreground to background color, isn't the only gradient available (Figure 4-23).

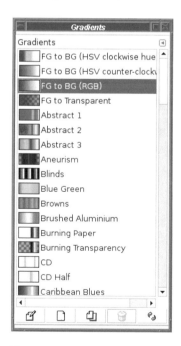

Figure 4-23. *The gradients chooser*

Most of the gradients available in the dialog have fixed colors regardless of the current foreground and background. Some gradients also include transparency, or partial transparency. You may find that some of them give a nice effect, or you may find most of them extraneous. Your call! But the basic gradient, *FG to BG (RGB)*, is useful for all kinds of effects, as you'll see in later chapters.

The Gradients dialog has buttons at the bottom similar to the ones in the Brushes dialog: *Edit, New, Duplicate, Delete,* and *Refresh.* As with Brushes, you can create new gradients and save them to use later (see Chapter 9 for the details).

Other Gradient Options

The usual drawing tool options, *Opacity* and *Mode*, are available in the Gradient tool options you saw back in Figure 4-22.

Mode is more interesting here than in most of the other tools since it can create some wild effects. For instance, try using *Difference* mode and applying the same gradient repeatedly (with a colored gradient—it's not very interesting in black and white). Then try it on a gradient of a different shape (see *Shape*, described in this section).

What *Mode* actually does will be explored in more detail in Chapter 9. For now, just play around and see what you can make.

Reverse transposes the colors of the gradient. Instead of starting with the foreground color and blending into the background color, it will start with the background color. Of course, you could just drag in the other direction to get the same effect; but some of the other gradient shapes only draw in one direction. With them you *will* need the *Reverse* button.

Offset controls where the gradient actually starts, as a percentage of the total distance you drag. If it's 0 (the default), then GIMP will create a gradient from your start point to your endpoint. If *Offset* is 40, then GIMP will draw the foreground color as a solid color for the first 40% of the distance, and only then will start the gradient. You can get the same effect by simply starting your drag in a different place, so this option isn't usually needed.

Shape offers a wealth of other ways GIMP can orient the gradient. *Linear* is the default, but GIMP can also make gradients that look like circles, cones, or spirals, or (the most fun) it can make a gradient following any shaped selection you make.

Try making a shaped selection using the Lasso tool; then set the gradient to *Shaped (Spherical)* and drag inside the image (Figure 4-24A). Then change the gradient to *Reverse* and drag again (Figure 4-24B).

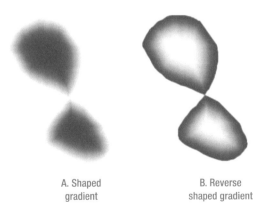

A. Shaped
gradient

B. Reverse
shaped gradient

Figure 4-24. *Shaped gradients (spherical) on a free selection*

Even if you drag over only a small distance, the Gradient tool will fill the whole selection (or image, if there's no selection active). *Repeat* gives you control over what happens outside of the region you dragged. The default setting, *None*, will simply use the beginning and ending colors of the gradient. If you select *Sawtooth wave*, GIMP will repeat the gradient, starting again at the beginning color; with *Triangle wave*, the gradient will be repeated in reverse.

Dithering offers higher precision in the way the gradient's color is calculated. Most of the time you won't notice a difference, but under some circumstances, you might see color-banding with this option disabled, especially on very large images.

Adaptive supersampling is another way of getting higher precision, at the cost of more computational work. Most of the time you probably don't need it, but if you notice unevenness or a stair-step effect, try it.

WHEN GIMP WON'T DRAW

GIMP is a great drawing program, but it can be frustrating too. Sometimes, you pick a drawing tool, try to draw, and nothing happens. What's up?

There are a lot of reasons that this can happen. Here are some of them:

- If you have a selection, GIMP will only draw inside it. When you try to draw outside the selection, nothing happens. Usually, it's obvious when you have a selection, because you can see the "marching ants" selection outline. But it's possible to have a selection and not know it. You might have done *View ➤ Toggle Selection* at some point to hide the selection boundaries, and then forgotten to turn them back on. The selection might be there but too small to see. Or, it might be scrolled off the visible part of the page, if your image is large or you're zoomed way in. When GIMP won't draw, try a *Select ➤ None* to make *sure* you don't have a selection in the image.

- GIMP will only draw to the current layer. Do you have the right layer marked as active in the Layers dialog? Is the layer visible? Is the opacity set to something more than 0%, so that the layer isn't completely transparent? Do the layer's boundaries extend to where you're trying to draw?

- It's also possible you've pasted recently and still have a floating selection. GIMP won't draw normally to a floating selection. You'll have to click the *New* button to make it a new layer, or the *Anchor* button to merge it into the previous active layer.

- While you're looking at the Layers dialog, take a look at the *Keep Transparency* button on the layer (the one to the right of *Mode*, with the checkerboard square next to it). If that's checked, then GIMP won't let you draw on currently transparent parts of the layer.

- Check the opacity of the tool in its tool options: make sure it's at 100%.

- Layers each have a mode, and some of the modes do strange things in combination with the layer beneath. Make sure the current layer's mode is *Normal* (unless you're deliberately creating an effect using a different layer mode, of course).

- Check the *Mode* in the tool options for the drawing tool you're using. If it's not *Normal*, unexpected things can happen. And usually will.

A Drawing Project

It's time to put all these techniques together and create a drawing.

So bring up a blank canvas, whatever size you like, with *File* ➤ *New*. If you already have a canvas you've been scribbling in, *Edit* ➤ *Clear* (the Delete key in GIMP 2.4, Ctrl+K in earlier versions) will clear out everything and leave you with an empty canvas.

Drawing a Tree

For a first drawing project, how about a tree? A tree is fairly simple and doesn't require a lot of art experience.

What's the first rule of drawing?

Right—create a new layer. Name it "trunk." Choose a brown foreground color. It's not always obvious where to find brown in a computer's color chooser. Try setting the hue to orange, then drag left and down to make the color darker (Figure 4-25).

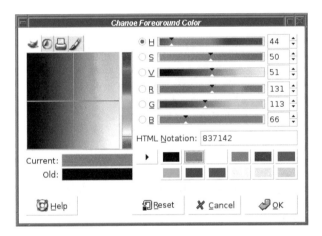

Figure 4-25. *Where to find brown*

Use the Paintbrush tool to draw the trunk. You can make the trunk a straight vertical line, if you like. But a real tree has a trunk that tapers a little, narrow at the top and wide at the base. You can accomplish this by using a narrow brush and drawing several near-vertical lines. Click where you want the top of the tree to be, and then click to the left side of the base and Shift-click. Now click again at the top, and Shift-click at the bottom-right (Figure 4-26).

Then fill in the trunk by drawing more lines just inside your original outlines until the trunk is a fairly solid brown color. Or just until you like it!

If you have trouble filling in small holes in the trunk, you can zoom in, but there's an even better approach: multiple views. *View* ➤ *New View* creates another window showing the same image. Any changes you make in one window will be reflected in the other. The advantage? One window can be zoomed way in to see fine detail while the other window is zoomed out so you can see the results at actual size (Figure 4-27).

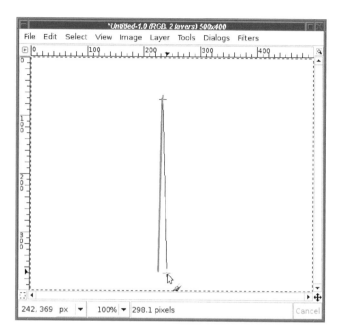

Figure 4-26. *The outline of the trunk*

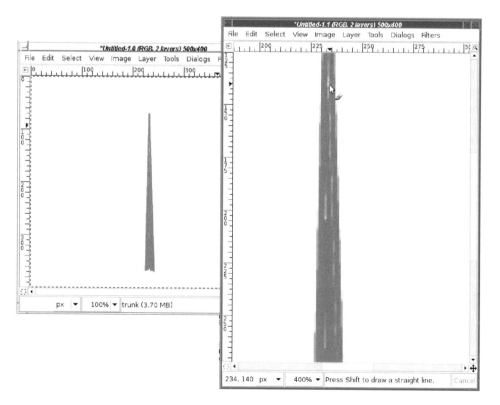

Figure 4-27. *Using two simultaneous views*

Once your trunk is ready, add some branches. Make a new "branch" layer. Then use the same click, Shift-click technique with the Paintbrush (Figure 4-28).

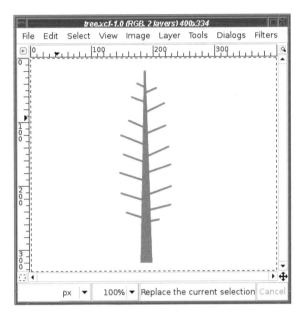

Figure 4-28. *Add branches in a separate layer*

Now it's time to add the leaves (or needles, if it's a pine tree), so switch to a green foreground color. Use a new layer for this! You may decide later that you don't like your leaves and want to change them. Or you might want to make an autumn or winter version of your tree.

For pine needles, use the Pencil tool and the smallest brush available, since you'll want to make thin lines. (Remember, the Paintbrush doesn't work well on the smallest brush. Making your drawing quite a bit larger would work around this and would give smoother lines than the Pencil tool.) For leaves, you might want a slightly larger brush (Figure 4-29). Experiment and see what looks right for your tree.

Continue putting in leaves, using short strokes, until your tree looks fairly well filled-in (Figure 4-30). Add more branches (switching to the "branches" layer, of course) if you need to.

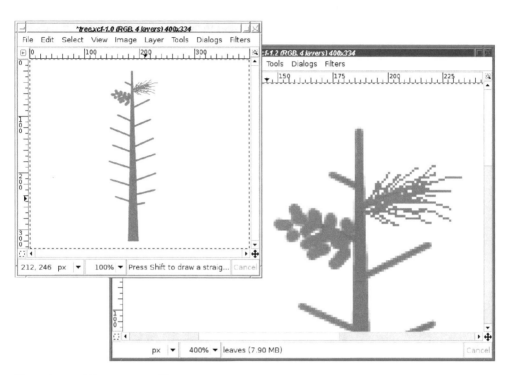

Figure 4-29. *Different types of leaves*

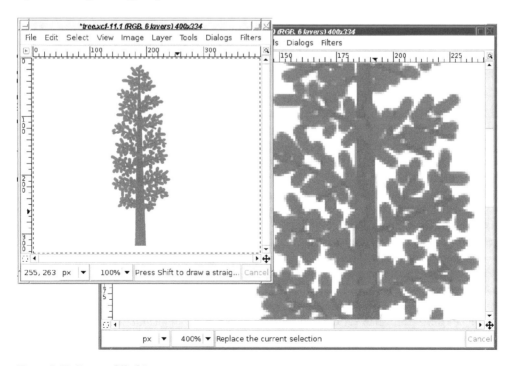

Figure 4-30. *Leaves filled in*

Real trees have a range of leaf colors. You may want to add some slightly darker leaves, and some slightly lighter ones. Use separate layers for each color, in case the blend of colors doesn't work out and you need to change it (Figure 4-31).

The tree looks pretty good now. But that solid brown trunk doesn't look right. It needs a shadow!

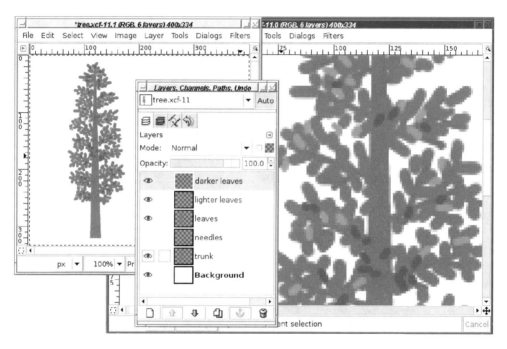

Figure 4-31. *Try using several different leaf colors.*

To make a shadow on the trunk, turn off visibility on all the branch and leaf layers so you can see what you're doing. Select the "trunk" layer and duplicate it to create a new shadow layer called "trunk shadow," just above the trunk layer but below the branches. Make this layer semi-transparent: try starting at about 35% opacity. You can adjust this later.

Select the Paintbrush tool (if it isn't already selected), a medium-sized fuzzy brush, and a dark foreground color. You can use black, but using a different dark color can give your shadow "depth," as though it's reflecting light from objects nearby.

You're going to draw a dark shadow line up the right side of the tree. But first, a tip: you can make sure the shadow doesn't spill off the side of the tree by using the *Keep transparency* toggle button in the Layers dialog.

With *Keep transparency* checked, draw a line up the side of the tree trunk (Figure 4-32). Keep the center of the fuzzy brush about at the edge of the trunk—you want it to be blackest at the right edge of the tree trunk, and fade away toward the middle. It's okay that the big fuzzy brush hangs off the edge of the trunk; the *Keep transparency* option will prevent any overhang.

You can add shadows to your leaves, too. Since they're too small and numerous for you to draw all the individual leaf shadows like you did with the trunk, take a shortcut: make a drop shadow of the leaf layer or layers, using small values for offset and blur radius.

Figure 4-33 shows the effect of the shadow. The tree is no longer flat—now it's a 3-D tree!

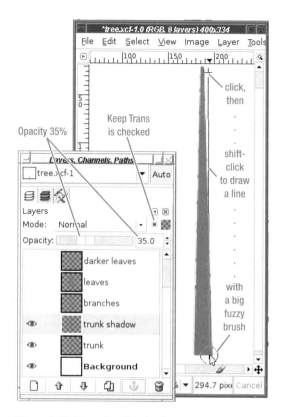

Figure 4-32. *Drawing the shadow*

Figure 4-33. *The completed tree*

Making a Planter Box Using Perspective Transformation

It's nice to have a tree. But wouldn't it be helpful to have a wooden planter box so you could carry the tree around or take it inside?

Make a new image to build your box. You can put the tree and the box together later. As with the tree, it's best to start with a blank image with a white background, and then make new transparent layers for each new piece you add. You'll want separate layers for each of the four sides of the box, so start with a layer called "box front" for the front face.

A box has a rectangular front. So make a selection using the Rectangle Select tool. You can fill that rectangle with a woodgrain pattern.

GIMP offers several woodgrain patterns to choose from. Some of them are better suited to a wooden box than others: the ones that look like wood paneling or a parquet floor look somewhat strange if you try to make a box out of them.

Just try lots of patterns until you find one you like. You can keep the Patterns dialog up while you choose a pattern, fill inside the image with *Edit* ➤ *Fill with Pattern* or Bucket Fill (or by dragging the pattern into the image window), and then choose another pattern. If you undo between each step, you won't fill up your Undo stack with all the patterns you tried.

I picked the birch-like pattern in Figure 4-34, which GIMP rather vaguely names "Wood of some sort."

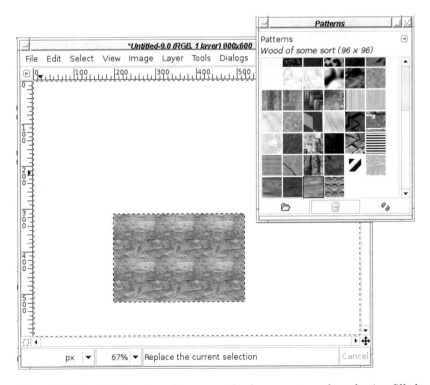

Figure 4-34. *The first step in making a wooden box: a rectangular selection filled with a woodgrain pattern*

Now the box needs sides. You could try to draw a side using the Free Select tool. But really, the side of the box should be just like the front, except rotated so that it looks like it's receding from you. GIMP has just the tool for that: the Perspective Transform tool.

First you need another layer. Make a duplicate layer of the box front, from the button in the Layers dialog. GIMP will name it "box front copy"; you'll want to rename this to something like "box right."

GIMP's perspective transformations work best if the layer is no bigger than the object you're trying to transform. (The image can be any size; it's only the size of the layer that matters.) You can crop the layer to eliminate all the extra transparent areas using *Layer* ➤ *Autocrop Layer* from the image window menus.

Note If you still have your rectangular selection now filled with your pattern, another way to make a new layer containing only the selection is to copy, paste, and click *New Layer* in the Layers dialog to turn the floating selection into a normal one.

Use the Move tool to move the "box right" layer over to the right, so that its left side touches the right side of the "box front" layer. It's not critical that they line up exactly; just get them close.

Now activate the Perspective Transform tool and click somewhere near the upper right of the box's right side (Figure 4-35). Drag to where you think the far top-right corner of the box will be.

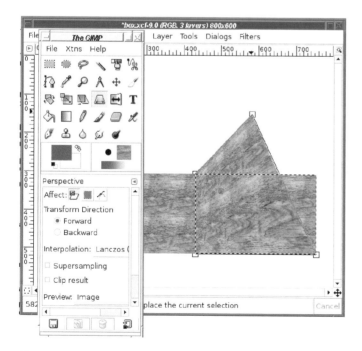

Figure 4-35. *Beginning a perspective transformation*

Meanwhile, the *Perspective Transform Information* dialog pops up, giving you a bunch of data you probably don't need, as well as buttons for *Help, Reset, Cancel,* and *Transform.* The last button is the one that will actually save the operation once you're happy with it.

The Perspective Transform tool has roughly the same options as the Rotate tool you already used in Chapter 2. Most important, you can preview the actual *Image, Grid, Image+Grid,* or *Outline.*

Notice that the Perspective Transform tool gives you boxes at each of the four corners of the layer. These are *grab handles.* When you clicked near the upper-right corner of the layer, GIMP assumed you wanted that grab handle, so that's the one that was dragged along with your mouse. (The blue dot shows you where the center of the layer will end up. It won't necessarily be blue; GIMP will show it in a color that contrasts with the color already there.)

Now click near the lower-right corner's grab handle, and drag that up until it looks like it's in about the right place for the box side (Figure 4-36).

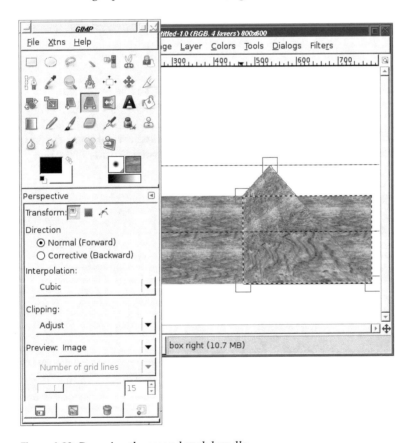

Figure 4-36. *Dragging the second grab handle*

For a box like this, you want the far grab handles directly on top of each other: the line between them should be straight up and down, and should contain no "jaggies." However, the diagonal lines—the "top" and "bottom" of the box as they recede—will not look right if they're parallel: they should be closer together at the far end, just as the sides of a railroad track look closer together where the track is further away. (See Chapter 9 for a detailed discussion of perspective drawing.)

When you're happy with the perspective, click *Transform* in the dialog.

You may find that it doesn't look quite as good after you've clicked *Transform* as when you were previewing. If so, just undo and try again.

The next step is to make the left side of the box, pretty much the same way as you made the right side. Start by copying the box front. Crop the layer if necessary, then use perspective transform.

Bonus! On the left side you don't need to move the layer, because the *left* side of the "box left" layer should touch the *left* side of the box front. That will happen automatically as soon as you copy the layer.

You might think you can just copy the "box right" layer to make the box's left side, but that won't look quite right. The sides of the boxes need to appear closer together at the far end than they are at the near end (they need to converge) in order for the perspective to look right. If you make the two sides exact copies of each other, it'll look wrong. (Don't take my word on this. Try it and see!)

Using Guides

To make the box look right, it's best if the far top ends of the two box sides line up at the same height. A *guide* can help you with that.

Guides are horizontal or vertical lines you can put anywhere in the image to help you draw in exactly the right place. Guides don't show up in the final image; they're strictly there to help you draw, and you can *Show* or *Hide Guides* from the *View* menu.

To get a horizontal guide, click on the ruler at the top of an image window, and drag downward (Figure 4-37). For a vertical guide, click on the ruler at the left side of the window and drag to the right. When you're moving a guide, GIMP will automatically select the Move tool, so you may have to switch back to the tool you were using previously.

In addition to giving you a visual indication of where you are, guides have another useful property: when you drag near them, the mouse will "snap to the guide." When moving a layer or working on a transform, this makes it easier to get the exact right spot. (You can disable *Snap to guides* in Preferences, but you probably won't want to.)

After the perspective transformation is finished (Figure 4-38), you'll want to move the layer down in the layer stack, using the up and down arrows in the Layers dialog. The left side should be *behind* the front side, so it needs to be below the front side in the layer stack.

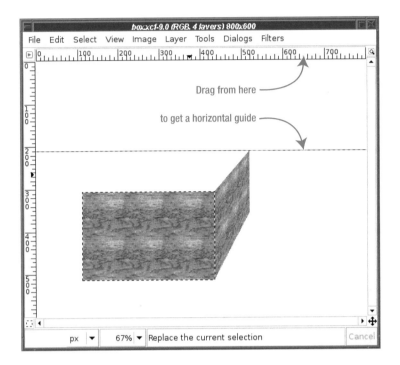

Figure 4-37. *A horizontal guide*

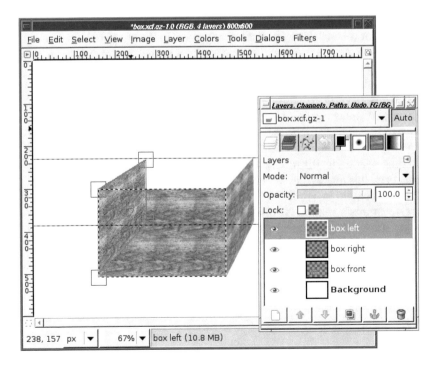

Figure 4-38. *Transforming the left side*

Finally, it's time to make the back side of the box. Use the Scale tool this time on another copy of the "box front" layer (Figure 4-39)—that way, the woodgrain pattern will be scaled a little smaller (since the back of the box is farther away). If you have trouble matching the new selection to the corners that are already there, it may help to set up vertical guides so that your selection will snap to them.

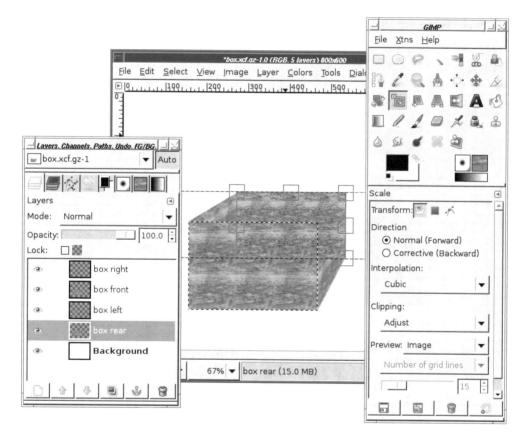

Figure 4-39. *Selecting the back side of the box. It's ready to be filled.*

It's not important whether the bottom of the selection matches anything: the bottom will be hidden by the front side of the box, so no one will ever see it. You could hide anything you want at the bottom of your box, and no one would ever know—except other GIMP users who look at your XCF.

You have all four sides of your box now. But it still doesn't look right, does it? The problem is lighting. A real box will have some sides brighter, and others darker, depending on where the light is.

Your tree had the shadow on the right side of the trunk. If the box will be in the same image, it needs to match that. You need to leave the front of the box bright, but darken the left and right sides since they are both in the shade.

You already know how to make something darker using Brightness-Contrast, Levels, or Curves (from Chapter 2). These operations work on one layer at a time, so it's easy to adjust each part of the box individually.

Select the layer for the box's right side, and then bring up your favorite brightness tool. (Which one you choose isn't important. You won't be making any subtle changes here, just general brightness.) I'll use the simplest one, *Layer ➤ Colors ➤ Brightness-Contrast*. Then make that layer darker. Do the same with the left side and the back (Figure 4-40).

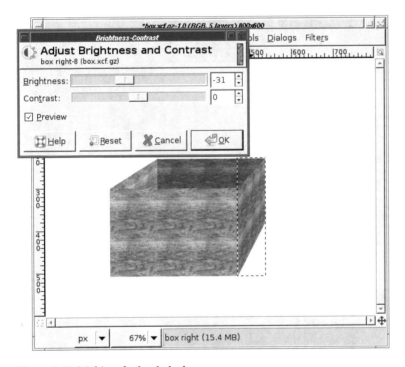

Figure 4-40. *Making the back darker*

You don't have to darken them all exactly the same amount as you did the right side: with a real box, the darkness of the two sides would depend on the color of the table it's sitting on and the color of whatever's inside it. (Really! Try it with a real box and prove it to yourself.)

You'll probably want to make the back a little darker than the front, too, if only to keep it from blending into the box front where the two layers meet. But play around with the four colors until it looks realistic to you.

Preparing the Planter Box

Finally, it's time to combine the two images and plant the tree in its planter box.

If you drew the box the right size for the tree, good for you! If not, no problem: use *Scale* to make them the right size.

Tip Make sure you're viewing both images at the same magnification setting.

Should you paste the box into the tree image, or the tree into the box image?

In order for the tree to go *into* the box, it has to be *behind* the front of the box, but *in front of* the back of the box, so the box needs to stay as multiple layers. The tree, however, can be pasted all as one layer. So it's easier to copy the whole tree using *Edit* ➤ *Copy Visible* in the tree image, and then paste it into the box image, than it is to paste all those box layers one by one into the tree image.

Wait! Before you use *Copy Visible*, turn off the white background of the tree image. You want to paste a tree with a transparent background. Now aren't you glad you made a new layer when you started the trunk, instead of drawing it on the white background? (In Chapter 5, you'll learn how to separate objects from their backgrounds, but it's a lot more work.)

Increasing Canvas Size

You've turned off the background and copied the tree. But there's one more problem to solve before you can paste: there isn't enough room in the box image for that tall tree!

Solving that is easy but it requires a few steps. First figure out how much space you need. You can use the Measure tool, or just combine the sizes of the two images. Too big is not a problem—you can always crop later.

Now resize the box image to be larger, using *Image* ➤ *Canvas Size…*. This dialog's elements should look familiar to you now. It has a chain link icon, which you can click to unlink width and height if you want to increase just one or the other (as in this case). Go ahead and type in your new size now (or use the increase arrow for a *long* time). Then press Tab or click in another text field to tell GIMP you're finished typing in the sizes.

Now you should see something like Figure 4-41. There's a preview below the *Offset* fields, showing the new size of the image. It also shows the current location of the existing layers in the new, larger image. You can drag the image thumbnail around in this box.

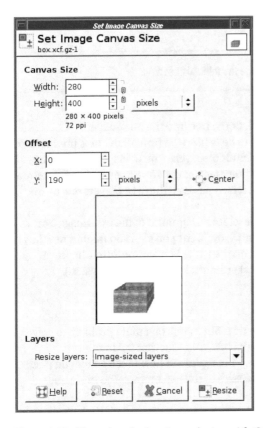

Figure 4-41. *Changing the box image's size with Canvas Size*

In this case, the goal is to get more space on top of the box, so drag the box thumbnail down to the bottom of the preview area. You can also type the offset of the layers directly in the *Offset* fields, but dragging the thumbnail around is usually easier.

If you're using GIMP 2.4, below the preview is *Resize Layers,* to specify which layers should be resized along with the image. In this case, you want the white background to cover the whole canvas. So set this to *Image-sized layers.* (The preview doesn't show that the white layer will be resized, but it will.) You can also leave this at *None* and resize the background layer later, too, using *Layer to Image Size* from the Layers dialog's context menu. Depending on whether your background layer has transparency, you may need to fill it with white after resizing the canvas. Click *Resize* to get your new larger image (Figure 4-42).

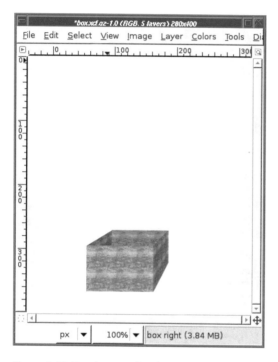

Figure 4-42. *Box image after increasing the canvas size*

Plant the Tree

Finally, it's time to paste the tree into the box!

In your tree image with the background layer made invisible, *Edit ➤ Copy Visible* will copy all visible layers. Then paste into the box image, and click *New* to make it a new layer.

Put it *inside* the box: use the arrow buttons to move the layer down until it's above (in front of) the box's back and left side, but below (behind) the box's front and right side (Figure 4-43). Or just drag the layer's line to the right place in the stack.

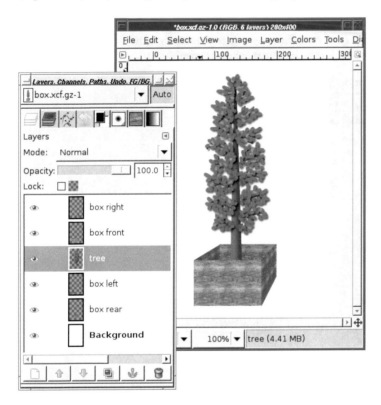

Figure 4-43. *Tree planted in box*

Final Touch-Ups

You can make the drawing look a little more realistic by adding some dirt or moss around the base of the tree.

Make a new layer just above the tree layer. Choose a dark green or brown color, fill in where you'd expect to see dirt, and try scribbling in different colors with different brushes (the Pencil Sketch (32 × 32) brush can add some randomness). Using two different views can help quite a bit here (Figure 4-44).

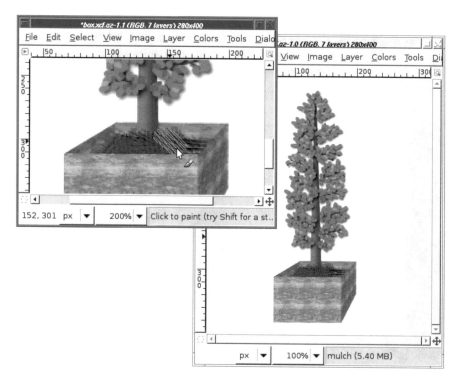

Figure 4-44. *Adding some mulch*

Finally, try adding a shadow. There are fancy ways of drawing shadows based on the shapes already in the image (you can use the Rotate and Perspective tools—you'll learn more about those in Chapter 9), but even adding a rough shadow drawn with the Free Select tool will make most images look more three-dimensional.

Start by making a new layer, named "shadow." Put it above the background, but below all the other layers. Give the layer some transparency, maybe about 50 to 70%, and set the foreground color to black.

Now choose the Free Select tool and turn on feathering. Shadows always have fuzzy edges, but you'll have to guess how fuzzy. Try to eyeball where the shadow should be (it may help to put a real physical box on the table in front of you and see where its shadow falls). Then use the Free Select tool to drag out the shape of the shadow.

Once you have a shadow shape selected, you can fill it with black (which will look fuzzy gray, not black, because of the layer transparency). But for a little more realism, try filling it using the Gradient tool. Make the shadow start out black close to the box, but lighten it farther away. Experiment with different shadow shapes, and with starting the gradient at different places to see the different types of shadows you can generate. Your tree is planted (Figure 4-45)! You're now an expert GIMP artist.

Figure 4-45. *The final tree in a planter*

Summary

Now you know how to draw on layers, and have an idea when to make a new layer. You can draw lines, curves, and shapes such as rectangles and circles, and you can outline them or fill them. You've seen the various types of brushes GIMP offers, and how to use them with each of GIMP's painting tools. Finally, you've learned techniques of drawing, shading, filling with patterns, and using the Perspective Transform tool to model real-world objects.

You can use these techniques to draw practically anything you can think of. Just use a little patience, and a lot of layers.

Armed with this knowledge, it's time to go back to working with photographs to learn how to select specific pieces so that you can use them in your own projects.

CHAPTER 5

■ ■ ■

Selection

You've already worked a little with GIMP's simplest selection tools: Rectangle, Ellipse, and Free (Lasso) Select.

So far, you've used selections primarily for drawing. But selections are more commonly used to choose one part of an image and ignore the rest.

It comes up in all kinds of situations. Perhaps you have a photo of a person against a complicated background, and you want to make the person stand out more, or paste a portrait onto a simpler background. Or you might want the opposite of that: to erase someone or something from a photo.

You may want to change or enhance part of an image—remember how the Bucket Fill tool could change the sky but not the rest of the photo in Chapter 4?

Sometimes it's just a simple touch up. For instance, you might need to take black text on a white background and change it to green text on a yellow background.

These are all selection issues.

If you've ever tried to use the Free Select (Lasso) tool to cut out parts of an existing image, you probably reached its limitations quickly. It takes a very steady hand, and if you make a mistake you have to start all over again.

Never fear! GIMP has quite a few tools for selecting shapes in existing images, in as much or as little detail as you need.

In this chapter, you'll learn about

- Working with selections

- Select by Color and Fuzzy Select

- Bezier paths

- The Intelligent Scissors tool

- Modifying selections with selection modes

- The QuickMask

- Highlighting foreground objects

- Using channels to save a selection

- Layer masks

- Extracting foreground objects with SIOX

Working with Selections

You know you can copy a selection and paste it somewhere else—like selecting Mars and pasting it into the poodle image in Chapter 3. But what else can you do with a selection, and how can you tell when something is selected?

Marching Ants

When you have a selection in an image, be aware of the selection boundary. It's a black-and-white dashed outline around whatever is currently selected. The dashes along this line move, making the selection outline seem to shimmer. This changing outline is dubbed the *marching ants*, and you'll see the term used a lot.

The marching ants are helpful for telling you when you have a selection and where it is. But they can also get in the way, particularly when you're trying to blend in an object pasted from somewhere else, as you'll see. For this reason, it's very helpful to be able to hide the marching ants using *View* ➤ *Show Selection*.

Squashing ants like that is so often useful that you may want to learn its keyboard shortcut, Ctrl+T (T stands for *toggle selection boundaries*). Another Ctrl+T will bring the ants back.

As useful as this is, though, it's also a major source of confusion. Once you've hidden the marching ants, you have no way of knowing whether anything is selected. (If you want another way of keeping track of what's selected, try the Selection Editor dialog, available in the *Dialogs* menu. You can even add it to one of your existing docks.) If you try a GIMP operation that works only on the selection—which means *most* GIMP operations—you may be surprised when nothing happens.

■**Caution** When you hide the selection boundary, try to remember to show it again as soon as possible. If you forget, you may regret it.

The *Select* Menu

Take a quick look through the *Select* menu (Figure 5-1), which contains a number of operations affecting the current selection.

All and *None* select the whole image, or make sure nothing is selected. You'll use these operations a lot, and it may be worth learning the keyboard shortcuts for them (Ctrl+A and Ctrl+Shift+A, respectively).

Invert reverses the selection: whatever is selected becomes deselected, and vice versa. You'll see why this is useful later in this chapter.

Float cuts out the selected area (leaving white or transparent behind) and pastes it as a new floating layer. (Ctrl+Alt-dragging a selection can also float it, but only under certain conditions—see the "'Confirming' Rectangle and Ellipse Selections" sidebar in the next section.) *Float* may seem very similar to *Cut* followed by *Paste*. So why use it? One reason: *Float* keeps the selected area in the same location in the image. *Paste* usually centers whatever you're pasting, losing any information about where the selection was.

Figure 5-1. *The Select menu*

By Color switches to the Select by Color tool, discussed later in this chapter.

From Path converts the current path to a selection.

Selection Editor brings up a dialog with a few options that mostly duplicate other functions.

Feather makes the edges of the selection fuzzy.

Sharpen does the reverse, making a fuzzy selection sharper. However, if your selection is fuzzy because you've just feathered it, you're best off undoing that feathering step to get back exactly what you had before.

Shrink and *Grow* make the selection larger or smaller.

Border replaces a selection with a new one that follows the border of the old selection (Figure 5-2). You can fill this with a color or pattern using the Bucket Fill tool to create an effect much like stroking the selection; or you can use it to blur the edges of a pasted selection that wasn't feathered; or you may find other uses for it.

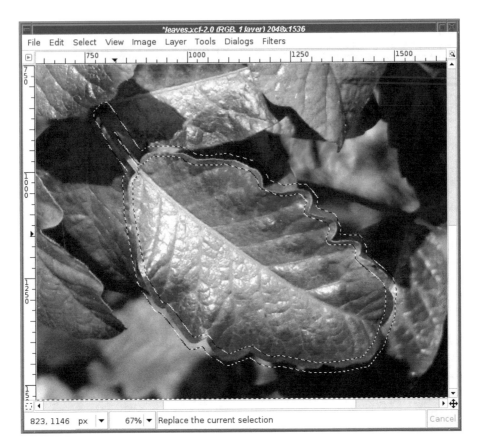

Figure 5-2. *Bordering a selection*

Rounded Rectangle rounds the edges of a rectangular selection. Making a rectangle with feathering is another way of rounding a rectangular selection; but *Rounded Rectangle* gives you nice rounded edges that are still sharp, while feathering will make the edges fuzzy. (You could sharpen the edges afterward, but that's more work.) You'll learn about the QuickMask and channels later in this chapter.

To Path converts a selection to a path. Then you can edit it using the Bezier Paths tool (explained later in this chapter), stroke it, or save it in a vector-graphics format.

Moving Selections

In GIMP 2.4, dragging a selected rectangle or ellipse moves the boundaries of the selection, not the part of the image inside it. If you've used earlier versions, this may seem like a big change.

The important distinction is between moving the *boundaries* of the selection and moving the *contents* of the selection. Here's how it works in GIMP 2.4: in the Rectangle and Ellipse Select tools, starting a drag from the middle of the selection will move the selection boundaries, without changing the image at all. It just means a different part of the image will be selected. Dragging near the edge of the selection (in the areas called *drag handles*) lets you change the size of the rectangle or ellipse. This makes it easy to make a selection exactly where you need it.

Dragging with the Ctrl and Alt keys pressed from inside a selection will automatically float the selection and then move it along with the mouse, leaving a hole behind…but only once the selection is "confirmed" (see the sidebar). It's the same as doing a *Select* ➤ *Float*, making the floating selection into a new layer, and moving that layer.

"CONFIRMING" RECTANGULAR AND ELLIPTICAL SELECTIONS

GIMP 2.4's new Rectangular and Ellipse select tools have two modes. When you first drag out an area, you'll see the marching ants plus one or more drag handles on the sides or corners of the box defining the selection. (Which drag handles you see depends on where you move the mouse.) You can adjust the size of the box by dragging the corner or side handles, and you can move the box by dragging from closer to the center of the box.

Clicking (without dragging) inside the box or pressing the Enter key "confirms" the selection: the drag handles disappear and all you see are the marching ants. Operations that affect the selection, such as the operations in the *Select* menu, will also confirm the selection.

Once a selection is confirmed, you can no longer move or resize it by dragging. Instead, dragging inside an existing confirmed selection will cancel the selection and start a new selection. Certain operations, like dragging the selection contents with Ctrl+Alt, work only after the selection is confirmed.

You can easily go from confirmed back to unconfirmed if you decide you want to adjust the selection's size or location some more. Just click (without dragging) inside the selection with either the Rectangle or Ellipse selection tool active. This will set the selection to a rectangle or ellipse big enough to contain the previous selection—even if the selection wasn't previously a rectangle or ellipse.

You can tell whether you're in confirmed mode by checking whether any drag handles are drawn and noting the shape of the cursor inside the selection. In unconfirmed mode, you will see an arrow when the mouse is inside a drag handle, or the Move tool's crossed arrows with the mouse closer to the middle of a selection. Outside of the selection box the cursor will revert to crosshairs. In confirmed mode, the cursor will always show crosshairs, regardless of where the mouse is. Make a selection and click inside it several times to go back and forth between committed and uncommitted mode, and notice the change in the cursor shape.

Some other selection tools, such as Lasso (Free) Select and Select by Color, don't need confirmation—they always behave like a confirmed selection. With these tools, starting a drag inside an existing selection will cancel the old selection and start a new one, while Ctrl+Alt-drag will float the selection contents and move them.

Some modifier keys also have an effect on the current selection mode (see the "Modifying selections with selection modes" section later in the chapter). Keep an eye on the tool options area when you first press a modifier key—if a modifier has an effect on the mode, the tool options will change to reflect that. The cursor, too, will change to give you hints on what mode you're in and what you can do.

Tip If you ever start dragging a selection and wish you hadn't, GIMP has a fancy way to cancel a mouse operation. Press the right mouse button while you're still dragging with the left button. Keep holding the right button down as you release the left. Whatever you were dragging should pop back to where it started. (You can release the right button now, too.) Hitting Esc while dragging may also work in some versions of GIMP. Of course, if you forget these, undoing always works.

In versions of GIMP before 2.4, dragging from inside a selection moved the selection contents, leaving a hole behind, while Alt-drag moved the selection boundary. If your computer uses Alt-drag for something else, you can sometimes use Alt+Shift-drag for the same purpose.

If all these modifier keys are too confusing to remember, you can always move a selection boundary by using the Move tool with its mode set to Transform Selection.

Select by Color and Fuzzy Select

Select by Color is a very valuable tool in your selection arsenal. You can use it on images where you want to separate a foreground from a simple background.

For instance, the Hubble Space Telescope folks offer a poster showing several views of Saturn (Figure 5-3). I'd like to cut out the central image to make a Saturn that I can paste anywhere.

Figure 5-3. *Saturn, from the Hubble Space Telescope*

The first step is to single out just one of the Saturns. Since that doesn't involve any fine detail, I'll use the Lasso (Free Select) tool (Figure 5-4), and then use *Copy* and *Paste as New*.

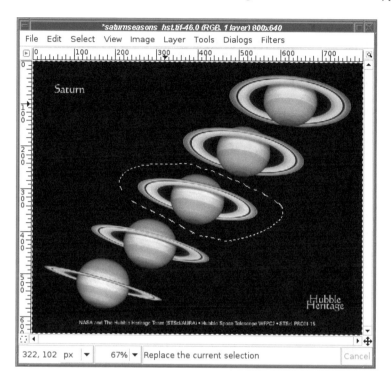

Figure 5-4. *Separating the middle Saturn from the rest with the Lasso tool*

Now it's time to use Select by Color. There's a button for it in the Toolbox (Figure 5-5), or you can use the *Select* ➤ *By Color* menu.

Click in the image, on the color you want to select. In this case, I'll select the black sky: I'm trying to select everything that *isn't* Saturn. Why? Because that's easier than selecting Saturn. The sky is all one color; Saturn isn't.

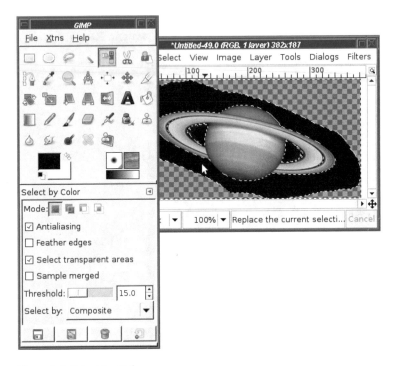

Figure 5-5. *Select by Color*

Notice the tool options.

The *Finding Similar Colors* options work the same way as they did for Bucket Fill in Chapter 4. With *Threshold* at 0, only colors exactly the same as the one you click will be selected. With a higher threshold, GIMP will include colors that are similar but slightly different.

The marching ants appear as soon as you press the mouse button down in the image. If you don't like the threshold when you first click, don't let up on the mouse button: you can change the threshold by dragging. Drag down or right to include more in the selection, and drag up or left to include less. (In GIMP 2.2, Select by Color didn't offer this option.)

If you aren't happy with what you're getting, you can always release the mouse button and click somewhere else. (If you undo first, the operation won't clutter up your undo stack, but it's not mandatory.) When you're trying to select an area that isn't all exactly the same color, like a sky, *where* you click in the image can make a big difference in what gets selected. Try clicking in different places with the same threshold to see how that changes the selection.

Select by Color offers the usual selection tool options you used in Chapter 4, *Antialiasing* and *Feather edges*. It also offers the option *Select transparent areas*—which allows the tool to include transparent parts of the image (they don't match the color you've chosen, of course, but they might be included if you've turned on feathering). *Sample merged* means that GIMP will look at the color that you see displayed, even if it comes from a layer that's not the active one.

Finally, new for 2.4, there's a menu that lets you select the method GIMP will use to decide which colors are similar. *Composite* is the default, and looks for colors that are similar in all respects. *Hue, Saturation,* and *Value* come in handy for many different tasks: they can help you separate a blue sky from green grass (*Hue*) even if there are lots of shades of blue and green, or to separate a bright sky from a dark tree (*Value*), or even to choose clouds out of a blue sky (*Saturation*). *Red*, *Green*, and *Blue* are not quite as useful: they let you restrict the comparison to only one hue.

But we don't need any of those options to select the simple black background from Saturn. Now that everything that *isn't* the planet is selected, you can make a transparent Saturn image by clearing with *Edit* ➤ *Clear* (the Delete key in GIMP 2.4, or Ctrl+K in earlier versions). This erases the black sky you just selected, leaving transparency instead (assuming the image has an alpha channel). Alternately, you can select Saturn and nothing else. Remember that *Select* ➤ *Invert* menu item, which selects everything that isn't selected, and vice versa? If you use it now, you can copy just Saturn. Either way, you end up with a Saturn that you can paste into other images.

Besides selecting solid-color backgrounds, Select by Color is particularly useful for extracting text or other single-colored elements out of logos, screenshots, or other computer-generated images.

Select Contiguous Regions

Select Contiguous Regions, also known as Fuzzy Select or the Magic Wand tool (from its Toolbox icon) is very similar to Select by Color, and its tool options are basically the same. The main difference is that it only selects areas that touch each other (Figure 5-6).

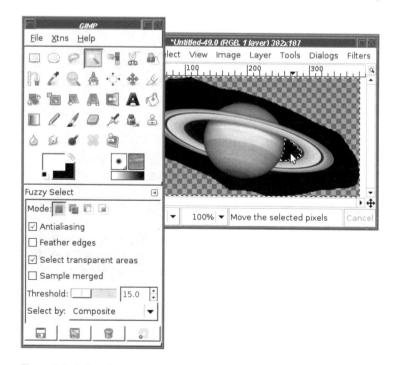

Figure 5-6. *Select Contiguous Regions*

In GIMP versions before 2.4, there were two other very important differences between Fuzzy Select and Select by Color. First, in Fuzzy Select, if you got the threshold wrong and wanted to try again, you had to cancel the previous selection (with Undo or *Select ➤ None*) first. If you didn't undo, you would end up moving the contents of the first selection you made.

The other difference was that Select by Color didn't let you fine-tune the selection by dragging with the mouse (as described in the previous section), while Fuzzy Select did.

Like Select by Color, Fuzzy Select is quite useful for text, especially when you need to select a single letter.

Bezier Paths

The Bezier Paths tool lets you define *control points* (also called *anchor points* or *nodes*) outlining your object. Then it "connects the dots" to create a path. You can even bend the lines between the dots to create a smooth curve.

■**Note** *Bezier* curves, pronounced *BEZ-ee-ay*, are named after Pierre Bezier, a French engineer who developed the concept while working on computer systems for automotive design.

A Bezier path isn't a selection by itself. But once you have a path, it's easy to tell GIMP to select everything inside.

You can also use paths for other purposes. You can stroke a path, just as you can a selection. You can even export it to a vector-graphics format such as SVG.

However, for the purposes of this chapter, you'll mostly use paths to define the outlines of a selection.

Defining a Path

The easiest way to understand Bezier paths is to see them in action. So open a photo and choose something you want to cut out of it. Then select the Bezier Paths tool in the Toolbox (Figure 5-7).

I'm going to cut a single leaf from this photo so that I can paste it into other images. (It's poison oak! Picking a leaf and taking it home was *not* an option.)

Rule 1 for making a good path is zoom in. Zoom *way* in. You probably want a zoom factor of 200% or more, depending on hand steadiness and how good your close vision is. Zooming in lets you place your control points *exactly* on the edges of the object you're choosing.

Figure 5-7. *The Bezier Paths tool*

It doesn't matter if the object you're trying to select becomes larger than the window. The biggest advantage of Bezier paths versus a simpler tool like Lasso Select is that you can stop between points. That means you can rest for a while (making a complicated selection can be a tiring and time-consuming operation). You can also scroll the image or resize the window as much as you need to see exactly what you're selecting. Best of all, if you don't get it perfect the first time, you'll be able to go back and edit it later.

Time to get started!

Just click in the image window, selecting points you want to connect (Figure 5-8). Use as many or as few control points as you need, depending on how precise you want your selection to be.

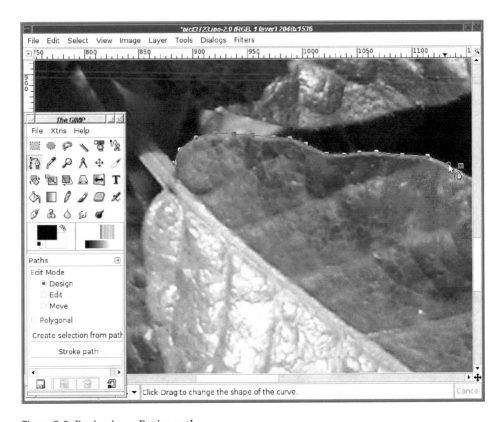

Figure 5-8. *Beginning a Bezier path*

Keep clicking to place points around the outline of the image until you get back to the starting point. You can zoom and scroll as much as you need between points.

If you place a control point in the wrong place, you can click on the point again and drag it to the right place. You can even go back and click on points you added earlier, and drag them to new positions. As always, watch the cursor carefully as you move your mouse near the point. When it changes to show crossed arrows, similar to the Move tool, that's your cue that you're over an existing control point and can drag it. (However, it can be difficult to tell the crossed arrows cursor from the simple cross cursor you see when you're adding a new point. If you look closely enough, you'll see the difference.) Undo (Ctrl+Z) also works to remove the last point you added, and further undos will remove earlier points.

When you have gone all the way around, Ctrl-click on the starting point (hold the Ctrl key while clicking on it) to close the path.

You don't actually need to Ctrl-click if you're just making a selection. Converting a path to a selection will usually work fine if you just click normally on the original point. But for other path operations such as stroking, it makes a difference whether your paths are open or closed—so remember that Ctrl-click is the way to close a path.

The Paths Dialog

In addition to being visible in the image, your path appears in the Paths dialog. That dialog is usually docked as a separate tab in the same window as the Layers dialog (Figure 5-9).

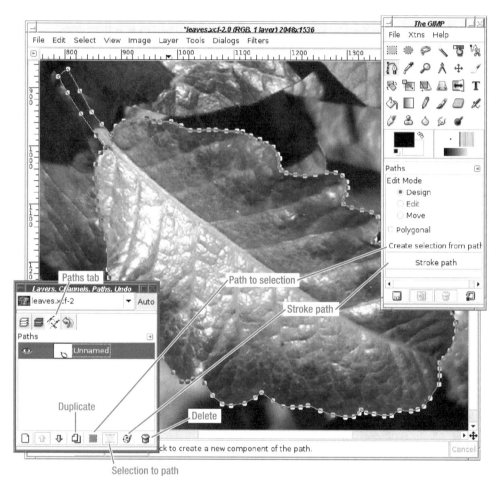

Figure 5-9. *The completed path, showing the Paths dialog*

Most of the components of the Paths dialog should be familiar to you from working with layers. You can manage multiple paths just as you would manage layers in the Layers dialog. Each path has the following:

- A small preview showing the general shape of the path

- A visibility icon (the "eyeball")

- Space for a "chain link" between the eyeball and the preview, so you can link several paths and move them together

Most of the time, you probably won't need to use more than one path at one time, but it's good to know you can link them if the need should sneak up on you.

Paths are preserved when you save to GIMP's native file type, XCF. So if you spend a long time creating a path, it's a good idea to save the image as XCF.

You can *Duplicate* a path (make a copy of it) in case you accidentally destroy what you spent so much work creating. Of course, there's a *Delete* button for paths you no longer need.

Selection to Path converts an existing selection to a path. This is useful if you want to edit the path further, or use the shape for some other purpose, such as saving to a vector-graphics format like SVG. *Stroke Path* does much the same as *Stroke Selection*, which you used in Chapter 4.

But our immediate interest in the Paths dialog is *Path to Selection*.

Creating a Selection from a Path

There are several ways to create a selection from a path.

The easiest way is to hit Enter. Voilà! You can also use the *Selection from Path* button in the Paths tool options, the *Path to Selection* button at the bottom of the Paths dialog (it has a pink square on it), the *Path to Selection* menu item in the context menu you get when right-clicking on a path in the dialog, or the *Select* ➤ *From Path* item in the image window's menu.

Try it! Once you've defined your path, convert it to a selection. At this point, you'll see both the path and the selection. If you find that distracting, you can hide the path by clicking the visibility eyeball button in the Paths dialog. Or simply switch to any other tool in the Toolbox (paths are only visible when the Paths tool is active, unless you turn on the visibility eye).

To see what you've created, copy the selection and (from the image window menus) open *Edit* ➤ *Paste as New*. GIMP will create a new image containing only your selection, on a transparent background (Figure 5-10).

Figure 5-10. *The selection, pasted as a new image with a transparent background*

Of course, you can also paste the selection into another image, or anywhere you want (Figure 5-11).

Figure 5-11. *The leaf pasted into another image*

The boundaries of the leaf are sharply defined, and it looks okay pasted into other images. But often the boundaries don't work out quite so well, and the selection looks odd when pasted somewhere else. Other times, there is no sharp edge—imagine trying to select a photo of a shadow, or a cloud, or a furry dog.

You can also have problems if you make a relatively sloppy path. For instance, the path in Figure 5-12 doesn't follow the contours of the dog's fur very well.

Figure 5-12. *A sloppy path*

If you make that path into a selection and paste it somewhere, the sharp edges show up and the result looks artificial (Figure 5-13).

You can make a sloppy selection look better by *feathering* it to make its edges softer. It's not a complete solution—but sometimes it's the best bet.

Most of the selection tools (such as Rectangle, Ellipse, and Lasso) offer feathering as a tool option. But the Paths tool doesn't, so you'll have to feather the selection after the fact, using *Select ➤ Feather…* from the image window. (Some people prefer feathering after selection anyway as it gives you more chance to increase or decrease the feathering as needed.)

This brings up the Feather dialog (Figure 5-14), which lets you choose the amount of feathering, specified in pixels.

Figure 5-13. *A sloppy selection looks artificial when pasted into an image.*

Figure 5-14. *Feathering a selection*

The amount of feathering you need depends on how large your selection is, how ragged it is, and where you're pasting it. You will probably have to experiment and try several different settings to find the perfect value, undoing each feather before trying something different.

In this case, the selection was so far off that a large feather of 40 pixels was needed to make it look better (Figure 5-15). You can still see that the selection isn't perfect, but now it looks more like a furry edge, or artistic soft focus, than an image-editing artifact.

Figure 5-15. *Feathering a sloppy selection makes it look better when pasted.*

Curved Paths

So far, you've only used straight lines between path nodes. But a Bezier path can include curves as well. The easiest way is to drag from the middle of a line segment—the line bows into a curve, and you can adjust the shape of the curve by dragging it.

You can get somewhat finer control over the shape of the curve with the drag handles (Figure 5-16). Each control point on a Bezier path can have two handles that control the curvature of the lines on either side. These handles will appear automatically if you drag a straight line segment to make it curve.

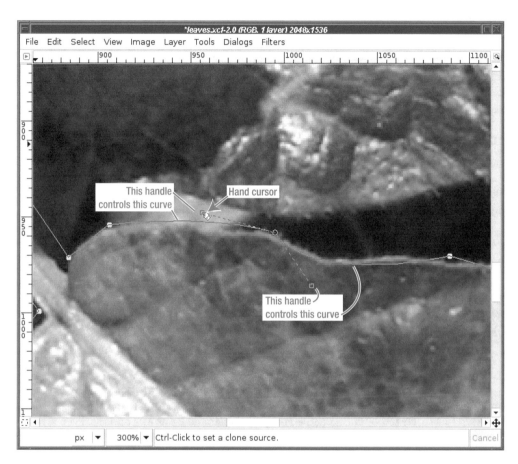

Figure 5-16. *The handles for a Bezier control point*

GIMP changes the cursor to a "pointing hand" when you're over a handle (although not all GIMP versions use the same cursors for editing paths, so watch what your own GIMP installation does). Drag the handle in the direction you want the curve to go. Experiment and get a feel for the sorts of curves you can make.

Basically, making the handle longer will add more curvature, while rotating the handle around its axis (the control point) will move the apex of the curve.

You can use paths that are composed of all straight lines, all curved lines, or any combination of the two. Experts in Bezier paths use mostly curved lines, adjusting the handles as they go. But when starting with paths, it's usually easiest to use straight lines for most of the path, and curve only the few segments that follow tricky outlines. (Or you can just use more points for the tricky sections, and never use handles or curved segments at all.)

■**Tip** A path consisting only of straight lines is called *polygonal*. You can prevent handles from appearing on new points by checking the *Polygonal* box in the Paths tool options. (If you have any curved segments already, checking *Polygonal* won't remove their handles.)

Adding Nodes or Segments and Moving Paths

You can also add new control points in between two existing ones, or remove points you don't need. The key is the three edit modes in the tool options: Design, Edit, and Move. By default, you're in Design mode, which is best for adding points at the end of a path or for moving existing points. Switch to Edit mode to add or delete control points.

■**Tip** Pressing the Ctrl key while clicking between two control points will switch to Edit mode and let you create a new point; Ctrl+Shift lets you delete points. As always, watch the mouse cursor when you press the Ctrl key with the mouse over the control point. GIMP will tell you, via the cursor, which mode you're in. To add a new control point between two existing points, just click along the path (make sure the cursor is a "+") wherever you want the new point.

This can be slightly confusing, because Edit mode assumes you want handles, so the new point will be created with two handles already visible. If you don't intend to use handles, you can avoid this confusion by checking the *Polygonal* box in the Paths tool options. Even if you *do* intend to use handles, you can still use this trick. Check *Polygonal* first, lay out your path, and then uncheck *Polygonal* and make handles for any control points you wish to use for curves.

To remove a point, Shift-click on it while in Edit mode.

You can also make a path that includes several disconnected path segments. Pay attention to which points are drawn with a closed circle versus an open or dotted circle. Any point that's open or dotted is *selected*.

Most of the time when you're creating paths, only one node, the last one created, will be selected. Creating a new point draws a line from the selected point to the new one.

But you can deselect a node by Shift-clicking on it, or select more than one node by Shift-clicking on each new point you want to select. If there are no nodes selected, or more than one, or a node that isn't the end of a path, then clicking in a new location will begin a new disconnected path segment.

Disconnected paths are useful mostly for making discontinuous selections or figures. They can be a time-saver since you can stroke or fill several areas at once. They're not generally used for making selections, but they can be handy if you want to select several disconnected areas—like both eyes.

If you have multiple points selected, dragging any one of them will also move other selected nodes by the same amount.

Moving or Modifying an Existing Path

The Paths tool has a third mode: Move mode. This allows you to move the entire path (not just one point, as in Design mode). Just click anywhere on the path and drag it to a new location. If you have more than one path segment, only the segment you drag will move. If you want all path segments to move, using Shift-drag will move them all at once.

If you change windows or choose another tool after working with a path, when you go back to the window the path is no longer visible. How do you go on working with an existing path?

First, make sure that the right path is selected in the Paths dialog, and that its visibility icon (the eyeball) is on. This will show the path, but not its control points, in the image window.

Now, with the Paths tool selected in the Toolbox, click on the path in the image. The control points should appear, and you're ready to continue editing it.

The Intelligent Scissors

The Intelligent Scissors tool (Figure 5-17), or "I-Scissors" for short, works somewhat like Bezier paths, but with a twist: it tries to follow the boundaries of an object. Use it the same way you would the Paths tool: click near where you want your selection boundary to be, and in theory, GIMP will make a more complicated path that follows the edges it can detect in the image. The result will be a selection, not a path.

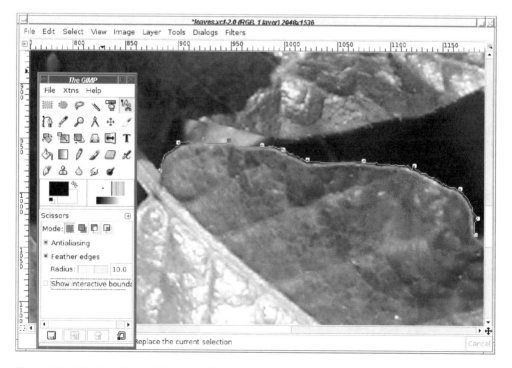

Figure 5-17. *The Intelligent Scissors tool*

When you've finished defining the outline of your selection, click on the first point to close the path (the cursor changes to show a circle-slash, meaning "no more points"), and then click inside the path (or hit Enter) to select.

Caution With Intelligent Scissors, you *must* close your selection by clicking on the first point; that's not optional like it is with the path tool.

When it works, Intelligent Scissors can make a selection that's more accurate and detailed than you would likely make yourself using the Paths tool. But unfortunately, it doesn't always get it right. Do try the tool, but most people find the regular Paths tool more useful. If you find that the cursor sometimes "jumps" to put a point somewhere where you didn't want it to be, Shift-clicking might help that.

If the Intelligent Scissors tool isn't quite on, don't give up! You can go back and move existing points (any point except the last one) or add extra control points to fine-tune your work—at least until you click inside the selection to finish it. Even after you finish the selection, you can still rework it by converting it to a path, or through other means such as the QuickMask (which will be discussed later in this chapter).

Intelligent Scissors only makes selections. You can't use it to make paths for other uses. Therefore, it has the normal selection tool options: *Mode*, *Antialiasing*, and *Feather*.

It also has an additional option: *Interactive boundary*. With this enabled, you can see as you mouse down where the tool would put the boundaries, then drag the mouse left, right, up, and down before you release the button to get the selection exactly where you want it. On anything except a very slow machine, you'll probably find this option helps a great deal.

UNDOING "HALFWAY" SELECTIONS

Sometimes you're partway through making a selection when you change your mind and want to start over. But Undo doesn't help when you're halfway through an Intelligent Scissors selection, or a path. How can you get rid of those distracting control points you no longer want?

There are several ways to cancel an operation in progress, First, as long as you haven't completed a selection, switching tools works. Just click on the button for some other tool, like Rectangle Select. That'll cancel any path or I-Scissors selection you've started and get rid of those distracting lines and points from your partial selection.

You can also use the Esc key. In the I-Scissors, hitting Esc cancels any pending selection and lets you start over. (This is not undoable, so don't hit Esc unless you mean to cancel.) It also works with the Foreground Select tool (discussed later in this chapter), but not with Paths.

Esc also works with the shape-selection tools like Rectangle, Ellipse, and Free Select—but only if you release the mouse button before releasing the Esc key.

Finally, in any mouse-driven selection tool *except* Foreground Select, you can cancel a left mouse button operation by adding the right mouse button. Here's how it works: while you're dragging with the left mouse button pressed, press and hold the right button, too. Then release the left mouse button, and then the right one. That will cancel that particular mouse operation: the current control point for I-Scissors or Paths, or the current rectangle, ellipse, or free select shape.

Modifying Selections with Selection Modes

It often happens that you use one of the selection tools and it gets it *almost* right—but there's a little bit that's wrong. If you could just add a little to the selection, or subtract a little, it would be perfect.

For example, I used Fuzzy Select on the sky in this image of the observatory domes on Mauna Kea (Figure 5-18).

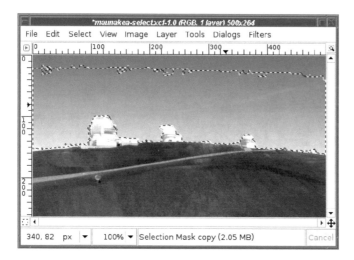

Figure 5-18. *Sky partially selected with Fuzzy Select*

The hard part—the selection around the domes and near the ground—is fine. But the very top of the sky isn't included. (Changing Fuzzy Select's *Threshold* doesn't help—it just selects the domes and the road in addition to the sky.) If I could just add the top part of the sky to the existing selection, everything would be perfect.

Modes come to the rescue. Every selection tool has four modes (Figure 5-19) represented by buttons at the top of the tool options area.

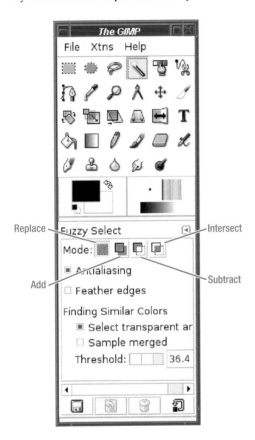

Figure 5-19. *Selection modes*

The default mode, on the far left, is *Replace*. Making a selection in Replace mode removes the current selection and replaces it with the new one.

STARTING SELECTIONS

In GIMP 2.2, with most selection tools, clicking *inside* an existing selection moved the selection contents rather than beginning a new selection. So Replace mode only replaces in 2.2 if you start the new selection *outside* the boundaries of the old one. The same holds for the other selection modes: any new selection must usually be started outside the boundaries of the existing one. In 2.4, that distinction no longer exists: you can start inside an existing selection to add to, subtract from, or intersect with it.

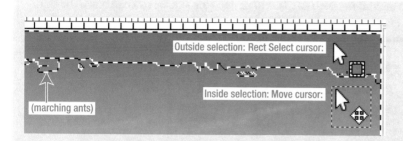

In 2.2, watch the cursor carefully whenever you start a selection, if there's already a selection active. The "Move" component of the cursor will tell you when you're still inside a selection. If you're outside, the cursor will show the icon for the selection tool you're using (Figure 5-20). You can't depend on the marching ants to tell you: if the selection is feathered, it may extend beyond the marching-ants boundary.

Add mode adds the new selection to the existing one. In the Mauna Kea example, that's what I want: to keep the existing selection, but to add the sky at the top of the frame.

The easiest way to do this is to choose the Rectangle Select tool, and set the mode to Add. Then make a rectangular selection that includes everything from the top of the frame down into the existing selection (Figure 5-20). A fast way to do this is in GIMP 2.4 is to start inside the existing selection and drag upward and over to one corner, and then adjust the other side of the rectangle so that it covers the other corner. With earlier GIMP versions, you can't do that because starting a new selection inside an existing one, even in Add mode, moves the contents of the existing selection; and you can't adjust the size of a rectangular selection once it's made.

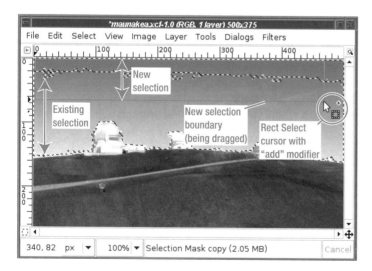

Figure 5-20. *Use the Rectangle Select tool to add a selection at the top of the sky to the existing selection.*

The two selections are added together. Consequently, the entire sky is selected.

Now you can do operations such as *Clear* to remove the sky. Or you can make the sky a separate layer (with *Float*, or just cut and paste it), put it at the bottom of the layer stack, and interpose another object between the foreground and the sky (Figure 5-21).

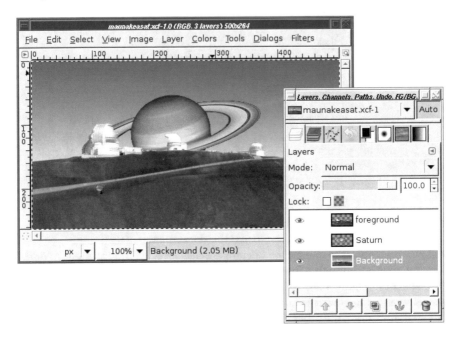

Figure 5-21. *Interposing another object between foreground and sky*

One way to obtain this effect is to invert the selection (*Select* ➤ *Invert*) so you'll now have the foreground selected. Copy, then paste the foreground and make it a new layer. After that, you can paste the transparent Saturn (or anything else you want) between the two layers.

Subtract mode is the inverse of Add mode: it subtracts from the selection. This is particularly handy when you're confronted with the opposite of your previous problem: an automated tool has selected just a little bit too much.

Intersect mode selects only the area where your new selection overlaps with the existing one.

USING MODIFIER KEYS FOR SELECTION MODES

Pressing the Shift key before dragging out a selection will enable Add mode. However, the Shift key also has another meaning in some selection tools: in Rectangle and Ellipse Select, it constrains the selection to be a square or circle. (If you find this confusing, use the Mode buttons in tool options when you want to add to or subtract from the selection.)

Then how do you constrain a selection to a square or circle if you *don't* want Add mode? The trick is to start dragging, and *then* press Shift. This will turn on the constraint without changing the mode.

Likewise, pressing the Ctrl key will enable Subtract mode, but in some tools it has another effect. In Rectangle and Ellipse Select, Ctrl makes the selection expand outward from the starting point, instead of using that point as the upper-left corner. The trick is to hold down the Ctrl key while you start the drag, and then release it while still dragging. Shift+Ctrl means intersect—find the place that the current selection intersects with your new one. As always, look at the cursor to see what you can do. In Rectangle and Ellipse select, the box and adjustment handles represents your new selection, not the result of the intersection.

The QuickMask

Sometimes, outlining just isn't the best way to select an object. You may catch yourself wondering, "Isn't there a more direct way to say that I want to select *here* and *here* but not *there*?"

GIMP has an answer: the QuickMask.

The QuickMask lets you see the selection visually superimposed on the image instead of the usual "marching ants" view. Everything selected will look normal; everything *not* selected will have a translucent red mask over it.

You can paint on the mask with all the normal drawing tools, like the Pencil and Paintbrush. Everywhere you paint in white will be selected; paint black to deselect. Painting in gray, or with the edge of a fuzzy brush, will partially select.

The QuickMask is one of those mind-bogglingly useful features that lots of people don't know about. It's easy to miss. I used GIMP for years before I stumbled onto it. Don't make that mistake, because the QuickMask can make complex selections easy. Just remember that red means *not* selected.

Flip to QuickMask mode by pressing the small square button at the bottom-left corner of the image window (Figure 5-22). You can flip back and forth between QuickMask mode and normal (marching ants) mode at any time with that button.

Figure 5-22. *The QuickMask button. A rough selection of the biplane has already been made with Free Select.*

___

■ **Note** Areas that are partially selected (such as the edges of a feathered selection) will have some red, but the mask will be more transparent than usual. This is not always easy to see, particularly on color images which themselves have red; but it still gives you a better idea than the marching ants would. You can make the QuickMask use a different color by right-clicking on the QuickMask button and choosing *Configure Color and Opacity.*

___

So how do you use the QuickMask?

It's often best to use some other tool to make an approximate selection, and then use the QuickMask to clean it up. For instance, remember the biplane from the animation back in Chapter 3? I made it by using the QuickMask to select from a photograph (Figure 5-22).

I'll begin by making a quick outline with the Free Select tool, as Figure 5-22 shows. My selection isn't very accurate; I just want something close.

Now press the QuickMask button. The marching ants disappear, and everything that wasn't selected before is overlain with a translucent red mask (Figure 5-23). Notice that the appearance of the button has changed, to show you that you're in QuickMask mode. Press the button again, and you'll go back to seeing the marching ants.

Figure 5-23. *The QuickMask view of the biplane Lasso selection*

When it's time to draw on the QuickMask, Rule 1 is the same as for paths: *Zoom in!* You want to be able to see individual pixels, so you can paint precisely even if your hand isn't that steady.

If you want a feathered selection (which is usually best for selecting an object out of a photograph), use a fuzzy brush. For a sharp-edged selection, stick to a sharp-edged brush. The size of the brush you choose will depend on the size of your image and the complexity of your subject.

Then start painting! (See Figure 5-24.) Shift-clicking to draw straight lines will come in handy here.

Figure 5-24. *Painting on the QuickMask with the Paintbrush tool*

Use short strokes. That way, if you draw somewhere you didn't intend to, Undo will correct the mistake without losing much.

Remember, when you paint on the QuickMask, use black for areas you *don't* want selected. For areas you *do* want selected, use white or the eraser (assuming your background color is white). Using gray, or any other color, will only darken the QuickMask partially: the area will be partially selected.

You might think you can't select areas and fill them—after all, the QuickMask defines an existing selection! If you make a new selection, won't that destroy the one you're trying to refine?

Fortunately, GIMP lets you make "selections" and fill them while you're painting in Quick-Mask mode. So go ahead and use the drawing techniques you learned in Chapter 4, including making shapes to be filled with black or white (Figure 5-25).

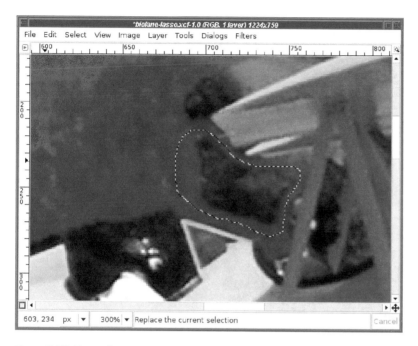

Figure 5-25. *Free select areas while in QuickMask mode to fill in gaps quickly.*

Tip It often helps to use a drawing tool such as the Paintbrush to outline an area, and then use Free Select to fill the remaining real estate. That way, you can fill large areas quickly using only crude Free Select strokes. Figure 5-25 shows a free selection about to be filled.

Continue painting, switching tools as needed to cover areas and fill gaps until you're happy with the result (Figure 5-26). Then click on the QuickMask button to return to the normal view.

Figure 5-26. *The QuickMask is finished, and ready to be turned back into a selection by pressing the QuickMask button again.*

Then you can use *Copy* and *Paste as New* (Figure 5-27), or use your selection any way you choose.

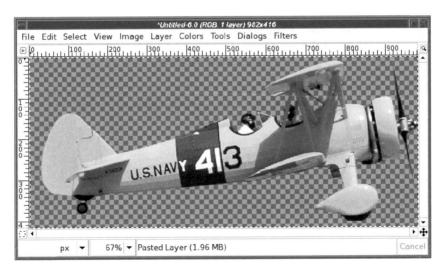

Figure 5-27. *The object selected with the QuickMask is now pasted as a new image.*

Highlighting Foreground Objects

What can you do with a selection, besides copying it and pasting it somewhere?

Pretty much anything, as it turns out. Nearly all of GIMP's operations will operate only on the selection, if one exists. For instance, GIMP's brightness tools, discussed in Chapter 2, will lighten or darken only the selected part of an image.

Figure 5-28 has a background that distracts from the flower in the foreground. Can GIMP de-emphasize the clutter to make the subject stand out more?

Figure 5-28. *Nice flower, distracting background*

First, select the flower using any combination of the techniques already discussed. Select by Color gets most of it, and correcting with the QuickMask fills in the rest. Then invert the selection: since the goal is to change the background, you want the background selected, not the flower.

Now bring up your favorite brightness tool. In this case, Curves is particularly helpful, because it lets you reduce the brightness of the white wall with respect to the green leaves (Figure 5-29). After darkening the background, you may also want to try blurring it a bit with *Gaussian Blur* (see the section in Chapter 6 on Gaussian Blur for more details).

Tip You'll probably want to make the selection invisible with *View* ➤ *Show Selection*. Then you can make sure the boundary between the flower and the background isn't too obvious. If you can see a line at the selection boundary, or the object looks like it has a "halo" around it, you probably need to feather the selection more.

Figure 5-29. *Use Curves to dim the bright background.*

Using Channels to Save a Selection

Sometimes it would be really nice to be able to save a selection.

Perhaps you have a selection you've spent a lot of time refining, but you temporarily need to make another selection somewhere else in the image. Or maybe you've made a selection in one image, but you want to be able to use that selection in another related image.

Of course, you can convert the selection to a path, and give the path a name. But a path won't store all the information about your selection: if you've spent oodles of time feathering the edges just right, converting to a path will forfeit all that work.

The answer is to use a channel as a mask.

Channels are black-and-white images (similar to the QuickMask—in fact, the QuickMask is actually just a special channel) that represent some aspect of an image. To work with channels, you need the Channels dialog, usually docked as a tab between Layers and Paths (Figure 5-30).

Figure 5-30. *The Channels dialog*

Notice that there are three channels already there, for the three colors in an RGB image: Red, Green, and Blue. If your image has transparency, there will also be a channel for Alpha. Each channel has a visibility button next to it, just like layers do. Click on the eyeballs to turn off individual colors and watch what happens to the image.

But you won't be using color channels now (for more on color manipulation, see Chapter 8). Instead, you'll be creating a special channel to hold the selection.

Note If you view the Channels dialog when you have the QuickMask active, you'll see that the QuickMask is also a channel.

To save a selection as a channel, use *Select* ➤ *Save to Channel* (Figure 5-31).

Figure 5-31. *The selection is now saved as a channel.*

Initially the selection channel doesn't have its visibility button turned on—by default it's invisible. You can show it by clicking in the spot where the "eye" would be.

The channel will appear as a translucent overlay, like the QuickMask, except it will be dark gray, not red. (You can change the color with *Channel Attributes*, as you'll see.)

Like the QuickMask, you can paint on a channel using the normal drawing and filling tools, with a few caveats:

- A channel must be visible (show an "eye") in order to paint on it.

- If you still have a selection active, you won't be able to paint outside the selection. If you convert a selection to a channel, and then paint on it, you'll want to use *Select* ➤ *None*.

- When you're finished painting on a selection, go back to the Layers dialog and click on the layer preview to select it. It's very easy to forget that you were editing a channel, and then wonder why none of your operations are working on the current layer.

You can save as many selection channels as you wish. You can rename a channel in the same way that you rename a layer: double-click on its name in the channel dialog and type in a new one. Once you've saved a selection, you can make another selection and save that, too (Figure 5-32). The small preview in the Channels dialog will give you an idea of what each selection channel looks like.

Figure 5-32. *Two selections saved (and renamed)*

To convert a saved selection channel back to an active selection, right-click on the channel to get a context menu (Figure 5-33).

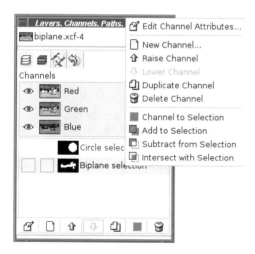

Figure 5-33. *The Channel dialog's context menu*

Channel to Selection is the simplest operation: just replace any existing selection with the selection saved in the channel. But you can also use the other selection modes: *Add to Selection*, *Subtract from Selection*, and *Intersect with Selection*. They let you combine several selections in fairly complex ways. Of course, you can also make a copy (*Duplicate Channel*) or *Delete Channel*.

You can also make a *New Channel*. By default, it will be all black (which will appear as a gray overlay), and then you can paint on it. In Figure 5-34, I've scribbled on the biplane's fuselage with the Paintbrush tool and a large brush.

Figure 5-34. *Painting on a new channel*

The first item in the context menu, *Edit Channel Attributes*, gives you another place to change the channel's name. In addition, it lets you change the *Fill Opacity* (Figure 5-35).

On some images, it may be nearly impossible to see what you're doing when the image is covered by the translucent dark gray of a channel. Changing *Fill Opacity* can make the overlay lighter or darker.

You can also change the color by clicking on the color box. Figure 5-36 shows the result.

Channels don't get in your way because you can switch them off at any time. They won't disturb your current selection until you explicitly ask for that using the context menu.

Of course, channels are included when you save as XCF, so all your stored selections will still be there the next time you edit the image.

Figure 5-35. *Channel Attributes. Click on the color button to bring up a color dialog.*

Figure 5-36. *The channel's overlay is now a different color.*

Layer Masks

A layer mask defines how much, and which parts, of a layer will be visible.

Layer masks are not actually a selection tool. But you can use them in many of the same ways you'd use a selection. For some jobs, a layer mask may be easier and more intuitive than using a selection.

A layer mask is actually a black-and-white image, like a channel or the QuickMask. It represents the "alpha channel" of the layer. The whiter the mask is, the more the affected layer shows through—the less transparent it is. Wherever the channel mask is dark, the image will appear transparent.

It may help to think of the mask as a film negative placed on top of your image. Anywhere the film is black, you can't see your image; anywhere the film is clear (or in this case, white), the layer can be seen.

Layer masks are particularly useful when combining images. For instance, I have an ostrich (Figure 5-37) and a giraffe (Figure 5-38). What if I want to make an ostraffe?

Figure 5-37. *An ostrich*

Figure 5-38. *A giraffe*

Start by pasting the ostrich onto the giraffe image. Copy from the ostrich photo, paste over the giraffe, then go to the Layers dialog and click the *New Layer* button. Rename the layers so you'll remember which is which.

The next step is to line up the two images. But that's hard since you can't see the giraffe once the ostrich is on top of it. The *Opacity* slider in the Layers dialog saves the day. Set the opacity to about 50% (or whatever makes it easy to see both images), and it's no problem to line them up (Figure 5-39).

Figure 5-39. *Make the top layer translucent in order to line up the two images.*

Now it's time for the layer mask. Right-click on the ostrich layer in the layers dialog and select *Add Layer Mask…* (Figure 5-40).

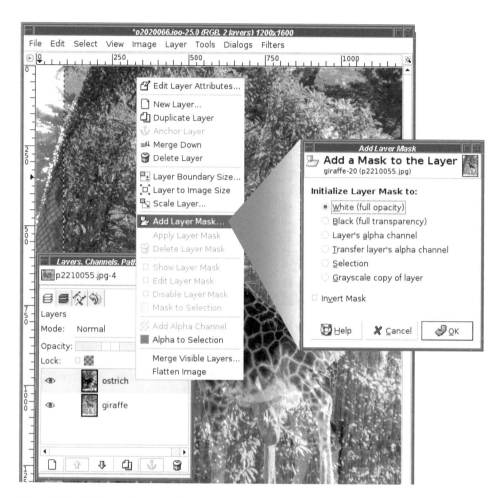

Figure 5-40. *Adding a layer mask*

The Add Layer Mask dialog lets you specify the color of the new layer mask. The default, white, means the full layer remains visible at first (until you change that by painting some black onto the mask). White is usually the best starting place, but the other options are there if you need them.

The new layer mask shows up as a thumbnail preview in the Layers dialog (Figure 5-41). There are two important points to note about the layer mask preview.

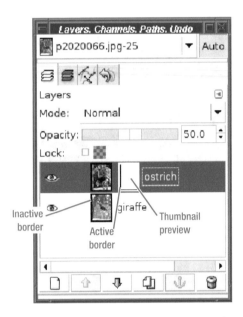

Figure 5-41. *A preview appears for the new layer mask.*

First, it shows you what the layer mask looks like. The new mask is all white, so it looks like a white rectangle. Once you start drawing in the mask, you'll see that the preview will give you an approximate idea of the mask's appearance.

Second, and more important, the border of the preview is white, indicating that it is *active*. That means if you draw in the image, you'll be drawing on the layer mask (just as you drew on the QuickMask or on a selection channel), not on the image itself.

This can be quite confusing. An image normally shows no visible indication of whether there's a layer mask active. When working with layer masks, it's important to keep the Layers dialog visible. Use the preview border colors to tell you whether you're working with the layer or with its mask. The one that has a white border is the one that's active.

You can activate the layer at any time by clicking on the layer preview in the Layers dialog. Click again on the mask to activate it. Or use *Edit Layer Mask* in the context menu to toggle between the two.

■**Caution** When a layer mask is active, drawing isn't the only GIMP operation that will be affected. The Move tool will move the mask, not the layer (if you had the mask lined up with the layer, it won't be lined up any more). Fortunately, Undo fixes minor mistakes like that. Also, saving to some file types will issue warnings if you try to save when you have a layer mask selected. If that happens, you can cancel the save, go back and select the layer instead of the mask, and then save again.

Now try drawing on the layer mask to see for yourself how it works. Gradients are particularly useful with layer masks. I'm going to keep the head, neck, and back of the ostrich, while making the legs invisible. The ostrich's upper body should blend in to the giraffe's lower body. That means I need the top of the ostrich's layer mask to be white, the bottom black, and a fade (a gradient) in between, right where I want the two images to merge.

With the layer mask still selected, I choose the Gradient tool in the Toolbox and drag a vertical line where I want the fade (Figure 5-42).

Figure 5-42. *Drag where you want the gradient to be.*

It's fairly easy to forget in which direction to draw a gradient, and end up blackening what you wanted to whiten, and vice versa. (Remember, the layer mask preview will show you a thumbnail of what the mask looks like.) Fortunately, that's easy to fix: just draw another gradient in the opposite direction.

Don't forget that holding the Ctrl key down as you drag a gradient constrains it to a multiple of 15 degrees. That's an easy way to get a gradient that's exactly vertical or exactly horizontal.

Once you've drawn on the layer mask, the image doesn't look that different, because of that translucent top layer. It's finally time to slide the opacity of the top layer back to 100%. You could have done that earlier, but without being able to see the bottom layer it would have been difficult to see where to place the gradient.

With the top layer made fully opaque again, now the image becomes Figure 5-43.

Figure 5-43. *A gradient on the layer mask, and top layer back to fully opaque*

Notice the layer mask preview has become fuzzy on the bottom: this is the gradient that has been drawn on the layer mask.

Don't forget to save your work as you go along. GIMP's XCF format will save layers, layer masks, and selections, so you can save at any time and continue later from wherever you left off.

To see the layer mask at full size, use *Show Layer Mask* from the right-click menu in the Layers dialog (Figure 5-44). A shortcut for *Show Layer Mask* is to Alt-click (or Alt+Shift-click) on the layer preview; another Alt-click will show the image normally again. Notice that the layer mask's boundary changes to green in the dialog preview. Also notice that the layer mask applies only to the area where the ostrich image is; the edges, from the giraffe photo, are not affected.

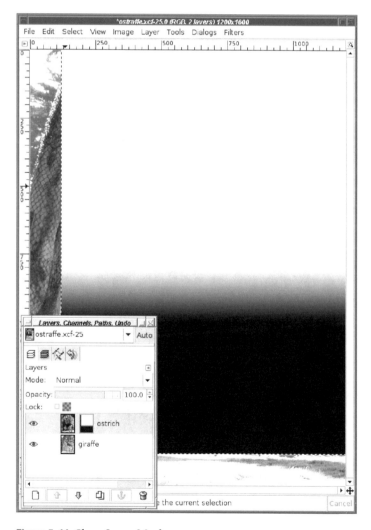

Figure 5-44. *Show Layer Mask*

Now play with the image. You may want to change the location of your gradient slightly (by drawing a new gradient higher or lower), or use the Move tool to adjust the relative positions of the two layers. (Don't forget to select the layer, not the mask, before moving.)

When you're satisfied that you have everything aligned just right, it's a good time to crop the image. The idea is to get rid of any overhang from either original that might be noticeable around the borders. For instance, the netting-covered tree on the left side of Figure 5-43 doesn't blend well with the bush to its right.

Now it's time to tune the mask a bit with a little hand-painting. Notice the area under the ostrich's neck where the layer is partially transparent and doesn't blend well into the giraffe's chest? Remember, a mask is just a black-and-white image. You can paint on it with paint tools, just as you painted on the QuickMask and channels earlier in this chapter. Anywhere you paint white will become opaque.

Choose a fuzzy brush with the Paintbrush tool, or use the Airbrush, and paint in the area where you want more of the upper image to show up (Figure 5-45). You may find it helpful to flip back and forth between "Show Layer Mask" mode and normal mode to see what you're painting. A quick way of doing that is by Alt-clicking on the layer mask preview (Alt+Shift-click will also work on systems that use Alt-click for other purposes). The border of the preview will go green to show that you're seeing the layer mask itself, not its effect on the image.

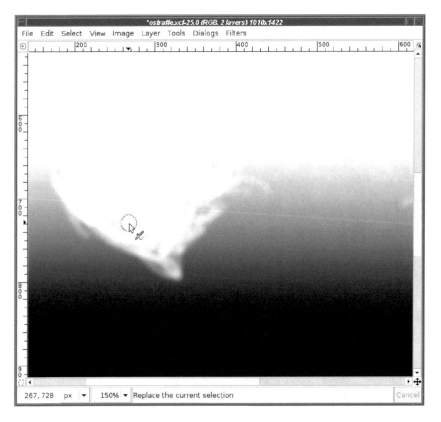

Figure 5-45. *Switching to Show Layer Mask after painting. Use painting tools to touch up areas where the gradient isn't quite enough.*

If you ever need to disable a layer mask temporarily, a quick way to do that is to Ctrl-click on the layer preview. The border will turn red to show the mask is disabled. Of course, you can always show, hide, enable, or disable layer masks through the context menu you access by right-clicking in the Layers dialog.

After touching up the layer mask, Figure 5-46 shows the final result.

Figure 5-46. *The only ostraffe in captivity!*

Of course, the backgrounds from your two images may not match up. You can paint on a layer mask—much as you would on a QuickMask—to hide one background completely and use only the other. Or you can hide the backgrounds on *both* images with layer masks, and then add *another* background layer to place your creation anywhere you want. The choice is yours!

Extracting Foreground Objects with SIOX

A brand-new tool in GIMP 2.4 is the Foreground Select tool (Figure 5-47). It's also called the Foreground Object Extractor, or sometimes SIOX, which stands for *Simple Interactive Object Extraction*.

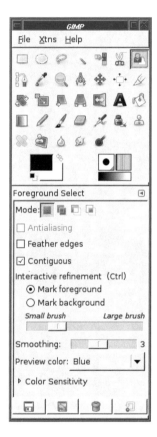

Figure 5-47. *The Foreground Object Extractor*

There are two steps to using SIOX. First, draw an outline around and outside the object you want to select. You have to do this in one motion, as if you were using the Free Select tool.

Don't try too hard to get close to the borders of the object. Just make sure that every bit of your object is inside the border. When you're finished, release the mouse button: everything outside the region you selected will be masked off in dark blue (Figure 5-48).

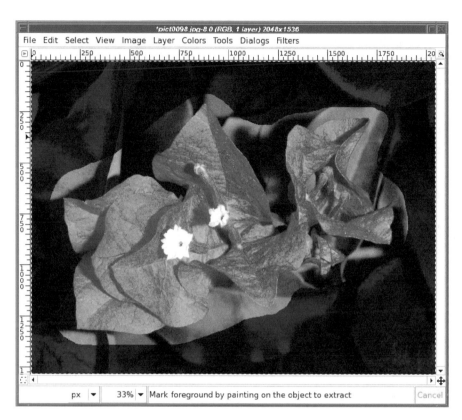

Figure 5-48. *Define the region of interest.*

The second step is marking the foreground. Drag the mouse across the part of the image you *do* want to select, being careful to stay away from parts of the image you *don't* want. Don't try to cover the whole object, but do try to make sure you cover all the representative colors in the object. The tool will draw a black trail wherever you drag, so you can see what you've already marked (Figure 5-49).

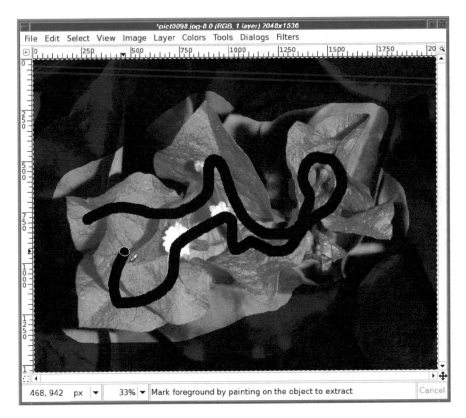

Figure 5-49. *Drag to define parts of the object you want to select.*

You can drag multiple short trails or one long one. I usually find that one long trail works best—sometimes as I add new trails, I lose parts of the image that were previously marked. But each image is a little different, and you'll have to experiment. With some images, you can refine the selection by using background select (use the *Mark background* setting in the dialog, or hold the Ctrl key while you drag over the green leaves).

When you release the mouse button after drawing a trail, the tool goes to work finding all parts of the region that are similar to the parts you dragged (Figure 5-50).

This may take a few seconds, or longer for a large image or a long trail.

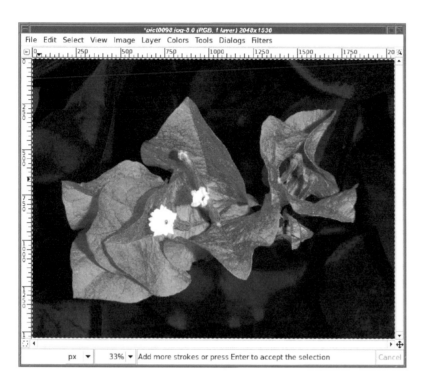

Figure 5-50. *The tool has done its work.*

Once you're happy with the result, hit the Enter key to turn the mask into a selection.

The tool options (back in Figure 5-47) include the usual *Antialiasing* and *Feather* options, and an adjustment for the brush size (you will want to adjust this if you're trying to select very small objects, or to mark thin structures like branches). There's also a *Smoothing* control, which lets you adjust the coarseness of the areas selected, and a *Color Sensitivity* expander that lets you play with how the tool determines what's close enough to the trail you dragged.

The SIOX tool is very young, but it shows a lot of promise. Since it's new, the GIMP developers are still adjusting it, and it's likely to evolve over the next few versions. It doesn't work for everything. I find it works best when you have significant color differences (like a magenta flower against a green background), and not so well for objects that include colors similar to the background (like a brown squirrel perched in a tangle of brown branches).

Try it out. For certain types of images, the tool works very well indeed, and should be a part of your selection arsenal.

Summary

By now, you should be familiar with a wide range of selection techniques. You're familiar with the marching ants, but you know how to turn them off when they get in the way. You can make selections using color or contiguous regions, Bezier paths, the Intelligent Scissors, or the QuickMask. You can make simple selections more complex by combining several selections in Add or Subtract mode, or by editing them in the Paths tool, the QuickMask, or as a channel mask.

In addition, you've seen how you can change the appearance of an image by using tools on only a selected part of that image, and you've worked with layer masks and seen how you can use gradients in a layer mask to combine two layers smoothly. You can save a selection to a channel or path, and restore earlier selections you saved that way.

Selections are useful in every aspect of image editing, but nowhere are they more useful than when working with digital photographs—especially photos that have something wrong with them that needs correcting. In the next chapter, let's take another look at digital photographs, and explore some techniques for touching them up…or editing problematic objects out of an otherwise good photo.

CHAPTER 6

■ ■ ■

Erasing and Touching Up

In Chapter 2, you learned some basic GIMP operations for improving photographs: the cropping, rescaling, and brightness/contrast tools.

But what if you have a photograph that needs more help than that? I know I sometimes take a photo that comes out just as I'd hoped…except for the lamppost growing out of someone's head, or the overflowing garbage can right behind the subject. Or maybe that photo of the Grand Canyon would look so much nicer without the guy in Bermuda shorts talking on his cell phone.

In an ideal world, we'd notice these things before taking the picture. We'd be able to move a little and re-frame the photo to eliminate any distractions. But in practice, we all take at least some photos like that. Fortunately, GIMP can help!

This chapter will introduce you to the following concepts:

- Darkroom work with Dodge and Burn
- Smudging blemishes away
- Using the Clone tool for more difficult jobs
- Copying small regions
- The Heal tool
- Perspective cloning
- Sharpening specific regions using the Convolve tool
- Blurring backgrounds with Gaussian Blur

Darkroom Work with Dodge and Burn

I don't know about you, but I take a lot of bad shots of people. Casual "models" like to stand with their backs to the sun, or wear a hat with a visor to keep the glare out of their eyes. I fire away, thinking it'll be a good portrait. But when I look at it later, it's a shot of someone whose face fades into darkness (Figure 6-1).

The answer, as any book on portrait photography will tell you, is to use fill flash: turn on the flash even though it's daylight. It illuminates the face even if the sun is in the wrong place. I've read those books—and I still forget to do it. Do you?

Figure 6-1. *Forgot to use fill flash…again!*

Fortunately, GIMP has the perfect tool to fix that, along with a host of other exposure errors: the Dodge/Burn tool. Typically, it's used when some small part of the image is too dark or too light.

Dodge and *burn* are terms from film photography. When making a print from a negative, some areas may come out too bright, others too dark. Photographic film can record wider *exposure latitude* than can be easily seen by viewing either the negative or the print directly.

The developer turning that negative into a photographic print gets to choose whether to use a long exposure (which will show detail in the light areas, but leave the dark areas too dark) or a shorter exposure (which will make the light areas solid white, but show more detail in the shadows).

That's not always good enough. When professionals make prints, they correct light and dark areas by hand. They place masks over small parts of the image to keep bright areas from becoming too white (*burning*), and to make sure dark areas get a little lighter (*dodging*).

The great photographer Ansel Adams often said that the photographic negative was like a musical score but the print was the performance. The time he spent making his prints perfect was a big part of what made his photographs so famous.

A digital camera can record exposure latitude roughly comparable to film. Your photographs contain a lot more information than you can see just by looking at them. GIMP's Dodge/Burn tool lets you adjust your digital photographs in much the same way that professional film photographers adjust their prints. And unlike Ansel Adams' technique, it doesn't require years of experience to learn! Or cost a bunch if you mess up.

Dodging

The Dodge/Burn tool starts in Dodge mode by default. It uses a brush, like the drawing tools you used in Chapter 4—try a fairly large one to begin with.

The Dodge tool lets you choose between three modes: Shadows, Midtones, and Highlights. By default, it's set to Midtones, and that will work for many dodge or burn problems.

However, if you're trying to brighten a very dark shadow area, you may be better off choosing Shadows. Then the Dodge tool will selectively brighten the dark zones much more than other areas. That lets you be slightly sloppier with your brush technique: if you slide a little outside of the shadow, it won't be very noticeable.

Try that with Midtones and you'll see some of the area that's not in shadow also get brightened. However, Midtones may sometimes bring out a little more detail than Shadows.

Take a look at the Dodge tool's options, as shown in Figure 6-2.

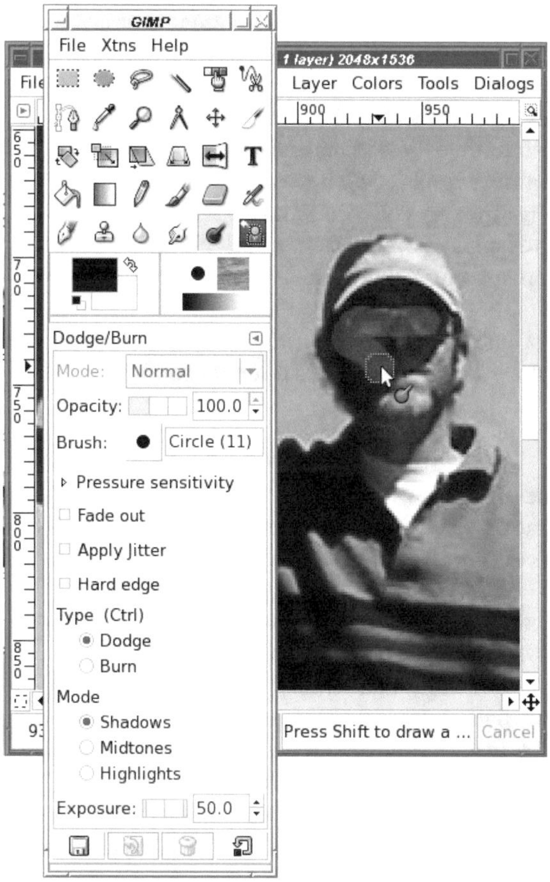

Figure 6-2. *Use the Dodge tool to lighten areas that are too dark.*

Opacity makes the tool's effect more subtle—as if the brush were more transparent (the default setting is 100%).

The *Pressure sensitivity* options control how the tool can respond to pressure if you're using a drawing tablet. Mouse users can ignore them.

Fade out makes the stroke end after a certain distance. That's one way to ensure that you use short strokes!

Apply jitter is a new option in GIMP 2.4 that makes the effect less regular. On some images it may give a more natural effect.

The Dodge tool normally makes the edges of the brush slightly fuzzy, even if you're using a hard brush. *Hard edge* turns this off.

Finally, an *Exposure* slider controls the strength of the effect.

Time to get started! Choose Shadows or Midtones depending on how dark the area is, and then start scribbling.

The trick to dodging? Hold the mouse button down and try to cover a contiguous area all in one sweep. The Dodge tool is smart: it won't brighten the same area twice, so if you cross back over an area you've already covered, it won't get too bright. However, if you use separate strokes, you can brighten the same area more with each stroke.

Dodging can turn a failed portrait into a better one. It still won't look as good as if you'd used fill flash or the correct lighting, but it can make the difference between seeing someone's face and not seeing it.

But wait—can't you do all of this by making a feathered selection that covers the shadowed area, then using one of the brightness/contrast tools to make the area brighter?

Sure! In fact, by selecting and using brightness tools you'll have more control: you can use a tool such as Curves or Levels to brighten just the way you want. And if you use the Quick-Mask to define the selection, you can have full control over *how much* brightening happens and *where*, by making the selection more transparent in areas where you want the effect to be less pronounced.

But all that takes time. Dodging is a shortcut—a quick way to brighten small dark areas, especially areas that are hard to select. It can be a lot quicker—and often it's good enough.

Burning

Burning is the opposite of dodging—it makes light areas darker. Unfortunately, it's more difficult to use. The problem? In digital photographs, bright areas are often so "blown out" that there really isn't any detail left. The camera's electronics have reached their saturation point, and all they can do is record white.

When you use the Burn tool on areas that are completely white, all it can do is turn them gray, since it has no way to tell what colors or textures should be there.

That means that the Burn tool is best used on fairly small areas, or on areas that are only a little too bright rather than completely white. If you use it on a large white area, you'll end up with a large gray area, which will be surprisingly noticeable. But if you burn small spots of brightness, you can make them detract less from the subject of the photo.

For instance, in Figure 6-3 the glints off the water aren't adding anything to the image. All they do is distract from the subject and lead the eye away from the geese. The Burn tool can help.

Figure 6-3. *The glints off the water distract from the geese.*

When using Burn, it's especially helpful to open a second view, like you did in Chapter 4 when you were drawing: *View ➤ New View.* That way, you can see the effect of your changes in the full image, even while you work with a nice zoomed-in view.

Note When burning completely white areas, the mode makes a greater difference than it did when dodging shadow areas. You *must* choose *Highlights*; the other two settings will have no effect on the white areas. (Try it and see!)

Now use the Burn tool in the zoomed window to burn in the bright areas (Figure 6-4). It's hard to watch both versions at once, but fortunately there's no need: only the zoomed view will be changed while you're dragging. When you release the mouse button to finish the burn, *then* the other view will change. You can see the full effect of one burn operation. If it isn't what you want, undo and try again.

Figure 6-4. *Open a new view and zoom in. Use the zoomed view to burn.*

Notice that the edges of the burned area in Figure 6-4, burned with the largest hard-edged brush, don't blend in very well with their surroundings. Sometimes this doesn't matter, while other times it does—it depends on the image.

If you burn with a large hard-edged brush and the edges are too harsh in the final image, try using a fuzzy brush and being more careful with your brushstrokes. It takes longer, but you'll get a better end result.

Don't forget that you can burn the same area twice if it's still too bright after one burn. Of course, you can also change the tool's *Exposure* setting if you want a stronger effect every-where. Be cautious of too much burning, though: it can create flat gray areas that become quite conspicuous in the final image.

DODGE/BURN AS A DRAWING TOOL

In the GIMP manual, the Dodge/Burn tool is considered a drawing tool because it uses a brush and lets you drag around the image. Although I find it most useful for touching up photographs, Dodge/Burn can come in handy in drawings too.

In particular, you can use it to make shadows along one side of an object you've drawn, for a more three-dimensional look. Remember drawing a dark line down the side of the tree trunk in Chapter 4 to give the trunk depth? You can do that even better with the Burn tool.

Smudging Blemishes Away

Many images only need a bit of easy correction. For instance, consider Figure 6-5. The power pylon on the right spoils the tranquil image.

Figure 6-5. *Bucolic image spoiled by a power tower*

One way to get rid of simple problems like this is by using the Smudge tool. Its icon in the Toolbox is a finger smudging, and that's exactly what it looks like when you drag the Smudge tool across an image (Figure 6-6). If you ever made finger paintings in kindergarten, the Smudge tool should seem familiar.

Figure 6-6. *The Smudge tool*

Notice that the Smudge tool picks up color underneath it, and distributes those colors as you continue to drag.

For this reason, most of the time you'll want to use short strokes when you smudge. Work from the color you want to keep (in this case, the sky) and gradually replace the colors you don't want (the power tower). Drag the sky color in on top of the power tower, and when it starts to turn dark, stop dragging, go back, and start again in the sky. Usually a large brush works best on photographs, because it takes too long to smudge with a small brush. Sometimes you can start with a large hard-edged brush, and then clean up any problems with a smaller fuzzy brush.

Eventually, after many short strokes, the unwanted object is gone (Figure 6-7).

Figure 6-7. *The power tower is gone.*

After smudging an object out of a photograph, you may have residual color that you can't seem to get right. If you look closely at Figure 6-7, you may notice a faint darker area in the sky where the power tower used to be. It's difficult to end up with completely smooth color using the Smudge tool. Often, it's "good enough," and the tool is simple and fun to use. But if you want cleaner results, fear not! You'll learn several more accurate ways to paint out images.

Smudge is useful in drawing as well as image touch-up. For instance, if you draw a white blob (by filling a rectangle or an oval with white) and then smudge in small arcs, you can make new clouds (Figure 6-8). Smudging outward from the white area expands the size of the cloud; smudging inward from the sky into the growing cloud adds some darker "shadow" highlights that can make a cloud look more realistic.

Figure 6-8. *Smudging to make larger puffy clouds*

The Smudge tool has the same *Opacity, Pressure sensitivity, Fade out*, and *Hard edge* options as the Dodge tool. In addition, it has a special option of its own: *Rate*.

Rate controls the strength of the smudge effect. The default setting of 50% is good for most touch-up work. But you can get some interesting effects by increasing the rate. The 100% setting isn't very useful for image touch-ups, but it gives a strong smudge with a hard edge and no transparency that can be useful for drawing cables, shoelaces, caterpillars, or other stringy subjects (Figure 6-9).

Figure 6-9. *Strange effects from a smudge rate of 100% and a large hard-edged brush. The blue on top of the "tubes" is just the sky from above the branch when starting the smudge.*

The Clone Tool, for More Difficult Jobs

The Smudge tool is fun and easy, but if you've used it you've probably already hit its limitations. It's hard to keep control of colors when you're smudging. More important, smudging smoothes out any textures that should be in the original. It's okay for clear blue skies and other evenly colored areas, but it wouldn't work to remove an object on a more complicated background, like the cars in Figure 6-10.

Figure 6-10. *I waited and waited for a clear moment, but the cars just kept coming!*

If you try to smudge objects out of areas like this, you'll just make a mess, like in Figure 6-11 (and give yourself a repetitive stress injury from pressing the mouse button too much). This inaccuracy is why finger painting never caught on in professional art circles, even though it was lots of fun to do in kindergarten.

Figure 6-11. *Smudging just makes a mess.*

The answer is the Clone tool. The Clone tool lets you duplicate a small area over and over, to paint an object out of a picture.

The first time you try to use it, you'll probably be frustrated. You click and drag, expecting patterns from nearby areas to be copied—just like with Smudge, only smarter. But nothing happens! The cursor shows a crossed-circle (Figure 6-12) saying "No"! Why won't it let you paint?

Figure 6-12. *At first, GIMP won't let you clone.*

Setting the Clone Source

The key to the Clone tool is that it copies bits of image from one place to another. Before you can start replacing anything, you have to choose a place from which GIMP will copy—the "clone source."

Choose the clone source by clicking while holding the Ctrl key down. GIMP will mark the spot with a small cross. The source doesn't have to be near the area you're trying to cover; in fact, you can even clone from a different image, or a different layer in the same image.

The size of the brush isn't important when specifying the source—you're only choosing a starting point. Each time you begin a cloning stroke, GIMP will start copying from the clone source. Then as you drag in one direction or another, GIMP will clone whatever's in that direction from the source…until you release the mouse button. Then when you start the next stroke (by pressing the mouse button again), you'll start from the source again. (But see the discussion of alignment modes under "Clone Tool Options" later in this chapter to learn the various ways you can change that.)

Tip As you paint with the Clone tool, keep an eye on the source region: GIMP will show you (with a subtle crosshair that moves) exactly which region is currently being cloned, which can be helpful if you're ever surprised at what's being painted.

For instance, suppose that you Ctrl-click to choose a source region in the bushes just to the right of the lead car. Then move down a bit and drag along a line from right to left (Figure 6-13).

Getting the bush at the beginning of the dragged line was great, but you can see the drag got carried away. It went too far left in the original source region, grabbing the car, the centerline, and a lot of road.

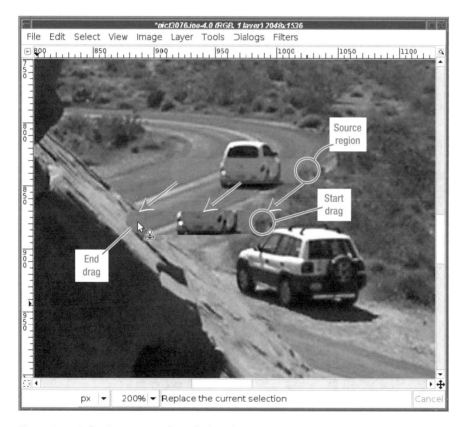

Figure 6-13. *Selecting too much with the Clone tool*

For that reason, try to choose a source region that has a fairly large chunk of the pattern you're trying to clone (though that's not always possible), and use short strokes. Be careful not to drag too far, or you'll find the Clone tool paints something you didn't want, like the way it cloned part of the car in Figure 6-13. Also, if you're trying to paint a specific object out of the picture, use direction to your advantage. For instance, if you clone from below the car, painting with downward strokes (starting at the top of the car and dragging down) will pick up more road, while if you drag upward you'll just copy the car onto itself.

In the case of the lead car, this technique doesn't work so well: the road ahead of the car is curving, while the road behind it is straight. There's no source region that would curve just the right amount at the right place. The best bet is to find a source region somewhere else in the road (for instance, the empty road behind the car) and use lots of short strokes, being careful about the placement of the road's centerline.

As with most touch-up techniques, a fuzzy brush usually works best, unless you're cloning near a sharp boundary like the edge of a rock or tree trunk against the sky.

Tip When covering an area, particularly a long thin area like this one, using Shift-click is helpful. Remember drawing lines in Chapter 4? Click on a point, and then hold down the Shift key while clicking to draw a line to your next point.

Change the source region whenever you need to. You'll probably need to grab from several different source areas (in this case, road, centerline, gray dirt, red dirt, and bushes, as in Figure 6-14).

Figure 6-14. *Cover the unwanted object(s), changing the source region as many times as you need to.*

Finally, it's as cloned as it's going to get. But, as usual, it's not perfect.

Fine-tuning a Clone Job

You may have noticed in Figure 6-14 that the centerline doesn't go around the bend. That's because the Clone tool copies regions at least as large as the brush. With a large brush, it will always copy a centerline that's pointing in the wrong direction. How can you fix that?

One way is to switch to a much smaller brush, Ctrl-click on the centerline to use it as the source region, and then click repeatedly around the corner, making dots of centerline color (Figure 6-15).

Figure 6-15. *Using one dot at a time to make the curve in the centerline*

Use enough dots to fill in the line completely. Or, if you start feeling too dotty, use the Smudge tool (still with a small brush) to close the gaps between the dots.

Voilà! I don't know why I kept waiting for a gap between cars to take that photo. Getting rid of cars is easy (Figure 6-16)!

Figure 6-16. *Cars, gone!*

Clone Tool Options

I haven't said much about the Clone tool's options. That's because most of the time, you won't need to change anything.

The collection of settings should be familiar from other tools you've already used: *Mode*, *Opacity*, *Pressure sensitivity*, *Fade out*, and *Hard edge*.

In addition, you can clone from one of GIMP's built-in patterns instead of from an image by changing the *Source*.

The only complicated option is *Alignment* (Figure 6-17). The default is *None*: for each stroke you make, the pattern GIMP will paint begins at the source origin (the place where you Ctrl-clicked) and proceeds from there.

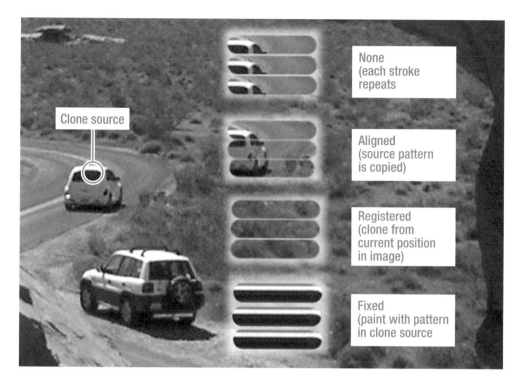

Figure 6-17. *Alignment modes in the Clone tool*

In *Aligned* mode, the first stroke you make after setting the source will begin from the source origin, just as in *None* mode. But for subsequent strokes, GIMP will make each stroke relative to the last, so you can paint an exact copy of the source region as you keep making strokes.

In *Registered* mode, painting will clone from wherever you are painting, rather than from where you chose the source image. This is primarily useful for painting parts of one layer into another layer at the same position, or for copying parts of an image into a different image.

Finally, *Fixed* mode works a lot like the clipboard brush (described in Chapters 4 and 9): it uses only what's inside the brush outline, over and over.

Copying Small Regions

Cloning works great for filling in small areas, or for painting patterns. But there are times when it's easier to copy a pattern all at once, in a single block.

For instance, the dune view in Figure 6-18 would look better without the figure standing at the lower-left corner.

Figure 6-18. *Dunes, with a person in the way*

You could use the Clone tool to get rid of the person, but there's a faster way: copy a region shaped like the object you want to remove, and then paste it over the object.

Start by making a selection around the object. The selection doesn't have to be perfect—just make sure it's big enough to cover the unwanted object completely. With some feathering, the Lasso tool is usually fine for this job.

Now move the selection boundary to the area you want to copy. You can use Alt-drag to move the selection boundary (use Shift-Alt-drag if your system uses Alt-drag for something else). Or use the Move tool with *Affect* set to *Transform Selection*, and then just drag from inside the selection.

With the selection boundary in the right place (Figure 6-19), you can copy and then paste. Move the pasted selection back on top of the object you're trying to remove, and then fine-tune its position with the arrow keys until everything meshes (Figure 6-20).

Figure 6-19. *Move the selection boundary, not its contents.*

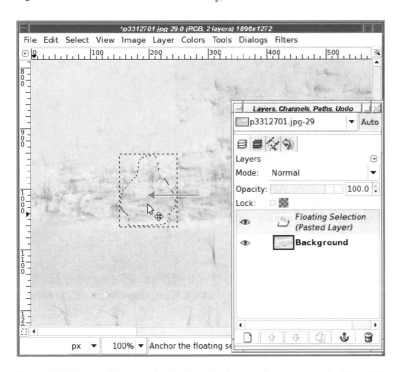

Figure 6-20. *Move the pasted selection back over the unwanted object. The selection and layer boundaries are shown.*

You will probably want to turn off both the selection boundary (*View ➤ Show Selection*, or Ctrl+T) and the layer boundary (*View ➤ Show Layer Boundary*) temporarily, in order to see the edges of the pasted layer better.

That's all there is to it! Quick and easy. If you need to clean up any details around the edges, the Smudge and Clone tools are good for making small corrections.

Tip This technique also works well with "finger-in-front-of-the-lens" mistakes. Not that you'd ever do that!

The Heal Tool

The Heal tool (new in 2.4) is similar to the Clone tool, but with a difference: it combines the texture from the source layer with the color and lighting of the destination layer.

Confused? An example makes it a lot clearer.

Suppose you wanted to erase some of the petroglyphs in Figure 6-21. How would you do it?

Figure 6-21. *Rock art*

You could use the Clone tool—but from where? The petroglyphs cover almost the whole wall. There's a relatively unmarked area down near the bottom, but it doesn't match the color of the rest of the rock (Figure 6-22).

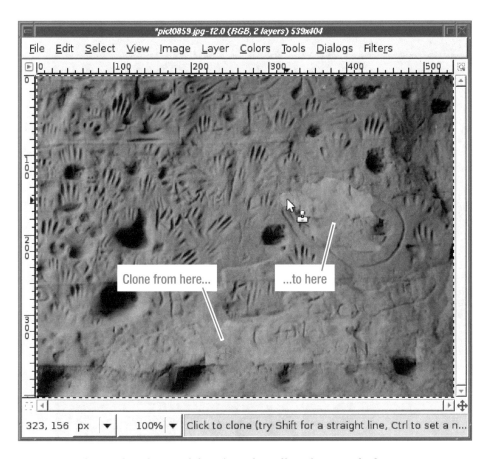

Figure 6-22. *The regular Clone tool doesn't work at all on the petroglyphs.*

The Heal tool is perfect for a case like this. It can take the texture from the bare rock source area and let you paint it on top of the texture you want to erase. Just as with the regular Clone tool, you need to choose a source region by clicking somewhere with the Ctrl key held down. Then paint onto a destination region. Heal will take the color from the destination area where you're painting, so your new petroglyph-free rock will match the rock around it (Figure 6-23). Like the regular Clone tool, Heal will draw a moving crosshair on the part of the source region being used.

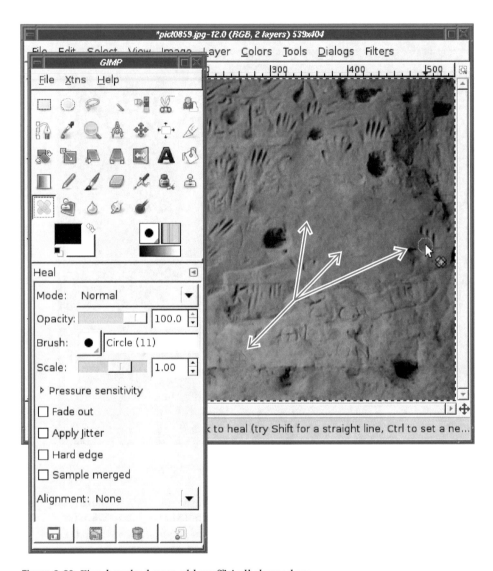

Figure 6-23. *Five-hundred-year-old graffiti all cleaned up*

Heal's options are almost the same as those of the regular Clone tool, including the Alignment options explained earlier in this chapter. You may find that experimenting with different Alignment settings is useful, more so than with regular cloning.

The Heal tool is quite new in GIMP, and it isn't always as smart as you might hope. In particular, it can be difficult to cover large areas with it. On the other hand, it excels at small areas like skin blemishes or spot flaws such as dust marks. But whenever you need to clone an area to somewhere that's a different color or brightness, it's definitely worth trying Heal. After a while you'll get a feel for the sorts of images where it works well. It might even become your favorite touch-up tool.

Perspective Cloning

There's another new cloning tool introduced in GIMP 2.4: Perspective Clone. Its specialty is images with perspective—images of scenes or objects that extend away or up from the viewer, as in Figure 6-24.

Figure 6-24. *Using the regular Clone tool to copy one of the existing windows to the bottom of the tower results in a window that's way too small.*

Perspective Clone comes to the rescue. It needs an extra step before starting a cloning operation: setting the perspective. Make sure the *Mode* option is set to Modify Perspective; then drag inward from each corner of the image, one by one, to make the perspective box line up with something in the image (Figure 6-25).

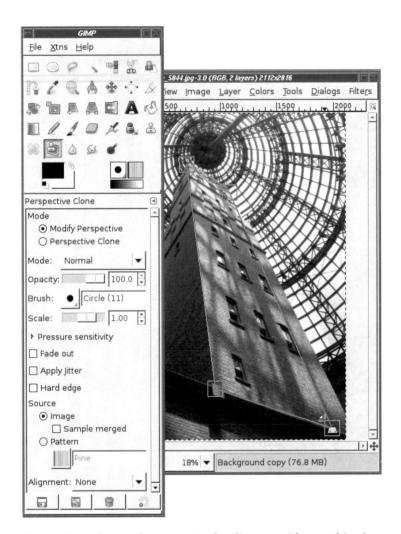

Figure 6-25. *Make sure the perspective box lines up with something in your image. In this case, I've used the right edges of the windows rather than the tower itself only because that keeps the lower-right corner inside the image.*

Caution You may have noticed that Perspective Clone has two options named *Mode*. In addition to the Mode option discussed here, you can also set the drawing Mode option to the usual set of drawing tool options, as discussed in Chapter 4.

Once your perspective is set, change *Mode* to Perspective Clone and proceed as with a standard clone (Figure 6-26). Whatever you clone will be modified appropriately based on the perspective you've set. You can clone anywhere in the image—no need to stay inside the perspective outlines you defined. You can even choose a small object (such as a single window in this photo) to define your perspective, and the tool will still apply it to the whole image.

Figure 6-26. *With Perspective Clone, the new window is a much more appropriate size.*

Your source region can be inside the same image and layer, as in this case where I cloned from the last row of windows to make windows lower down. But you're not limited to that: you can clone from another image that shows no perspective. You can even clone from one of GIMP's built-in patterns by choosing that pattern in Tool Options—but (at least as of GIMP 2.4.5) the pattern isn't modified to fit the perspective, so it's not clear how useful this is.

Like the Heal tool, Perspective Clone is new and doesn't always work as you might expect. But for certain types of photos, it can be a real time-saver.

Enhancing Specific Regions: The Blur/Sharpen Tool

Don't you hate it when you take a picture of something, and it turns out the focus was on the wrong place in the photo (Figure 6-27)?

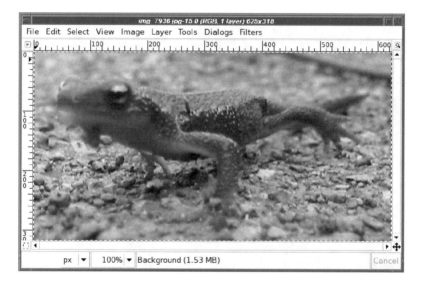

Figure 6-27. *The focus is good on everything except the newt's face.*

You already know about Sharpen and Unsharp Mask from Chapter 2. But if you used those tools on an image like this, the parts that are already sharp would turn grainy. What you really need is something that can sharpen just the newt's face.

That's a job for the Blur/Sharpen tool (Figure 6-28), the tool formerly known as Convolve (and you may still see this term used in places, like the official GIMP manual).

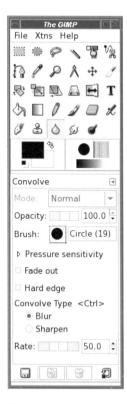

Figure 6-28. *The Convolve (Blur/Sharpen) tool*

The Blur/Sharpen tool lets you change small regions of an image just by dragging over them. The more you go over an area, the more it will blur or sharpen.

The tool's options include the usual drawing and touch-up choices, plus a switch for *Convolve Type* (this is where you choose between *Blur* and *Sharpen*). There's also a *Rate* slider to let you choose the strength of the effect. Since you can drag over the same area repeatedly, *Rate* doesn't matter as much as it does in some tools.

Sharpening with the Convolve Tool

Dragging the Sharpen tool around the newt's head produces Figure 6-29.

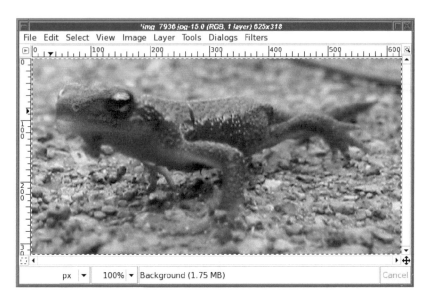

Figure 6-29. *The newt is much sharper now.*

You may notice that the area around the head, and especially the eye, has become a bit grainy. That's what happens when you sharpen something too much (as you may remember from Chapter 2, with Unsharp Mask). If necessary, you can zoom way in and clean up some of that with the Smudge or Clone tools and a very fine brush.

By the way, why was it called "Convolve"?

The name comes from *convolution*, the mathematical operation used to blur or sharpen an image.

Blurring with the Convolve Tool

The flip side of the Convolve tool is Blur. Why would you ever want to make something more blurry?

One good reason to blur is to de-emphasize a distracting background, like the second meerkat in Figure 6-30.

A little judicious use of the Blur tool on the rear meerkat's face, and suddenly the front one stands out much more (Figure 6-31). As with Sharpen, you can drag back and forth over the area you want to blur until it's as blurry as you like. (This technique also works well for hiding license plates or other incriminating details.)

Figure 6-30. *One meerkat tries to distract your eye from the other.*

Figure 6-31. *Now the meerkat in the foreground stands out.*

DEPTH OF FIELD

The visual property that makes closer objects stand out is related to an effect photographers call *depth of field*.

Some cameras let you control the *aperture* of the lens, or how wide open it is. The *f-stop* is related to the aperture: the bigger the f-stop, the smaller the aperture. At an f-stop of F/2.8, a lens is fairly wide open, whereas at F/11, most of the opening has been closed off, as shown in the figure.

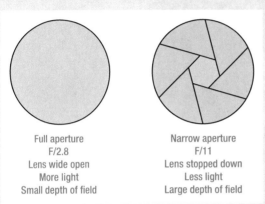

Full aperture
F/2.8
Lens wide open
More light
Small depth of field

Narrow aperture
F/11
Lens stopped down
Less light
Large depth of field

The curious "division" notation used, F/number, is actually somewhat descriptive. It's the result of dividing the focal distance of the lens by the current aperture diameter.

A wide open lens lets in a lot of light, so you can take photos in dimly lit rooms or with fast shutter speeds, but the larger the aperture of the lens, the smaller its depth of field.

Depth of field is the range of distances that are in focus. If your subject is a person five feet away from the camera, the photo might actually have good focus for everything from three feet away to the mountains in the distance ("infinity")—a large depth of field. Alternately, if the depth of field is very small, perhaps only the range from 4'11" to 5'3" away will be in focus—the person's nose may be in focus while his ears might not be!

Wouldn't having everything in focus be a good thing? In fact, it's often useful to have a shallow depth of field. If your subject is the only object in focus, then the eye is naturally drawn to that subject and away from the rest of the photograph.

Looking back at the meerkats, the original Figure 6-30 shows a large depth of field: both meerkats are in sharp focus. The modified Figure 6-31 simulates the effect of a shallow depth of field: only one meerkat is in focus, and the other one is blurry.

One problem: the photo now looks somewhat strange, because the background meerkat is fuzzy while the wall behind him is sharp. In the next section you'll see a better way of simulating a shallow depth of field over a wider area.

Blurring Backgrounds with Gaussian Blur

The Blur mode of the Convolve tool was an easy way to make part of a subject stand out. But what if too much of the background is busy and confusing, as in Figure 6-32? You could run the Blur tool over and over the background, but that gets tiresome. There's an easier way.

Figure 6-32. *I want to blur the branches on which the butterfly sits.*

First, select the background (everything but the butterfly) using any combination of the techniques from Chapter 5, such as Paths, QuickMask, Foreground Select, or Intelligent Scissors. Then bring up the Blur filter: *Filters ➤ Blur ➤ Gaussian Blur...* (Figure 6-33).

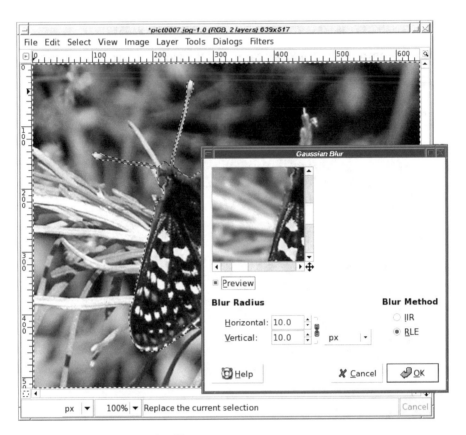

Figure 6-33. *The Gaussian Blur filter*

Gaussian Blur can use either of two Blur methods: *IIR* and *RLE*. It doesn't matter which one you use. They produce the same results, but switching to RLE may be slightly faster for images that are computer-generated or have large areas that are all the same color. IIR is a little faster for photographs.

Adjust the *Blur Radius* (which controls the amount of blur) while watching the preview. Make sure the *Preview* button is checked (it should be, by default). You can scroll around in the preview window if you need to.

As with most effects, the right amount of blur depends on how large (in pixels) your image is, as well as how strong you want the effect to be. Sometimes blurring too much can create an unrealistic, dreamy effect. This could be either good or bad, depending on your goal.

Usually you'll want to keep the *Horizontal* and *Vertical* numbers the same (they're linked together by default), but if you ever need them to be different, you can unlink them.

Tip Sometimes that tiny preview window is annoying and you want a bigger one. With Blur it's particularly obvious, since it's hard to tell the overall effect of blurring the background from viewing only a small piece of an image. With most GIMP filters like Gaussian Blur, resizing the plug-in's dialog larger will also increase the preview area. To increase it permanently, see the section "Changing Preview Sizes with gtkrc" in Chapter 12.

When you're happy with the blur amount, click *OK* (Figure 6-34). You'll probably want to toggle the selection off temporarily (*View* ➤ *Show Selection*) or eliminate it completely (*Select* ➤ *None*) to see the effect. Make sure you don't have any halos around the selected object!

Figure 6-34. *The butterfly stands out more when the grass is blurred.*

But you can overdo this effect, too. Figure 6-34 doesn't look quite right, because there's a lot of grass that's the same distance from the camera as the butterfly is (it's at the same "depth"), which wouldn't be so blurry in a real photograph. To make your blur effects more subtle and more realistic, try deselecting a little of the nearby background, as shown in Figure 6-35.

Figure 6-35. *Use the QuickMask to deselect some of the branches at the same distance as the butterfly for a more subtle effect.*

Summary

By now you should have a fairly good collection of tools for touching up any problems you might see in your photos.

You can dim bright highlights, and enhance areas that are too dark. You can sharpen or blur specific points, or large regions of an image. You know quite a few ways to paint unwanted objects out of a photograph or copy patterns or textures from another part of the image (or even from a different image)

These techniques can keep you busy for quite a while, especially if you have a large collection of photographs that could use some minor touch-up work of one sort or another.

But this is only a tiny sample of what GIMP has to offer! In the next chapter, let's explore some of the other filters, plug-ins, and tools buried within GIMP's menus.

CHAPTER 7

■ ■ ■

Filters and Effects

GIMP has a huge collection of special effects, tools, and techniques you can use to modify your image or create something brand-new.

You've probably already experimented with some of GIMP's plug-ins, but there may be some interesting toys that you haven't seen yet.

In this chapter, I'll take you on a tour of some of GIMP's filters and special effects. I won't cover everything—there's always more to explore—but this chapter should give you a taste of the sorts of effects you can create. You'll learn about the following:

- Image window filters vs. Toolbox *Xtns*

- Filters for images

- Scripts and plug-ins that make new images

Image Window Filters vs. Toolbox Xtns

Most of GIMP's fun special effects are located in two places: the image window's *Filters* menu (plus a few in other menus, such as the *Colors* menu), and the Toolbox window's *Xtns* menu. What's the difference?

Simply, filters operate on an existing image, while items in the Toolbox's *Xtns* menu will create a new image.

Note In GIMP 2.6, the Toolbox *Xtns* functions will move to the image window's *File* ➤ *New* menu.

The Toolbox options generally create buttons, arrows, bullets, and other items usable in web pages or applications, fancy text that you can use for logos or posters, or patterns that you can use as the background to an image or for effects in other images. Plus, there are a few miscellaneous items you can create, like a shaded sphere.

Filters can change an image in all sorts of ways. There are straightforward operations you've already used such as blurring, sharpening, or adding drop shadows. Various artistic filters are available that can make your photo look like a painting or a sketch. There are filters to handle edge detection or noise reduction, and distortion filters that can bend your image like a pretzel.

I'll cover filters first, and then move on to the operations in the Toolbox that can create new images.

Filters for Images

Filter is a general term for anything that can operate on an existing image. Filters will always be found in the menus of an image window, but they aren't all in the *Filters* menu.

First, in GIMP versions prior to 2.4, *scripts* (filters written in GIMP's built-in *Script-Fu* language, or certain other languages such as Perl or Python) appeared in their own top-level menus named for each language: *Script-Fu, Perl-Fu,* and *Python-Fu*. In addition, certain plug-ins may also create new menus: for instance, if you install GAP, the GIMP Animation Plug-In, it creates a top-level *Video* menu.

Finally, other image window menus provide some filter operations, such as *Colors* (in pre-2.4 versions, these might appear in *Layer ➤ Colors* or *Image ➤ Colors*).

■**Tip** Many image filters work only on RGB images, because they need a full range of color. Other filters will only work on a layer with an alpha channel. If you want to use a filter and can't figure out why it's grayed out, check your image's mode (in the title bar of the image window) and make sure it's RGB, not indexed or grayscale. Also check the Layers dialog to see whether the current layer has transparency. (Right-click on the layer and see if *Add Alpha Channel* is still available: if it is, the image doesn't have transparency yet. This is generally only an issue on the bottom layer.) In Chapter 11, you'll learn how to find out a plug-in's requirements using the Plug-In Browser.

Tools vs. Plug-ins

Most filters are implemented as plug-ins. If you install a plug-in you've downloaded from the web (you'll learn more about that in Chapter 11), it will most often appear in the *Filters* menu, and will look just like the filters that come installed with GIMP.

The *Colors* menu contains a mixture of tools and plug-ins. You know about tools: they're operations that have buttons in the Toolbox, like the selection and drawing tools. But did you know that some of the other operations you've used, such as Brightness-Contrast, Levels, and Curves, are also tools?

What's the difference between a tool and a plug-in? Tools can respond to clicks in the image window. When you use a drawing tool, you drag your mouse across the window and leave a trail behind you. When you use a selection tool, you click or drag in the image to indicate where you want the selection to go. Plug-ins can't do that: any adjustment must be done from within the plug-in's own dialog.

Equally important, tools can give you a full-sized preview of their effect in the image window. Plug-ins can only offer a miniature preview in the plug-in's dialog.

Finally, tools display their options in the Tool Options dialog (usually docked below the Toolbox), while plug-ins must use a separate dialog. In menus, tools generally have an icon next to them. Plug-ins usually don't.

There are quite a few tools that don't show up in the Toolbox. You can always get to them from the *Tools* menu in the image window, or from the *File* ➤ *Dialogs* ➤ *Tools* dialog in the Toolbox, which gives a list of every tool GIMP knows about. You can use the Tools dialog to customize your Toolbox, adding or hiding tools using the "eye" icon in this dialog.

If you forget the difference between tools and plug-ins, don't worry about it. You can use all these filters just fine without remembering which is which.

This chapter won't cover the filters in the *Colors* menu; you've already used some of them, and you'll meet the rest in Chapter 8.

The Filters Menu

The *Filters* menu is where most GIMP plug-ins live. It's a collection of fun functions that can transform your image in all sorts of ways. You can spend hours exploring and barely scratch the surface.

The first two items in the *Filters* menu let you repeat the last filter operation. *Repeat Last* will run whichever filter you ran last (the menu entry will change to tell you what that filter was, e.g., *Repeat "Gaussian Blur"*) with the same settings you used last time. *Re-Show Last* will bring up the dialog for that filter, so you can run the same filter but use different parameters this time around. (Not every filter shows up in the *Repeat* menus, though; scripts usually don't.)

Reset all Filters lets you back up all the filter dialogs to their default values. Normally, if you run a filter and change any of its parameters from the default, GIMP will remember those settings until you quit GIMP. Unfortunately, there's no way to reset just a single plug-in back to its default values, though a tool can be reset with the *Reset to default values* button in the Tool Options dialog.

The rest of the *Filters* menu is divided into functional areas. Remember, if you're using a version prior to 2.4 and a function isn't where you expect it to be, try looking under the *Script-Fu* menu.

Tip In many of these filters, the dialog will show you a preview region. But you may not actually see a preview unless you turn on the *Preview* checkbox underneath. If you're ever in doubt about whether you're seeing a live preview, look for a box marked *Preview*. With any luck, in some future version of GIMP it will be possible to say "Always preview."

Blur

You learned about the Blur tool and the very useful *Gaussian Blur* in Chapter 6. The first item in the *Blur* menu, *Blur*, is similar to *Gaussian Blur* except that it offers a bit less control. But there are several other ways to blur an image.

Motion Blur is the most interesting (Figure 7-1). It blurs in only one direction (specified by *Angle*) to give an impression of motion.

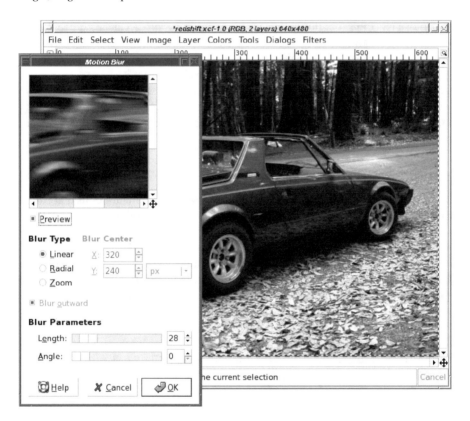

Figure 7-1. *Motion Blur makes a blur in only one direction, giving an impression of movement.*

Of course, in addition to giving an impression of motion, this will also make your image look—well, blurry! You can try selecting and blurring just the background, but you have to be fairly precise with the selection. Alternatively, you can get a nice effect by making another layer containing only the foreground object (like the car in Figure 7-1) before you blur the layer underneath.

Select the object and copy it (you don't have to be particularly precise with your selection as long as you feather it a bit). Paste that on top of the layer that you will blur (don't forget to click *New Layer* to turn the floating layer into a real one), then click on the lower layer again. Run the Motion Blur, then go back to the pasted layer and adjust its transparency and position so it looks like it's leading, with the blur trailing behind. Experiment and see what sorts of effects you can create.

By default, Motion Blur spreads the image along a line (*Linear*). But it offers two other types of blur. *Radial* is particularly useful for car images like this one: if you select just a wheel, you can make it look like the wheels are turning. *Zoom* is good for making diagrams showing the expansion of the universe or the jump to light speed—or just when you want a "zoom" effect for a poster.

For either *Radial* or *Zoom*, you will have to specify the *Blur Center*, the coordinates of the central point for the rotation or zoom. If you know where you want the center, you can easily figure out the coordinates by moving your mouse over the image (without clicking) while watching the status line at the bottom of the image window.

In addition to Motion Blur, the *Blur* menu offers *Pixelize*, which replaces the image with a mosaic of squares, as though you had blown up a much lower resolution image.

You can also choose *Selective Gaussian Blur*, which is similar to Gaussian Blur except that it tries to keep edges sharp while blurring everything else. Try it on a photo and see if you like the effect.

Finally, there's *Tileable Blur*, which gives you a Gaussian-blurred image whose edges can be combined to make a tiled background (you'll learn more about tiling in Chapter 9). It works best if you start with an image that's already tileable.

Enhance

The *Enhance* filters are used to correct problems in images. The menu contains *Sharpen* and *Unsharp Mask*, which should already be familiar from Chapter 2. But what are those other filters?

Antialias looks for jagged edges and tries to make them look smoother…like changing a jaggy line drawn with the Pencil tool into the smoother sort of line the Paintbrush tool would draw. Unfortunately, it doesn't offer any controls to adjust the strength of the effect. *Deinterlace* is intended for images from certain types of video cameras that *interlace*: they record every other line of an image—say, the odd-numbered lines—and then go back and make a second fill in the even lines. If you're capturing a fast-changing scene, this can create still images that look slightly odd. Deinterlace tries to compensate by creating an image using only the even—or only the odd—lines.

Despeckle is used to remove small elements of "noise" from an image, particularly specks or small lines caused by dust or scratches on a scanned film image. It can also remove the "moiré" effects sometimes seen in scans of prints. That sounds great; of course in practice, it may also remove detail from your image that you wanted to keep. Use it with caution, but it can be helpful when you have a noisy scanned image. (A trick that can help is to duplicate the original layer, despeckle it, and then use the Opacity slider in the Layers dialog to mix the despeckled layer with the original.)

You can control the size of the defects Despeckle will look for with the *Radius* parameter. *Black level* and *White level* control how dark or how light a defect has to be for it to be removed. *Adaptive* tries to detect the proper *Radius* setting automatically. *Recursive* makes the filter repeat itself for a stronger effect.

Destripe removes vertical lines that are left by some older scanners. Usually a better solution is to use a decent scanner.

NL Filter tries to do everything: it's a combination of smoothing, despeckle, and sharpen in one filter. It always works on the whole image, unlike most filters that operate only on the selection (if there is one) and the current layer. If you have an image with all these problems, fiddle with the NL Filter settings. Maybe you can make it better.

Distorts

Distorts is a fun filter category that offers all sorts of toys that can change the shape of your image.

Blinds makes it look like your image is painted on venetian blinds, and you're adjusting the angle of those blinds.

Curve Bend is useful for changing the shape of nearly any layer. It gives you a dialog with a line you can drag to warp the top of your layer to any shape.

But that's not all—you can adjust the bottom of the layer too, by clicking on *Lower* (Figure 7-2). Click *Copy* and you'll get a lower curve that matches the upper curve. *Reset* will make the current curve flat again. *Mirror* will give you a lower curve that's a mirror of the upper. *Swap* will exchange the upper curve with the lower one.

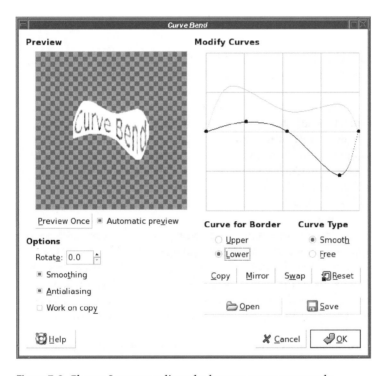

Figure 7-2. *Choose Lower to adjust the bottom curve separately.*

Choosing *Free* instead of *Smooth* lets you make a spiky curve between your points. *Rotate* lets you turn the result, though it's not as effective as you might think—you might be better off using GIMP's free rotation tool (as described in the "Free Rotation" section in Chapter 2) to rotate your image after you've bent it. *Smoothing* and *Antialiasing* do much the same as in drawing tools (most of the time you'll want to keep them enabled). *Work on copy* creates a new layer in the image and leaves the original layer unchanged. (The new layer will have visibility disabled, so you have to go to the Layers dialog and make it visible.)

Either way, if you started with a layer that was the size of your image, the distorted layer is probably too big to fit. You may have to do an *Image* ➤ *Fit Canvas to Layers* in order to see all of it. Too bad *Curve Bend* doesn't do that for you, but don't let that minor inconvenience stop you from trying a useful distortion tool.

Emboss is another nifty filter (Figure 7-3). It makes your image look as though the picture has been embossed onto metal.

The three adjustments are straightforward: *Azimuth* is the direction of the light source in the resulting image, starting from 0 at the right and going counterclockwise from there (90° is up). *Elevation* is the angle of the light above the image plane (90° means that the light will appear to come from overhead). Play with it and see what it does (usually it makes the effect darker or lighter). *Depth* controls how much relief the emboss will seem to have—that is, how strong the effect is. Finally, selecting *Bumpmap* instead of *Emboss* gives a smoother effect that preserves colors. (It's actually just regular *Emboss* combined with the original layer in Multiply mode. You'll see how to create effects like this in Chapter 10.) Don't confuse this with the extremely important *Bump Map* plug-in, which you'll meet later in the Map group of filters.

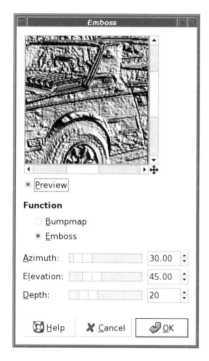

Figure 7-3. *The Emboss filter*

Engrave creates the black-and-white "engraved" look that you sometimes see in old illustrations. It has two options: *Height*, which controls the height of the lines used, and *Limit line width*, which keeps the lines from bleeding together completely in the dark areas (such as in the car's shadow).

Engrave requires that the image already have an alpha channel. If it's grayed out, try *Layer* ➤ *Transparency* ➤ *Add Alpha Channel.*

Erase Every Other Row (previously located under *Script-Fu* ➤ *Alchemy*) does just that. It can be useful for certain effects, such as creating the illusion of a television screen, or combining an image with modified versions of itself.

■**Caution** If the result of *Erase Every Other Row* looks odd to you, check your zoom level. If you're zoomed less than 100%, you may not see the effect properly. It also may not work right if the layer goes outside the boundaries of the image.

IWarp, the Interactive Warp filter, is one of GIMP's best toys. Occasionally it's even useful. It brings up a dialog like Figure 7-4.

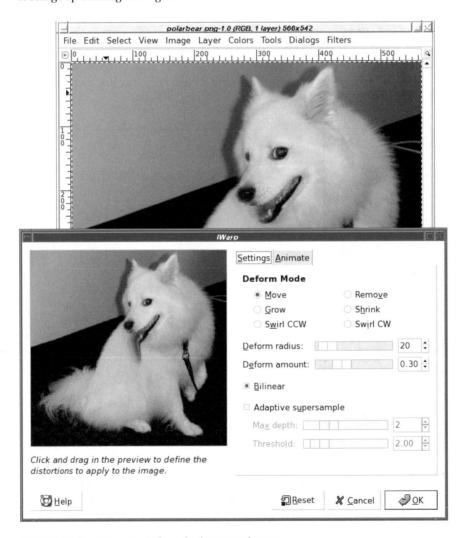

Figure 7-4. *Use IWarp to make a dog's tongue longer.*

Click and drag in the preview area of the dialog. Parts of the image will drag along with your mouse, "stretching" the image as though it was printed on a rubber sheet and you were deforming the rubber. Use short, repetitive strokes.

You can use IWarp in all sorts of creative ways: you can change animals into other animals, chubby cheeks into gaunt ones, or a human into a Vulcan. It can also be useful as part of other transformations, such as the panoramic images you'll make in Chapter 10.

IWarp has quite a few *Deform Modes*. The default, *Move*, stretches the image wherever you drag the mouse.

Remove lets you remove the distortion in one area of the image. There's no Undo for the strokes you make inside IWarp, so if you go too far in one place but you like the changes you've made everywhere else, a quick switch to *Remove* mode might help.

Grow inflates a round area, as though you placed a magnifying lens only over the area where you're dragging. *Shrink* does the opposite.

The *Swirl* options mix up the image under the mouse as you drag—as though you were dragging a cake beater through the image. You can make neat paisley swirls out of any picture.

Deform radius is like a brush size: it controls how many pixels to either side of the mouse position will be distorted. *Deform amount* controls the strength of the effect.

Bilinear makes the effect smoother (it's selected by default), while *Adaptive supersample* and its suboptions *Max depth* and *Threshold* can smooth the effect even more, at the cost of extra CPU work.

IWarp does have one problem: you have to make your changes in the small preview in the dialog. You can make the preview a little larger by resizing the dialog, but since there's no image-sized preview, it's often difficult to tell when you've gone too far. But don't let that stop you from having fun with one of GIMP's most enjoyable distortion filters.

Back to the *Distorts* menu, *Lens Distortion* lets you correct for the way wide-angle camera lenses can warp an image; it can also take an un-warped image and bend it the way a fisheye lens would. It has quite a few options (Figure 7-5).

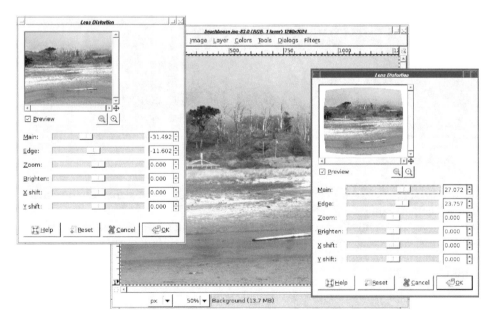

Figure 7-5. *Lens Distortion: negative correction (left) compresses the center and expands the edges (note the way the stream in the foreground bends), while positive correction (right) expands the center and compresses the edges.*

Main controls how much "spherical correction" to add (imagine you're taking your image and stretching it on the outside or inside of a sphere). Positive values make the image convex as in Figure 7-5; negative values make it concave. *Edge* lets it add some extra spherical correction to the edges without affecting the center. *Zoom* lets you zoom in (magnify) or zoom out. *Brighten* controls whether the image should be brightened or darkened at the edges (many wide-angle lenses "vignette" or darken the image a bit at the edges). *X Shift* and *Y Shift* let you shift the center of the lens warp effect away from the image's center.

The *Mosaic* filter does exactly what you'd expect: it creates a mosaic out of your image, as if made with random tiles (Figure 7-6). It has lots of options controlling the tile shape, size, height, spacing, and surface.

Figure 7-6. *The Mosaic filter*

The *Newsprint* filter creates an effect like zooming way in on a newspaper photo, with the individual ink colors visible.

Pagecurl gives the useful effect shown in Figure 7-7. You can control which part of the page is curled and what colors are used for the page. If you want less of the page to curl, try selecting a rectangle in the corner where you want the curl. The size of your selection will control the amount of curl.

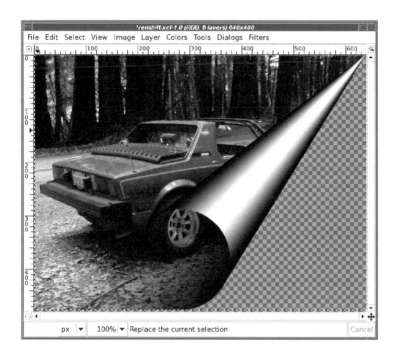

Figure 7-7. *The Pagecurl filter*

The *Polar Coords* filter wraps an image around a point at the top or bottom center. It can also take an image that is wrapped in this way and unwrap it. This is useful for looping text around in a circle (Figure 7-8). Images with straight lines in them can turn into nifty spiral patterns.

Figure 7-8. *Polar Coords can wrap text in a circle.*

The *Ripple* filter makes an image look as though it's being viewed through water waves. The options are fairly straightforward and fun to play with, though the *Waves* filter gives a better water effect. The *Border* options control what happens at the edges of the image.

Shift moves each row by a random amount, either vertically or horizontally, creating an interesting ripple effect quite different from the one *Ripple* makes.

Value Propagate is tricky. It finds areas of your image that are nearly black or nearly white (your choice) and expands them. You can set the amount by which areas will be expanded, and how close they have to be to black or white. You can also use it to expand colored areas by selecting *Only foreground* or *Only background*. You can even expand or contract areas of transparency.

Still, even with all these options, you'll probably only want it in specialized circumstances. It can be useful when working with layer masks.

The *Video* filter applies various patterns intended to make the image look as though it's being viewed on a television screen or various other types of low-resolution device. Curiously, unlike most filters, it doesn't have a real preview area; instead, it shows a picture of a fox with pregenerated examples of what each pattern should do.

Waves is similar to Ripple except that the waves are concentric around the center of the image, as if you'd thrown a rock into a swimming pool. It's a nice effect. You can adjust three parameters controlling the size of the waves: *Amplitude*, *Phase*, and *Wavelength*. The *Mode* (which can be either *Smear* or *Blacken)* controls what happens at the edges, much like *Border* did in the Ripple plug-in.

The *Reflective* option of *Waves* makes the waves bounce off the sides of the image and back in, where they interfere with waves coming from the center. It works best if you reduce the amplitude and increase the wavelength. Try it and see.

Whirl and Pinch is useful for several types of "funhouse mirror" effects. Its *Whirl* mode grabs the image from the center and stirs it like clothes in a washing machine. You control the amount with the *Whirl angle* slider.

Pinch of a negative amount bloats the image as if it's blown up like a balloon from the center of the image (Figure 7-9). A positive pinch does the opposite, compressing the center of the image as though all the pixels were sliding down a drain in the center.

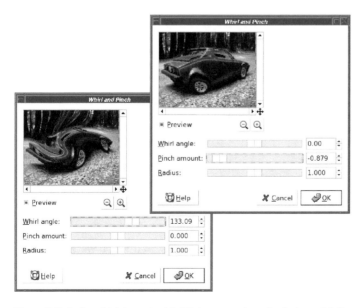

Figure 7-9. *Left: whirl (no pinch). Right: negative pinch (no whirl).*

Tip *Pinch* can sometimes be used to compensate for lens distortion, though the *Lens Distortion* filter gives a more easily controlled effect.

Radius controls how much of the image will be affected, with "2" meaning the entire image. This is deceptive, though, since the effect is applied smoothly and will usually look like it's affecting more of the image than it actually is.

The *Wind* filter gives a nice effect similar to Motion Blur, but it's much more specific. It finds dark or light lines in the image and makes "streaks" trailing in only one direction. *Strength* controls the amount of wind, while *Threshold* controls how many lines are drawn. *Blast* creates thicker lines than *Wind*, making for a less subtle (and often less effective) result. You can control the *Direction* from which the wind seems to blow. You can also control the *Edge Affected*—*Leading*, *Trailing*, or *Both*—but you may need the opposite setting from the one you expect.

Light and Shadow

GIMP offers quite a few filters relating to lighting and shadows. GIMP 2.4 collects all the lighting plug-ins in a single menu, *Filters* ➤ *Light and Shadow*. In earlier versions, they were scattered in four places: *Filters* ➤ *Light Effects*, *Filters* ➤ *Glass Effects*, *Script-Fu* ➤ *Shadow*, and *Python-Fu* ➤ *Effects*.

Flares and Sparkles

GIMP offers several ways to put a bright flare of light into your image: *Lens Flare*, *Supernova*, and *Gradient Flare* all have similar effects (Figure 7-10).

Figure 7-10. Comparison of Supernova, Lens Flare, and Gradient Flare

The *Lens Flare* (previously called *FlareFX*) has no options to speak of; just click or drag in the preview to set the flare where you want it.

Supernova is similar, but it makes a flare with spiky rays, and you can control the color of the flare.

If those two aren't quite right, *Gradient Flare* is more general: it lets you choose from a selection of different flare effects in the *Selector* tab. The *Settings* tab lets you change all sorts of parameters to adjust the flare exactly the way you want it.

Lighting Effects is even more general. It lets you add a beam of light in many different ways.

This plug-in has more options than there is space to cover them, but here are some tips. In the *Light* tab are three lighting *Types*. *None* always begins the light in the upper left. *Point* displays a blue point somewhere in the preview: you can drag it around, and you should see a beam of light passing through the blue dot to the center of the image. *Directional* is similar to *Point* but offers a bit more control. On the other hand, with *Directional* it's easy to lose the point as it slips off the edge of the image. The *Bump Map* option will make sense after you've worked with Bump Map (in *Filters* ➤ *Map*, and covered later in this chapter). *Environment Map* lets you specify a pattern that will seem to be reflected by whatever you're mapping. It's most often used to create the effect of a shiny metallic surface, though you can control how shiny the surface will seem to be with the controls in the *Material* tab.

Finally, the *Sparkle* filter works off the image. Instead of adding one big flare at a place you define, it adds small sparkles in any places that are bright in the image. You can control how bright that has to be with the *Luminosity threshold*. *Flare intensity* and the various *Spike* options control the way each sparkle is drawn. *Opacity* makes the sparkles translucent, making the effect a bit more subtle (higher numbers indicate more transparency, the opposite of what you would expect from the name).

Sparkle's *Random Hue* and *Random Saturation* allow for sparkles of different colors, but the effect is very subtle unless you also increase *Opacity*. *Inverse* puts dark sparkles on the dark areas. *Foreground color* and *Background color* can control the color of the sparkles; as with the *Random* options, the effect is much more pronounced if you add some opacity.

Shadows

You've already seen *Drop Shadow*, for a text layer in Chapter 3.

The *Perspective* filter (usually referred to as Perspective Clone) makes a shadow tilted at an angle to show perspective. Unfortunately, the plug-in currently has a bug: the shadow appears in a box that prevents you from seeing most of it, so it isn't very useful. Try it—but if you find the plug-in frustrating, you'll learn how to make this sort of shadow yourself in Chapter 9.

Lens and Glass Effects

Xach Effect gives the illusion of a translucent object (perhaps made of rough-ground glass) raised above its surroundings. It makes the most sense when you use it on a layer containing a few straightforward objects—for instance, letters in a text layer—above a separate background layer (Figure 7-11). Whatever layer is active in the Layers dialog when you run the effect is the one that will be used for the shape. Alternately, Xach Effect can use a selection, if you have one: you can create nice Xach effects by using the Free Select tool to make a selection of any shape you wish to use.

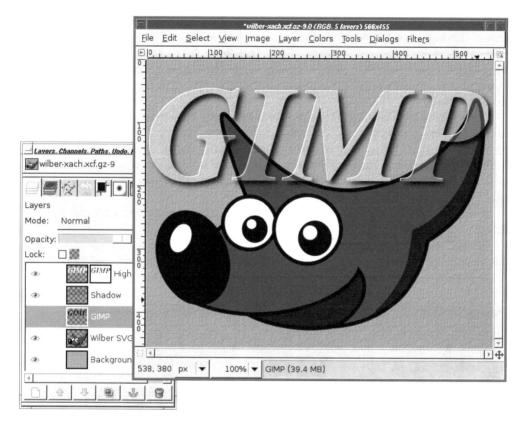

Figure 7-11. *Xach Effect on a hidden text layer*

Named for Zach "Xach" Beane, a GIMP contributor who came up with the idea, Xach Effect creates several new layers, leaving the existing layers untouched. If you use a foreground layer rather than a selection outline for your shape, you'll probably want to turn off visibility on the foreground layer. (Xach Effect can work on an invisible layer.)

Apply Lens warps the image in the way that a wide-angle lens might. You can get a similar effect by pinching with a negative number in *Whirl and Pinch*, or by using *Lens Distortion*, but *Apply Lens* is more specific and has only one parameter, the index of refraction of the lens being simulated.

Glass Tile makes the image look like it's being viewed through a wall made of many glass bricks, each of which refracts light a little differently.

Noise Filters

These filters add noise to an image. Why on earth would you want to do that? You'll see as you explore them.

HSV Noise (previously called *Scatter HSV*) creates colorful noise. It has four parameters. *Hue* controls the average color of the generated noise. *Saturation* and *Value* control the saturation and brightness of the noise. The other parameter, the oddly named *Holdness*, controls how much the color of the image is allowed to change. A low value of Holdness will preserve more of the original colors than a high value.

Hurl changes a random selection of pixels to random colors. *Randomization* is the percent of pixels to be changed; at 100%, the entire image will be replaced by random noise. *Repeat* runs the effect repeatedly, but you're usually better off just using a higher value for *Randomization.*

Pick replaces each affected pixel with a value randomly chosen from nearby pixels. So the image won't change nearly as much as it would with most of the other noise filters. Even with *Randomization* set to 100%, *Pick* can create an image that's quite recognizable and interesting.

RGB Noise (known in earlier GIMP versions as *Scatter RGB*) creates very natural-looking colored noise. You can set each color independently, or with *Independent RGB* turned off, you can slide the three sliders together.

RGB Noise can be used on a grayscale image as well; in that case it will show only a single slider.

Slur is a bit more fun: it randomly moves pixels downward, as though they were melting. That's not immediately obvious when you run it once, but try setting *Repeat* to a large number like 50 (Figure 7-12).

Figure 7-12. *Slur with a repeat of 65 and randomization of 100%*

Spread is somewhat like Pick, except that it replaces each affected pixel with one chosen at random from somewhere nearby in the image (how near it must be is controlled by the *Spread Amount* parameters). It makes the image look stippled, as though drawn with dots from blunt-tipped colored marking pens.

Edge-detection Filters

GIMP comes with five edge-detection filters (though there are other ways to detect edges— you'll learn a few in Chapter 10). They're all a bit different.

Difference of Gaussians gives a subtle pastel effect by blurring the image with two different radii, and then subtracting one from the other (Figure 7-13). You can tune it by adjusting the two radii.

Figure 7-13. *The original image, and after using Difference of Gaussians*

Edge is a real workhorse, and includes six different edge-detection algorithms, each a little different. It also lets you tune its sensitivity with the *Amount* slider. Most of its algorithms give a wild neon effect. The more colors in the original image, the better the neon effect will be. *Wrap*, *Smear*, and *Black* are options controlling the effect at the edges of the image, in case you're trying to make a tile that can be used as a repeated background.

Neon also gives a neon look, with fewer options and a somewhat different effect (Figure 7-14).

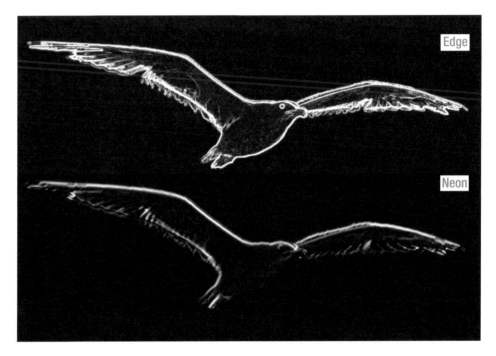

Figure 7-14. *Two ways of making a neon sign: the Edge plug-in with the Sobel algorithm vs. the Neon plug-in*

Laplace has no options at all. It simply replaces your image with a line drawing. *Sobel* gives a result somewhat like *Laplace*, but it gives you a chance to tune the algorithm slightly, with a preview. *Sobel* is a bit more generous in finding lines than *Laplace* is.

"Generic" Filters

The *Generic* category is a catchall for filters that can be used in many different ways. It currently contains only three filters.

Convolution Matrix is a general way for people working on mathematical image-processing algorithms to test those algorithms in GIMP. Under the hood, many of GIMP's plug-ins use a convolution matrix. If you don't know what that is, you may not find this plug-in very interesting, though of course you can try typing random numbers into the matrix to see what happens. You may occasionally see convolution matrix numbers on a web page describing a particular effect, in which case you can copy them. Be sure to enable at least one channel in the list, or the convolution matrix won't have any effect.

In GIMP 2.4, *Dilate* enhances light areas of the image, reducing dark areas. *Erode* does the opposite, enhancing dark areas at the expense of light areas. Earlier versions of GIMP reversed the meanings of *Dilate* and *Erode*, so *Dilate* made the image darker. They aren't as useful as you might think, since you can't adjust how much the image will be dilated or eroded; if you want more control, you can do something similar by making a selection and adjusting it with *Edit* ➤ *Shrink* or *Grow*.

Combine

The *Combine* group is another catchall, and contains only two plug-ins.

Depth Merge combines two images in a complicated way, specified by two other images called *depth maps*. All four images *must* be the same size (the plug-in will only let you choose depth maps the same size as the original images).

Source 1 and *Source 2* are the two images you want to combine. They can be any layer from any image currently open in GIMP (as long as they're the same size, of course).

The two depth maps specify which part of each image will be most prominent in the final image. It's best if the images contain only blacks, grays, and whites; color is meaningless in a depth map.

Depth Merge compares the two depth maps, and whichever one is darker "wins." Wherever a source image's depth map is black, you will see that source image. Where it's white and the other source image's map is black, you'll see the other source. To try out Depth Merge for the first time, try using two gradients: one that fades from white on the left to black on the right, and a second that is the reverse of the first.

Depth Merge is another way of combining images in a way similar to the ostrich and giraffe layer mask project in Chapter 5. You may find it quicker than setting up the masks yourself and it can be useful for combining three-dimensional images. On the other hand, it's somewhat limited and finicky: images must be exactly the same size, you can't do any editing after the fact, and the plug-in is prone to crashing if it's unhappy with any of the four images. Try it and see if you like it.

Filmstrip combines the layers in the image into a single image that looks like a strip of 35mm film (Figure 7-15).

Figure 7-15. *The Filmstrip plug-in*

It's most interesting when you use a set of similar but related images—perhaps different portraits of the same person, or scenes from a vacation. You can specify which images you want to include in the plug-in's dialog, and it will load each image layer as a separate image in the filmstrip. You can either load all your files as layers in the same image by using *File* ➤ *Open as Layer*, or open them all as separate images. (To open multiple image files at once, whether as layers or separate images, use Shift-click or Ctrl-click on the file list in the Open or Open as Layer dialog.)

Caution The Filmstrip plug-in insists that all the layers in the image be the same size. If they aren't, it may crash or otherwise misbehave. Fortunately, when a plug-in crashes, it doesn't take GIMP down with it, though you might be wise to save any open images after any plug-in crashes.

The Artistic Filters

GIMP's *Artistic* filter menu contains filters to make a photograph look like an oil painting, sketch, woven rug, or other work of art.

It's a great place to explore. Nearly all of the filters there do something fun, and most of them have lots of parameters to tweak. You can see easily what the parameters do by trying them, so it's easy to find an effect you like.

In GIMP 2.2, several of these filters lived in the *Script-Fu ➤ Alchemy* menu.

Apply Canvas gives a canvas-like texture to the image (Figure 7-16). *Clothify* gives a similar effect, but with a slightly different texture.

Figure 7-16. *Apply Canvas adds texture to the image.*

Cartoon simplifies colors and adds black outlines near edges with the intent of making a photograph look like a hand-drawn and inked cartoon. Most of the time, it doesn't look much like a cartoon, though. Try it and see what you think—it can give interesting looks somewhat similar to *Posterize* (which you may remember from the *Colors* menu). *Cubism* turns your image into cubist art. *GIMPressionist* will be discussed in the next section. *Oilify* blurs and flattens it in ways that make it look like a paint-by-number. *Photocopy* makes the image look as though it was subjected to a poor-quality copy machine, with burnt-out lights and overdone edges. It's not a pretty effect, but it may be useful for some projects.

Predator turns the image into something that should remind you of the movie *Predator*, or a video game from the 1980s (Figure 7-17).

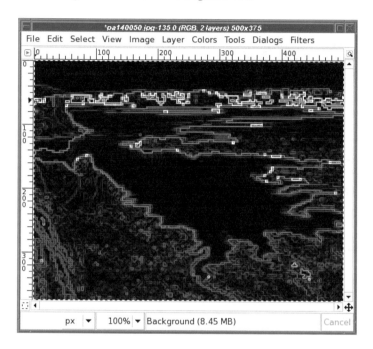

Figure 7-17. *Predator effect*

Softglow gives a "bathed in light" impression, as though the image was hazy and a bit overexposed.

Van Gogh (LIC) gives an image a rather subtle shift. Alas, it won't make your photograph look like Van Gogh painted it, but it can create some interesting effects, and it has all sorts of knobs to twiddle. Play with it and see what you can create. *LIC* stands for "Line Integral Convolution," the mathematical operation that is happening behind the scenes.

Weave is another texturing plug-in like *Apply Canvas* and *Clothify*. It gives the nifty effect that the image has been woven into a basket (Figure 7-18).

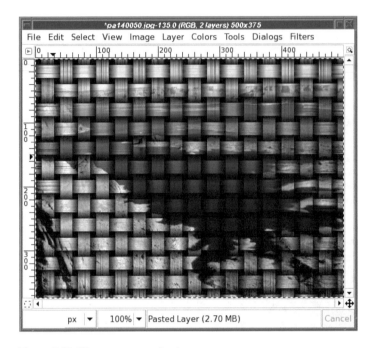

Figure 7-18. *Weave creates a basket.*

■**Caution** Weave is unlike most filters: its Undo doesn't work in one step. It takes three Undo operations to get rid of a Weave. Don't be too dismayed when the first Undo doesn't do what you expect; just hit a couple more and you'll be fine. You'll learn in Chapter 11 what this means in terms of how Weave was written—and how to fix it if it bothers you!

GIMPressionist

The crown jewel of the *Artistic* menu is *GIMPressionist*. It has an enormous collection of options and can duplicate the functions of several other plug-ins. The catch is that it's a bit harder to use (Figure 7-19).

Figure 7-19. *GIMPressionist offers many options, such as Cubism.*

GIMPressionist offers eight tabs, each full of options. *Don't panic!* You can accomplish most tasks simply by using the presets in the first tab, and never looking any farther than that.

When you first try GIMPressionist, you may wonder why it doesn't seem to be doing anything. You're exploring the presets, but selecting different options seems to have no effect. There are two reasons.

First, GIMPressionist doesn't have an automatic preview. Whenever you change an option and want to see it reflected in the preview, you need to click *Update* under the preview area.

But even then, changing presets doesn't do anything. If you click *Update*, you just get another version of the preset you used last, not the one you just selected. What's going on?

The answer is that the presets change values in all the other tabs: *Paper, Brush, Orientation, Size,* and so on. Since this would overwrite any changes you may have made in those other tabs—and there's no easy way to undo that—GIMPressionist requires you to take two steps in order to apply a preset: choose the preset in the list, and then click the *Apply* button to the right of the list. Now, when you click *Update* you'll see the new setup.

You can spend quite a while just viewing all the presets in GIMPressionist. It's often hard to tell from the small preview pane exactly what an effect will look like at full size, so you'll often want to click *OK*, then *Undo* and bring up GIMPressionist again (a fast way to do that is *Filters ➤ Re-Show "GIMPressionist"*, which is bound to Shift+Ctrl+F).

In your explorations, you may find a preset that is almost what you want except for one or two minor attributes. That's your cue to explore the other seven tabs.

If you've selected a preset you like and clicked *Apply*, the other seven tabs will show the settings that create that effect. For instance, the *Apply Canvas* preset uses a *paper* called struc.pgm that has a canvas-like texture; the other tabs are set to reasonable defaults to make the canvas texture look right when it's applied to your image. *Cubism* uses a much finer paper (though still with a canvas texture), but it uses a large graduated brush called grad01.pgm, while *Apply Canvas* used a much smaller brush.

You can tweak the settings as much as you like. You can make small changes: start from Cubism and change the paper to create cubist art drawn on bricks, burlap, or marble. Or you can make large changes.

Orientation adjusts the angle of asymmetrical brushes. You can make the brush strokes all go in the same direction, or make them change directions randomly within limits you set. *Size* controls the size of the brush: to see a strong example of its effect use the *Marble Madness* preset, click *Apply* then *Update*, and then go to the *Size* tab and make both the minimum and maximum size much smaller (Figure 7-20). Click *Update* again to see the effect of your changes.

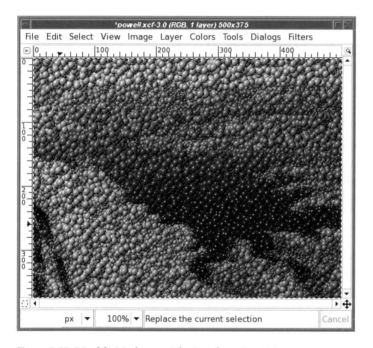

Figure 7-20. *Marble Madness with sizes from 2 to 14*

Placement controls how the brush strokes will be grouped on the page—whether they'll be clustered close together or distributed evenly. *Color* controls how precisely the color is laid; for most images it won't be obvious, but if you're using a large brush on an image with precise sharp bands of color, this setting might affect how sharp the lines are in the result.

The *General* tab has some useful options. In particular, adding a *Drop shadow* can add depth to an image. Try starting with *Cubism* and then adding a drop shadow: you get an effect like an explosion in a sticky-note factory (Figure 7-21).

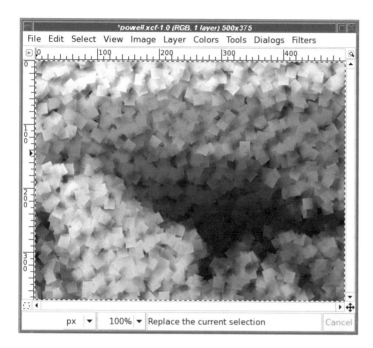

Figure 7-21. *Cubism plus a drop shadow gives you an explosion in a sticky-note factory.*

You can even make your own papers and brushes. Most of them have extensions of .pgm or .ppm. These files are a special format called PPM or *Portable PixMap*; PGM, or *Portable GrayMap*, is a special grayscale case of PPM. GIMP has no problem reading and writing PPM and PGM files. Try searching for one of the brush or paper images on your system, like blob.ppm, and opening it in GIMP. Make some changes to it and save it as the same type. GIMP will ask you whether you want *Raw* or *ASCII*; choose *Raw* (that makes the file smaller, so GIMP can load it faster).

Save it where? Find your GIMP profile (look in the Folders category of the Preferences window if you don't remember where it is—more on that in Chapter 12). Go to the folder called gimpressionist. Create folders inside it called Brushes or Papers if they aren't already there (it doesn't hurt to create both folders if you think you might ever need them). Then save the new brush or paper to the appropriate folder. You'll have to dismiss the GIMPressionist dialog and call it up again to see the new brush, but you don't have to restart GIMP.

You may wonder about the drop-down menu in the *Brush* tab with the *Save As* button next to it. Is that a way to choose a brush, or save one?

Well, sort of…but you may run into some bugs in trying to use that option (the details vary with GIMP version). Most people are probably better off ignoring the Brush tab's *Select* menu and *Save As* button.

Since GIMPressionist has so many different knobs to tweak, it allows you to save settings when you find a combination you like. *Save Current…* will write the current settings to your GIMP profile, along with a description of what the effect does. Then you can call up the same combination of settings in future GIMP sessions.

The only catch? You probably won't know for sure whether you like a combination of settings until you've seen them in full size on the image. It's hard to tell much from that little preview window. But when you *Re-Show "GIMPressionist"*, the *Presets* tab is back to *<Factory defaults>*. It looks like it's forgotten your changes!

Never fear. Although GIMPressionist doesn't remember your last preset, it does remember all the other settings. Click *Update* to verify that. If you're so happy with your settings that you want to remember them, type a name into the field above the preset list, next to *Save Current...*, and then click *Save Current...*. GIMP will prompt you for a longer description of your settings.

The Map Filters

The *Map* filters distort the image a bit, like the *Distorts* filters—but only in very localized and specific ways.

Bump Map

The first map filter is *Bump Map*, one of GIMP's most useful filters. It's used in many text and logo effects, but you'll find lots of other applications for it.

It's easiest to see what Bump Map can do if you start with a new blank image and fill it with a pattern (*Edit ➤ Fill with Pattern*). For example, use *Pink Marble*. Then, create a *white* text layer on top of that.

In the Layers dialog, select the background layer, not the text layer. Then call up *Bump Map* (Figure 7-22).

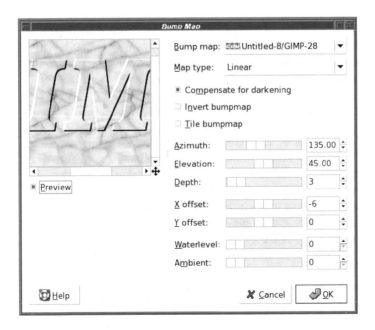

Figure 7-22. *The Bump Map filter*

Bump Map makes "bumps" in the active layer, as if another layer (called the *bump map*) was pushing up from underneath. Where the bump map is light, the layer will seem to be pushed up farther; where it's black, it won't be pushed up at all.

The map layer is chosen from the drop-down menu at the top of the Bump Map dialog. This menu lists every layer in every image that you have open in GIMP. It can be confusing: both the image name and the layer name are crammed into the menu. Sometimes there isn't room for both, so some letters may be left out. Use the tiny layer previews to the left of each image/layer name to help you figure out which layer is which.

Once you've chosen the text layer as the map, you can click *OK* to create the bump map. You'll probably have to make the map layer invisible in order to see the effect. (It's okay if you keep it invisible. You don't have to be able to see a layer in order for Bump Map to use it.)

Bump Map has several options. The *Map type* controls how abrupt the map will be and whether it has sharp edges.

Compensate for darkening brightens the image a bit after applying the bump map. The map is implemented using the *Multiply* layer mode (you'll work with modes in Chapters 9 and 10), and that has a tendency to darken the image. Normally, you'll want to leave this option checked to get the brightness back to normal.

Invert bumpmap makes the bump appear to go *into* the active layer rather than rising *above* it. If you want an effect like letters chiseled into marble or routed into wood, use *Invert.* *Tile bumpmap* makes the bump map repeat across the image. You can use it with a small map image to get a repetitive pattern all the way across a large background area.

Azimuth controls the direction of the illumination, with zero meaning a light coming in from the right. The default, 135, makes the light appear to come from the upper left, but you can light your bump map from any direction. *Elevation* controls how high off the page the light source will seem to be (within limits: lowering it won't give you long shadows).

Depth controls how tall or deep the bump will seem. *X offset* and *Y offset* shift the bump effect in relation to the position of the map layer. Most of the time, you'll already have positioned the bump map right where you want the effect to be, so you'll leave these at 0.

Waterlevel controls the "bottom edge" of the effect when your bump map layer has transparency, like a text layer would. Increasing *Waterlevel* can make the effect appear softer and more subtle.

Ambient makes the light source appear more diffuse (think of it as mixing in some ambient light). When it's set to 0, the light will appear to come from only one direction, but increase the value and some of the shaded areas will lighten a bit more to create a more subtle effect.

Displace

The *Displace* filter shifts pixels in the active layer according to a *gradient map.* The map layer must be the same size as the image you want to displace. (Images that aren't the right size won't appear in Displace's option menu.)

What's a gradient map? It's a monochrome image where the gray value at each point specifies what to do with another image; in this case, how much another image will be displaced from that point.

Horizontal and vertical displacements are handled separately: you can use different gradient maps for them.

For horizontal mapping, a white pixel in the gradient map means that the corresponding point in the image will be moved to the left. A black pixel means the point will move right, while a medium-gray pixel means the point will stay where it is. Vertical mapping is similar, except white means move up; black, down.

Confused? A couple of examples will help.

Make an image consisting of some text on a patterned background (Figure 7-23).

What sort of map would it take to lay this text out in a diagonal line from upper left to lower right?

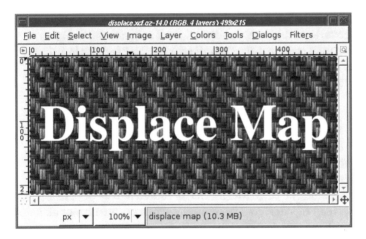

Figure 7-23. *Text on a patterned background*

That means only vertical displacement, so don't worry about what happens horizontally. On the left side of the image, you want text to move *up*—so that means you want white on the left side of the gradient map. You want the right side to move *down*, so that side needs to be black. A smooth gradient from white on the left to black on the right ought to do that. Make a new layer (call it **gradient**: it's important to give layers clear names to make it easy to choose them from plug-in menus). Choose the Gradient tool and drag from the right edge of the image to the left to make your gradient.

You can move the gradient layer down in the layer stack, or even hide it. It doesn't have to be visible to work as a displacement map.

Now make the text layer active and call up *Displace…* (Figure 7-24). Uncheck *X displacement* since you won't need it, but make sure *Y displacement* is checked. In the menu next to *Y displacement*, choose the layer with your gradient. You may not be able to read the full layer name in the menu, but look at the layer previews. You should be able to find your gradient there.

Once you've chosen the gradient, the preview shows that the text is indeed slanting from upper left to lower right, as intended. The background is also slanting, though that's more difficult to see. You can make the effect stronger by changing the displacement value from 20.00 to a larger number, like 60.00.

How would you go about displacing in both X and Y at once? For this, it's best to think about each direction separately.

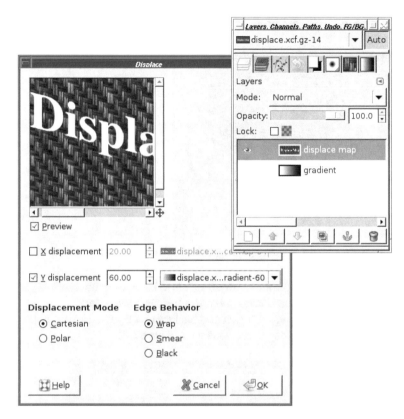

Figure 7-24. *The Displace dialog*

Suppose you want to make it look like you've laid a magnifying glass on the middle of the text. All the text under the glass should be magnified: text near the left edge should move left, text on the right should move right, text above center should move up, below center, down. Everything outside the lens should remain unchanged. How would you design Displace gradient maps to accomplish this?

Consider the horizontal problem first. Make a new layer for your horizontal gradient map—call it **hlens**.

Most of your text will be outside the magnifying glass, so it won't move at all. That means it needs to be medium gray. Set the foreground color to medium gray (V = 50% in the color chooser), and fill the layer with that color. As long as you have that foreground color handy, this is a good time to make a second layer (**vlens**) and fill that with gray as well.

Now, in your hlens layer, make a circular selection where you want your magnifying glass to be. Give it quite a bit of feathering so the effect will be gradual at the edges.

What should go inside this circular lens? Think about the goal: text at the left edge of the lens should move farther left, so the map needs to be white there. Similarly, the right side of the lens needs to be black so the text will move right. Set the foreground color back to black (the black/white button under the color swatches in the Toolbox is a handy shortcut) and drag the Gradient tool across your selection from right to left (Figure 7-25).

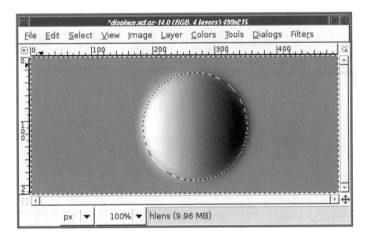

Figure 7-25. *The horizontal gradient map for a magnifying lens*

Now make your vertical lens gradient the same way. It needs to be black at the bottom, and white at the top. You can activate the vlens layer and reuse the same selection.

Cancel the selection (*Select ➤ None*), make the text and background layer active, and call up *Displace…*. Choose the hlens for X displacement, vlens for Y (Figure 7-26).

Figure 7-26. *Lens effect using Displace*

If you displace in *Polar* mode, the two maps are interpreted somewhat differently. Instead of X and Y, you're mapping *Pinch* and *Whirl*. In *Whirl*, white rotates the pixel clockwise around the center of the image, while black rotates it counterclockwise. In *Pinch*, white pinches the center of the layer in, while black bows it out. Polar mode is hard to visualize, but if you play with it you can get some good results. Try starting with 0 in both *Pinch* and *Whirl* numerical fields and changing just one of them by small amounts to get a feel for what it does.

Some Mapping Toys

Fractal Trace turns your image into a fractal. This is a class of mathematical equations that can produce all sorts of pretty pictures. There are several parameters to play with, but you can have a lot of fun tweaking them without worrying about the mathematics.

Illusion creates ghostly copies of parts of your image. There aren't many options to adjust, so give it a whirl.

Map Object is another wonderfully useful GIMP workhorse. It takes an image and wraps it around some other shape, such as a sphere or a cylinder (Figure 7-27). It has lots of options, but they're fairly self-explanatory.

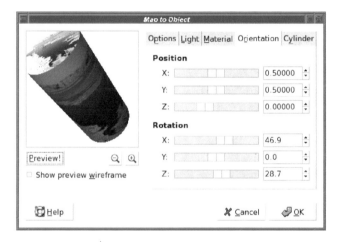

Figure 7-27. *Mapping an object to a cylinder*

Tiling

Make Seamless warps your image so that the right edge can match up to the left edge, and the top to the bottom. This is useful if you want to *tile*: use several repetitions of a small image as a background for a larger page. It doesn't always give a realistic result, but it's useful anyway. You'll use Make Seamless for making backgrounds in Chapter 9.

Paper Tile's description is that it "cuts the image, and slides the pieces." It's not a very realistic effect, though.

Small Tiles replaces the image with scaled-down versions of itself, repeated several times (2×2, 3×3, and so on).

Tile is similar but more flexible: it tiles the image at its full size into a larger image whose dimensions you specify. If you have a 320×240 image and you tile it to a 640×480 image, you'll see four copies of the original. You can specify any dimensions, though, not just multiples of the original image size.

If you've just run Make Seamless to create a background and want to see how it looks, either *Tile* or *Small Tiles* can help. They're also useful if you're printing many small copies of an image.

Warp

Warp is like Displace but with a twist—literally. Like Displace, it uses a gradient map to control how much each pixel will move. But Warp only needs a single map where Displace uses two. When warping, the *difference* between a pixel in the map and the pixels nearby controls the amount and direction of displacement in the source image.

It's most commonly used with random maps. To try it out, create a new layer the same size as the one you want to warp, and then generate some noise (*Filters* ➤ *Render* ➤ *Clouds* ➤ *Solid Noise* works well). Use the noise layer as the warp map (Figure 7-28).

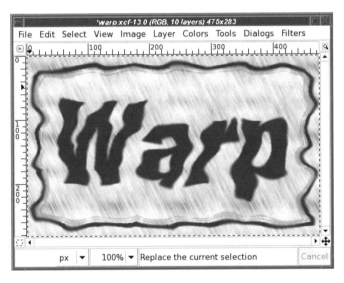

Figure 7-28. *25 steps of random Warp on some text and a rectangular border. The "Rain" pattern background was not warped.*

Under *Basic Options*, *Step size* controls how far a pixel can move in each step; *Iterations* controls the number of times Warp will be run. Usually, you'll want to run quite a few steps (Figure 7-28 used 25 steps). It's fun to watch the effect of the warp as it proceeds.

In *Advanced Options*, *Dither size* can add some extra randomness. *Rotation angle* is, according to the documentation, "The angle through which the local gradient of the displacement map (control matrix) will be rotated before displacing the pixel in that direction." (Well, the dialog *did* warn you that this was an advanced option!) The plug-in's author recommends staying with 90° in most cases. You can add a *magnitude map*, another monochrome image that adjusts the intensity of the effect at each point (white means maximum effect; black gives no effect). There are several even more advanced options: experiment if you're so inclined.

You don't have to use random maps. Try using a series of black feathered polka dots: start with a white background, choose the Ellipse Select tool and turn on feathering, and then make a small circular selection and fill it with black. Make another circular selection and fill it, and repeat until you have as many dots as you want and the layer looks like a Dalmatian. Use that as a map for Warp. It's a neat effect and it's fun to watch it run (Figure 7-29).

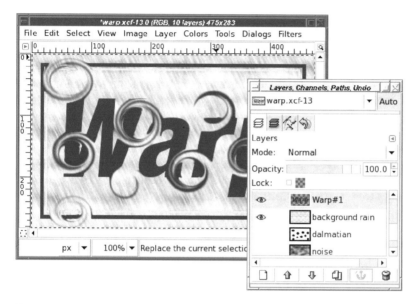

Figure 7-29. *Warping text with a "Dalmatian" polka-dot map*

Adding Patterns to a Layer

The *Filters* ➤ *Render* submenu offers you a collection of patterns you can add to the current layer. None of them are based on what's already in the image; they just add to the current layer or, in a few cases, create a new layer.

Clouds

Clouds provides several ways to get random cloudy patterns.

Plasma creates a wild blending of many colors. It doesn't look like clouds, but it makes a nice background.

Solid Noise looks like a lumpy surface photographed in black and white. It's useful in effects (you saw it used with the Warp plug-in in the previous section) even if it doesn't look that good by itself.

If you have GIMP-Python installed, you may also have Fog in this menu: by default the fog it creates is bright orange, but if you change it to gray you can get a good foggy-day effect.

Nature

Nature only provides two filters, *Flames* and *IFS Fractal*. They both use the mathematical concept of *fractals* to create intricate patterns.

Flame doesn't actually create flames. It creates arcs and loops like something you might see if you whirled a can of paint around your head. Experiment with the *Colormap* options to make the effect a bit more colorful. The *Edit* button lets you choose different patterns.

IFS Fractal is much more general. *IFS* stands for "Iterated Function System," and with this plug-in you can create fractal patterns that repeat in a variety of ways.

The dialog presents you with three triangles, which you can drag in various ways to affect the preview. Click on a triangle to select it, and then drag it. You can add another triangle by clicking the *New* button, or use fewer by clicking on one and then choosing *Delete*. You can change the shapes, sizes, and orientations of the objects with the *Move*, *Rotate*, and *Stretch* buttons, or you can edit the *Spatial Transformation* numbers. You can turn the triangles into quadrilaterals by adding another triangle and moving it a bit, into pentagons by adding a fifth and moving it, and so forth.

Choose *Full* in the *Color Transformation* tab to add a bit of color to the fractal you create, though controlling it is difficult.

Actually, controlling anything in the IFS Fractal dialog is difficult. The key is to make small changes one at a time. Happily, Ctrl+Z (Undo) works in the dialog, so you can back out changes that didn't work. There are also some interesting tutorials available on tricks you can do with this plug-in: try a web search for GIMP "IFS fractal."

If you want more general fractal patterns, keep reading: you may like *Fractal Explorer* better.

Pattern

Pattern offers a variety of—well, patterns. *Checkerboard* is obvious (and the *Psychobilly* option can be fun).

CML Explorer generates *Coupled Map Lattices*. Mostly, these are patterns that "bleed down" from the top of the image in complex ways. You can choose from a large variety of functions that will be of interest to mathematicians. Everyone else, try making random choices and watch how the image changes.

Diffraction Patterns is a real kick. Diffraction is the way light bends when it passes by an obstacle, or through a slit or a pinhole. This causes the light waves to interfere with each other in interesting ways. The *Diffraction Patterns* plug-in can simulate some of these behaviors, giving you mandala-like images that would look at home on a 1960s-style wall.

There's no automatic preview: when you make a change you'll have to click the *Preview!* button. Changing colors won't do what you expect: increasing a color won't necessarily show more of that color in the final image. Don't miss the values in the *Other Options* tab, which can change the image quite a bit.

Grid can draw lines on your image to divide it into pieces. You can choose the color of your grid lines, the spacing between the lines, and their offsets from the top and left sides of the image.

You can even make dashed grid lines by specifying a different color for the intersections of the lines. If you set the width of the grid lines to 0, Grid will draw "plus" characters at the intersections of the grid lines without drawing the lines themselves.

Jigsaw turns your image into a nifty jigsaw puzzle (Figure 7-30). You can control the number of puzzle pieces, whether they're square or curved, and how heavily they'll be shaded.

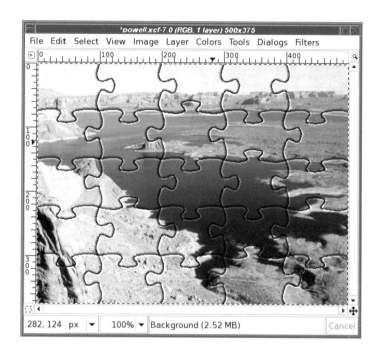

Figure 7-30. *Jigsaw turns an image into a jigsaw puzzle.*

Maze generates a random maze in black and white. You can even make one that's tileable so you can use it as a background for large images.

Qbist generates random colorful patterns. The dialog shows nine sample patterns. If you like one of them, click on it: that pattern will center, and GIMP will offer some other patterns similar to the one you chose. If you like one of those patterns better, click on it.

Continue until you have one you like; then click *OK*, and your layer will fill with a pattern similar to the one you saw previewed.

If you find one you *really* like, click *Save* to save the pattern to a .qbe file. You can *Open* it later if you want to use it again.

Sinus won't give you a headache—it makes patterns based on a combination of sine waves. It can produce anything from shaded bars to the grain pattern you see in a really nice piece of wood. It uses two colors, which you define in the *Colors* tab.

By default, you'll merely get straight bars shading into one another. But vary *X scale* and *Y scale* (make sure they're not the same value), and then play with the *Complexity* to get much more interesting patterns.

Circuit is outside the *Pattern* submenu, but it's similar to *Maze* except that it draws rounded traces in black and white. They look like the patterns on a printed circuit board.

Fractal Explorer

If you like beautiful fractal patterns like Figure 7-31, you can spend hours in *Fractal Explorer*.

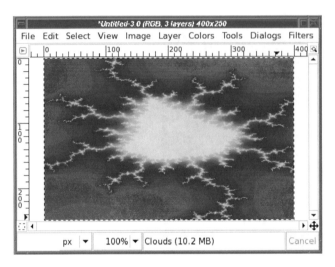

Figure 7-31. *"Energetic Diamond"—a type of Mandelbrot fractal*

If you've never played with fractals before, start with the *Fractals* tab. The list there gives you a sampling of patterns you can generate. Double-click on anything in the list to see a preview.

Once you find something you like, you can tweak it as much as you like. Go back to the first tab, *Parameters*. Twiddling any of the parameters will change the shape of the fractal. Make small changes: fractals are very sensitive, so a tiny bit of fudge in a parameter can mean a huge change in the image. The *Colors* tab lets you adjust how much of each color will be used in the image.

Fractals have an interesting property: the more you zoom in on a fractal pattern, the more detail you see. The *Zoom* buttons in Fractal Explorer let you home in on the center of a fractal—but that's not really the point. The most interesting detail may be in one of the fractal's outer arms, as it is in Figure 7-31. Fortunately, you can also drag in the dialog's preview area to zoom in on whatever area interests you most (Figure 7-32). If you don't like what you see, you can *Undo* or *Zoom Out* and try another region.

Since you can spend a lot of time tuning fractal parameters to get exactly the right curve, there are buttons to *Save* a pattern you really like in the *Parameters* tab, or *Open* one you've previously saved.

Figure 7-32. *Zooming in on a region in Fractal Explorer*

gfig

gfig is an odd beast: a vector-drawing program built inside a raster image-editing program.

Its dialog is a simple vector-drawing application all by itself (Figure 7-33). You can make lines, rectangles, ellipses, Bezier curves (like in GIMP's Path tool), stars, spirals, and other patterns. You can move objects around independently and change their fill or stroke style.

What's the catch? Well, gfig doesn't save to a standard format. It draws into its own layer in your GIMP image, but if you want to edit the shapes you made later as gfig objects, you'll have to save to gfig's own format, using *File ➤ Save* from the Gfig dialog.

You probably don't want to use gfig for creating elaborate vector-graphics art. But for adding a few figures to a GIMP image that you might want to change or resize later, it can be quite helpful.

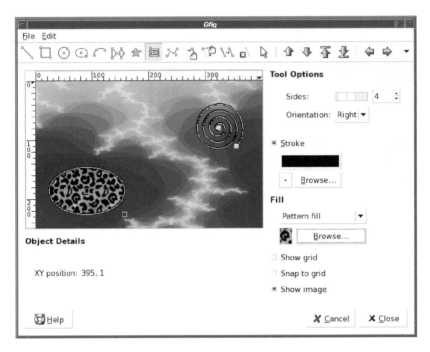

Figure 7-33. *gfig is a vector-drawing application built inside GIMP.*

Other Patterns

The *Render* menu ends with a few more interesting designs:

- *Lava* creates a red-on-black pattern that looks a bit like glowing lava at night.

- *Line Nova* creates a starburst pattern using the current foreground and background colors.

- *Sphere Designer* creates a sphere using a variety of complicated options. You can control all aspects of how the sphere is rotated and its apparent texture. In GIMP 2.2 and earlier, the options were difficult to figure out, but they've been simplified quite a bit in 2.4. Play around and see what you can make. (For a simpler sphere plug-in, keep reading: there's one in the *Xtns* menu of the Toolbox.)

- *Spirogimp* creates a pattern like a "Spirograph" toy. You can control the number of teeth each Spirograph wheel has, as well as the colors, drawing tool, and pen that will be used.

Filters to Help Make Web Pages

GIMP offers a few filters to help you prepare images for your web pages.

ImageMap lets you specify regions of the image that will link to other pages. You can specify rectangular or circular shapes, or use the Polygon tool to make any shape you want (Figure 7-34).

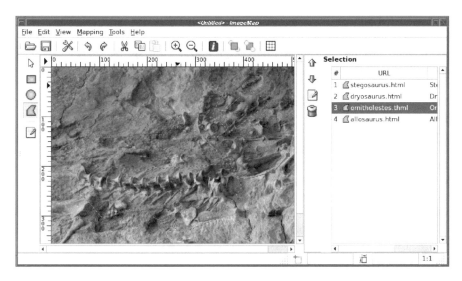

Figure 7-34. *Define regions in ImageMap that will take the user to different web pages.*

To define a rectangular or circular region, click at one corner, move to the other corner (don't drag), and click again. A dialog pops up to let you enter the web link you want for that region.

Polygonal regions are only slightly more complicated. Click on each point in turn, building up the region. When you get to the last point, double-click instead of single-clicking to complete the region and bring up the dialog.

You can select regions and edit or change them by clicking on them in the list to the right of the preview.

When you've defined all your regions, you can save the image map using the ImageMap dialog's *File ➤ Save....*

One function that's useful for the web isn't included with all GIMP installations. The filters *Py-Slice* and *Perlotine* are two ways of chopping up an image into a table of smaller images to put on a web page. Slice is written in Python and Perlotine in Perl, so you'll only see them in the *Web* menu if you have GIMP Python or Perl installed. (In GIMP versions prior to 2.4, look for them in the *Python-Fu* or *Perl-Fu* menus.) They're very similar in function: drag guides from the left and top rulers in the GIMP image window to define where you want to chop the image.

Either Py-Slice or Perlotine will chop the image into bits and then generate a web page in which the pieces are reassembled as a table. You can specify the type of image that will be saved (GIF, JPEG, or PNG), where the HTML and new images will be written, whether there should be space between the images in the table, and a few other details about how you want the web page to work.

This is useful for lots of different sorts of web pages. You can use an image of a keypad to let the user enter numbers, or you can split a map into quadrants and let the user explore them separately. Or you might just want to display extra space between pieces of your image.

GIMP won't show you the web page it wrote: it doesn't know how to show HTML! You'll have to open the HTML file in a web browser to see the result. Of course, there won't be any links on the individual images yet; you'll have to edit the page to make it do what you want.

If you specified no spacing between table elements, don't be too surprised if the web page looks exactly like the original image. It should! Nothing has been deleted from the image—it has merely been split with a very sharp knife.

The act of splitting up an image following the position of the guides is known as a *guillotine* operation. If you just want to split up one image into several smaller images but you don't need an HTML table, *Image* ➤ *Transform* ➤ *Guillotine* is for you. It will open all the new images in GIMP, and you can take it from there.

The final filter in GIMP's *Web* menu is *Semi-Flatten* (in some versions it can be found in *Filters* ➤ *Colors*). Semi-Flatten provides a solution for browsers such as Internet Explorer that don't support full PNG transparency. Semi-Flatten will preserve areas of full transparency, but pixels that are only partially transparent will be given some combination of their current color and the background color. Before you use this plug-in, be sure to set the background color to match the web page where the image will go.

Animation Helpers

The *Filters* ➤ *Animation* menu offers optimizers to make your animated image more efficient. *Optimize (for GIF)* was mentioned in the animation project at the end of Chapter 3: it attempts to reduce GIF file size, and adds layer names that help you control the speed of the animation. *Optimize (Difference)* performs more general optimizations, not specifically targeted at GIF animations. *UnOptimize* removes some of the optimizations that the other filters add; this simplifies layer names and can make the image easier to edit.

Playback is the way to preview an animation in GIMP. But it also has one unusual feature completely unrelated to animations: the *Detach* button. Run Playback on any image (even one with no layers) and click *Detach*. It looks like nothing happened, right? Wrong—try mousing down in the image and dragging it. The image moves without the window frame, and you can drag it anywhere on screen. You can use Playback's Detach as a quick way to see how your image would look on a web page or in a document.

The *Animators* menu offers a few filters that create animated images for you. Each of these starts from one or more existing layers and creates a new animated image.

Blend makes an animation that gradually fades between the layers of the current image. *Burn-in* takes an image that consists of two layers—like a text layer and a background layer— and creates an effect of the text being "burned" into the background, letter by letter.

Rippling and *Waves* each make an image look as though it's being viewed through rippling water. *Waves* is the better effect, though you'll want to run it on an image that has only one layer. *Rippling* works on the active layer and ignores any others.

Spinning Globe wraps your image around a globe and then rotates the globe. It works best on an image with a single layer: if there are multiple layers, you'll see flashes as the animation switches layers, but only one layer will be animated. It also works best if your image is tileable, or at least if the left and right edges join together smoothly.

Alpha to Logo

The *Alpha to Logo* scripts (in the *Script-Fu* menu of GIMP versions prior to 2.4) create interesting effects from a text layer (or any other layer with transparency). If you want some text in a fancy style, try some of these scripts. Figure 7-35 shows the collection, though of course they all have options to let you change fonts, colors, and other aspects of the effect.

All these logo scripts are also available in the *Xtns* ➤ *Logos* menu of the Toolbox (in earlier versions, *Xtns* ➤ *Script-Fu* ➤ *Logos*; in 2.6 they'll move to *File* ➤ *New* ➤ *Logos*). If you don't already have a layer you want to use, the Toolbox versions will create a brand-new image containing your fancy text.

Figure 7-35. *The logo scripts*

BENDING TEXT INTO OTHER SHAPES

One of the logo scripts isn't shown in Figure 7-35 because it does something a bit different: the very useful *Text Circle* bends text in a circle without adding any extra styles to it.

You may remember that *Polar Coords*, from the *Distorts* menu, is another way to bend text into a circle, and that *Curve Bend* can change the vertical height of a layer. But what if you want to bend text around a more complex shape?

The answer is a button in the Text tool options: *Text along Path*, which can take a text layer and warp it along any path you've defined with the Paths tool.

Define the path first, and make sure it's selected in the Paths dialog. Then create the text layer. If you're using a text layer you've already made, make it active by choosing the layer, selecting the Text tool in the Toolbox, and then clicking on the text in the image window.

This should enable the *Text along Path* button, which will create a new path consisting of the outline of the text, warped so that each letter follows the old path.

Since the result is a new path, you have several options for what to do with it. You can convert it to a selection and fill it with a color or pattern, stroke it, edit it further, or export it as an SVG file.

Be careful if you run this repeatedly: since Text along Path leaves the newly made text path active, if you invoke it again, perhaps for a second text layer, be sure that you have the right curved path active in the Paths dialog or you may create a very messy knot.

Decor

The final category of *Filters, Decor,* lets you dress up an image—or dress it down. You can add a bevel around the outside of an image, add a colored border or make the outside of the image look fuzzy, add splotches that look like coffee stains, or make the image look like an old photo you found in a drawer.

You can round an image's corners, or make it look like an unmounted 35mm slide—these two only work on images *without* an alpha channel. If they're grayed out, you'll have to use *Image* ➤ *Flatten* to use them, which will combine all your layers into one image and eliminate any transparency, or you can right-click on the image's bottom layer and choose *Remove Alpha Channel.*

If you have an image that's in grayscale mode, you can carve it into another (colored) image with *Stencil Carve,* or use it as a map to create interesting chrome effects with *Stencil Chrome.*

Experiment with these and see which ones you like. But there are some tricks you should know about *Add Bevel.*

The classic use for *Add Bevel…* is to shade the edge of rectangular boxes (like buttons for a website) to make them look more three-dimensional. But it can be even more useful on text. Adding a bevel and a drop shadow is a quick way to give boring, solid-colored text more life. But if you activate a text layer and run *Add Bevel…,* nothing happens. Why?

Some filters, including *Add Bevel…,* will work only on a selection. So before you can bevel your text, you'll need to select the text layer (or whatever it is you're trying to bevel) by using *Alpha to Selection,* available either in the right-click menu of the Layers dialog or in *Layer* ➤ *Transparency* ➤ *Alpha to Selection.* Of course, with the marching ants in the way you also can't see your bevel very well, so you'll probably want to hide them with *View* ➤ *Show Selection.*

But there's another way of getting a beveled-like look, a trick using drop shadows. You know what a drop shadow looks like on a text layer. But for this effect you'll use the opposite of that. After you've selected the text, invert the selection with *Select* ➤ *Invert.* Then run a drop shadow on that inverted selection, turning *off* the *Allow Resizing* box in the Drop Shadow's dialog. Figure 7-36 shows how the effect compares to a standard bevel.

Figure 7-36. *Beveled text (top) vs. adding a drop shadow on a selection containing everything but the text (bottom)*

Scripts to Make New Images: The Xtns Menu

The Toolbox's *Xtns* menu, like *Filters*, offers a collection of scripts and plug-ins for lots of different effects. The difference is that the Toolbox scripts all make a new image and don't require you to have an image already open. (In GIMP 2.6, these will all move to the image window's *File* ➤ *New* menu.) *Buttons* offers two scripts to make buttons with text on them, which you can use on web pages or in programs. You can probably make more interesting buttons by searching for web tutorials, however.

Logos offers the same list of logo styles as in *Filters* ➤ *Alpha to Logo*, except that you don't need an image open to use them. I usually find it more convenient to make a logo as a new image, and then paste it into another image.

Misc ➤ *Sphere* lets you make a sphere. It's a bit like *Filters* ➤ *Render* ➤ *Sphere Designer*, but a lot simpler. Set the foreground color and the image's background (alas, Sphere can't do a transparent background—but in Chapter 11 you'll learn how to fix that). Specify the lighting angle and the size of the sphere, and whether or not you want a shadow. Voilà! A nice sphere.

Patterns offers a collection of designs you can use as background images or for any other purpose you can think of.

A *Truchet* pattern (named for Dominican priest Sebastien Truchet, who first studied them) is a network formed by combining a series of tiles, each of which has a circular arc across two opposite corners. *Truchet* and *3D Truchet* create an image filled with two variants on a Truchet pattern.

Camouflage makes a pattern like you might see on army fatigues. You can change the colors and make camouflage for other environments, of course.

Flatland gives a random pattern rather similar to the one in *Filters* ➤ *Render* ➤ *Clouds* ➤ *Solid Noise.*

Land and *Render Map* create two different but equally interesting "artificial world map" views. *Land* gives textured green hills against a powder-blue sea (you can change the colors if you want by using a different gradient). *Render Map* looks more like something you might see on a globe of the earth. They look even better if you wrap the resulting image around a sphere by using *Filters* ➤ *Map* ➤ *Map Object*—make your own planet (Figure 7-37).

Figure 7-37. Make your own planet with Render Map (left) or Land (right), combined with Map Object.

■**Tip** You might want to take a look at the layer name after you run *Render Map*.

Swirl-Tile makes an interesting swirly pattern. You can tile it to a larger image to make a place mat.

Swirly gives a pattern of black-and-white squares with a swirl in one of the corners.

Finally, *Web Page Themes* offers several "looks" you might want to use on a website. Under each theme, you can make several types of element, such as arrows, buttons, or headings, all coordinated. If you happen to like one of the motifs, you might find this useful.

Summary

Well, that's quite a list of toys! When you first installed GIMP you probably played around with a few of the filters, but it's easy to miss some of the most useful functions GIMP has stuffed in its menus.

Now you know when to look in the Toolbox menus vs. the menus in the image window. You've experimented with GIMP's offerings for changing lighting and shadow, adding noise, and detecting edges. You can map images to three-dimensional objects with the Map filters and turn them into art with the Artistic filters. You know how to create interesting logos and other text effects, and how to make images for your web pages.

But there's one class of GIMP filter I skipped in this chapter: the filters in the *Colors* menu. There's enough to know about color manipulation that it needs a chapter of its own. So grab that psychedelic tie-dye T-shirt from the back of the closet and let's go on a tour of GIMP's color handling, channels, and layer modes.

CHAPTER 8

■ ■ ■

Color

In earlier chapters, you learned how to do simple color correction, how RGB and indexed color differ, and how to change the foreground and background colors in the Toolbox. But a deeper understanding of GIMP's color model can illuminate all sorts of useful image-processing tricks.

In this chapter, I'll describe the way GIMP represents colors, different color models, and techniques to manipulate colors.

Understanding color requires a more theoretical approach than you've seen so far. A familiarity with color implementation in digital images is helpful to understanding the sorts of advanced tricks that can be played.

If you feel overwhelmed by the theory, you can skip those sections and use this chapter for reference when you have questions about color. Later chapters will not require an understanding of color theory, though some of the techniques covered here will help in other projects.

This chapter will cover the following:

- RGB and CMY color

- Working in HSV

- Working for print: CMYK

- GIMP's other color choosers

- Correcting color balance

- Working with grayscale or black and white

- Coloring monochrome images and making sepia photos

- Using the Threshold tool to clean up scanned images

- Indexed color

- Picking colors from the image

- The color channels

- Selection using color decomposition

- Some color-mapping toys

- Color profiles

RGB and CMY Color

You've already worked with RGB images, and you know the letters stand for *red, green,* and *blue*. But do you know why those three colors are used? Why not red, yellow, and blue, like the paints you probably mixed as a child?

The answer has two parts. The first part has to do with the structure of the human eye. Our color vision is made possible by light-sensitive cells in the retina called *cones*. There are three types of cones: some are sensitive to red, some to green, and some to blue. Every color we can see, we perceive as a combination of these three *primary* colors.

The second part of the answer lies with how colors of transmitted light combine to make other colors. Transmitted colors are *additive*. The light of one color, combined with the light of another color, is perceived as a third color that is lighter than either component.

Additive Colors

Computer monitors use the additive technique to depict color. Each pixel in a computer monitor is a combination of red, green, and blue lights. These three colors combine efficiently into virtually any color that the eye can perceive.

If you hold a magnifying glass up to your screen, you should be able to see the separate colors. It's easiest to see in white areas—that's where all three colors are lit up.

Figure 8-1 gives you an idea of how the primary colors combine to make other colors.

Notice that the center of the circle, where all three colors combine, is white. (It may not look white to you, an optical illusion created by the other colors nearby. Try covering the other colors so that you see only the center portion. You'll see it really is white.)

Figure 8-1. *The primary (outer circles) and secondary (overlapping areas) additive colors*

Subtractive Colors

So what's up with those red, yellow, and blue paints you mixed as a child?

The red, green, and blue *additive primary* colors work for transmitted light. But ink or paint on paper follows different rules. As you add colors of transmitted light, the image gets brighter. But as you add shades of paint to a reflecting surface, the image gets darker. That's *subtractive* color.

The paint absorbs light of particular frequencies. The light that doesn't get absorbed is reflected to your eye. In other words, the paint subtracts colors from the white light shining on it. When you mix several colors of paint together, the paint absorbs more and more colors, subtracting from the colors that reach your eye. Reflected color is called *subtractive*.

Each of the additive colors that come from your RGB monitor has an opposite, or complementary color. The complement of blue is yellow, of green is magenta, and of red is cyan. You can see the relationships in Figure 8-1.

For subtractive colors, it works best to use those complementary colors as primaries: so the *subtractive primary colors* are cyan, magenta, and yellow, and the color model based around them is known as CMY.

Take some yellow paint and put it on white paper. The white surface reflects the full spectrum of magenta, cyan, and yellow light, while the yellow surface absorbs the magenta and cyan—what's left is yellow.

But wait! When you shine differently colored lights on a white screen, you're looking at reflected light, but it follows the "additive" rules. What's up with that?

That's confusing, but the reflection is a red herring. The color you see is still coming from transmitted light, even after it's reflected. It's not subtractive color because there's no tinted surface subtracting from the colors you see.

The Relationship Between Additive and Subtractive Systems

It's convenient to consider these two systems, additive and subtractive, as mirrors of each other. They have their own rules about how colors work, but the rules are exact opposites of each other.

For example, if you mix any two of the additive primaries (red, green, or blue), you get one of the subtractive primaries (also called the additive secondaries): magenta, cyan, or yellow, as you saw in Figure 8-1.

Conversely, mixing any two subtractive primaries of paint will yield the additive primaries: yellow + magenta = red, yellow + cyan = green, and cyan + magenta = blue.

Tip GIMP can help you experiment with combining colors, using the *Addition* and *Subtract* layer modes and the color picker. That's how Figure 8-1 was made. You'll learn how in the next chapter.

There's another way the two approaches mirror each other. If you keep adding transmitted light colors, eventually you'll get white. If you keep mixing colors of paint (subtracting reflected light), you theoretically end up with black. (In practice, with paint you get a muddy dark brown most of the time, but that's just reality refusing to conform to theory. You'll learn more about black in the discussion of CMYK color.)

Color Depth

Digital images have another property: *depth*, or how many different shades of each color the video system can display. You will sometimes see color depth abbreviated as bpp, *bits per pixel*.

You may hear the phrase *bits per channel*, the number of bits used per color in each pixel. Multiply by three (for the three primary colors) to get bits per pixel—or sometimes by four if the image has transparency.

Many early color computers could display only 256 colors—this is 2^8, the largest number that can be expressed in 8 bits, and hence this was sometimes referred to as *8-bit color*.

Later, computers were introduced that could display 16-bit color, or 65,536 (2^{16}) colors. Today, most computers can display *24-bit color*: 8 bits per color channel, or 16,777,216 (2^{24}) different colors. This is sometimes called *true color*. Figure 8-2 compares these three color depths.

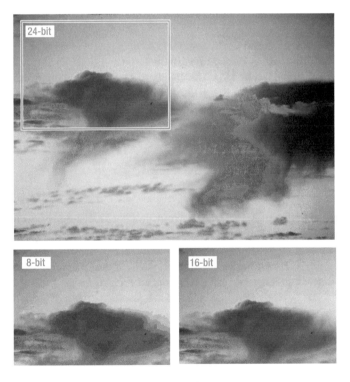

Figure 8-2. *24-bit, 8-bit, and 16-bit color*

Modern computers most often use 32 bits to represent a pixel. Generally, 32-bit color has the same number of colors as 24-bit color. The extra 8 bits may be used to represent transparency (as GIMP does), or it may not be used for anything at all.

■**Note** Macintosh computers show the color depth choices as "256," "Thousands," or "Millions," historically corresponding to 8-bit, 16-bit, and 24- or 32-bit color.

Some professional graphic artists and motion picture animators use even greater color depth: 16 or more bits per color channel. Normal computer monitors can't display this many colors—some video cards can display 10 bits per channel on a CRT monitor, but typical LCD monitors only manage 6 bits per channel. But extreme color precision can offer more control to the artist who must produce exactly the right color on professional output equipment. High-end digital cameras and some scanners can also produce images with 16 bits per channel, though you'll never see the difference on an ordinary computer display. GIMP 2.4 doesn't support these high color depths—it uses 32 bits per pixel internally—but support for higher color depths is in the works for future versions.

■**Caution** When someone says "8-bit color," they might mean 8 bits per pixel—only 256 colors total—or they could mean 8 bits per channel, or 24-bit true color. The same is true of someone saying "16-bit color": it could mean slightly less than true color, or it could mean high-depth color with 16 bits per channel. Usually you can tell from the context, but the terminology can be quite confusing.

The 24-bit model is pretty easy to understand. Divide 24 by 3, and you get 8 bits to assign to each color. However, 16-bit color is not so easy to figure—you can't divide 16 by 3 so conveniently. What gives?

In 16-bit color, the usual technique is to assign 5 bits each to red and blue, with the remaining 6 going to green. It turns out our eyes are more sensitive to green light, so distinguishing fine differences of intensity is most useful in that part of the spectrum.

The Indexed Palette

Eight-bit color is even weirder. Because there just aren't enough bits to do a good job, there never was a truly common standard bit assignment for those 256 colors. The usual trick was to create a *palette* of colors, assigning the values however the designer saw fit. If a program needed to show a color that wasn't in the palette, it picked the closest match (which sometimes wasn't very close).

Since monitor phosphors could show far more information than the system could supply, the palette could be redesigned with different goals in mind: making text and windowing systems look good, making computer graphics such as logos look good, making photos look good, and so on. Each window on a display might use a different palette, and when you went from one application to another, every window on the display would suddenly shift colors.

Fortunately, you probably won't have to deal with palette headaches any more except for GIF images (see the section on "Indexed Color" later in this chapter).

Representing RGB Color in Web Pages

Knowing RGB notation can help you understand color in web pages written in hypertext markup language, or HTML. Although HTML lets you specify the most common colors by name, such as "red," many web page authors prefer something more flexible. Instead, they specify colors by their RGB values.

Figure 8-3 shows what the color notation looks like. *HTML notation* shows six digits representing three two-digit numbers in base 16 (called "*hexadecimal*," or just "*hex*" for short), ranging from 00 (darkest) through 99 to ff (brightest). Bright red is shown: the first two digits are *ff*, meaning as much red as possible. The second and third pair are both *00*, meaning no green and no blue, only red.

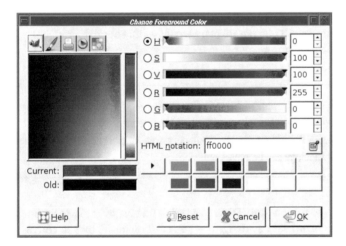

Figure 8-3. *HTML notation for "red"*

In HTML, you add "#" in front of the number GIMP gives you. So red would be #ff0000 in HTML notation. (You can also write this in a more compact three-digit form, as #f00.)

Notice that you can also read the R, G, and B values off the sliders in GIMP's color chooser. R is 255 (ff is hexadecimal for 255), while G and B are both 0. If you don't know how to convert between hexadecimal and decimal numbers, that's not a problem: just use GIMP's color chooser to pick a color, copy the number in the *HTML notation* field, and then put a "#" in front of it.

Working in HSV

RGB is straightforward, and it's the way the computer represents colors internally. But sometimes it works better to represent colors in some other way.

HSV, or *Hue, Saturation, and Value*, is a very useful color model. You've worked a little with HSV already if you've used GIMP's color chooser.

The HSV model, like RGB and CMY, uses three numbers to represent each color. But instead of splitting an image into separate color components, HSV uses conceptual properties of the image.

Hue is a measure of where that color falls in the spectrum—is it more blue, or more red, or more green? In GIMP's color chooser dialog, hue goes from 0 to 360, not 0 to 255 the way the RGB values do. The number represents degrees on a circle: a hue of 360 is the same as a hue of 0 (both are pure red). You can see the hue values laid out in the rainbow-colored vertical bar in GIMP's color chooser, from reds at the bottom (hue=0) through orange, yellow, green, blue, magenta, and finally back to red again (hue=360) at the top.

Saturation is how intense a color is. It ranges from 0 to 100. A color that's bright and vivid is *highly saturated* and has saturation of 100. A color that's pale and looks "washed out" will have a lower saturation, down to white at the bottom (saturation=0). In GIMP's color chooser, dragging up and down in the color square changes saturation; or you can drag the "S" slider by itself.

Value represents how bright a pixel is, from 0 to 100. A black pixel has value=0; a bright pixel (whether it's white or some other color) has value=100. Dragging left and right in GIMP's color square changes value, as does dragging the "V" slider.

Figure 8-4 illustrates these relationships.

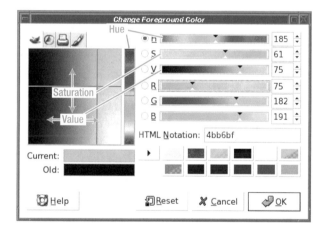

Figure 8-4. *Hue, saturation, and value in the color chooser*

Why Use HSV?

Why learn this model? Why not just stick with good old Red, Green, and Blue?

Experimenting with the color chooser will provide the answer. Think of a color, then try picking it using only the R, G, and B sliders. Then try again using the H, S, and V sliders.

Most people find that it's more intuitive to choose colors according to questions like "More red, or more yellow?" "How intense should the yellow be?" and "How bright do you want it?" That's much easier than it is to figure out how much red you need to mix with how much green to make the shade of brownish-yellow you're after.

In addition, other aspects of the HSV model can provide a shortcut to certain image-editing operations.

You've already seen the Hue-Saturation dialog in action: first in Chapter 2, where reducing saturation provided a quick fix for red-eye, and then in Chapter 6, where changing hue helped to get rid of a color error in a photograph. You'll learn other uses for HSV later in this chapter.

Working for Print: CMYK

Printers use the subtractive colors—with a twist. To represent dark colors in CMY, you would normally combine all three inks in fairly equal amounts. But due to the physical properties of ink, this often ends up as a muddy dark brown instead of a nice sharp black. It also uses up a lot of expensive colored ink. So most printers add a fourth color, pure black, and add that to the CMY mixture to get better dark colors.

This might have been called CMYB—but B is already used for blue when talking about colors. So, instead, black is represented by K, and the printing color space is known as CMYK.

■**Note** You might also sometimes see it written as CYMK.

CMYK for Professional Printers

People working primarily for print media, on professional equipment, want a lot of control over how much black gets mixed in when an image is printed. Therefore, they like to work directly with CMYK colors when they're editing images.

GIMP is limited in that respect. The Decompose function, which I'll talk about later in this chapter, has a CMYK option. The color chooser offers a CMYK tab, and the new Gutenprint print plug-in (see the section "Printing" in Chapter 12) allows adjustment of K. However, most tools and filters don't give you control over CMYK color, and most plug-ins can't yet save to CMYK. (That may happen in a future version of GIMP.)

But fortunately, most of us don't need this functionality. You can't see any difference at all on a computer monitor. Desktop computers and home inkjet and laser printers can print perfectly well from an RGB image, and so can most copy and print shops.

If you take your images to a professional for printing, you can use external programs to convert from RGB to CMYK. There's a GIMP plug-in that uses a program called *littlecms* to convert to CMYK. Or you can just let the printing house do it for you—they know the characteristics of their printers better than you do anyway.

GIMP's Other Color Choosers

Up to now, I haven't mentioned the tabs at the top of GIMP's color chooser dialog. What are they, anyway?

The tabs provide alternative ways of changing color, in case you don't like the standard Saturation-Value square with the Hue bar next to it. The number of tabs and their order may vary from system to system. Some systems may not show any tabs, if the extra color-selector modules weren't installed. Other systems may have more than four, if additional modules have been added.

The default color chooser is the one you've already used—the standard GIMP color chooser (which has a picture of Wilber on its tab).

The Triangle Color Selector

The "triangle" color selector provides an alternate HSV interface (Figure 8-5). Instead of a vertical slider, hue is represented by a circle (remember from the discussion of HSV how the Hue slider goes from 0 to 360, representing degrees around a circle?). The two small rings are grab handles that you can drag: one drags the point of the triangle around the circle to choose a hue, and the other drags into the triangle to choose saturation and value.

Notice that you still have the familiar set of sliders for H, S, V, R, G, and B on the right: only the left section of the dialog has changed.

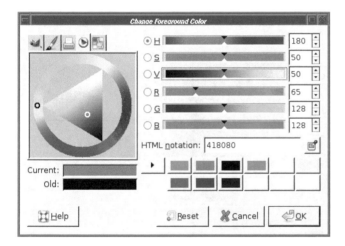

Figure 8-5. *An alternate set of HSV controls*

Once you've chosen the hue, drag the other white ring back into the triangle to choose saturation and value. Dragging toward the black corner reduces value; toward the white corner, saturation.

The interface in this tab is pretty. But it's sometimes a little hard to balance saturation and value—they don't follow equal scales (for instance, the point in Figure 8-5 has saturation and value both set to the halfway point of 50, but clearly it's not halfway between the dark and light corners of the triangle).

The interface is also a lot slower than the standard GIMP selector—on my machine I find that it can't always update as fast as I can drag the circle around. But if you have a fast system, you may prefer this color selector.

The CMYK Tab

The CMYK tab, with a picture of a printer, offers controls to set CMYK colors. If you're working for a print medium, and know exactly the CMYK hue you're after, you can choose it here. If you have a CMYK color profile set, GIMP will use it for this tab. But beware: GIMP does not use CMYK color internally, so the value you choose in this tab will be converted to RGB for most GIMP operations.

The *Black Pullout* parameter (GIMP 2.2 and earlier) lets you control how much the other colors can be reduced in order to use black instead. The maximum, 100, means use as much black as possible. Adjusting *Black Pullout* automatically adjusts the other colors (but not the reverse).

The Watercolor Selector

Finally, the trickiest of the selectors: Watercolor (Figure 8-6). When you drag the mouse in the square palette area, the color you drag gets "mixed with" the current color. At first, the color will be fairly pale; drag in small circles within the same color area to make the color gradually darker. Be careful not to slop over into other color zones, unless you want to mix in a different color.

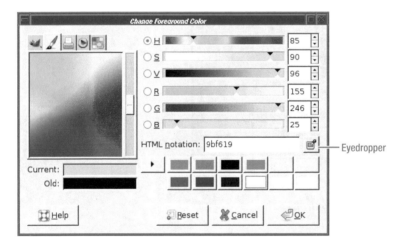

Figure 8-6. *The Watercolor selector*

The slider to the right of the palette controls how fast color is added. To be cautious, or to paint with pastel colors, slide it farther down, as in Figure 8-6. If you slide it down all the way to the bottom, though, no color at all will be added.

If you've done a lot of watercolor painting, this selector may seem familiar. If you've done a little watercolor painting, and when you mix colors, you usually end up with a muddy brown and have to start over—well, this interface may seem familiar!

To try it out, start with white and add color gradually to see what happens. It takes practice and parsimonious mouse use to get good color combinations without ending up at dark gray or brown.

What happens if you go too far? The watercolor selector is one of the few areas in GIMP where there's no Undo. So if you accidentally add the wrong color or your color gets too dark, you usually have to start over by going back to white. With any luck, one of the color presets to the right of the *Current* and *Old* color swatches will be white. If not, there's always the eyedropper.

Tip The "eyedropper" button to the right of the *HTML notation* field, new for GIMP 2.4, lets you set GIMP's color chooser to any color you can see on the screen—even in windows belonging to other applications. Click on the eyedropper in any GIMP color chooser, then click on the color you want. It's a fast way to get back to white…or to use a color out of a photograph or web page. GIMP has an eyedropper tool in the Toolbox, too, the Color Picker tool (described in the section "Picking Colors from the Image"), but it's much less flexible: the tool can only pick colors from open image windows, while the eyedropper in the color chooser dialog can pick colors from anywhere.

Correcting Color Balance

Cameras don't always record the same colors your eye sees. Photographs taken indoors under incandescent lights often come out looking yellow (though some cameras have settings to compensate for this effect). Fluorescent lights can turn photos blue. Long exposures can have strange effects as well, especially with film cameras.

For instance, Figure 8-7 was a relatively long exposure on color slide film. Although it was a beautiful storm (I was trying to capture lightning, but didn't manage it), the clouds were just ordinary gray, not the purple shade that showed up in the slide. To be honest, I rather like the purple sky in this photograph. But what if I wanted to make the colors more normal?

Figure 8-7. *Long film exposures can create strange color casts, such as this purple sky.*

Hue-Saturation

GIMP has several ways of adjusting color balance. The simplest is *Colors* ➤ *Hue-Saturation…* (in versions prior to 2.4, you'll find the *Colors* menu inside *Layer*).

For correcting color casts, *Hue* is the only slider you need. The effect of nudging the Hue slider slightly to the left shows up well in Figure 8-8. A subtle change can help eliminate a color cast in a photo.

Figure 8-8. *A small Hue shift fixes the magenta sky.*

However, you usually have to be very sparing with the Hue slider. Move it more than a trifling distance and you'll have huge color changes in your image, as Figure 8-9 shows.

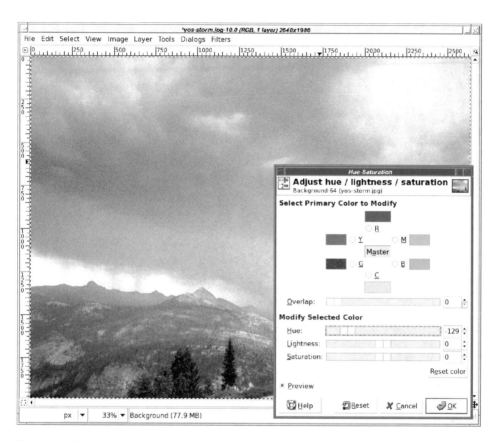

Figure 8-9. *Too much Hue change leads to drastic color changes.*

Color Balance

Layers ➤ *Colors* ➤ *Color Balance* is another tool for correcting color problems in photographs.

Choose to modify *Shadows, Midtones,* or *Highlights,* then slide the sliders in the direction you want to go—in this case, away from Magenta (toward Green) and away from Blue (toward Yellow). Figure 8-10 shows the result.

Figure 8-10. *Using the Color Balance tool*

How do you decide which range to adjust? It's not always obvious which is best. In this case, *Highlights* seemed like the obvious choice, because the strongest magenta cast was in the brightest part of the clouds. Wrong! Choosing *Highlights* created a grainy texture in that region, whereas choosing *Midtones* gave nearly the same color balance but without the unwanted texture.

When in doubt, start with *Midtones*. But you don't have to stop there; before you click *OK*, you can adjust all three ranges. The *Reset Range* button sets the current range back to zero, while *Reset* zeroes all three ranges at once.

Using Curves or Levels for Balancing Colors

You've already used the Levels and Curves tools for adjusting brightness and contrast. But they're also powerful tools for adjusting color.

The key is the *Channel* menu at the top of the Levels and Curves tools. By default, it's set to *Value*, meaning that the tool will adjust the brightness of the image. But you can also adjust levels or curves of the individual color channels: *Red*, *Green*, or *Blue*.

You can even adjust the transparency, or *Alpha*, channel. However, that is a more advanced technique and isn't generally useful for photographs.

Levels

You can adjust each channel in Levels by moving the Output sliders around, just as you would adjust the brightness of a photo. But Levels offers you a more powerful tool: the three eye-dropper buttons representing White Point, Gray Point, and Black Point. You can use them to adjust color casts as well as brightness. All you need is to find places in your image that should be pure white, pure black, or a neutral gray. Then click on one of the eyedroppers and a corresponding point in the image. It doesn't matter which channel is showing—the eyedroppers will affect all three channels. In this case, I've clicked on a white point in the clouds, viewing the red channel to see what the effect is there (Figure 8-11).

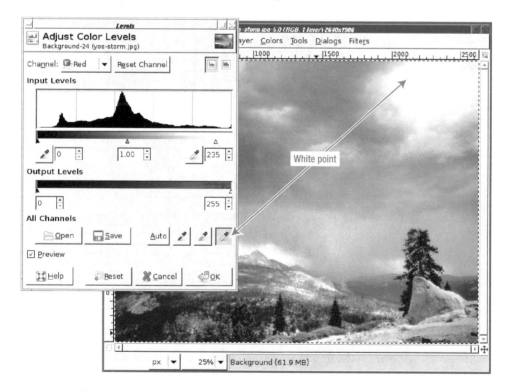

Figure 8-11. *Choose a White Point in Levels to adjust color balance.*

Experiment to find out which controls work best. In this case, I also tried setting the gray point to the color of the lowest band of clouds, but that didn't help much compared to setting the white point. And setting the black point didn't help at all.

Curves

Curves doesn't have White, Black, and Gray eyedroppers, but it gives you a lot more control over the amount of each color at each point in the curve.

Figure 8-12 shows the effect of a curve that reduces the amount of blue in the brightest areas of the picture without changing the other two channels.

Figure 8-12. *The right curve can make color adjustment easier, even if you adjust only one color channel.*

It often won't be obvious which channel you should adjust to correct a color problem. Don't be afraid to experiment!

Working with Grayscale or Black and White

How do you turn a color photograph into a black-and-white one?

It turns out there are lots of approaches. They all produce similar results, but they're not exactly the same. There are quite a few ways to map three color values into a single brightness value. If you want a specific effect, you may want to try several methods and compare the results. But why are there so many methods?

Mostly because it's not always obvious what brightness means.

Methods of Measuring Brightness

What are all the brightness values, and how do they differ?

Since each pixel in an image has a red, green, and blue value, these three numbers must be combined in some way to turn the pixel into a single gray value. The obvious way is to take the *average* of the three: *(R + G + B)/3*.

Another simple method is to extract the value of the most prominent color in the image: *max(R, G, B)*. This is *Value*, the *V* of HSV color.

But those methods don't always give you a result that matches what the eye sees. The eye is most sensitive to green, less so to the other colors. *Luminosity* (also called *luminance*) is a measure intended to match the way most people's eyes see colors on a computer display. Instead of just averaging red, green, and blue, luminosity is a weighted average that gives the most weight to green, and the least to blue.

In some cases, though, a slightly more complicated method can give better results. To find the *lightness* of a pixel, GIMP takes the value of the color that's most prevalent, and the value of the color that's least prevalent, then averages those two numbers. This usually gives a "flatter" result, with less dynamic range: the brights aren't as bright, and the darks aren't as dark.

How do you create all these grayscale images in GIMP?

Grayscale Mode

The most straightforward way to convert to grayscale is to change the image's mode from RGB (24 bits) to grayscale (8 bits) using *Image ➤ Mode*. Without asking any additional questions, this gives you a black-and-white version of your image.

Grayscale mode uses luminance. Often, this is all you need. It's the only method that converts the entire image; the others will convert only the current layer. It is also the only method that will save the image in grayscale mode (if the format you're using, such as PNG, allows such a concept). This can make a smaller image on disk.

Once you tell GIMP an image should be grayscale mode, it won't let you add any colors to it. If you want to add colors later (even in a new layer), you need to convert the mode back to RGB…which won't add the colors back; it will merely change the image's mode so that you *can* add colors.

Desaturate

The second grayscale conversion method is the *Desaturate* function found in the *Colors* menu. In GIMP 2.4, this gives you a dialog offering a choice between *Lightness*, *Luminosity*, or *Average*. (In earlier GIMP versions, the *Colors* menu was found in *Layer ➤ Colors*, and *Desaturate* always used lightness, without offering the other two choices).

Hue-Saturation

You may have noticed that, ironically, none of the *Desaturate* options do the same thing as reducing saturation to zero in the Hue-Saturation dialog. Figure 8-13 shows other uses for the Saturation bar. By reducing saturation in an image, you can create a pale-hued image that can make a nice background for a poster or greeting card. Increasing saturation creates a bright, garish image, which again could be useful for posters or other artwork.

Figure 8-13. *Reducing (center) or increasing (right) saturation*

Decompose

No, this isn't what happens when you leave your disk drive out in the rain too long! *Colors* ➤
Components ➤ *Decompose* is actually a cool way of seeing the color components of your
image. (In GIMP 2.0 and 2.2, you'll generally find this under both *Image* ➤ *Mode* ➤ *Decompose*
and *Filters* ➤ *Colors* ➤ *Decompose*.)

The Decompose dialog gives you lots of choices (Figure 8-14). Yikes!

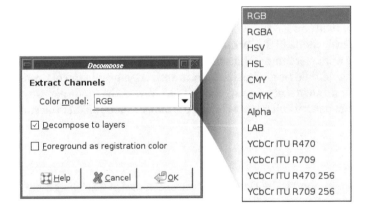

Figure 8-14. *The Decompose dialog*

The first five should already be familiar to you. RGB will give you the red, green, and blue
channels of your image; RGBA will do the same, but will include information about the alpha
channel if your image has transparency. HSV, CMY, and CMYK are all terms you've read about
earlier in this chapter; HSL is a variant of HSV that gives you a lightness layer in place of
value). Alpha gives you just the transparency and nothing else.

LAB is yet another color model. The L stands for luminance; A and B represent a color channel between red and green and another color channel between blue and yellow. Some images made in Photoshop and certain other programs use this model. If you don't need to convert LAB images, you probably don't need to worry about it, though it can be useful for certain effects, like sharpening.

The YCbCr ITU entries represent specialized color models used for digital video and for the internals of JPEG images. They're similar to LAB, but most people won't find much use for them.

Whichever color model you choose, *Decompose* will create a new image in which the layers correspond to the color channels (Figure 8-15). If you uncheck *Decompose to Layers* in the dialog, it will give you separate new images, instead of separate layers in a single new image. Either way, it will leave the original image unchanged. (The last option, *Foreground as registration color,* is for high-end CMYK printing; it maps the current foreground color to black.)

In the new image, what you see is the top layer—in this case, the blue layer. You can view the other layers by clicking on the visibility buttons in the Layers dialog.

Figure 8-15. *Layers dialog after decomposing to RGB*

Tip You can make changes to these layers, then recombine them into a color image using Recompose (located right next to Decompose in the menus). You can also build a color image out of several unrelated grayscale images using Compose. This will let you choose among all of the grayscale layers (and only grayscale layers) currently open in the GIMP.

Decompose is fun because it lets you see the components of your image in several different color models. But it's also useful: you can modify one or more channels then *Recompose*, or you can use one of the layers as your final monochrome image, if you like it.

Often, the green layer of an RGB decomposition makes a good approximation to what the eye sees. Or try the value layer of an HSV decomposition (which should be equivalent to using the Hue-Saturation dialog and reducing saturation to zero).

The saturation layer of an HSV decomposition is particularly interesting—it looks a little like a black-and-white negative of the original image. The K layer of a CMYK decomposition also looks like a negative. But they're not really equivalent to a negative: if you want to see what a black-and-white negative of the image would actually look like, you can do that by converting to monochrome using any of the methods already discussed, and then selecting *Colors* ➤ *Invert*.

Decompose is also useful in making tricky selections, as you'll see later in this chapter.

Channel Mixer

Finally, if you want complete control, try *Colors* ➤ *Channel Mixer* (Figure 8-16). Clicking on *Monochrome* gives you an opportunity to convert to grayscale using a weighted average like luminosity uses, but with complete control over the weights for each color. Setting red to 21%, green to 72%, and blue to 7% matches the standard luminosity in GIMP 2.4 (earlier GIMPs used 30%, 59%, and 11%). But if your image might benefit from a little more red and less blue, or any other combination, Channel Mixer is for you.

Figure 8-16. *The Channel Mixer*

Notice that you can make the image much brighter or darker by using the sliders in the Channel Mixer. If you just want to adjust the weights of the colors, without changing overall brightness, the *Preserve luminosity* checkbox will adjust all the values so that the image's luminosity remains unchanged even if the three slider values add to more or less than 100%.

Coloring Monochrome Images and Making Sepia Photos

Some cameras have a "sepia" setting, which makes a black-and-white photo and then colors it brownish, like a photographic print that's been "toned" to make it last longer.

But if you like the look of sepia prints and your camera doesn't do them, you can make your own with GIMP. Start with a color photo (Figure 8-17).

Figure 8-17. *A color photograph to be converted to sepia*

Automatic Conversion with the "Old Photo" Filter

First, let's do it the easy way. GIMP already has a plug-in to do this conversion. It's in *Filters* ➤ *Decor* ➤ *Old Photo…* (Figure 8-18). Earlier versions of GIMP located this feature in *Script-Fu* ➤ *Decor* ➤ *Old Photo*.

- *Defocus* makes the focus a little softer.

- *Border size* creates a fuzzy border around the image, making it look like the edges have been torn. Change this value to 0 if you don't want a border.

- *Sepia* converts the image to black and white, and then tints it sepia (without this, the image will remain colored).

- *Mottle* creates mottling all over the photo, making it look like it's been sitting in a dusty drawer for 50 years.

- *Work on copy* creates a new image, leaving your original unchanged.

By default, it will *Defocus*, add a 20-pixel border, tint sepia, add no mottling, and create a copy.

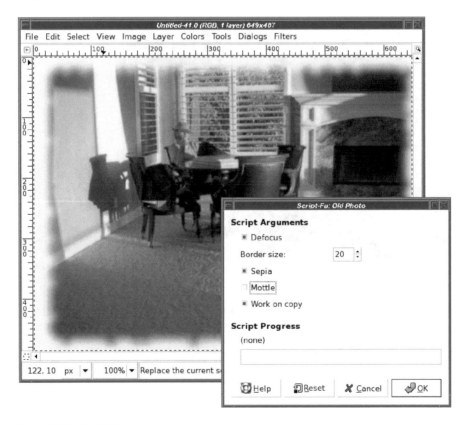

Figure 8-18. *The Old Photo plug-in*

Manual Conversion for Fine Control

How does it work? How can you use GIMP's color system to make your own sepia prints?

Let's try several techniques. They all begin by converting the color image to black and white. But make sure the image ends up in RGB mode, not grayscale, so you'll be able to add the sepia color.

Colorify

One method is by using the *Colorify* plug-in, accessed through *Colors* ➤ *Colorify* (Figure 8-19). Colorify tints an entire image as though you were looking through a filter. It starts with a small set of predefined colors, but by clicking on the *Custom Color* button, you can tint with any color you like.

Colorify tends to make images that are fairly dark. You have to make the tint color very light or you may end up with a muddy result.

Figure 8-19. *The Colorify plug-in*

Colorize

Easier to use is *Colors* ➤ *Colorize* (Figure 8-20). With the Hue, Saturation, and Lightness sliders, you get much more control over the image—and Colorize is a tool, so you get a full-sized preview. The only tricky part is finding the right hue. For sepia, you'll probably want to choose a hue down in the thirties, then increase lightness as needed to get the right effect.

Figure 8-20. *Tinting a black-and-white photo with Colorize*

Sample Colorize

Colors ➤ *Map* ➤ *Sample Colorize…* is like Colorify or Colorize except that it can take its input color range from any image. The image you're colorizing is on the left of the plug-in's dialog; on the right you can choose any image you already have open in GIMP or a gradient. Click on *Get Sample Colors* to calculate a color range from the image on the right. Then fiddle with the input and output level sliders, which work a lot like the ones in the Levels tool. When you like the look of the preview, click *Apply*.

Layer Modes

Finally, you can use layer modes. First, set the foreground color to a medium sepia color: **a28a65** (typed into the *HTML notation* box) works well as a starting point. Now, create a new layer that is entirely filled with this color by clicking on *New Layer* in the Layers dialog. Set the *Layer Fill Type* to *Foreground color*. This covers your original layer. But don't panic!

Go to the *Mode* menu in the Layers dialog and choose *Color* (Figure 8-21).

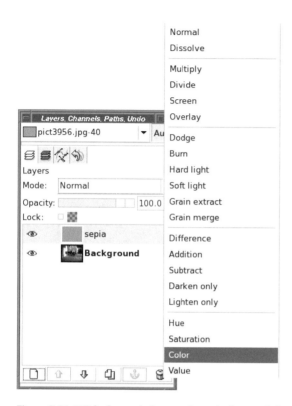

Figure 8-21. *With the sepia layer selected, choose Color in the Mode menu.*

This gives a sharper result than Colorize or Old Photo. Of course, you can use the Color layer mode to tint photos any shade, not just sepia; and you can create impressive effects by drawing different colors on different parts of the color layer. You'll learn more about colorizing with layer modes in Chapter 10.

Using Threshold to Clean Up Scanned Images

Have you ever tried to scan in a page from a book? It's especially tricky with an old yellowed book, or a page that has crumples and folds and dirt spots on it, or text showing through from the other side of the page. How can you clean up a page of text like Figure 8-22 into a nice black-and-white image?

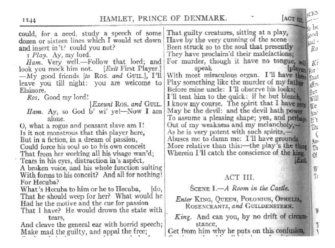

Figure 8-22. *A scanned page from an old yellowed book*

For anything that really ought to be black and white (with no shades of gray in between), the tool of choice is *Colors* ➤ *Threshold...* (Figure 8-23). Previous GIMP versions have it in *Layer* ➤ *Colors* ➤ *Threshold...*, and it can also be found in *Tools* ➤ *Color Tools* ➤ *Threshold....*

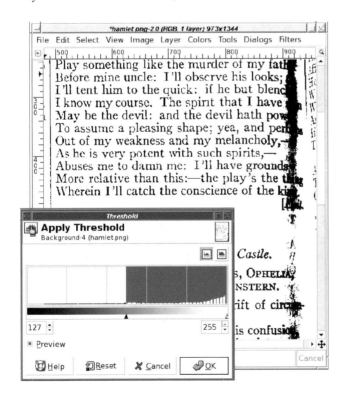

Figure 8-23. *The Threshold tool*

Threshold has two sliders, though most of the time you'll only need to adjust the left one. The sliders move along a bar showing a range of grayscales. The key to the Threshold tool: any pixel value between the two sliders—marked as blue in the tool—will be white in the resulting image. Anything that's darker than the left slider or brighter than the right slider will be black. (Yes, that's slightly counterintuitive. To give the image more white, you want less white—more blue—in the tool's dialog.)

To adjust the darkness of an image such as a scan, slide the left slider until you're happy with the result.

So what's the right slider for, anyway? Adjusting the right slider will take anything that's very bright in the image, and make it black instead of white. This may sound like an odd thing to do, and generally it's not useful in scans. However, you can also use the Threshold tool on a photograph to make selection masks—you'll see how later in this chapter. Occasionally being able to select a brightness region somewhere in the middle can help a lot in making a selection.

Threshold, since it creates an image that's purely black and white, will eliminate any "aliasing" smoothing the edges of lines, sometimes resulting in a "jaggy" look. When you want smoother edges and don't mind some gray in the image, Curves or Levels may be a better tool than Threshold. Try all of them to become familiar with the differences.

In Figure 8-23, Threshold works fine for everything except the right edge, where the page curves away toward the binding. Using Levels or Curves doesn't help with that, either. So how do you fix it? Easy: with layer masks.

Make a duplicate layer with the original scanned page. Run Threshold on that layer too—but set the threshold so that the text at the right edge comes out looking right. Now all you need to do is combine those two layers with a gradient layer mask…just like the "ostraffe" layer mask project in Chapter 5.

Indexed Color

An image with indexed color contains only a fixed set of colors, usually 256 or fewer. You've already read about indexed formats such as GIF and indexed PNG in Chapter 2. There, you saw an example of how the number of colors can change the quality of the image.

The list of colors in the image is called the image's *palette*, like an artist's palette holding the pigments to be used in a painting. The file size of an indexed image depends very much on the number of colors in the palette. Indexed formats can be efficient when they have only a small number of colors. They're ideal for small web images such as icons for buttons or forward/backward arrows.

Every image loaded into GIMP has a color mode, represented in the title bar of the image window. For instance, in Figure 8-24, the title bar shows that the image is in RGB mode.

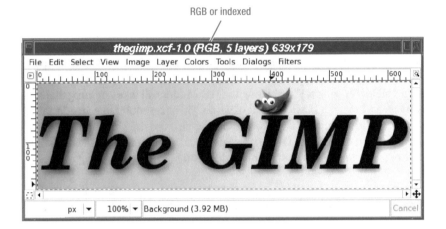

Figure 8-24. *The title bar for this logo shows that the image is RGB, not indexed.*

Saving an image as GIF will automatically convert it to indexed mode, since GIF images are always indexed. But you usually won't get the smallest possible image that way: GIMP will use 256 colors, when four might have sufficed. You're much better off converting the image to indexed mode yourself, even for GIF. To save in indexed PNG format, converting to indexed mode is your only option. Since PNG images can be either indexed or full color, GIMP uses the image's mode to determine which form of PNG to use.

A Typical Indexing Problem: Choosing the Palette

Suppose you've made a logo such as Figure 8-24, and want to save it in an indexed format. How do you make the image size as small as possible?

To convert to indexed mode, use *Image* ➤ *Mode* ➤ *Indexed....* Figure 8-25 shows the options.

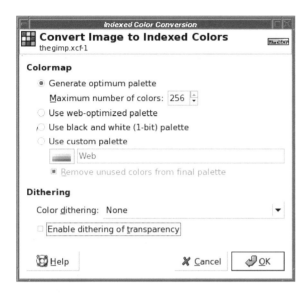

Figure 8-25. *Options when converting to indexed mode*

By default, GIMP chooses *Generate optimum palette*, which creates a palette of the colors in the image, and no others. Most of the time, this is your best choice. The other options offer palettes for special cases.

The black-and-white palette, which contains only those two colors, can save a lot of space if your image truly only contains those two colors (no shades of gray).

The web-optimized palette and the Web palette in the custom palette list use colors that used to be standard in web browsers. Today, nearly all web browsers and computers support 24-bit true color, so web palettes are much less important. You're usually better off optimizing a palette for each image.

The trick in converting to indexed mode is in choosing the right number of colors: the smallest number for which the image still looks good enough. Start with a small number, like four or eight (make a guess based on how many colors you think the image should need), and click *OK* (Figure 8-26).

Figure 8-26. *An eight-color palette*

Yuck! The image looks awful! That's clearly not enough colors, so undo and try a different setting. (Converting to indexed, alas, does not have a preview.)

Dithering an Indexed Image

Take a look at those options again. An image that has shades of color can often benefit from *dithering*: combining several colors in the palette to simulate colors that aren't there. Dithering will increase file size significantly, but not as much as increasing the number of colors.

The dialog offers several dithering options:

- The two *Floyd-Steinberg* options differ only subtly.

- *Positioned* dithering is usually best for animated GIFs.

- *Enable dithering of transparency* can help if you have any partially transparent layers.

Figure 8-27 shows the effect of starting with that same 8-color palette and adding *Floyd-Steinberg (reduced color bleeding)* dithering plus dithering of transparency. The shadows around the letters are now dithered with black dots, but they still don't look at all like a shadow. There's good news too: the transition in the color background looks much smoother now, as you can see in the zoomed image (Figure 8-28).

Figure 8-27. *An 8-color palette with Floyd-Steinberg (reduced color bleeding) dithering and dithering of transparency*

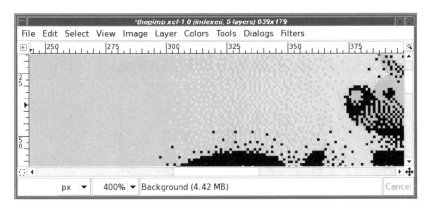

Figure 8-28. *Figure 8-27 is zoomed in to show how dithering helps the background look smooth.*

Flatten for Better Dithering

What's the problem? Well, part of the problem is that converting an image with multiple layers to indexed mode often doesn't work very well. This image has five layers: the background, the text, the text's shadow, Wilber, and Wilber's shadow. GIMP is trying to index each of these layers separately—and so the dithering on those shadow layers looks very poor. There are two solutions.

First, get rid of the layers. *Image ➤ Flatten Image* or *Merge Visible Layers* (both of them also available from the context menu in the Layers dialog) combine all layers into one. That means it will be difficult to do any further editing on the image, so it may be best to make a copy of the image (*Image ➤ Duplicate*). Then flatten and convert the copy so that you can keep all your layers in your original XCF.

Note What's the difference between *Flatten* and *Merge Visible Layers*? They differ in two ways. First, *Flatten* will remove any invisible layers and leave you with only one layer in the image, while *Merge Visible Layers* will leave any invisible layers untouched. Second, *Flatten* will also remove any transparency, while *Merge Visible Layers* keeps it. If you don't have any transparency or invisible layers in your image, you can use either one—they'll both do the same thing.

The flattened image looks much better when indexed, even with only eight colors (Figure 8-29).

Figure 8-29. *Flattening the image helps quite a bit.*

Redesigning for Better Indexed Results

But sometimes, if the goal is to make a very small image, simplifying the design can help more. The sad fact is that those lovely, subtle color fades you can make in GIMP don't translate very well to indexed formats.

If you can change the design to eliminate shading, you can make a *much* smaller image. In Figure 8-30, all the shading (except in Wilber himself) has been removed and the image converted to indexed with no dithering. This resulted in a GIF file less than 5K, as compared to 6.1K for the dithered version and 15.8K for the image in Figure 8-29.

Figure 8-30. *Shading removed, converted as eight colors with no dithering*

Doubtless you're wondering, "Why all this fuss over a mere 10 kilobytes?" Of course, for a single image there isn't much point trying to make your images this small. But some web pages have hundreds of images on them. If you design your icons to have small file sizes, that can make the difference between a web page that loads instantly and one that loads so slowly that users give up on it and go someplace else.

Tip Do you ever find that the GIMP function you want to use is grayed out when you're working with an image you loaded from a GIF file? Most often, it's because your image is in indexed mode, perhaps because it was originally a GIF image. Many of GIMP's color functions will only work on an RGB image (or sometimes a grayscale image), and will be disabled for indexed images. This is because an indexed image does not allow a full range of colors. If you see color functions disabled and wonder why, check the title bar of the image window and see if it says "Indexed." If so, a quick conversion (using the *Mode* menu) back to RGB mode will solve the problem. If that doesn't enable the function, check whether the image has an alpha channel; some filters require one. Of course, if you ultimately want to save to GIF or indexed PNG, you'll have to convert back to indexed mode before you save.

Editing the Palette

What if you want to change one of the colors in an indexed image?

Dialogs ➤ *Colormap* brings up the colormap editor (Figure 8-31). This window shows every color currently in the image.

To change a color, simply double-click on the color square to bring up a color chooser. Alternately, click on a square and then edit the *HTML notation* box and press Return. Or click on a color, and then click the lower-left button in the dialog (its tooltip calls it *Edit color*).

Figure 8-31. *Editing a colormap*

Color index lets you move to the next or previous colors, though clicking on the appropriate square is usually just as easy.

The + button in the lower right is *Add color from FG*. It adds a new entry in the colormap, using GIMP's current foreground color. Note that this will slightly increase the size of your colormap, and therefore your image.

Between the colormap editor and making corrections with the Pencil tool, you can usually fix any dithering problems in your indexed image. In the end, you get a clean image to put on the web.

Picking Colors from the Image

While cleaning up that indexed image, the Color Picker tool was awfully helpful. It was introduced back in the animation section of Chapter 3, but it comes in especially handy here.

One problem you may have with indexed images is difficulty in using GIMP's normal color chooser. For instance, in the indexed Wilber image, if I set GIMP's foreground color to bright red and try to draw on the image, what actually appears is a muddy brown. What gives?

An indexed image can display *only* the colors in the palette. If you attempt to draw with a color that's not in the palette, GIMP will try to pick the closest color—almost certainly not what you want.

The solution is to use GIMP's Color Picker tool to grab a specific color from the image, as in Figure 8-32. That way, you'll be sure of getting a color from the right palette.

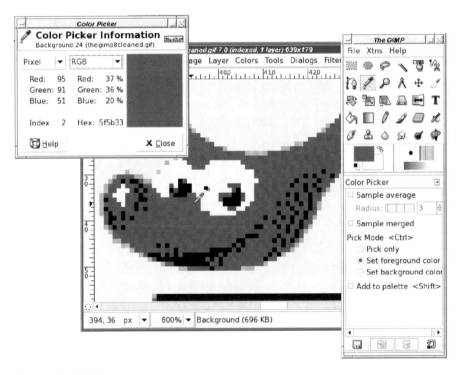

Figure 8-32. *Picking a color*

The Color Channels

GIMP maintains three special color masks that show the red, green, and blue components of the current image. You can see them in the Channels dialog, usually docked as a tab with Layers and Paths (Figure 8-33). Light colors means a lot of the indicated color; dark means less. Notice the white flower in the blue channel (the flower petals have a lot of blue in them), the general lightness of the green channel (there's a lot of green in the photo), and darkness of the red (there's a little red in the flower but not much anywhere else).

Figure 8-33. *The color channels*

However, the previews in the dialog are too small to see much detail. You can make them a bit larger using the *Preview Size* item in the tab configuration menu—to the right of the Layers label in the dialog—but they'll still be small compared to the full-sized image. Also, not many operations work directly on the color channels. You can turn a color channel into a selection (via the context menu in the Channels dialog), but for more detailed work with color channels, you're usually better off using *Decompose* to create an image with red, green, and blue layers.

Selection Using Color Decomposition

Remember *Colors* ➤ *Components* ➤ *Decompose*, discussed earlier under "Working with Grayscale or Black and White"? There, you saw how to use it to convert images to grayscale in several ways. But it's far more useful than that. What interesting things can you do with color decomposition?

Well, for example, you could select that flower from Figure 8-33.

If you right-click on the blue channel (in the Channels dialog) and choose *Channel to Selection*, the "marching ants" make it look like you have a pretty good selection of the flower. But that's deceptive.

There's a problem: nothing is *completely* selected. The flower was mostly blue, but not pure blue, so it gets mostly selected. The grass around the flower has some blue, so a little bit of that gets into the selection too. Instead of getting all of the flower and none of the grass, you get a mostly opaque flower and mostly transparent grass.

If you paste the selection onto a white background, you'll see something like Figure 8-34. It might make a nice background for stationery, but it's not what you thought you had selected.

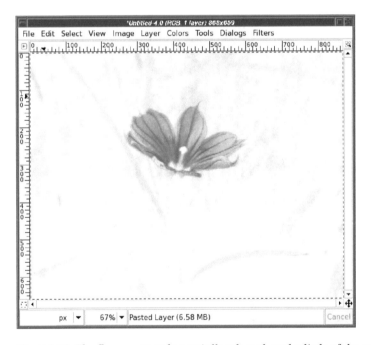

Figure 8-34. *The flower was only partially selected, and a little of the grass was also selected.*

Decomposing to RGB can give a better result. Figure 8-35 shows the blue layer, which is basically the same as the blue channel. You can see lots of pieces of the background, not just the flower. But since it's in a layer now, you can modify it to be more useful.

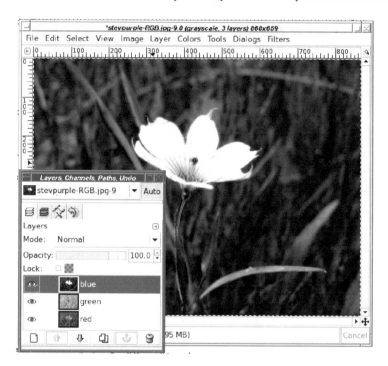

Figure 8-35. *The blue layer of the RGB decomposition*

Use Threshold and QuickMask to Improve the Selection

To turn the blue layer into a useful selection mask, use the Threshold tool (Figure 8-36). A tool such as Levels or Curves will also work.

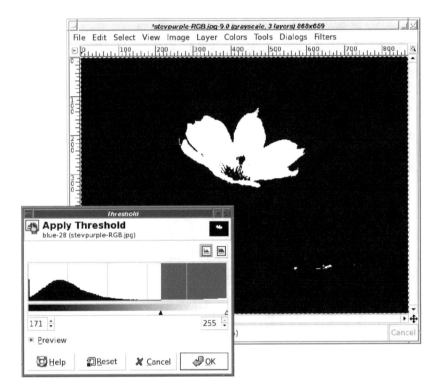

Figure 8-36. *Threshold on the blue channel gives a much cleaner selection.*

Once you've set the threshold, you can use drawing tools to clean up the selection. Paint out (in black) anything you don't want, like those white bits in the bottom right; and paint in (in white) anything you do want, like the center of the flower. Once you're happy with your selection mask layer, copy it (Ctrl+C).

Now go back to your original image, and activate the QuickMask (remember it from Chapter 5?) by clicking on the dotted square at the lower left of the image window.

A simple paste (Ctrl+V) onto the QuickMask, then click the *Anchor* button (this is one of the few times you want to anchor a floating layer rather than make it a new layer) and your selection is ready (Figure 8-37). Switch from QuickMask mode back into normal mode and copy, and you have a perfect flower that's ready to paste anywhere.

Tip This method also works well for creating a layer mask. To avoid the sharp edges that the Threshold tool can create, try Levels instead.

Figure 8-37. *The flower is now selected.*

Decomposing to HSV

With Decompose, though, you aren't restricted to using just the RGB color channels. HSV decomposition can be even more useful in extracting a glaring overcast sky (Figure 8-38).

Figure 8-38. *The overcast sky ended up overexposed, spoiling this photo.*

Decompose to HSV, and then run Threshold on the value layer (Figure 8-39). Clean up any stray pixels with a drawing tool such as the Paintbrush, and you're ready to select the sky.

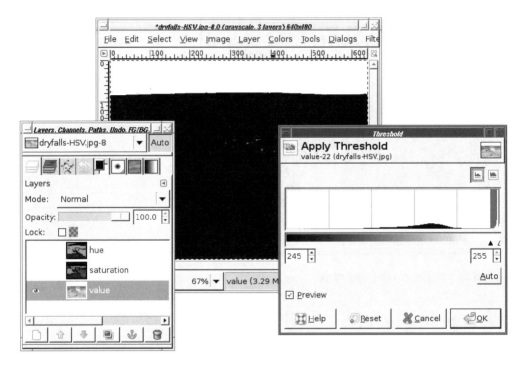

Figure 8-39. *Run Threshold on the value layer.*

Once the sky is selected (you may also want to *grow* or *feather* the selection by a few pixels), you can make a replacement light blue sky (Figure 8-40). But it doesn't look right.

Figure 8-40. *Solid-colored skies don't look realistic.*

What's wrong with the sky in Figure 8-40? Real skies are darker and bluer up high, fading to lighter colors down low. So use a gradient and two similar shades of blue to make a more realistic sky (Figure 8-41).

Figure 8-41. *A gradient between two shades of blue makes a much more realistic-looking sky.*

But it's not always the Value channel you want. For the photo in Figure 8-42, the Hue channel works better than Value for selecting the sky. But that's not all you can do.

Figure 8-42. *For some skies, the hue layer works better than value.*

The saturation layer is even more useful: it can separate the clouds from the blue sky, because the sky is much more saturated than the clouds are. For selecting clouds you'll want to use Levels (Figure 8-43) or Curves, not Threshold, because to select fuzzy edges you need levels of gray, not just black and white.

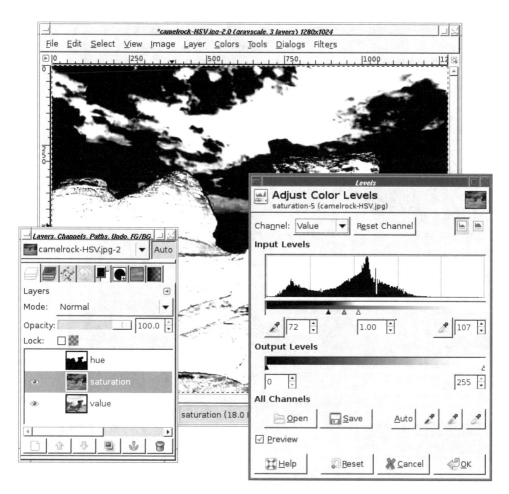

Figure 8-43. *Use Levels on the saturation layer to separate clouds from sky.*

You may notice that the layer in Figure 8-43 is also selecting some of the rock, not just the sky. But that's okay because I'm using it as a layer mask for the sky layer I pasted earlier—that layer contains only sky, no rock. Copy the saturation layer, then right-click on the sky layer and choose *Add layer mask…* (the initial value doesn't matter since you're about to paste into it). Paste the saturation layer, and click the *Anchor* button to make it replace the layer mask. And now you're ready to use Brightness/Contrast, Hue/Saturation, or any other operation you like on the sky. By using the saturation of the sky compared to the clouds, you can select just the blue sky, and make it darker blue…or any other color you like (Figure 8-44).

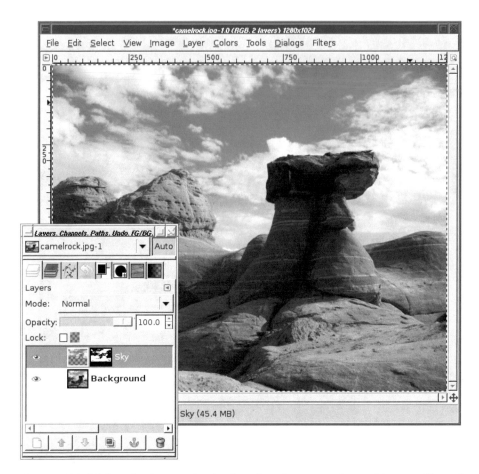

Figure 8-44. *With just the sky (not the clouds) selected, you can do anything you like to the sky color.*

Some Color-mapping Toys

The *Colors* menu has a few interesting entries remaining.

Filter Pack is a complex plug-in that gives you a choice of several operations you can apply to your image. It can change *Hue*, *Saturation*, and *Value*, or you can edit the color curve directly (under *Advanced*). Of course, you can already do all those operations using separate color tools, but Filter Pack lets you combine several operations at once. It also gives you a choice of operating on any combination of Shadows, Midtones, and Highlights; and you can pick those shadows, midtones, and highlights according to Hue, Saturation, or Value. You can even apply the same effect over and over again: for instance, turn on *Saturation* and click the button for *More Sat,* then click it again, and again, to get a wild, oversaturated view.

Find all these buttons too confusing? You might prefer individual tools—but play around with Filter Pack and see what you can create.

Hot finds bright areas that might give problems on TV screens.

Maximum RGB intensifies every color in the image to its brightest and most saturated—or, if you choose *minimal channels*, its least saturated.

Retinex is a useful filter that can bring out detail in dark images taken in very low light. The effect is quite different from the simple brightening you might get from Levels, Curves, or Brightness/Contrast. Its results are sometimes grainy, but if you're trying to squeeze detail out of a dark photo, it's definitely worth a try.

Colors ➤ *Map* also has some plug-ins I haven't mentioned yet. Most of them aren't very useful for everyday work with real images, but they can help you create some wild special effects.

Rearrange Colormap… lets you adjust the order of colors within an indexed image's palette. *Set Colormap…* lets you change the palette of an indexed image to one of GIMP's named palettes. You can also add palettes of your own, in the *palettes* folder in your GIMP profile.

Adjust Foreground and Background only works if you set GIMP's foreground and background colors to something other than black and white. It takes no arguments, but changes the image's dark pixels to shades of the foreground color, while changing light pixels to shades of the background. Why? Nobody knows…the filter may be removed in future GIMP versions.

Alien Map… can shift all the colors in your image in unpredictable and psychedelic ways. It offers two modes, RGB or HSL (similar to HSV, with L meaning luminosity), and a handful of sliders. It rotates each channel as many times as you specify with the *frequency* slider, while the *phase shift* sliders can make it start at a different place. But honestly, it's difficult to predict what any combination of settings will do. You'll probably do best by sliding knobs at random to see what happens.

Color Exchange… lets you exchange one color with another (similar to *Select by Color* followed by *Fill with FG*, or to the color exchange found on some digital cameras). You can select the color to be replaced by middle-clicking in the preview window. But beware: by default it's very picky about only replacing the exact color you've selected, so on a photograph, you may not see any replacement at all. To make Color Exchange more lenient about what it considers a match, set the three Threshold sliders to numbers larger than 0.0.

Color Range Mapping… is a bit easier to use (though whether it's actually useful is arguable). It maps all colors in the range between the background and foreground colors (you can't choose the color from the plug-in's dialog as you can with Color Exchange), so choose your two colors first, perhaps by using the Color Picker tool to choose colors from the image. But beware: it doesn't map only colors that are between the two colors you specify. It maps all colors in the image, extrapolating from the colors you've specified. If you only want to map the colors of part of your image, select the part you care about first, or use *Rotate Colors*, described in a moment.

Gradient Map replaces the image with colors taken from the current gradient. The darkest parts of the image will map to the left side of the gradient, and the lightest parts to the right side.

Palette Map is similar, except it takes colors from the current palette. If you don't work much with indexed images, you might not even know that you have a current palette. You can see it, or choose another, with *File* ➤ *Dialogs* ➤ *Palettes…* from the Toolbox window.

Rotate Colors… is a powerful way to map a color range to another. It's what you probably hoped *Color Range Mapping* would do. Don't panic at the complexity of the dialog—it's surprisingly easy to use. Drag the arrows on the upper ("From") color wheel to span the color range you want to replace. Pay attention to the arc between the two arrows, so you know which arrow is the starting point and which is the end point. If you want to reverse them, you can click on *Change Order of Arrows* or you can just drag one arrow past the other one. Then set the new color (which will replace the "From" color) the same way, and keep an eye on the preview to see if it's doing what you expected. Figure 8-45 shows how to replace a range of blues with reds.

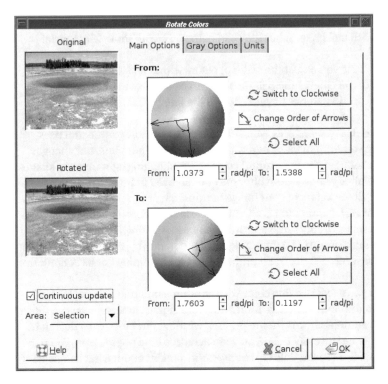

Figure 8-45. *Rotate Colors is an easy way to turn water and sky red.*

The *Gray Options* tab of Rotate Colors lets you specify what to do with gray areas in the image, since the Main Options color wheel can't represent them. *Gray Threshold* specifies how desaturated a color has to be before it's considered to be gray. These gray areas will be mapped to whatever color you set in the *Gray Options* color wheel. *Gray Mode* lets you specify whether to do this substitution before or after doing the color rotation: with *Change to this* GIMP won't do any further substitution, while with *Treat as this* the replacement color will be mapped to a color in the output range.

Sample Colorize…, already discussed in the "Sepia Photos" section earlier in this chapter, rounds out the *Colors* ➤ *Map* menu.

Color Profiles

Different computer systems display colors very…differently. If you've ever viewed the same photo on both a Mac and a PC, you've probably seen how much the colors and brightness can vary.

One way to compensate for that is by using color profiles. These are files (usually with an .icc or .icm extension) that represent the difference between a standard baseline (called the *sRGB* profile) and the capabilities of a particular device like a monitor, printer, or scanner.

Some devices such as monitors and scanners come with a color profile included, and if you install the driver that comes with the device, it may install a profile as well. However, that can backfire: sometimes device profiles are wrong. If you notice odd colors—say you try to paint in white but the result looks yellow, or you notice images are much darker or lighter when viewed in GIMP than they are when viewed with other programs—the culprit might be a color profile.

You can choose profiles in the Preferences window's *Color Management* category (Figure 8-46). *Modes of operation* can be *No color management* (GIMP won't look for color profiles at all), *Color managed display* (use color profiles), or *Print simulation* (temporarily switch to using the printer's profile—this is also called *soft proofing*).

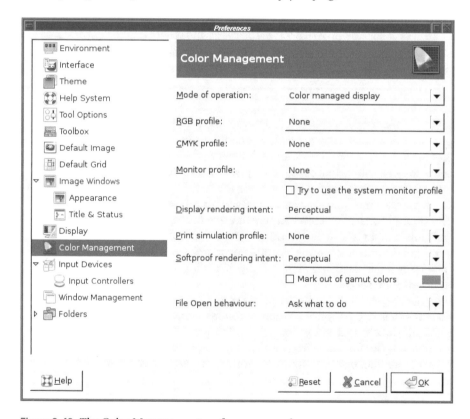

Figure 8-46. *The Color Management preferences panel*

Then there's a list of profiles to set. *RGB Profile* is GIMP's notion of the "standard" sRGB working space. Normally it should be set to None to use GIMP's built-in sRGB space, but you can set a profile explicitly if you have a newer or slightly different version. *CMYK profile*, too, is GIMP's notion of the default CMYK color space; it's used primarily by the CMYK color chooser and when loading image files that use CMYK.

Monitor profile describes your monitor, but there's a problem: monitor profiles are very dependent on ambient lighting conditions, so ideally you should use a different profile for a monitor located near a window vs. the same monitor used in a windowless room lit with fluorescent light. Since the manufacturer doesn't know what your computer room is like, any profile shipped with the monitor is at best a compromise. At worst, it might be just plain wrong.

A common source of problems, especially on Windows, is the *Try to use the system monitor profile* checkbox. If that option is on, GIMP will use whatever it finds in the standard system location—probably somewhere under *C:\windows\system\color* on Windows, or */Library/ColorSync/Profiles* or */Library/Printers/[manufacturer]/Profiles* on Mac. Linux doesn't have a system color profile.

■**Caution** A lot of monitor profiles installed with a Windows driver package are just plain wrong, and can lead to all sorts of odd color problems in GIMP. If you find that all images opened in GIMP have a color cast—white looks yellowish or greenish—the first thing you should try is switching *Mode of operation* to *No color management* and see if the problem goes away. If it does, you may have a bad monitor profile installed.

If you really care about exact color, you can buy monitor calibration devices that can measure your monitor's output under the lighting conditions you use most, and create an exact color profile for it. For making quick-and-dirty color profiles without any specialized hardware, there's an open source tool called *lprof*, part of the LittleCMS color management package. Or you can use your system's color profiling tool: on Mac, go to *System Preferences* ➤ *Displays*, click on the *Color* tab, and then click the *Calibrate* button. On Windows, the Microsoft Color Control Panel applet lets you generate and manage color profiles. If your system has it, you'll find a Color tool in the Windows Control Panel. If it's not already available on your system, you can download it from Microsoft.com: search for *WinColorSetup.exe*.

Display rendering intent describes different ways of dealing with colors that can't be shown in the current color space.

Print simulation mode is the place to set your printer's profile (if you have one) so that you can predict how an image will print out (and *Softproof rendering intent* and *Mark out of gamut colors* describe how to treat colors that are hard to convert to CMYK). Printer profiles are usually accurate only for one set of inks and one type of paper, so if you print to different papers or with ink other than the manufacturer's, you may need an updated profile.

Embedded Color Profiles

The last item in the *Color Management* preferences is *File Open behavior,* which tells GIMP what to do when it encounters a file with an embedded color profile.

Many imaging devices, like digital cameras and scanners, include a color profile whenever they save a file. If GIMP detects such a color profile when you open an image, it will ask you whether to convert the image to the sRGB workspace. Usually it's a good idea to let GIMP convert the file. The alternative is for GIMP to work on the file without converting (the colors may look slightly wrong to you) and keep the color profile attached when saving the image. If you always want to do one or the other, you can set a preference here so GIMP will no longer ask.

Summary

By now, you probably know more about color than you ever wanted to know.

You're familiar with all of the common color models and some of the theory behind them. You know about indexed color, grayscale, RGB, and alpha; how to tell the color mode of your image, and how to change it.

You've worked with GIMP's different color choosers, and you've probably picked a favorite that you use most of the time. You may even switch among several of them depending on the sort of project you're working on.

You know several methods to correct a photograph's color cast, to change a color image to black and white, or to reduce the amount of color in an image. You've also seen several ways to add color to monochrome images.

When you need to use an indexed image, you know how to optimize it so you can get a good-looking image that only requires a very small file size. You can clean up scanned images by adjusting their color levels. You know how to decompose an image into its component colors, and how you can use that to help you make tricky selections. And finally, you know a little about color management and how to tune GIMP's handling of color profiles.

You'll find many of these techniques helpful as you move on to the next chapter and explore some advanced drawing tricks.

CHAPTER 9

■■■

Advanced Drawing

In Chapter 4, you learned the basics of drawing with GIMP. But there are still quite a few tricks that can give your drawings more polish.

In this chapter, you'll learn how to use layer masks, gradients, and layer modes to create great-looking drawings and logos. You'll learn how to control the Perspective tool, and create shadows and highlights. Finally, you'll learn how to create your own brushes, gradients, and other GIMP resources. The chapter will cover the following:

- Useful mask tricks

- Layer modes

- Creating depth: drawing with layer modes

- Drawing realistic shadows

- Realism and multipoint perspective

- Adding reflections and shading

- Making brushes, patterns, and gradients

Useful Mask Tricks

You learned about the basics of layer masks in Chapter 5, and saw one use for them. But there are all sorts of interesting effects you can create with layer masks.

Making Text "Fade Out"

One of the easiest uses of a layer mask is to make some text (or any other layer) fade out.
Just follow two easy steps:

1. Add a layer mask. Right-click on the layer in the Layers dialog and choose *Add Layer Mask....* Initialize it to *White (full opacity)*, the default setting.

2. Draw a gradient on the mask. The layer mask should already be selected since you just created it. If not, click on its thumbnail in the Layers dialog. Choose the Blend (Gradient) tool in the Toolbox, and the standard foreground and background colors of black and white, respectively.

Then just drag in the image to draw the gradient. You can drag exactly vertically or horizontally (remember, holding down the Ctrl key while you drag will help by constraining the gradient's angle to a multiple of 15 degrees), or you can drag in any direction you like.

In this case, I started with a layer that had the text and drop shadow already merged together, and then dragged diagonally, from the lower right toward the upper left of the text-and-shadow layer (Figure 9-1). You can see the gradient in the layer mask's thumbnail in the Layers dialog.

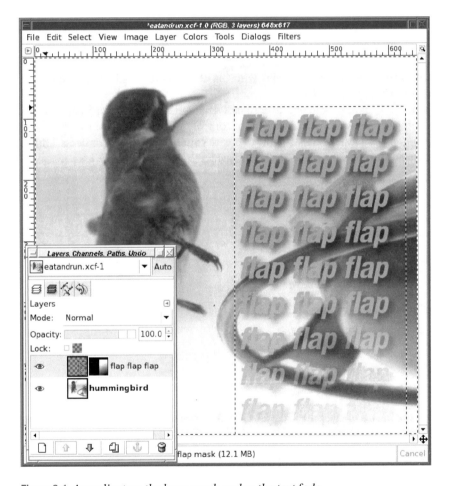

Figure 9-1. *A gradient on the layer mask makes the text fade.*

Making a Fuzzy Border

A layer mask can also give an image a fuzzy border, so that it fades into the background. This gives a nice effect for images included on web pages.

The procedure is straightforward. First choose your favorite selection tool. Turn on feathering (you'll probably want as much feathering as possible), and then make a selection where you want your border to be (Figure 9-2).

Figure 9-2. *Make a selection where you want the border to be.*

Now add a layer mask to the image layer: right-click on the layer in the Layers dialog and choose *Add Layer Mask….* (In some GIMP versions, you may not be able to create a layer mask unless the image has transparency. If *Add Layer Mask…* is grayed out, use *Layer* ➤ *Transparency* ➤ *Add Alpha Channel* for that.) Under *Initialize Layer Mask to:* choose *Selection* (Figure 9-3). This will make the new layer mask white inside the selection and black outside of it, which is exactly what you want.

Now you have an image with a fuzzy boundary. Everything outside the selection is transparent, so GIMP will show it with a checkerboard pattern.

To find out how the image will really look on a website, there are two additional steps. First, hide the selection with *View* ➤ *Show Selection* or Ctrl+T. Second, make a new layer of white (or any other background color you prefer) and move it below the image layer. That will give you a much better idea of how your fuzzy border looks (Figure 9-4).

Figure 9-3. *Make a new layer mask, initialized to "Selection."*

Figure 9-4. *Adding a white background layer and making the selection invisible gives you a much better idea of how the border will look.*

If you're happy with the result, make the selection visible again (that way, you won't be surprised the next time you try to select something), and then cancel it (*Select* ➤ *None*). Save the image as JPEG since it's full color—unless you absolutely need the transparency. If you do, make the background layer invisible (you won't want to save that part), and then save in a format that allows transparency, such as GIF or PNG (refer back to "Image File Types" in Chapter 2 for a discussion of the trade-offs).

Even Bigger Fuzzy Borders

What if you want more feathering than the 100 pixels that GIMP allows in its selection tools?

While you still have the selection, you can use *Select* ➤ *Feather....* But that doesn't let you preview what the border will look like.

A better solution is to make sure the layer mask is selected (it will have a white border, as in Figure 9-5)—and then blur it with *Filters* ➤ *Blur* ➤ *Gaussian Blur....*

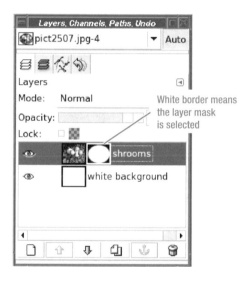

Figure 9-5. *A selected layer mask has a white border.*

Blurring the existing 100-pixel feathering by another 250 pixels gives a more gradual border, as shown in Figure 9-6.

Figure 9-6. *Blur the layer mask to get a more gradual border.*

But wait—what's wrong with Figure 9-6? Notice what happens at the edges. All this blurring has made the border extend beyond the edges of the image. If you put the image on a web page, you'll see squared-off edges, as in Figure 9-7.

Figure 9-7. *Blurring beyond the size of the image creates squared-off edges.*

This happens because the oval frame gets bigger when it's blurred, and the image isn't big enough to contain it. For a really fuzzy border, you have to leave quite a bit of room around your original selection. If you want a *lot* of fade at the boundary, your best bet is to avoid cropping much until the very end.

Note You can do the same sort of operation on GIMP's QuickMask: select the image with a fuzzy border, and then paste it onto a white background. Why use a layer mask? Because that makes it easier to see the effect of the operation. With the QuickMask, you have to modify the mask, change it to a selection, copy it, and paste it somewhere else—only then will you see whether you need to go back and modify the Quick-Mask.

Of course, since the layer mask is just a black-and-white image itself, you can modify it in a variety of ways to make all sorts of borders, like the ones in Figure 9-8. Experiment! You may not like most of the effects, but you might also find the perfect look.

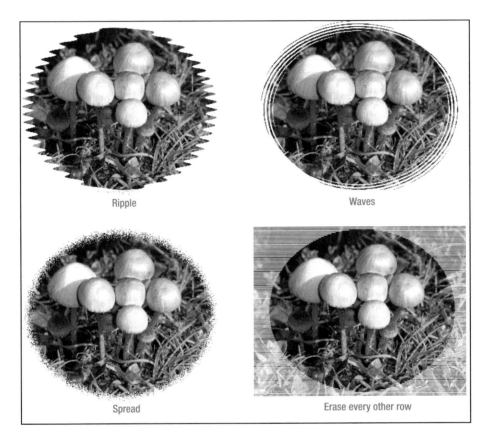

Figure 9-8. *You can make all sorts of frames using layer masks.*

INTERPRETING THE MASK BORDER COLOR

Sometimes it's hard to tell the mode of a layer mask. But it's a lot easier if you learn to decode the colors of the mask thumbnail's border in the Layers dialog:

- *Black*: Not selected.

- *White*: Selected. If you draw, you will draw on the mask.

- *Green*: Displayed. GIMP will display the contents of the layer mask, rather than applying it as a mask. When in this mode, the border color doesn't help you tell whether the mask is selected for drawing; to find out, check the color of the layer preview next to the mask preview. If the layer preview is black (unselected) but the layer is highlighted in the dialog, the layer mask is selected.

- *Red*: Disabled. Again, you can't tell whether or not the layer mask is selected if it's disabled, so check the layer preview's border color.

Layer Modes

By now, you should be comfortable with adding layers to an image. Generally, when you put one layer on top of another, the top layer is what you see. Lower layers only show through when the upper layer is at least partially transparent.

But layers can be combined in many other ways, using *layer modes*. You'll find them in the *Mode* menu in the Layers dialog. GIMP will use a layer's mode to determine how to combine each pixel from the top layer with the pixel in the same location in the layer below. Layer modes are also called *blending modes*, because they specify how to blend the colors in a layer with the colors in the layer below it (this has nothing to do with the Blend tool, however).

Note The *Mode* drop-down menu in the drawing tool options, which you've already seen in Chapter 4, works basically the same way that layer modes do. It also adds a few special modes that are only used for drawing tools.

Confusing? Let's look at an example.

Figure 9-9 shows a red swirl on a white background. Of course, the swirl is in a separate layer from the background.

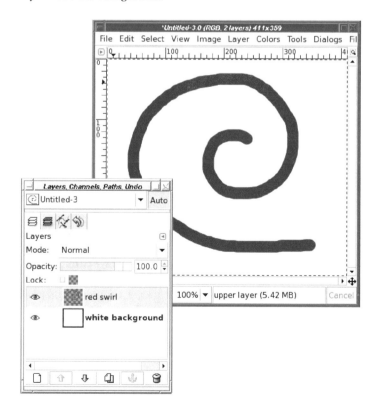

Figure 9-9. *A red swirl layer on a white background layer*

Where the swirl is red, you're seeing just that—red. The layer mode is *Normal*, so GIMP takes each pixel in the top layer (the red swirl), determines that it's not transparent, and shows you only that. Outside of the swirl, the top layer is transparent, so GIMP shows you the next layer down. Simple!

But what happens if you set the layer mode to *Subtract* (Figure 9-10)?

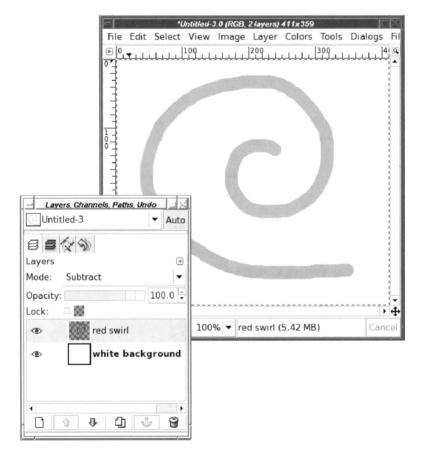

Figure 9-10. *The red swirl with Subtract mode*

Why did the red swirl turn that color?

In Subtract mode, the color you see is the result of subtracting the front layer (the swirl) from the back layer (the background). Each color channel is subtracted separately.

Remember that white is the combination of the three primary colors: red, green, and blue. Each color has a range from 0 to 255 (8 bits, in computer terminology). A white pixel is (255, 255, 255) to GIMP. A red pixel is (255, 0, 0): all the red, with no green or blue. So:

```
white - red = (255 - 255, 255 - 0, 255 - 0)
```

or (0, 255, 255).

The result has no red at all, but full green and blue: it's cyan. That's why the red swirl on top of a white background becomes cyan in Subtract mode.

A lot of the modes don't do anything interesting when the background is white. For instance, in *Addition* mode, the colors of the two layers are added together. But white already contains a full complement of each color. You can't get any whiter than white, so in Addition mode, the red swirl just becomes white and disappears in the background. For the same reason, other modes won't seem to do anything useful if the background is black.

A Quick Tour Through All of GIMP's Layer Modes

Figure 9-11 shows all of GIMP's layer modes, using the tree from Chapter 4 against a background of light blue/cyan.

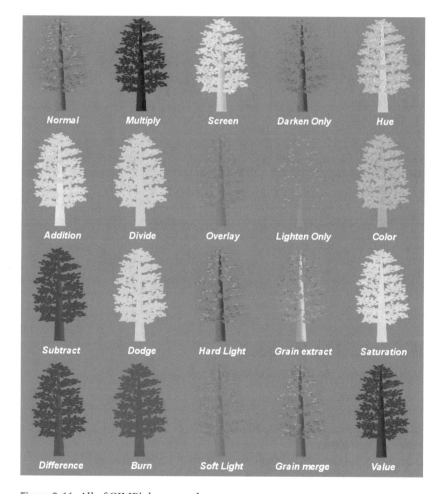

Figure 9-11. *All of GIMP's layer modes*

Be careful not to draw too many conclusions from this one diagram, though. The effects of each layer mode can vary considerably depending on the colors of the layers involved, as you'll see. Also, though it may not seem like it as you read through, all these modes have their uses—which are often not what you'd expect at all! But more on that later.

Dissolve and the two special drawing tool modes Behind and Color Erase were discussed in Chapter 4. Now I'll cover the other modes, what they do, and some ways to use them. You'll learn even more uses for the layer modes in Chapter 10.

MATHEMATICALLY SPEAKING

In the discussions of the individual modes, I'll give equations for what each mode is actually doing "under the hood." If you're mathematically inclined, this can help you to better understand what the modes do.

If that doesn't describe you, don't panic! You don't have to understand the equations to "get" layer modes. Many talented artists use GIMP's layer modes to create beautiful art without ever worrying about the mathematical underpinnings. If you're not comfortable thinking about colors as vectors, or with the mathematical operations, just skip the equations (and the rest of this sidebar).

When equations are given, rather than using the (R, G, B) notation used previously, I'll use a shorthand notation, where each pixel is referred to as a single vector with three color components. The two layers will be referred to as F, for the layer in *front*, and B, for the layer in *back*. For instance, in the Subtract mode example above, a shorter way of writing the operation is

```
B - F
```

This is just a shorthand way of saying "For each of the three colors in B and F, subtract the Front color from the corresponding Back color."

Colors must always range from 0 to 255. If not otherwise stated in an equation, you can safely assume that if the result of an operation results in a negative color, 0 will be substituted; if an operation results in a value greater than 255, GIMP will use 255. So the result of subtracting bright red from medium gray is:

```
(128, 128, 128) - (255, 0, 0) = (0, 128, 128)
```

In other words: no red, half green, and half blue will give you a dark cyan.

Addition, Subtract, and Difference

Addition mode is straightforward: the two pixel values are added together:

$$F + B \hspace{5cm} \textit{(Addition)}$$

If that makes any of the colors greater than 255, then that color is set to 255. Addition will nearly always make the image lighter.

Subtract is the opposite: the front layer is subtracted from the layer below it:

$$B - F \hspace{5cm} \textit{(Subtract)}$$

Anything that would become negative will be set to zero. This will make colors darker, naturally. You'll often end up with a lot of black or near-black from using Subtract mode.

Note Why is it "Addition," but "Subtract" rather than "Subtraction"? Historical reasons. Which usually means, "No one remembers any more why they're named that way."

Taking the difference of two numbers is the same as subtracting, isn't it? Usually that's true. But in GIMP, *Difference* mode is, well, different. Difference is a subtraction too: but after subtracting, if any color values are negative, GIMP uses the absolute value of that color instead of truncating it to zero. Think of it as showing the difference between two colors regardless of the direction of that difference.

$$|B - F| \qquad\qquad\qquad (Difference)$$

This means that instead of a lot of dark areas, the regions that would have been black become lighter again—especially in the colors that would have been absent. You can see that in Figure 9-11: areas of the trunk that were dark blue in Subtract mode become magenta in Difference mode.

Difference sometimes creates strange, garish colors and unusual transitions between colors. It can be useful when you need that sort of effect. In Chapter 10, you'll see several other uses for Difference mode.

Multiply and Divide

Multiply multiplies the value of the pixels in the two layers (bet you already guessed that). This generally makes the image darker.

Why should that be? Multiplying two numbers should make a bigger number, shouldn't it? And bigger numbers are lighter?

The trick is that the result is *normalized* to 255 (in other words, divided by 255). Otherwise, too much of the image would end up being too bright.

So, the equation for *Multiply* is

$$\frac{F * B}{255} \qquad\qquad\qquad (Multiply)$$

Note This ends up being darker than the front layer because B / 255 is less than 1 (except where B is white). So when it's multiplied by F, you get a number that's usually less than F.

Divide is a little more complicated. As you learned in grade school, you can't divide by 0 (at least without getting infinity). To guard against division by 0, GIMP adds 1 to the front layer's pixel values. Like Multiply, Divide is normalized, though this time it's normalized to 256 (1 is added to the normalization because of the 1 that was added to the front layer's pixels).

$$\frac{B * 256}{F + 1} \qquad (Divide)$$

Divide mode often results in nearly white pixels that look "burned out."

Dodge and Burn, Screen and Overlay

These four modes are closely related to Multiply and Divide. *Burn* and *Overlay* are similar to Multiply and make the image darker; *Dodge* and *Screen* are more like Divide, and make an image brighter.

Dodge divides the back layer by the inverse of the front layer (the inverse comes from subtracting the front layer from white, just like *Colors* ➤ *Invert* would do). This usually lightens the image about the same amount as Divide mode does, though sometimes it doesn't whiten the image quite as much…but it inverts some colors. (Unfortunately, that's hard to tell from Figure 9-11.)

$$\frac{B * 256}{256 - F} \qquad (Dodge)$$

In Burn mode, it's the back layer that is inverted rather than the front layer; then after the division, the result is inverted again:

$$255 - \frac{(255 - B) * 256}{F + 1} \qquad (Burn)$$

Burn ends up looking a lot like Multiply, though there are some differences. In Figure 9-11, you can see that they both got darker, but Burn took on the blue color of the background layer, while Multiply turned black. With another color combination, though, Burn might end up darker.

In Screen mode, the values of the visible pixels in the two layers are inverted, multiplied, and the product inverted again:

$$255 - \frac{(255 - F) * (255 - B)}{255} \qquad (Screen)$$

This sometimes results in a washed-out look and a bright image with muted colors.

Overlay is a combination of Multiply and Screen modes. The back layer is inverted, multiplied by twice the front layer, added to the original rear layer, and then multiplied by the original rear layer. (If you didn't follow that, don't worry about it.)

$$\frac{B}{255} * \left(B + \frac{2 * F * (255 - B)}{255} \right) \qquad (Overlay)$$

It usually doesn't darken nearly as much as straight Multiply, though in this case, it has taken on so much of the background color that you can scarcely see the tree any more.

Hard and Soft Lights

Hard light is another combination of Multiply and Screen modes. Depending on the color of the rear layer, you can sometimes think of it as an opposite of Overlay mode.

The formula is complicated because it has two parts: one for dark colors, and another for bright ones.

$$255 - \frac{(255 - B) * 255 - (2 * B - 256)}{256} \quad\quad F > 128$$
$$\frac{F * B * 2}{256} \quad\quad F < 128$$

(Hard light)

Hard light can sometimes be a useful mode for combining two photographs when you want bright colors and sharp edges.

Soft light is not the opposite of Hard light, but it does tend to soften edges and dim colors. It's yet another mixture of Multiply and Screen modes, and its effect is most similar to Overlay mode. In fact, in some versions of GIMP, Soft light and Overlay modes are identical due to a bug.

If Rm is the result from Multiply mode, and Rs is the result from Screen mode, the equation for Soft light is

$$\frac{R_m * ((255 - B) + (R_s * F)}{255} \quad\quad\quad\quad \textit{(Soft light)}$$

Darken or Lighten Only

These two are easy: they do just what their names imply. For each color component of each pixel, GIMP will show you the darker (or lighter) of the two components. So *Darken only* will make the image darker, while *Lighten only* will make it lighter. So Lighten only would be

$$Max(B, F) \quad\quad\quad\quad\quad \textit{(Lighten only)}$$

To get Darken only, just use *Min* instead of *Max*.

Grain Extract and Grain Merge

Grain extract is supposed to produce something akin to the "grain" you might see in photographic film. In reality, I find it's more useful for giving images an embossed and desaturated look.

Its equation is surprisingly simple:

$$B - F + 128 \quad\quad\quad\quad\quad \textit{(Grain extract)}$$

Grain merge adds texture to an ordinary image, as if adding film grain or texture from an artist's canvas. The equation is the mirror of Grain extract:

$$B + F - 128 \quad\quad\quad\quad\quad \textit{(Grain merge)}$$

You can use these two modes together to combine the texture of one image with the color of another, as you'll see in the next chapter.

Hue, Color, Saturation, and Value

These modes are straightforward once you understand what they do, but their names can be a bit confusing.

Hue mode takes the hue from the front layer (unless the front layer's saturation is 0), but takes saturation and value from the back layer. *Saturation* and *Value* modes, likewise, take the named value from the front layer and everything else from the back layer.

■**Note** Some graphics programs offer a Luminosity mode instead of Value. It's the same thing.

Color mode gives you the color of the front layer with the lightness of the back layer. It's like Hue, except that it takes saturation as well as hue from the front layer.

You'll see in the next chapter how you can use this mode to colorize an image, using a photograph as the back layer and a solid color as the front layer. It's as if you took a black-and-white version of the back layer and covered it with a colored filter—only it works better than simply using a translucent-colored layer in Normal mode, since that would darken the image unacceptably.

Saturation and Value modes aren't needed very often (though Saturation can be used to remove color from selected parts of an image), but Hue and Color modes can be quite useful for colorizing images, as you'll see in Chapter 10.

Creating Depth: Drawing with Layer Modes

So far, layer modes probably seem mostly an academic exercise. But there are some surprisingly interesting things you can do by combining them.

For instance, suppose I start with a happy face drawn with circular selections, stroking, and the Paintbrush tool with a fuzzy brush (Figure 9-12). Of course, in keeping with the first law of drawing (*Make a new layer!*), the face is on a layer by itself, separate from the white background.

Figure 9-12. *A simple happy face*

Make a copy of the face layer, and offset it a few pixels up and to the right. All you'll see initially is a face drawn with slightly thicker lines.

But look what happens when you use layer modes on the top copy of the face (Figure 9-13).

Figure 9-13. *The effect of different layer modes on a duplicate of a layer, shifted over slightly*

As you can see, layer modes can give some nifty three-dimensional effects to simple lines with very little effort on your part.

But it gets even better. Layer modes control how a layer combines with everything visible below it—not just the next layer down. In the case of the two face layers, with each layer transparent along the borders of the lines, the color of the background makes a difference.

Figure 9-14 shows what some of the modes look like if the background layer is changed to a medium gray: (128, 128, 128). The effects are even more interesting than the ones on a white background—and very different.

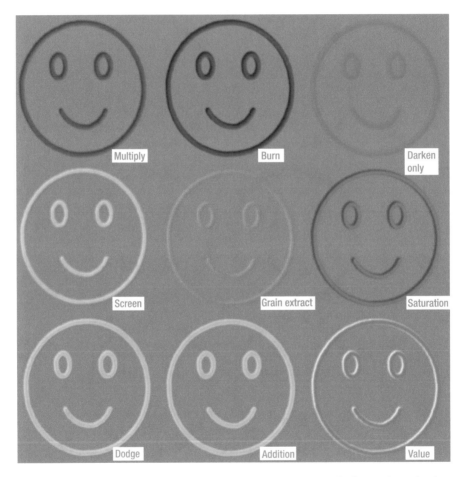

Figure 9-14. *Layer mode depth effects are even more pronounced when using a background other than white.*

Tip Medium gray is often useful when combining layers to get depth effects. Medium colors, not particularly bright or dark, can work well too. Blurring one of the two layers can make the effects even more pronounced.

By now you're probably worried. "How can I possibly remember what all the different layer modes will do with every possible color combination?" Fear not. You don't need to remember all the possible combinations. Just make two similar layers (one a copy of the other, but shifted, blurred, or otherwise modified), and then start trying layer modes until you see an effect you like. Once you've clicked on the *Mode* menu in the Layers dialog, the down-arrow key will change to the next mode, saving you a lot of mouse clicking.

Tip There's a problem with using a gray background. Ultimately, you'll probably want your pretty 3-D image on a layer of its own, so that you can paste it into other projects, or on a nice color that works for the project. Since the background color is inherent to the effect, you can't just make the background invisible: if you do, the interesting effect will disappear too. (Try it!) You can try selecting the background with Fuzzy Select, but sometimes you'll have trouble at the edges of letters. The solution: *Colors* ➤ *Color to Alpha*, which turns every instance of GIMP's current foreground color transparent. First *Merge Visible Layers*, use the Color Picker tool to choose the unwanted background color, then run *Color to Alpha*. Depending on how complex your effect is, you may need a few more adjustments (like making a selection mask to keep *Color to Alpha* from turning some of your effect transparent as well)…but that's a small price to pay for nifty jelly-bean effects!

Combining Layer Modes: Making 3-D Letters

Here's a straightforward example of how to use layer modes to create interesting logos. Start by making some text in basic black on a white background (Figure 9-15).

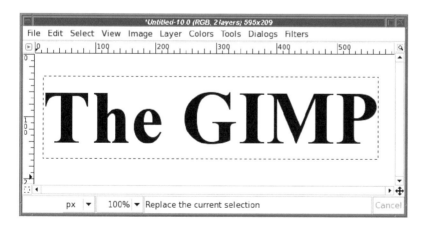

Figure 9-15. *Start with some black text.*

For once, rather than keeping the text layer separate, in this exercise you should merge the two layers. Right-click on the text layer in the Layers dialog and select *Merge Down* (Figure 9-16).

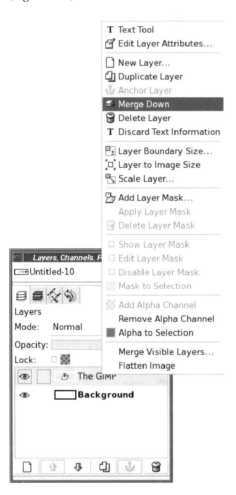

Figure 9-16. *Merge the text layer into the background.*

Make a duplicate of the text layer, Gaussian Blur it (*Filters ➤ Blur ➤ Gaussian Blur…*), and then invert it (*Colors ➤ Invert*) to get Figure 9-17.

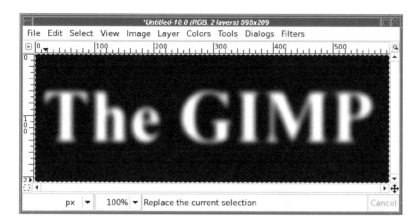

Figure 9-17. *The duplicate text layer has been blurred and inverted.*

For the next step, you need to replace the original white background on the bottom layer with a medium gray. (Remember your old friend medium gray?) Turn off visibility temporarily on the blurred and inverted layer so that you can see what you're doing on the lower layer. Then select a medium gray foreground color: in the color chooser, set H and S to 0 and V to 50, or type **808080** into the *HTML Notation* box.

In theory, you should be able to use GIMP's Select by Color tool to select all the white background, and then use *Edit ➤ Fill with FG Color* to turn it gray. Unfortunately, this isn't enough. When you made the text, you probably used *antialiasing*. (Remember that term from Chapter 3?)

Antialiasing smoothes the text by making pixels at the edge slightly transparent, blurring the interface of type and background. That means that along the edges of the letters, the color isn't exactly black or exactly white, but some in-between shade of gray. Select by Color will leave some of these areas unselected, and when you fill with gray, you'll end up with speckles left over (Figure 9-18).

Figure 9-18. *Light speckles left behind when you try to use Select by Color on antialiased text*

You could clean those up by hand, or by using operations like *Select* ➤ *Blur* or *Select* ➤ *Grow*, but that's a lot of work.

So what *can* you do? Layer modes to the rescue! Make a new layer with the *Layer Fill Type* set to *Foreground color*, so you have a layer of solid gray. Use the down arrow in the Layers dialog to move that layer to the bottom of the stack, below your black-text-on-white-background layer.

Then set the text layer mode to Multiply, and magically, the white background turns to gray (Figure 9-19).

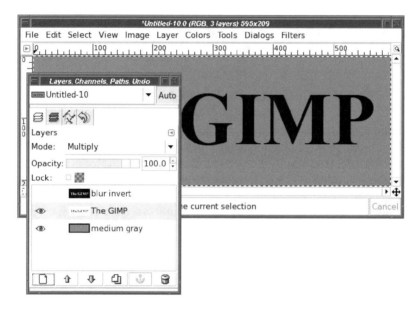

Figure 9-19. *Multiply mode changes the white background to gray smoothly, without any unwanted speckles.*

Why does that work so well? How does Multiply get rid of the speckles so cleanly?

It's a trick. No antialiasing speckles are harmed in the generation of this background. Instead, it's darkening the white to become the background color, without changing the black text (or its gray antialiasing) very much. "Darken only" works as well as Multiply, and the trick works for colored backgrounds as well as gray ones. On a gray background like this one, you could also use Burn; but with a colored layer underneath, Burn will change the color of the black text. (As always, if you're not sure, try several layer modes—or all of them—and see what works best.)

Note For this project, since you started with just a text layer, you could also make this black-on-gray layer by making a duplicate of the original text layer and merging it with a medium gray layer. But there are times when you only have a black-on-white image to start with. This trick using Multiply mode works any time you have a dark shape on a light background and you want to eliminate the background. It even works if you're replacing the background with a pattern.

Getting back to the 3-D letter project: turn visibility back on for the top layer (the one you blurred and inverted). Then set that layer to *Difference* (Figure 9-20).

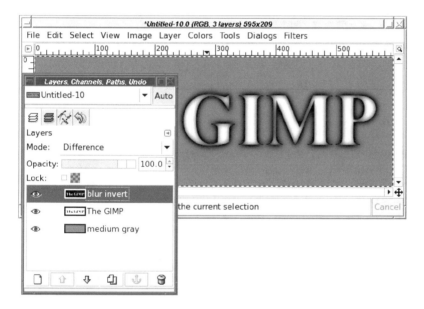

Figure 9-20. *Set the top (blurred, inverted text) layer to Difference mode.*

Nice effect! But you can get an even nicer, more 3-D effect by using the Move tool to move the top (blurred, inverted) layer a few pixels in any direction.

Don't like the gray color? No problem. Make another solid-color layer, any color you like, put it on top, and set it to Overlay mode (Figure 9-21).

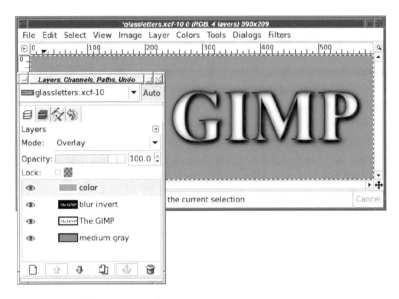

Figure 9-21. *Add a color overlay.*

Or set it to Darken only, which maintains a medium-gray background while turning the text your desired color (Figure 9-22). That might be useful if you want to select the text and paste it somewhere else. (If you need to paste the text without the background, try using a copy of the original text or blurred text to paste into the QuickMask or use as a layer mask. Don't forget that you need to click the Anchor button in the Layers dialog after pasting into either the QuickMask or a layer mask.)

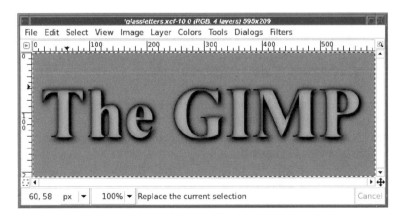

Figure 9-22. *Try Darken only mode for the top color layer.*

Tip Try all the available modes for your color filter—remember, the up and down arrow keys in the Layers dialog are good for trying every mode. Quite a few of the modes give interesting results.

I'm sure by now you realize that I've only given you a tiny idea of the useful effects you can get by combining modes. It would be an epic task to list all the possible combinations. So, make lots of layers and experiment for yourself!

Drawing Realistic Shadows

Remember adding a shadow to the tree-in-a-box in Chapter 4? Did you find that you had to try over and over to get a shadow that looked good?

There's an easier way to give a complicated object a shadow than by drawing it by hand. Just make a copy of the object's layer, turn it black, blur it, and then use the Perspective tool to make it point in the right direction.

Pasting an object into a photograph is a great way to show this. First, make sure you know in which direction the shadows are pointing in the original photo. In Figure 9-23, that's easy because of the figure of the hiker. I've livened up the picture by adding Tux, the Linux penguin.

Note Tux was drawn by Larry Ewing using GIMP version 0.54. Larry has an excellent "Penguin Tutorial" page describing the methods he used: *http://www.isc.tamu.edu/~lewing/linux/notes.html*.

Figure 9-23. *Notice the direction of the hiker's shadow. Tux looks somehow artificial without a shadow.*

Tux is cute and all, but he just doesn't look…realistic. The reason is the lack of a shadow. (Well, okay, maybe it's not the *only* reason.)

Using an Object to Cast Its Own Shadow

Start by making a drop shadow from the Tux layer.

Now use the Perspective tool to drag the shadow off in the right direction (Figure 9-24). Try to match the shadow angle that you see on other objects in the same photo. Don't worry if the base of the shadow doesn't quite match the base of the pasted object; you can fix that separately.

Figure 9-24. *Use the Perspective tool to drag two corners of the shadow box in the right direction.*

Until now, the shadow layer has been on top of the Tux layer. Obviously that's not right. Now is a good time to move the shadow layer down in the layer stack. Then use the Move tool to move the shadow so that its base is in the right place (Figure 9-25).

Figure 9-25. *With the shadow layer under the Tux layer, move the shadow to the right place.*

■**Note** This is basically what the Perspective Shadow plug-in does. However, it can be hard to get the plug-in to work right; it's usually easier just to make a perspective shadow by hand.

Transparency: Add the Final Tweak

That looks pretty good—but you're not quite done yet. Change the transparency of the shadow layer so that it's not completely black. Then you can see some of the texture and color underneath it (Figure 9-26).

Figure 9-26. *Give the shadow layer some transparency, so you can see the colors and textures underneath.*

Of course, sometimes you may need more work to make a shadow look perfect, especially if it's being cast onto a curved or irregular surface. But for most of your shadow needs, the Perspective tool combined with Blur and layer transparency will give you everything you need.

Realism and Multipoint Perspective

There's a little fib in the last section. Remember where it said to match the shadow angle of other objects in the photo? That's close to true—but sometimes not close enough.

The problem is perspective (the name of the tool you used to warp Tux's shadow to the right shape and angle!).

If you look carefully, you can see the problem. In Figure 9-25, both the hiker's and Tux's shadows are at roughly the same angle. If you have a sharp eye, Tux's shadow will look just a bit out of line—tilted down. However, in the final Figure 9-26, his shadow is rotated up a bit—and somehow that looks more natural.

Why is that? It's actually a nearly ideal representation of the effect of perspective. But it's easier to start any discussion of perspective with the most elementary version.

Single-Point Perspective

You probably remember your introduction to perspective in Chapter 4, when you drew the box for the tree planter. That was a reasonable introduction to *single-point* perspective (Figure 9-27).

Figure 9-27. *A classic example of single-point perspective: three boxes drawn with one vanishing point*

The "point" in question is the *vanishing point*. This is the place where parallel lines seem to converge in the distance. Imagine looking down the lane stripes on a long stretch of road. You'll note after some distance you can no longer distinguish them as separate stripes. If you can see far enough, the entire road disappears to a point in the horizon.

Since there are three boxes in Figure 9-27, you can see what happens when foreground objects are offset to one side or another. But that tells you something else: the vanishing point does not have to be in the center of the image.

Use any object (such as your hand, or the opposite page of the book) to block out two boxes. Now you have an example of a drawing where the vanishing point is offset to one side.

This is similar to the effect at work in the Tux image. But in Figure 9-26, the point where the shadows converge is *way* off to one side. Why is that, and how do you figure out where the vanishing point should be?

Two-Point Perspective

In Figure 9-27, all the horizontal lines are parallel to each other, and so are the vertical lines. The only lines that have a different angle are lines that recede "into the paper." Real images are often more complicated; we can do better.

How? By adding another vanishing point, as in Figure 9-28.

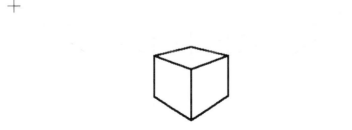

Figure 9-28. *Perspective using two vanishing points. Note the guide layout is very different from single-point drawings.*

Not coincidentally, the box has been drawn so that the angle from it to the left vanishing point is similar to the angle the shadows follow in Figure 9-26. What happens if you scale up part of the two-point drawing and paste it onto the Tux picture (as in Figure 9-29)?

Figure 9-29. *Centered on Tux (the focus of the image), the two-point cube's perspective lines show the relationship of Tux's shadow to the hiker's.*

An understanding of perspective will help not only with drawing, but any time you have to make an alteration to an existing image. Getting the angles, warps, and shapes "just right" can seem impossible using LARTM ("Looks About Right To Me"), but is easy when you know how to draw perspective lines.

GIMP doesn't let you set up guides that aren't exactly vertical or horizontal to help with the Perspective tool. But that's okay: by drawing lines in a separate layer, as shown here, you can still find your vanishing points, and then let them guide you when using the Perspective tool. Then make the layer invisible before you save.

In many cases (such as this one), the vanishing point is so distant, it's off the edge of the picture. That's perfectly normal. Sometimes old-world draftsmen (in the days before computers) would stick a pin into their drafting board way off the work, and line up their guides with a ruler.

Not so easy with a screen! But you can use the same trick you see in Figure 9-29. Make your guides smaller on a separate layer, and then scale them up to the proper size.

By using vanishing points with GIMP's Perspective tool and adding a realistic shadow, you can convincingly stick just about any object into even the most distorted background.

Adding Reflections and Shading

To draw Tux's shadow on the dunes, you had to have an idea of where the light was coming from. If you wanted to make an object look really three-dimensional, you'd want more than just a shadow: you'd want highlighting on the side of the object that faces the light, and shading on the other side of the object.

Remember shading the tree and box in Chapter 4? This is similar, but with curved objects a few other details are involved.

Rather than using Tux, I'll use a simpler example: I'll show you how to make a sphere.

Note GIMP has a plug-in to make a sphere for you, in the *Xtns* menu of the Toolbox. But once you know how to shade a sphere, you can use similar techniques to shade any object. In Chapter 11, you'll learn more about how the Sphere plug-in works.

Start by making a colored circle. Make a circular selection, and then fill it using *Fill with FG Color* or the Bucket Fill tool (Figure 9-30). Use a fairly dark color: this will be your shadow color. Of course, put your circle in its own layer.

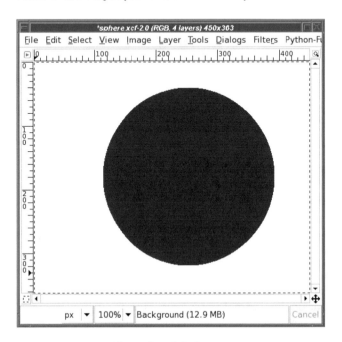

Figure 9-30. *Start with a colored circle.*

Bring up the color chooser and make the foreground color quite a bit brighter (increase its Value by sliding the V slider to the right). This will become the lighted part of the sphere.

You'll need a selection that's a bit bigger than the current circle, and feathered quite a lot. Your choice: either enable *Feather edges* in the Ellipse Select tool and make a new circular selection, or use the existing selection, enlarge it with *Select ➤ Grow…*, and then feather it with *Select ➤ Feather…*. For my relatively small example, I'll *Grow* by 20 pixels, and then *Feather* by 45.

Move the selection toward your light source: in this case, I'll move up and to the right (Figure 9-31). Remember, you can move a selection with Alt-drag or Shift-Alt-drag, or by using the *Transform selection* tab in the Move tool options.

Once the selection is moved, fill it with your new brighter foreground color (Figure 9-32). Then change the layer mode to any mode that looks good. Screen and Dodge are good for bright colors; Soft light gives a more subtle and darker effect.

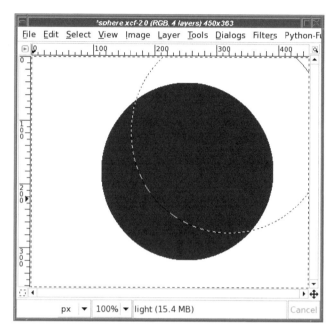

Figure 9-31. *Move the selection boundary toward the light source.*

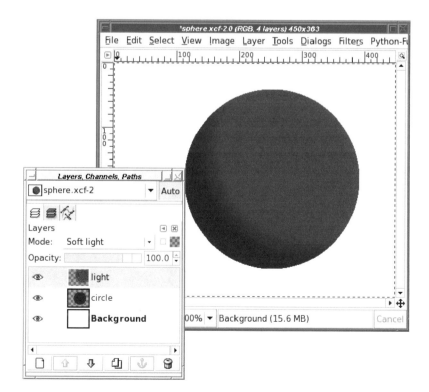

Figure 9-32. *Fill with the lighter color, using an appropriate layer mode.*

Add a bright highlight: make a small, feathered circular selection up near the light source, and fill it with white (Figure 9-33).

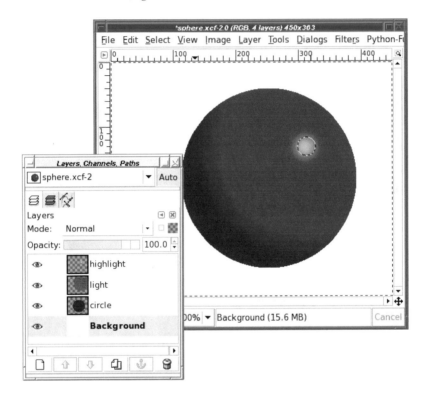

Figure 9-33. *Fill a small circular region with white to add a highlight.*

Finally, add a shadow, the same way you did with Tux. There are two slightly tricky aspects to this step. First, if your perspective drag handles end up off the screen, it can sometimes be difficult to get them back. Second, it's hard to tell when the perspective is right just by looking at the shadow's preview, so look instead at the box drawn by the Perspective tool (Figure 9-34).

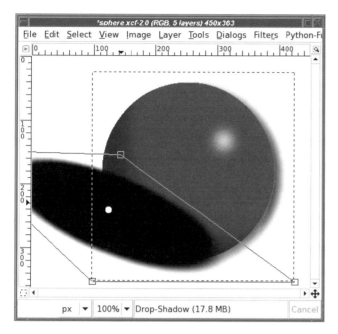

Figure 9-34. *Add a shadow.*

Drag the shadow to where it looks right and adjust its transparency, and you're all set (Figure 9-35).

Figure 9-35. *The finished sphere*

Of course, you can modify this technique in all sorts of ways. When you need to shade a complex object, you can draw shadows along one edge of the object using the Paintbrush tool with a fuzzy brush (in a separate layer, of course), or fill complex selections you've made with tools such as the Lasso tool.

You can make spheres with different textures such as glassy, metallic, or leathery: vary the feathering of the selections you fill, and then add textures or reflected objects, perhaps warped with one or more of the Map plug-ins discussed in Chapter 7.

You can add color to the shadow, or to the highlighted areas, to emphasize color being reflected from other parts of your artwork. Try different approaches! The more you experiment with light and shadow, the better your art will look.

Making Brushes, Patterns, and Gradients

GIMP has a great collection of brushes, gradients, and patterns. But sometimes you need something really specific. How do you make your own?

Making Brushes

In Chapter 4, you learned how to create simple parametric brushes. But what if you want to create a brush of a different type?

The Clipboard Brush

The easiest way to make a brush out of an image is the Clipboard brush (new in GIMP 2.4). Simply copy anything in GIMP, then look at the list of brushes either in the Brushes dialog or in the *Brush* menu in the Toolbox. The first item will be a brush made of whatever you copied (Figure 9-36).

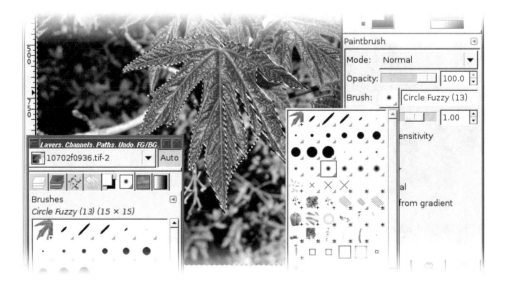

Figure 9-36. The Clipboard brush puts whatever you last copied as a brush in the Brush menu and Brushes dialog.

Simple Image Brushes

Any image can become a brush. But GIMP has two types of image brushes: color and grayscale.

A grayscale image brush works like most of GIMP's standard brushes: anywhere the brush is black, GIMP will paint in the current foreground color. Anywhere that's white will not affect the image. Be sure to use white rather than transparent for grayscale brushes: GIMP will refuse to save a grayscale brush with transparency.

■**Caution** If you try to save an image as a grayscale brush and you get an error message, check to make sure the image is really in grayscale mode, not RGB (it should say grayscale in the window's title bar). If not, use *Image* ➤ *Mode* ➤ *Grayscale*. If you still have trouble, make sure the image doesn't have transparency: *Layer* ➤ *Transparency* ➤ *Remove Alpha Channel*.

Color image brushes keep their color when you paint with them (like the Vine brush discussed in Chapter 4). Most good color image brushes will be small and will have transparent backgrounds.

Hey—that describes Wilber! How would you go about making Wilber (Figure 9-37) into a GIMP brush?

Figure 9-37. *Wilber, the GIMP mascot*

Making an image into a brush is easy—just save it in the right place using the right image type (Figure 9-38). The right place is the folder check-marked *Writable* in *Preferences* ➤ *Folders* ➤ *Brushes*.

■**Tip** If you have trouble finding your GIMP profile folder in the Save as dialog, try clicking on Browse for other folders; then right-click in the file list and select Show Hidden Files.

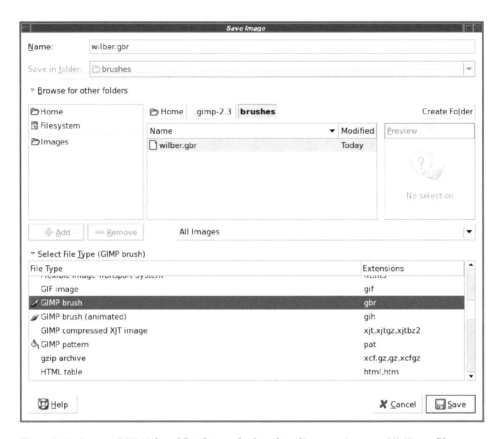

Figure 9-38. *Save as "GIMP brush" (.gbr) to the brushes directory in your GIMP profile.*

The right type is GBR, for "GIMP brush." You can expand GIMP's *Select File Type* list and click on *GIMP brush*, or just save it to a file ending in .gbr and let GIMP figure out the type.

Once you click *Save* in the dialog, you'll be prompted for a *Spacing* and *Description* (Figure 9-39).

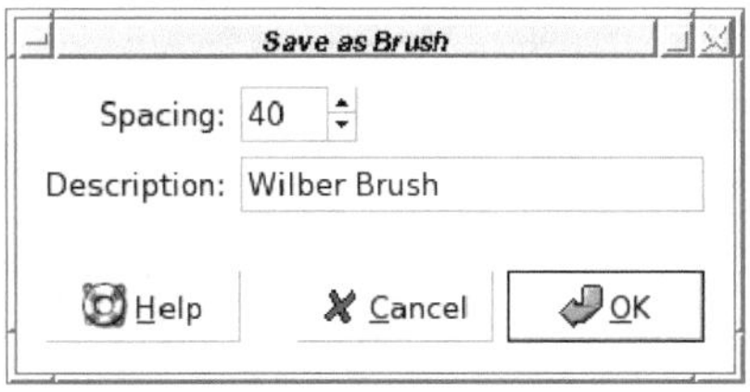

Figure 9-39. *Options when saving a brush*

Spacing is how far apart the images will be when you draw lines and curves with the brush (Figure 9-40). The *Description* is the name that will show up when you choose the brush from the Brushes dialog.

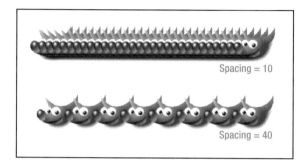

Spacing = 10

Spacing = 40

Figure 9-40. *Spacing controls how far apart the images will be drawn.*

After you've saved a brush, you need to *Refresh brushes*—the button in the lower right of the Brushes dialog—before GIMP will see the new brush. Of course, exiting GIMP and starting again also works. Then you can use your brush.

Although it's fun to draw silly lines made of Wilbers, a more practical use for simple custom brushes is as a *stamp*, or an image you need to use frequently. Suppose you have a signature that you like to add to your artwork. You could keep your signature in a file and open it every time you needed to use it, copy it, and then paste it into the new image. But if it's already loaded as a GIMP brush, it's always accessible through the Brushes dialog. Much easier, and you don't need to remember where you stored the file.

Animated Brushes

The real power of custom brushes is in *animated brushes*. These are made from images with multiple layers, just like the animated image you made at the end of Chapter 3. As you drag the mouse across the canvas, instead of seeing the same object repeated many times, you'll see slightly different objects. GIMP's Vine brush, and others such as the Pencil Sketch brushes, Felt Pen, Confetti, and Galaxy, all use animation to give you a random-looking, constantly changing line. The animated brushes have a red corner in the Brushes dialog, so you can tell them from other types of brushes.

To illustrate, I'll demonstrate how to make a simple animated brush: some cartoon grass.

Start with a small image. I'll use 50 × 50 pixels. It shouldn't have any background, just a completely transparent image. (If you start with an image that has a background, *Add Alpha Channel* followed by *Clear* can fix that.)

Now draw a blade of grass (Figure 9-41). Notice that I zoomed in the window to 400%: it's hard to draw in a 50 × 50 window at normal size.

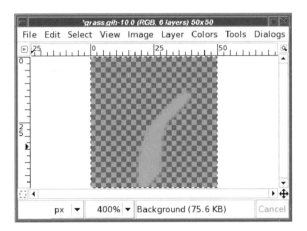

Figure 9-41. *A single blade of grass against a transparent background*

▪ Tip Since GIMP doesn't offer any way to draw a line that starts wide and then tapers to a point, I drew each blade as a constant-width line, then zoomed in and used Lasso Select and *Clear* to taper their tips.

Make a new layer, and draw another blade of grass. Grass will look more realistic if each blade is a slightly different shade of green as well as a different shape.

Continue adding new layers until you're happy. I'll stop at six layers (Figure 9-42).

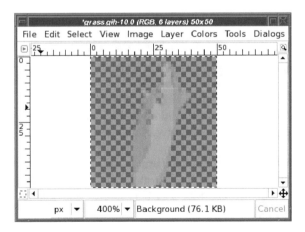

Figure 9-42. *Six blades of grass, each a different color and shape and in its own layer*

Now it's time to save the brush. Use the same folder you used for simple brushes—the brushes folder in your GIMP profile directory—but this time use the *GIMP brush (animated)* type, a .gih extension (Figure 9-43).

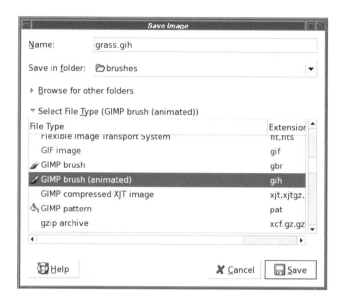

Figure 9-43. *Save with a .gih extension: type "GIMP brush (animated)."*

This brings up the *Save as Brush Pipe* dialog (Figure 9-44). *Pipe* is another term for an animated brush.

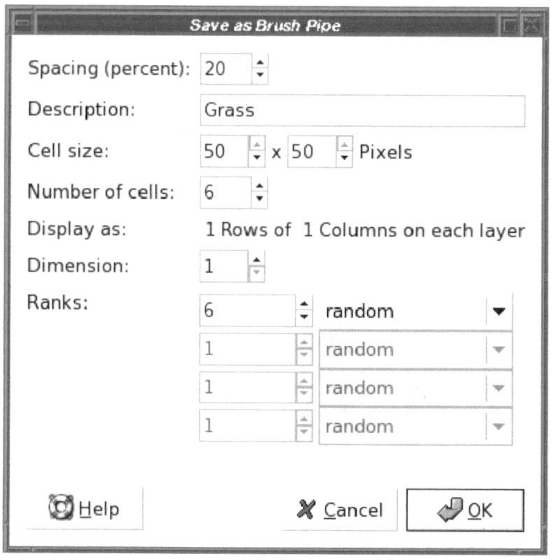

Figure 9-44. *Options when saving an animated brush*

Spacing is the distance between consecutive brush marks, just as it was with simple brushes. It's specified as a percentage of the brush size. You'll have to experiment with this setting to find the right one for your brush. For grass, 8 or 10 works fairly well.

Description is simply a text description you can give to your brush. *Number of cells* is the number of layers in your image. GIMP should initialize this for you.

The rest of the options—*Cell size*, *Display as*, *Dimension*, and *Ranks*—control how the frames of the animated brush are chosen from the image, and in what order. For a simple animated brush like this, leave *Dimension* at 1 and set the first *Ranks* column to the number of cells (6, in this case).

▪**Note** For more complicated brushes, you can choose to divide each layer into a grid, and then use each grid cell as a frame in the brush. Dimension and the other Ranks fields tell GIMP how the grid is set up and in what order to choose the frames. These make brush design more complicated; you're probably best off ignoring them until you get comfortable with animated brush design. They're used for fancy effects like changing orientation according to the direction you're drawing.

The menu next to the *Ranks* entry controls the order in which cells are chosen. *Random* picks a random layer each time; *Incremental* uses the layers in order; *angular* and *velocity* let you create more advanced effects, such as changing the brush image according to the direction or speed the mouse is moving. The other options, *pressure*, *xtilt*, and *ytilt*, use those values from a drawing tablet if you have one. If you don't, you're better off sticking to *Random* or *Incremental*.

Figure 9-45 shows the effect of drawing with the grass brush.

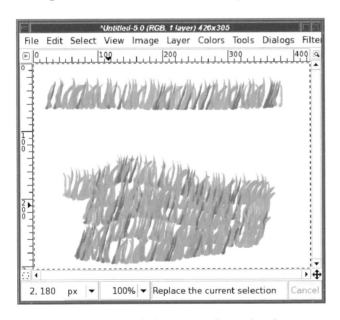

Figure 9-45. *Drawing with the animated grass brush*

Importing Animated Brushes

GIMP can also import animated brushes from certain other programs. Paintshop Pro calls them *tubes* and uses the .tub extension. Convert them to GIMP animated brushes by opening the .tub file as an image and saving as GIH. For other programs, you may be able to find plug-ins or external programs to convert a brush to GIMP's GIH format.

Note You'll sometimes see the term *image hose* to refer to animated brushes, especially in the Paintshop Pro world. The idea is that the brush is a hose that sprays out a stream of constantly changing images. *Pipes* (as in GIMP's dialog) and *tubes* are other ways of referring to animated brushes.

Making Patterns

You've probably used some of GIMP's built-in patterns by now. But you can get a pattern from a photo too. For instance, what if you want a pattern of spots copied out of a cheetah photograph (Figure 9-46)?

Figure 9-46. *Cheetah spots to use as a pattern*

The easiest way to test a pattern is to use the Clipboard pattern, which works just like the Clipboard brush. Copy your pattern, and it will automatically appear as the first item in the Patterns dialog, or in the *Pattern Fill* checkbox you get in the bucket fill tool (Figure 9-47). Drag from the Clipboard pattern into an image window, or use *Edit ➤ Fill with FG Color*.

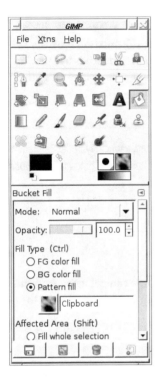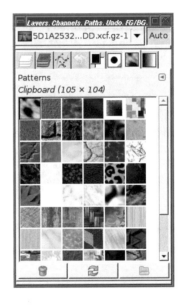

Figure 9-47. *The first pattern is a copy of whatever's in the clipboard.*

Well, of course there's a catch. When you fill with a new pattern, you'll almost always see a *tiling* effect, as in Figure 9-48.

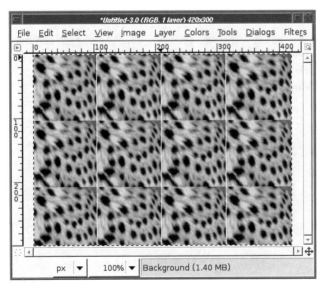

Figure 9-48. *You can see seams at the edge of each tile.*

What went wrong? There's a sharp boundary where the bottom edge of one copy of the pattern doesn't match the top edge of the next copy (and similarly with the left and right edges, though the effect is less obvious). The eye is very good at picking out boundaries. That won't do!

Fortunately, GIMP has a filter to help with creating patterns which can be found at *Filters ➤ Map ➤ Make Seamless*.

After running Make Seamless on the cheetah pattern, copying it, and filling with it, you get something more like Figure 9-49.

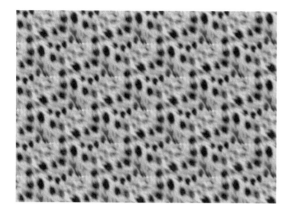

Figure 9-49. *After running Make Seamless, you can't see the boundaries as easily.*

Running Make Seamless sounds easy, and it is. But it's not perfect—notice the repeating group of spots you can see in the cheetah pattern when it's tiled. Patterns with straight lines, such as bricks, may end up warped or blurred in unnatural-looking ways. Even fairly random patterns like cheetah spots can become blurry or blotchy. If I move the selection over just a few pixels in the original cheetah image, copy it and use the Make Seamless command, it comes out like Figure 9-50.

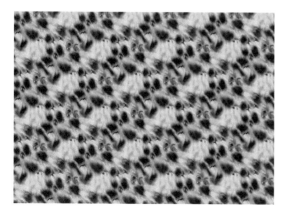

Figure 9-50. *Moving the selection over slightly can make a big difference in how realistic a pattern looks, even with Make Seamless.*

The key to choosing a good pattern is finding one that doesn't change much from one edge to the other. If it's brighter in one corner, if there's a big dark spot in the middle or a line along the bottom, if there's an obvious shape inside...it will be obvious where one tile ends and the next begins. Sometimes this is acceptable (and even some of GIMP's built-in patterns show obvious edges), but most of the time you won't want that.

There are also plug-ins you can download, such as Resynthesizer, and other techniques such as a high-pass filter and the Clone tool, that can go beyond Make Seamless to help make your patterns tileable.

After making brushes, I'm sure you can guess how to save your pattern once you're happy with it. Navigate in the Save as dialog to the brushes folder in your GIMP profile, and save it as type "GIMP pattern" (with a .pat extension). When you're prompted for a description, choose a name that makes sense. Then open the Patterns dialog and click the *Refresh* button in the lower right.

Making Gradients

You can make your own gradients, too, by using the *Gradient Editor*.

The easiest way to learn the Gradient Editor is to edit an existing gradient. Select a gradient similar to your goal, make a copy of it by clicking the *Duplicate* button, then click *Edit* to get the Gradient Editor (Figure 9-51). You can also use the context menus of the Gradients dialog (right-click on any gradient in the list, and then select *Edit* to edit that gradient, or *New* to make a new one).

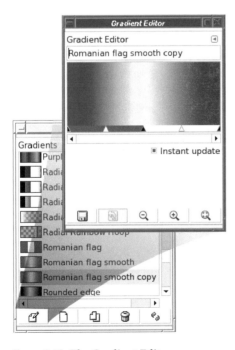

Figure 9-51. *The Gradient Editor*

Caution Make sure you duplicate an existing gradient before running the Gradient Editor. If you try to edit one of GIMP's built-in gradients, many functions in the dialog won't work because the gradient will be opened as read only.

At the top of the Gradient Editor is the name (for a new gradient, "Untitled"). You can change this to the name of your new gradient.

Below the name is an image of the gradient as it currently looks, and below that, an area for *range selection sliders*—the blue-and-white bar with black-and-white triangles.

In the range selection area, black triangles define *segments*. Each segment has two endpoint colors. White triangles represent the midpoints of ranges. The currently selected range is blue; the others are white.

In Figure 9-51, there are two segments. The first (leftmost) segment is active, since that's the one with the blue bar below it. Its left endpoint color is blue, and its right endpoint color is yellow. The second segment has a yellow left endpoint, and a blue right endpoint.

Each segment will fade from the color at one endpoint to the other. How fast it will fade is controlled by dragging the midpoint slider (the white triangle). Drag it to the right, and you'll see more blue; to the left, and you'll see more yellow. You can also drag the black endpoint sliders, or even drag the entire selected zone.

Tip To make an abrupt cutoff, like "Romanian Flag" (as opposed to "Romanian Flag Smooth"), make segments where the left and right endpoints are the same colors, so there's no fade from one end to the other.

You can control many aspects of blending, and add or delete segments, by right-clicking in the gradient to get a context menu (Figure 9-52). The most important entries are *Left Endpoint's Color* and *Right Endpoint's Color* to choose the colors used in the current segment.

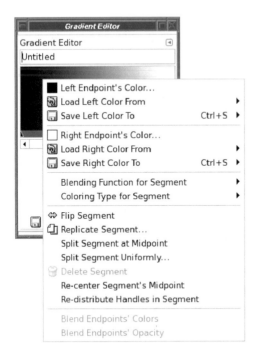

Figure 9-52. *The Gradient Editor's context menu*

When you've edited a gradient to your liking, the *Save* button adds the gradient to your GIMP profile. You don't need to choose a file name or file type for it: GIMP will handle that for you.

Most people won't ever need to create or modify a gradient. But for those who do, GIMP's Gradient Editor gives you plenty of power to do whatever you need. Experiment and see what it can do for you.

Summary

By now you know how to create your own brushes, patterns, and gradients. You know all about perspective and how to use it when drawing, how to make shadows, and how to make text or other objects fade out using layer masks. And you have some idea of the effects you can achieve by combining GIMP's many layer modes in your drawings.

Next, it's time to revisit photographs, and see how you can use some of these same techniques to make your photos better, or to combine several photographs together—a process called compositing.

CHAPTER 10

■ ■ ■

Advanced Compositing

*C*ompositing is a fairly general word. In its most basic sense, it means combining two or more images of any sort—even small elements such as a circle, a shadow, or a text layer—to make a new image. You've already been doing that throughout much of this book.

In this chapter, I'll cover a more specific meaning: blending two or more existing photographs to make a new image. (In some cases, the two photographs may be copies of the same photograph, as you'll see.)

You'll learn some tips for improving photos that weren't covered in the chapters on photo retouching, and tricks for extracting detail from a photo that you may not have known was there. You'll learn to create artistic renderings of your photos (without needing GIMPressionist or similar plug-ins), and how to combine photos in interesting ways. You'll learn how astronomical photographs are made, and how to use astrophotography techniques to take photos you didn't think your camera could capture. Finally, you'll learn how to make panoramic images, including some tips on how to shoot them in the first place. The chapter will cover the following:

- Colorizing images

- Combining patterns with textures or grain

- Using layer modes to improve photos

- Making photos into art using layer modes

- Compositing unrelated images

- Stacking images

- Stitching panoramas

Colorizing Images

Did you ever have an old black-and-white photograph you wished was in color? Or maybe you have a color photograph, but you don't like the real colors. You may want to colorize a whole image, or perhaps just a part.

Colorizing a black-and-white image is just a variation on the sepia photo techniques you learned in Chapter 8. Instead of using a light brown tone, just experiment with various colors until you hit the combination you're after.

But what if you want to alter the colors in an image that already *has* color?

For instance, have you ever wondered what your car would look like in another color? A professional paint job costs a fortune, but with GIMP it's both cheap and fun (Figure 10-1).

Figure 10-1. *The car is okay in blue, but would it look better in red?*

Begin by selecting the part of your photo you want to colorize using the techniques you learned in Chapter 5. In this case, that would be all parts of the car that are blue.

Tip For this kind of operation, you'll often find that a combination of selection techniques works best. On the car, it was easiest to start with Fuzzy Select (Select Contiguous Regions), which caused some overrun. Then use the Lasso or the QuickMask to fill in selection gaps and cut away any excess.

Copy your selection and paste it, which will make a new floating layer. As usual, convert it to a regular layer with the *New Layer* button (at the lower left of the Layers dialog). If you made the background layer invisible, your new layer might look like Figure 10-2.

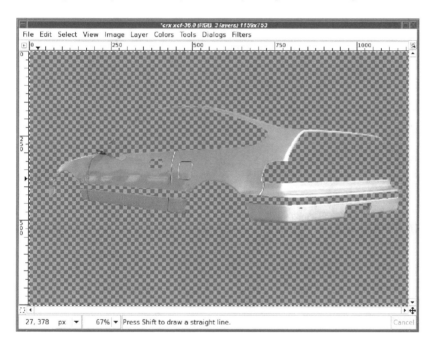

Figure 10-2. *Make a layer consisting of just the colored part of the car.*

Now, color the layer. You can start with the *Colors ➤ Colorify* filter and get a pretty good result (in GIMP versions prior to 2.4, it's in *Filters ➤ Color*). But you can get more interesting results if you use *Fill With FG Color* to get a flat color. It won't look good right away, but it will look fine when you combine it with layer modes. Try every mode to see what happens, using the up and down arrow keys after clicking on the *Mode* menu—you'll find that the solid color you used will change to different, sometimes surprising shades depending on the mode you use. A solid red layer in Color or Grain Merge mode gives you a nice red factory paint job (Figure 10-3). Overlay mode turns the car purple while keeping the metallic look of the original, while that same red layer in Difference mode gives you a lovely pearl-purple effect.

Figure 10-3. *A solid red layer in Color mode—now that looks racier!*

But don't stop there. Since all you're doing is painting solid colors on the top layer, you can just as easily paint patterns, or make a two-tone by drawing a gradient with the Blend tool (Figure 10-4).

Figure 10-4. *A gradient—red above, green below—combined in Overlay mode*

Of course, you can make several copies of each part of the car and color them differently. Try adding stripes or other shapes. Then switch layers on and off to see which color or pattern you like best. (This is also a good way of testing hair colors on a photo of yourself before you take the plunge and dye your hair magenta!)

Some modes, such as Multiply, will probably look strange at first. Sometimes you can fix that by reducing the layer's *Opacity*. It's difficult to predict the effects of the layer modes on various color shifts you may make, even if you're experienced with these modes. The bottom line? Try them all and see.

Combining Patterns with Textures or Grain

Colorizing with layer modes is fun, but on some images you need more. For instance, if you try to use modes like Overlay on an animal like a squirrel (Figure 10-5), you'll lose a lot of the fur detail. You can keep some of that detail by using the Heal tool (Chapter 6), but it's tedious, and works better for correcting small spots than for covering large areas. Fortunately, there's a better way, using the Grain Extract and Grain Merge modes.

Figure 10-5. *Fur detail in this squirrel won't show up well with simple compositing like you used for the car.*

Start by selecting the part of the image you want to colorize. For the squirrel, it works best to select just the gray fur, omitting the eye, the white belly, and the tail. Use the *Copy* and *Paste* commands, and make it a new layer, just as with the car. Then click the *Duplicate* button in the Layers dialog to make a copy of the gray fur layer (you'll need it later). Turn off visibility on the upper of the two copies and make the lower one active: that's where you're going to put your new color or pattern, so name it something appropriate. I'd like to give this squirrel a leopard-spot pattern, so I'll name the layer *leopard*.

Choose the pattern you're going to use. There's a pattern called Leopard in GIMP's built-in pattern collection, but the spots are quite small—for the squirrel, I'd prefer bigger spots. To fix that, right-click on the Leopard pattern in the Patterns dialog and choose *Open Pattern as Image*. Then scale it as much as you want: 175% works well in this case.

You can save the result as a new pattern file (.pat) if you think you'll use it for other projects. But for one-time use, the easiest way to use your scaled pattern is simply to choose *Edit* ➤ *Copy* to copy the pattern. Then it will show up in the Patterns dialog as the Clipboard pattern, the first pattern in the list. Click on it to make it the active pattern.

Back in the squirrel picture, turn on the *Lock alpha* button in the Layers dialog, just under *Opacity*. That way, you'll get the leopard pattern only where the gray fur is. Then choose *Edit* ➤ *Fill with Pattern* (Figure 10-6), or drag the Clipboard pattern from the Layers dialog into the image. (The Bucket Fill tool will also work—your choice.)

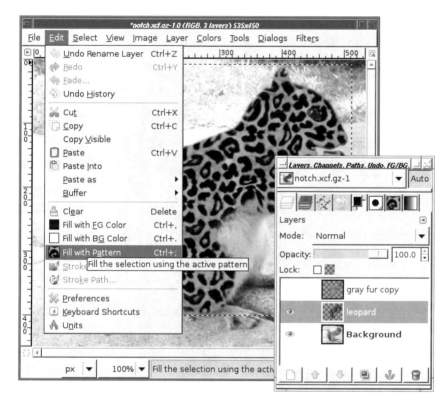

Figure 10-6. Fill with Pattern. Notice that the leopard layer is active in the Layers dialog, Lock is checked, and the active pattern (in the tab in the Layers dialog window and in the Edit menu in the image window) is the scaled-up leopard pattern from the clipboard. (The image is shown as it appears after being filled.)

At this point, you can try some layer modes on the leopard pattern layer. Overlay works pretty well on this image, but it doesn't look realistic enough—the pattern overwhelms the fur detail. It's a good start, but what you need is a way of adding more of that furry texture.

That's where you'll use that copy you made of the gray fur layer. Turn off visibility of the Background and pattern layers and make the gray fur layer visible and active. Click *Duplicate* to make a second copy of it.

Choose the upper of the two gray fur copies and blur it with *Filters* ➤ *Blur* ➤ *Gaussian Blur…*. Blur it enough that you can't see any more fur detail (a blur radius of 10 is about right for the squirrel). You might want to name this layer "gray fur blur." Then set the blurred layer to *Grain extract* mode. It will look like texture embossed onto metal, with not much color visible (Figure 10-7).

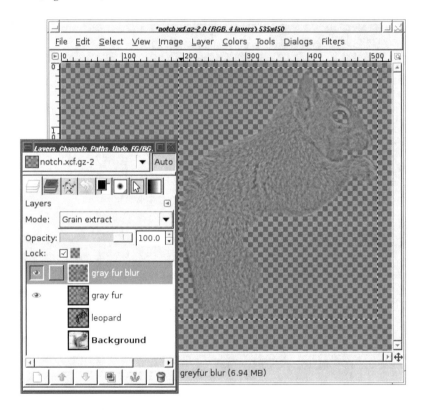

Figure 10-7. *Set the blurred layer to Grain extract mode.*

To use Grain merge, you need to store the result of Grain extract in a single layer. So merge the gray fur blur layer with the gray fur layer below it by right-clicking on the blur layer and choosing *Merge down*. Set the resulting layer to Grain merge mode.

Turn the Background and leopard layers back on (Figure 10-8) to see the result. You can still see the pattern, but the fur texture is much more evident than it was before. Try turning visibility of the grain merge layer off and on to see the difference it makes. You can even enhance the texture more by duplicating the grain layer. (I've also added a layer mask to make the pattern less evident on the squirrel's face, ears, and "hands," and you can improve the result further with a bit of *Filters* ➤ *Distorts* ➤ *IWarp* along the squirrel's back to distort the spots there as they curve away.)

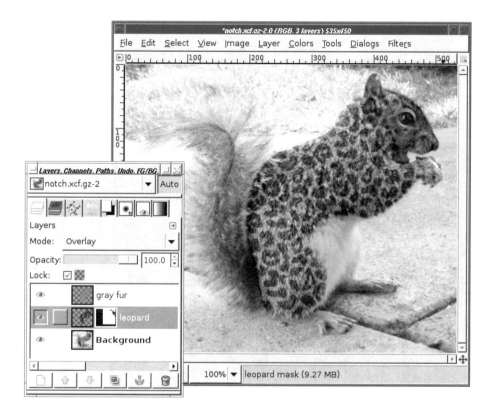

Figure 10-8. *With the grain layer in Grain merge mode, the furry texture is much more obvious even through the pattern.*

What happened? Let's review how you can use Grain extract and Grain merge together. When you need to save or emphasize the texture of some part of an image, start by making a copy of your target that has the texture removed (that's the blurred layer). Combine that, in Grain extract mode, with the original to make a "grain" layer. That grain layer, used in Grain merge mode, will add the original grain wherever you need it.

Using Layer Modes to Improve Photos

Think way back to Chapter 2, where you used tools such as Levels and Curves to improve the brightness of an image.

You can make similar changes by using layer modes, sometimes with a much better result. Just make a copy of the image, right on top of the original, and experiment with the layer mode of the top copy.

Let's take a look at some of the corrections you can make by compositing an image with itself.

Using Screen Mode for Dark Images

Sometimes you pick the wrong f-stop. Sometimes the camera guesses the exposure wrong. Especially aggravating, sometimes there just isn't enough light where you want to shoot—such as in Figure 10-9.

Figure 10-9. *A dark indoor shot from Las Vegas*

When your picture comes out too dark, you can try to adjust the color, brightness, and contrast to get the perfect balance. But there's a much quicker way to get nearly ideal brightening.

First, go to the Layers dialog and duplicate the Background layer. Next, change the result-ant layer to Screen mode. Usually that's all you have to do.

In some cases the result will be too light, but you can adjust that by turning down the *Opacity* slider. Other times, such as with this picture, the original was so dark you need to lighten it further. In that case, just duplicate the second layer and you'll get a third layer, already in Screen mode. The picture will become even brighter. Figure 10-10 is the result of two additional screen layers.

Of course, if your second or third layer goes too far, you can adjust *Opacity* on just the top layer until it looks just right.

Figure 10-10. *Look at all the detail you can see in areas that were previously just mud, particularly the building at the center right.*

■**Note** In some cases, especially when you're just trying to lighten up a portion of a photo, you'll find Dodge mode works a little better. But most of the time, Screen is just right.

Using Overlay or Hard Light When Light Is Flat

When you find yourself confronted by an image that's just way too flat and has no significant bright areas, self-compositing with Overlay or Hard light mode can help bring out color and detail.

Hard light will tend to overwhelm any bright areas in the photo, so confine it to dull, washed-out images only. Figure 10-11 shows the striking difference it can make to a dull image. For images with very bright colors or a lot of detail, Overlay is more versatile.

Figure 10-11. *Hard light is an easy and fast way to bring out color in an image that has no bright areas. The left half of the image is the original; the right half has been self-composited with Hard light.*

Using Overlay or Burn to Cut Through Haze

I live near a major city, and it's frequently smoggy or hazy. When I try to take long-distance shots with my camera, I'm often disappointed: objects that seemed perfectly clear to the eye are buried in haze in the photograph, as in Figure 10-12.

Figure 10-12. *You can barely see the city for all the haze.*

Overlay mode excels at cutting through haze. Make a layer copy, and then set the top layer to Overlay. The city becomes much clearer (Figure 10-13).

Figure 10-13. *Overlay mode cuts through the haze a little.*

But that's just the beginning. With the Overlay layer selected, click the *New Layer* button again. GIMP makes another copy, already in Overlay mode—and the distant city becomes sharper. Click again, and it becomes sharper still. You can keep adding Overlay layers until the image gets as sharp as you need (Figure 10-14).

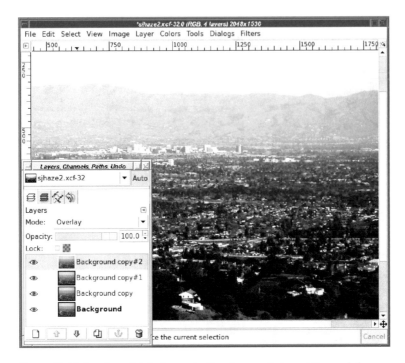

Figure 10-14. *Stack multiple layers in Overlay mode to cut through haze even more.*

If that effect isn't strong enough for you, try turning off all but the first two layers and using Burn mode on the upper layer (Figure 10-15).

Burn mode gives excellent detail and color on the city that previously was shrouded in haze. The downside is that the rest of the image becomes black and you no longer have those nice green hills in the foreground.

Figure 10-15. *Burn mode cuts through the haze much better than Overlay—but now the rest of the photo has way too much contrast.*

Of course, you can adjust the strength of the effect by changing the *Opacity* of the upper layer. But with Burn, you may find that light areas are still too dark and you can't get the nice green hills you had when you started.

Adding a layer mask to the burned layer can fix that. The goal is to make the layer opaque where you want the effect, fading to transparent in places you don't want to change. To do that, either paint in the area you want burned, leaving the rest black, or draw a gradient separating the part you want burned from the part you don't. Figure 10-16 shows the effect of a white oval, blurred by 300 pixels, covering just the city.

Figure 10-16. *A layer mask that emphasizes just the city can preserve the foreground hills while still showing detail on the distant city.*

Making Photos into Art Using Layer Modes

As you've seen, compositing an image with itself usually affects the contrast, colors, and apparent sharpness of the image. It's a useful technique for changing iffy photos into better ones.

But if you modify one of the copies of the image before you combine it with the original, you can create many other interesting artistic effects.

Making "Drawings" and Other Effects Using Layer Offset

The idea is to start with any photo you like, duplicate the layer, and then move it just a little bit. It's easier to describe what's going on after you see an example of the technique.

In the first series, you'll see three effects applied to the same image (Figure 10-17). The top (duplicated) layer will be moved down and to the right by a few pixels.

Figure 10-17. *A drawing capturing all the petal detail could take quite a long time.*

Tip A good way of moving a layer by small amounts is to click on the Move tool, and then use the arrow keys to move the layer one pixel at a time.

Each caption will tell you the exact number of pixels moved to achieve the effect shown. Your own experiments will probably use different shifts. Less movement will make finer lines; more will add detail and color. Sometimes you'll like more vertical movement, sometimes more horizontal. Fortunately, it's cheap and easy to experiment!

Colored Pencil Drawings: Divide Mode

Generally, you'll move the image only moderately when using *Divide* mode. Figure 10-18 is a fairly strong example of the effect, showing heavy shadow detail by moving the top layer *down* more than sideways.

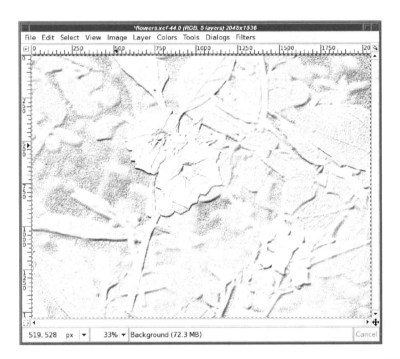

Figure 10-18. *The top layer was moved three pixels right and six down in Divide mode.*

It's striking that such a dark image results in such a light drawing. Also, the complexity in the dark areas has created an effect very much like you would see when an artist draws with colored pencils on heavily textured paper. Figure 10-19 shows another example, with a more complex landscape photograph.

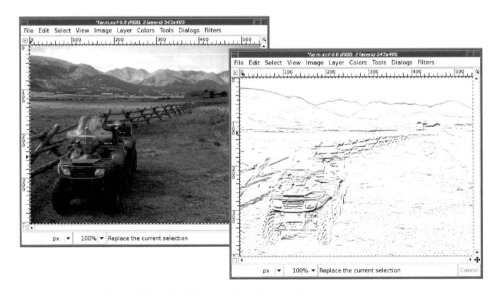

Figure 10-19. *The "pencil sketch" effect on a landscape photo*

Less complex images will generate fewer lines, and can be moved less to get a more sketched look. You can further modify your "drawing" by playing with the colors, or turn it into a graphite pencil sketch by converting it to grayscale.

Black Velvet Paintings: Difference Mode

Sometimes, you want a dark result rather than something bright. In that case, use *Difference* mode on the same picture to create Figure 10-20.

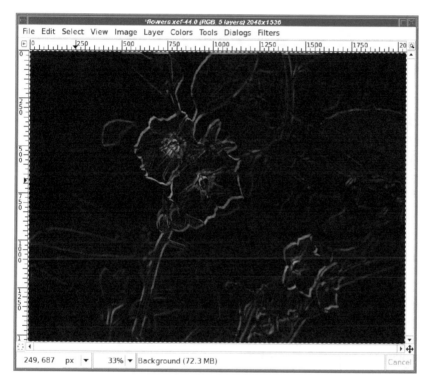

Figure 10-20. *Difference mode makes a neon line drawing on black. The top layer was moved eight pixels to the right and ten pixels down while in Difference mode.*

That's a neat effect, almost like neon lights. But playing with the *Opacity* of the difference layer can make the effect more interesting, and turns the artwork into a "black velvet" painting (Figure 10-21). Too bad I don't have any photographs of Elvis to use as examples!

Difference usually requires you to move the top layer more than you would for other layer mode effects. This picture is no exception, having moved only a little further right than Figure 10-21, but almost three times as much to the right. (When moving a layer over larger distances than a few pixels, remember that holding down Shift while pressing an arrow key moves the layer by a larger distance than by using the arrow key alone.)

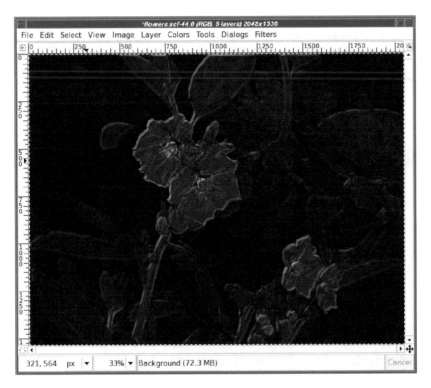

Figure 10-21. *Reducing the top layer's Opacity to 75% brings out some of the details within the lines.*

The result will often change dramatically as you vary the offset of the two layers, sometimes in surprising ways. If you go too far, particularly in Difference mode, the "painting" will start to become blurry. It's an interesting balance that looks like what might happen if Van Gogh had tried to imitate Rembrandt's dark realism.

You can get a similar effect by using Subtract mode, but in most cases, Difference will give a more pleasing image. However, it's worth a try—when Subtract does work, it's spectacular.

If you look closely, sometimes you can see the exposed edges of the background layer at top and left. Of course, you can crop the image to eliminate those edges before saving your painting.

Embossing: Grain Extract

Although *Grain extract* was originally intended for storing information to be used in simulating photographic grain or other textures, as in the squirrel example, it's also useful for making an *embossed* version of an image. It works with almost any image.

Normally, you'll need very little layer movement with Grain extract. The image in Figure 10-22 uses more offset than you'd normally want—partly to make sure the effect shows up well, and partly because the color accents are attractive.

In a real embossed work, of course, the image would be colorless. Many other "emboss" conversions will use as little as one or two pixel shifts, and won't show much color at all. You can always convert to grayscale to eliminate the color, of course.

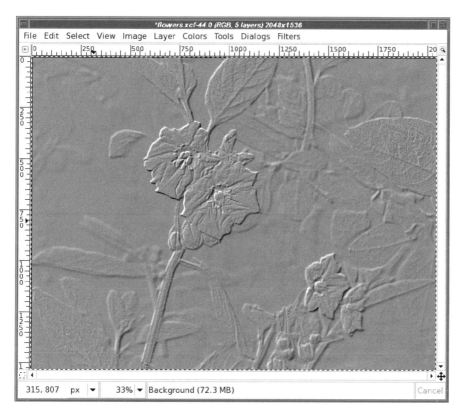

Figure 10-22. *The top layer was moved five pixels to the right and five pixels down while in Grain extract mode.*

Adding Blurs and Other Tricks for Artistic Effects

Sometimes you can use Gaussian Blur instead of an offset when using layer effects. Typically, a blur gives a somewhat weaker, more subtle effect than an offset. Edges won't be emphasized as strongly.

Gaussian Blurring the top layer in the Grain extract example, instead of offsetting it, gives an effect like a tintype photo (Figure 10-23). Reversing the layers—putting the blurred layer beneath the original rather than above it—gives a similar effect except that the colors are reversed (the flowers are darker than the background, instead of lighter).

There's a compromise between the offsetting and blurring: use a *Motion Blur*, which blurs in a specific direction. Since it's directional, Motion Blur acts a lot like an offset; but it smoothes out the effect, giving less emphasis to the edges and more to the gradations within the image. The color accents are also muted. The difference can be subtle, but try it to see whether you like it better.

By now, you probably see what's going on. Most images will have sudden changes in color where they transition from one object (a flower) to another (the background). These artistic effects all capitalize on those transitional edges. Anything that causes the edges to spread or interfere will give an interesting—and sometimes unexpected—result when you use Divide, Difference, Subtract, or Grain extract.

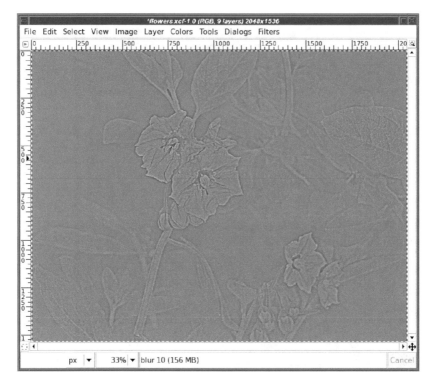

Figure 10-23. *Use Blur and then Grain extract for a tintype effect.*

Compositing Unrelated Images

So far, you've used layer modes to combine an image with itself (perhaps after minor modifications such as blur or offset). But, of course, you can use layer modes to combine two different images as well.

Using Soft Light for Combining Images

Soft light mode is a real workhorse for combining just about any two images (Figure 10-24). Copy an image and paste it as a new layer over a different image, and you'll probably get a fun result (Figure 10-25). As a rule, use the less distinct image as the background, since it will slightly dominate the combination. You can also use Soft light to give the effect of objects reflected from water or glass.

Compositing with Soft light doesn't do what you'd expect from the name: it doesn't soften the image. Instead, you'll get a nice increase in brightness and contrast. Even pictures you think are just fine can be surprisingly enhanced, with no fake look at all.

Figure 10-24. *Two unrelated images to be composited*

Figure 10-25. *Combine the two unrelated images with Soft light.*

Using Overlay for Dark Images

Overlay has an effect quite similar to Soft light, and is always worth trying to see how the effects compare. Overlay is also good for adding elements of an image on top of darker areas in another image, like the photographs in Figure 10-26. You'll still see elements of both, of course—it's not a substitute for painstakingly selecting an object and pasting it into another picture.

Figure 10-26. *Unrelated images: Shiprock, New Mexico, plus sailboats*

But sometimes you might not mind "ghostly images." For instance, the ghostly sailboats in front of dark, looming Shiprock give a nice effect (Figure 10-27).

Figure 10-27. *Overlay tends to make dark images, creating a moody effect.*

Using Screen to Get a Lighter Effect

Screen, too, is a useful tool for combining images—but it has a very different effect. Screen brightens the image, so instead of ghostly, looming figures, the brighter image will stand out (Figure 10-28).

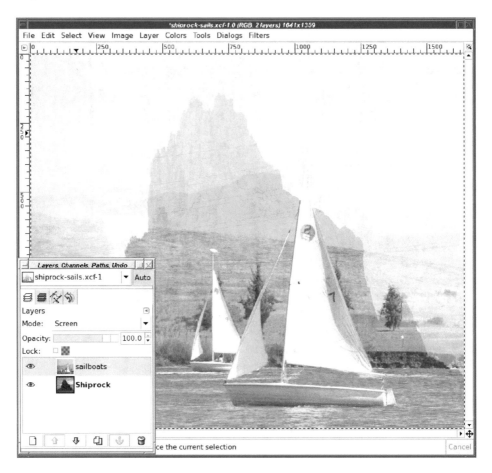

Figure 10-28. *Sailboats in front, in Screen mode; Shiprock in back*

Using Addition to Complement Light and Dark

Addition mode can be useful when you have two dark images that might work together, or two images with complementary light and dark areas (one is light where the other is dark), such as in Figure 10-29. Combining them in Addition mode gives the result in Figure 10-30.

Figure 10-29. *It's hard to see how these could relate.*

Figure 10-30. *Addition mode can combine dark areas of two images.*

Using Subtract to Make a Cutout Mask

Subtract usually inverts dark and light on the layer being subtracted. You can use it to take an image that has light and dark areas, such as the gull in Figure 10-31, and make a mask for another image, as shown in Figure 10-32.

Figure 10-31. *The gull's light and dark areas can make a mask for the building.*

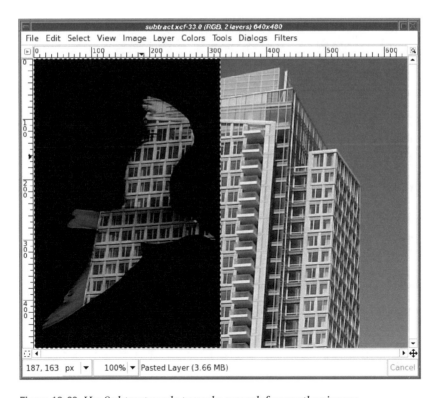

Figure 10-32. *Use Subtract mode to make a mask for another image.*

Difference will give a slightly different and weirder effect, turning the dark colors bright again (Figure 10-33).

Figure 10-33. *Difference adds color to the previously dark areas of the mask.*

Making Eerie Colors with Burn

When the background picture has very distinct darker and lighter areas, like the tree silhouettes in Figure 10-34, it can seem to turn into a mask when Burn mode is used (Figure 10-35). In this case, the trees blot out the strange rock formation, but the lighter sky alters its colors to appear otherworldly. You've probably seen effects like this used to illustrate science-fiction book covers.

Figure 10-34. *Burn works best when one image has distinct light and dark areas.*

Figure 10-35. *Burn mode can combine a sky or other light, colored area with another image for an interesting effect.*

Using Grain Merge to Add Texture

You've already seen, in the squirrel project, how to use Grain extract and Grain merge together. But you can use Grain merge with other patterns as well. To add texture to a photograph, use the photo as the lower layer, and fill the upper layer with a tileable pattern.

For instance, using GIMP's built-in pattern named "Crack" as the upper layer in Grain merge mode, on top of the sailboats, gives the result shown in Figure 10-36.

As always, when dealing with layer modes, the results of any particular combination tend to be unpredictable. These examples can point you in the right general direction, but experimentation will often give surprising results. You can duplicate layers and use multiple modes with varying degrees of opacity to create almost *anything*. It's fun and easy to try several options, and it's almost always rewarding.

Figure 10-36. *A pattern in Grain merge mode adds extra texture to an image.*

Stacking Images

Have you ever marveled at a space shot, like the ones from the Hubble Space Telescope? Did you know that the "raw" images straight from the camera are hardly ever that good?

Astrophotography is one area where image compositing is an essential tool. Professional observatories, NASA, and amateurs in their backyards all use a set of related techniques known collectively as *stacking*.

The first image stacks were just that: photographic negatives or slides stacked directly on top of each other. When these stacks were viewed on a light table, or printed, the result was a photograph with much higher contrast. With stacking, details that weren't visible in any single original became easy to see.

Of course, today, stacking is usually done by computer. Stacking multiple images of the same object is similar to the self-compositing you've already used earlier in this chapter. But compositing several different but similar images is better than self-compositing in many cases, as you'll see.

Sometimes astronomers get carried away with stacking. The famous "Hubble Deep Field" photo captured more than 1,500 distant galaxies in a tiny patch of sky 1/30th the diameter of the full moon. The Deep Field project shot 342 images over 10 consecutive days, and used 276 of them in the end. Of course, the Hubble team uses much more complex stacking and compositing methods than simple layer modes. But many of the basic principles are the same.

Although stacking techniques were developed first for astronomy, you can stack earth-bound images as well. You can boost the light level of a dim image, improve contrast, or even increase resolution. It can also be fun to stack several different images into an "average." But stacking will always add another benefit: reduced noise.

Reducing Noise

Every photograph includes some unwanted interference, from thermal activity in the camera's sensor chip or various other sources. (Such as cosmic rays. Really!) Collectively, these spurious signals are called *noise*.

Noise is random: it shows up in unpredictable places. If you take two images of the same scene, the scene may not change, but the noise will be different.

Suppose you shoot an image that has a light speck due to noise. If you composite that image with itself, or use a tool such as Levels or Curves to boost the contrast, you will increase the speck of noise as much as the object you're trying to capture. If you've tried boosting contrast on a very dark photograph, you've probably seen that already.

But if you composite two *different* images of the same object, chances are that the second image's noise will be in different places. The noise in the first image will be partially cancelled out by the second image, and vice versa. The result is a less noisy image.

So how do you go about making a stack? There are three steps:

1. Open the images as layers.

2. Register the layers.

3. Combine the layers.

Loading All the Images As Layers

Load each image in the stack as a separate layer. Open the first image normally, and then use *File ➤ Open as Layer...* for the rest. If you have more than two images, use Shift-click or Ctrl-click in the file selection dialog to select all your images at once, and they'll all open as separate layers.

Once all the layers are loaded, make all but the first two layers invisible. Next, before you stack the two layers, you have to register them.

Registering the Images Using Difference Mode

Stacking won't work well unless the images fit over each other exactly. If the subject of the photograph isn't in the same place, or isn't the same size, then it will look blurry when the two images are combined.

You can make this step much easier if you use a tripod when shooting images you plan to stack. If you try to shoot hand-held, you will almost certainly move or rotate the camera. That can be fixed, but it's tedious: use GIMP's Measure tool to measure sizes and angles in the two images, and then Scale by the ratio of the two measurements and Rotate by the difference in the angles. Eek! It's much better to use a tripod and get them right in the first place.

Note Even the best tripod will not give you perfectly registered photos of the night sky. Why? The earth is turning, which means, from the camera's point of view, that the sky is moving—about a degree every four minutes.

Once the images are approximately aligned, select the Move tool in the Toolbox and set the mode of the upper layer to Difference. This will show every place the two images differ. Two perfectly registered, identical layers will look totally black when the top layer is in Difference mode. Otherwise, move the upper layer around (remember the arrow keys for moving by one pixel at a time) to make the combined image as black as possible.

Now it's time to make a stack, using one of the methods I'll describe next. After you've stacked one layer, make the next layer visible, register it, and stack it. Repeat until you're out of layers.

Increasing Light by Additive Stacking

There are times when a flash just isn't appropriate. Did you ever go out at night with your little digital camera and wish you had a fancy SLR that could take time exposures?

With stacking, you can—even if your camera can't. Just take a lot of short exposures, and then stack them in Addition mode.

For instance, I shot some photos of a fence near a local reservoir. The camera I was using wouldn't do an exposure longer than four seconds. At that setting, the original images just look black. It's hard to tell that there's anything in the shot at all.

If I take a single image and use Curves or Levels on it, I can see that I do indeed have a shot of the fence. But I have to enhance the image so much that it becomes extremely noisy and grainy.

I can do a little better by making 10 or 12 copies of one image and compositing them all in Addition mode. But it's still very noisy.

But what if I take 12 *different* images of the fence, and then stack those?

Stacking different images allows you to increase the light level a lot with hardly any increase in the noise. You can even duplicate some layers: Figure 10-37 shows a stack of 24 layers total, two copies each of 12 different layers, all in Addition mode.

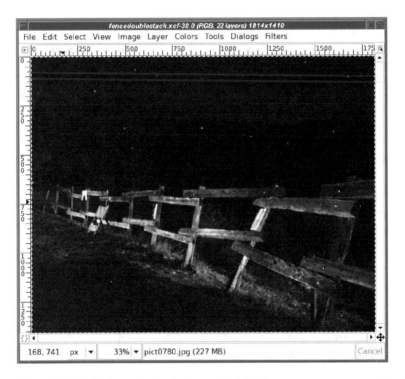

Figure 10-37. *A 24-layer stack of a fence at night. You can even see some stars!*

This technique reduces noise so well that you can boost the brightness even more using Levels or Curves (after merging or flattening all the layers into one) without hurting the image much.

So grab a tripod (even one of the little plastic ones with legs a few inches long, if your camera is small enough), wander off to a dark place, and try taking some shots!

Increasing Contrast by Multiplicative Stacking

Those great shots that you see from NASA spacecraft aren't just snapshots downloaded straight from the camera. They take a lot of processing before NASA puts them up on public websites. (If you watch NASA TV, sometimes you can even see GIMP windows on screens at Mission Control! Of course, NASA uses a wide assortment of tools, not just GIMP.)

Figure 10-38 shows an original photo of Saturn's largest moon, Titan, taken from the Cassini spacecraft. (You can find unprocessed images by looking for "raw images" on the Cassini website.) You can see that there's a little detail there, but it's hard to see it well. The contrast is very low.

But Cassini actually shot four of these Titan shots, and you can download all four and stack them.

Register the frames, and then set each layer's mode to Multiply (Figure 10-39).

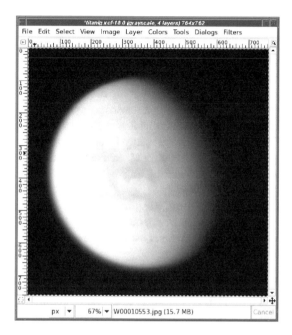

Figure 10-38. *Saturn's moon, Titan, from NASA's Cassini spacecraft*

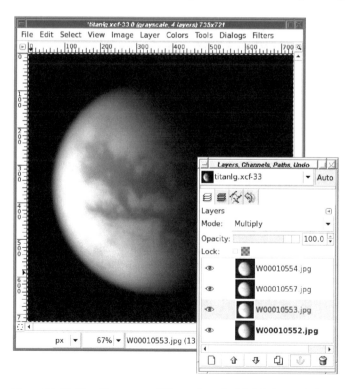

Figure 10-39. *Stacking several Titan shots in Multiply mode boosts contrast, so you can see Titan's cloud details.*

Increasing Resolution by Averaging

When the Titan images were stacked, they didn't get sharper, merely more contrasty. But stacking, carefully done, can also increase sharpness. Technically, what you're increasing is *resolution*, the size of the smallest detail that can be distinguished in the photograph.

In recent years, video astrophotography has become very popular. Astrovideographers take cheap webcams or security cameras, modify them to mount on a telescope, and then take videos of bright objects such as the moon, Jupiter, or Mars. Each individual image is awful, and it doesn't make a very interesting movie. But if you split the video into its component frames—several hundred separate images—you can stack those frames to make an amazingly sharp photograph. Using these techniques, amateurs are now getting images as sharp as the professional observatory photos from just a few decades ago.

First you have to remove the bad frames. Turbulence in the atmosphere (even on a clear night) means that some images in these "movies" will be too blurry to be worth keeping. Then stack the remaining frames using an averaging technique. Each layer is in normal mode, and the stacking is done with GIMP's Opacity slider.

The bottom layer, of course, is at 100% opacity. Click on the layer above it, and change the opacity to 50%. Now you're seeing an image that comes half from the first layer and half from the second: they're averaged. The resulting image won't be any brighter or darker than the components, but it will share pixels from both.

Now make the third layer visible and active. Set its opacity to 33%. That means that it'll be contributing only a third to the final image; the combination of the first two images will contribute two-thirds. So you're still seeing an average of the three.

Turn on the fourth layer, and set its opacity to 25%. And so on through all the layers. The rule you're following is that layer N gets opacity 1/N: 1/1, 1/2, 1/3, 1/4, and so on.

Of course, you wouldn't want to do this by hand if you had 200 layers. Astrovideographers usually use dedicated programs that handle both stacking and registration. Within GIMP, for a large number of layers, you'd be better off writing a script (you'll learn how to write simple scripts in Chapter 11).

Stitching Panoramas

Ever find a beautiful sweeping view and feel frustrated that your camera's lens isn't wide enough to fit it all in?

Even if you have an SLR with replaceable lenses, sometimes you'll want to shoot vistas that are just too wide for the camera to capture in one shot.

Back in the film days (remember film?), I sometimes used to shoot several overlapping pictures, and then take the prints and tape them together and pin them up outside my office. They might have ended up looking something like Figure 10-40.

That might have been good enough a decade or so ago, but you can do a lot better than that now!

Figure 10-40. *An old-style panorama, before GIMP*

Combining several images into a panorama is called *stitching*. The process is straightforward, but it includes several steps, and requires some patience to get a result that looks truly seamless.

Let's take it one step at a time.

Shooting the Images

Perhaps you already have a collection of images you'd like to stitch together. If not, here are some handy tips for taking a panoramic series. Some people find this stage the most intimidating part of the process, but it's not a problem if you follow a few guidelines.

Overlap Photos for Panoramas

Overlap quite a bit. At first, you might be tempted to put the left edge of image 2 right where the right edge of image 1 was. There are two problems with that.

First, camera lenses (especially wide-angle lenses) distort the image (a phenomenon known as *lens warp*). The distortion is especially pronounced at the edges. If you use a lot of overlap, you'll be using mostly the centers of each frame where there isn't so much distortion. (GIMP does have a plug-in to remove lens warp—*Filters ➤ Distorts ➤ Lens Distortion*—but that adds extra work.) Second, a lot of overlap means that if one image turns out to be bad, you can discard it and still make a usable panorama from the remaining images.

Overlap at least a third of each image (as in Figure 10-40), but more is better, especially if you're using a digital camera: "bits are cheap."

Keep the Horizon Level

Keep the camera level: don't tilt it between shots. If you have a tripod, or a flat surface like a picnic table, that makes it easy.

If you have to hold the camera by hand (and let's face it, most of the time when you see a spectacular vista worthy of a panoramic shot, you probably won't have your tripod with you), try standing in a stable position and twisting your body as you take each shot.

Pay attention to the horizon in the camera's viewfinder: try to keep it parallel to the top and bottom of the frame. If you accidentally tilt the camera, you can use GIMP's Rotate tool to make it level after the fact. However, rotating images so that they all match well enough to make a panorama is more difficult than it sounds, and you can save yourself a lot of work by shooting them level to begin with.

It's less important that you keep the horizon at the same height for each photo. You can have more sky in one shot, more ground in another, and the panorama will still look fine. The downside: to get a rectangular picture you may have to trim more from the top and bottom than is ideal.

Match Exposure Levels

If you can shoot all the images at the same exposure setting, that may save a little work later. Otherwise, the individual photos may vary in color or brightness. Notice the different colors of the sky and the ground between the left and middle pictures of Figure 10-40.

Some cameras offer a panorama setting which does this automatically, or manual exposure controls. If yours doesn't, you may be able to simulate it by *metering* on a point somewhere around the middle of your panorama: hold the shutter button halfway down, rotate the camera (still holding the button halfway), and press the button the rest of the way to take the picture. Repeat as necessary.

This isn't crucial. You can adjust brightness in GIMP, of course. And a panorama whose components have slightly different brightness levels may still look okay. Try it both ways and see whether it's worthwhile for you.

Once you've shot all your images and uploaded them to GIMP, it's time to start stitching.

Decide on a Resolution

Although it's normally best to work at the full resolution of your camera and scale the final image down after you're finished, that's not necessarily true for a panorama.

Panoramic images combine a lot of photos into one humongous GIMP image. Using three-megapixel or larger images for a big panorama (say, five or more images) can take up so much memory that it slows the machine to a crawl. The saved XCF will take up a lot of disk space, too (don't forget that you can use a compressed XCF format by saving to a file name ending in .xcf.gz or .xcf.bz2). You might use full resolution if you need an image that large—for instance, if you plan on printing to a banner three feet long. But otherwise, if you notice slowness, consider scaling down a bit.

Once you know the resolution of the individual images, how many of them there are, and the overlap you used, you can calculate how big an image you'll need to hold the panorama.

Calculate Your Expected New Image Size

The next step in building a panorama is to make a new image of the right size. What is the right size? That's something you'll have to figure out.

Tip If you'd rather not do the calculations, I've written a script called Pandora to automate the first few steps of panorama stitching. Find it under "Scripts" at *http://gimpbook.com*.

The easy way out is to simply take the width of your images and multiply by the total number you'll stitch together. There's not much penalty for starting with a new image that's too big—you'll just crop it in the end anyway. GIMP may complain if you try to create a new image larger than the parameters set in your preferences. The default is 128MB (up from 64MB in GIMP 2.2). Should you need to change this setting, you'll find it in Preferences under *Environment*.

If you're feeling lucky, subtract whatever you think you can get away with, say 20% to 25%. Don't stress over it. If it's too big, crop it later. If it turns out you need more space, a simple *Image* ➤ *Canvas Size* will fix it in a jiffy.

Once you've decided on a size, create the new image with a white background. I'll refer to this image as the "panorama image."

Load the First Two Images

Open the first image as a new layer and move it (using the Move tool) all the way to the left side of the image (assuming your panorama is left to right). The panorama image will look something like Figure 10-41.

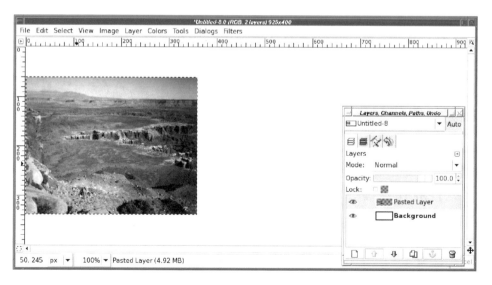

Figure 10-41. *The first image is loaded.*

Next, load the second image as a new layer, just as you did the first, and use the Move tool to move the new layer to where it approximately overlaps the first one. Don't worry about getting it perfect...yet.

Make a Gradient Layer Mask

How do you get rid of the sharp edge between the first picture and the second? By using a layer mask.

In the Layers dialog, right-click on the second layer and choose *Add Layer Mask…*. Initialize it to *White (full opacity)*, the default.

Now use the Gradient tool to draw a gradient on the layer mask. It should be white everywhere to the right of the overlap, shading to black at the left edge of the second image. If you have the usual black foreground and white background, and the Gradient tool is in normal mode (not *Reverse*), this means starting your drag from the left edge of the second image, and then dragging right for some distance, not all the way to the point where the first image ends. You'll end up with a result like Figure 10-42.

Tip Use the Ctrl key while dragging your gradient, to help you get a gradient that's exactly horizontal.

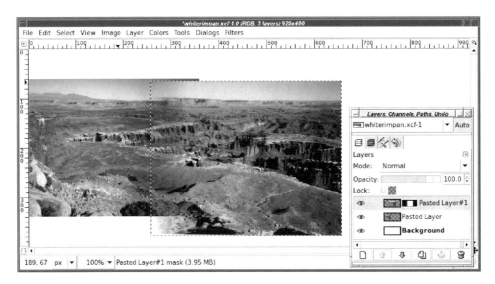

Figure 10-42. *Draw a gradient on the layer mask so that the left edge of the second image fades into the first.*

Fine-tune the Position of the Second Image

Now that the second image has transparent areas, you can position it more accurately. Switch to the Move tool, but there's a trick: if you simply click and drag with the Move tool, you'll move the layer mask rather than the layer itself, since the mask is still selected in the Layers dialog (indicated by the white boundary around it in Figure 10-42). Click on the layer preview in the Layers dialog to select the layer and not just its mask.

Zoom way in so that you can see details, and scroll so you can see the region of the image where the two layers overlap. Then use the Move tool to move the second image around until it matches the first image as well as possible. (Don't forget about the arrow keys.)

It'll usually be obvious when the images mesh. When you have two overlapping images (one partially transparent) that don't quite match, the image will look a bit blurry, as though you had a few too many beers before beginning the stitching process. When you find the right position, suddenly the image will seem to snap to focus, and all the blurriness and double vision will go away.

The catch? It won't happen everywhere in the image. Most of the time, the two images won't match up perfectly. If you line them up in the center, the top and bottom won't match. You're seeing lens warp. If you overlapped the images a lot (50% or more) or zoomed in when you shot the images, you'll see less lens warp, but there will always be some.

Usually, you're best off matching two layers at the vertical midpoint, and not worrying about the top and bottom (you can fix that in the next step). But if your panorama has a pronounced horizontal line somewhere—say, the horizon in an ocean panorama, or the canyon rim in my Canyonlands shots—you may want to use that as the location to match.

Adjust the Layer Mask

The gradient in your layer mask was great for a first step, but now it's time to eliminate parts of the image that don't match well. You don't want to replace the gradient, just add to it.

In this canyon panorama, the first priority is getting rid of those mesa tops that don't line up. To do that, a bit of black added with the Paintbrush tool in the upper left of the second image's layer mask will make the ghostly floating mesa disappear. (Remember, black in the layer mask makes that part of the image invisible.)

Watch the double images gradually go away as you scribble—it's fun.

If you need to get rid of a whole corner of an image, you can add another gradient to the existing gradient. Use the *Mode* menu in the Gradient tool: any of the darkening modes, such as Multiply, Subtract, or Darken only, will do (they'll give slightly different results at the edges where the two gradients meet, but you probably won't see the difference).

Tip Remember that you can use Show Layer Mask from the Layers dialog (or Alt-click or Alt-Shift-click on the layer preview) if you get confused about what your mask looks like.

When you've finished adjusting the mask, click on the layer preview in the Layers dialog so the mask won't remain selected. That way, you won't be surprised if you try to do anything with the layer later.

Figure 10-43 shows the mesa-top area cleaned up (I cheated a little and made a new butte). Notice that the sky now looks patchy. Don't worry about the sky—you can clean that up later.

Figure 10-43. *The area around the mesa top is cleaned up. The sky still needs work.*

Adjust with Other Tools If Necessary

Most of the time, you can get what you need (except the sky) by drawing on the layer mask. But in a few cases, you'll have something—perhaps a branch, or a road—that just doesn't meet in the two images.

Sometimes, you can use other tools to fix this. Of course, you can draw directly on the image, using your cloning and smudging skills from Chapter 6. But first, try IWarp (described in Chapter 7, in the section "Distorts"). Sometimes careful use of IWarp can do exactly what you need.

Add the Rest of the Images

You're done adding the second image! Now, repeat the steps for each of the pieces of your panorama: load the image, add a layer mask, move it into place, adjust the layer mask, and make any additional adjustments you need.

■**Tip** You can also load all the images in one step at the beginning, using *File* ➤ *Open as Layers*. If you do that, I recommend turning off visibility on all but the first two layers, then make each new layer visible when you're ready for it.

Sometimes you'll find that one image is a *lot* harder to stitch than the others, especially if it's rotated. If you used a lot of overlap between photos, you can probably discard the problematic ones and save yourself a lot of time. Don't get wrapped up in the need to use every photo.

Final Adjustments

Ironically, skies are particularly hard to get right in panoramas. Differences in exposure seem much more obvious in a clear blue sky. So go ahead and cheat: select the sky using your favorite selection technique (for instance, use Select by Color with *Sample Merged* turned on, or just paint on the QuickMask), and then make a sky in a new layer using a gradient between two shades of blue, just like in the "Decomposing to HSV" exercise in Chapter 8.

Finally, crop the panorama. The top and bottom edges of the component images probably won't quite line up. It's your choice: you can leave the edges ragged (Figure 10-44), to show off its panoramic nature, or you can crop to an even rectangle so it looks like the whole thing was taken in one shot.

Figure 10-44. *Crop the panorama. Leave the ragged edges if you like: sometimes it's fun to show how many images went into your creation.*

Summary

Now you know all sorts of ways to composite several images. No book could possibly list all the amazing things you can do compositing images in GIMP, but now you know the important tools and a collection of different techniques. You should have a solid base from which to begin experimenting with your own images.

You'll also be able to apply techniques you find in web tutorials. If you experiment with these ideas, and try them on the sorts of images you use yourself, you'll be an expert in no time.

But for now, take a break from fiddling with images by hand. During the course of this chapter you've done quite a lot of repetitive operations that would have been so much easier if they were automated. In the next chapter, you'll learn how to automate GIMP processes yourself, using plug-ins and scripting.

CHAPTER 11

■■■

Plug-ins and Scripting

GIMP is a supremely flexible image-editing program. But sometimes you may need to do something unusual, something that isn't built-in. Or maybe you just need to do the same repetitive operation over and over on many different images.

Either way, don't give up just because the function you need isn't in the menus anywhere. GIMP's flexible architecture means it's easy to add plug-ins and scripts to do nearly anything you need to do. There are dozens, maybe hundreds, of plug-ins readily available. But if you can't find one to do what you need, you can even write your own, using a choice of several languages.

Many plug-ins are written in the C programming language, the same language used to write GIMP itself. But other plug-ins are actually scripts.

Scripts are a special type of plug-in, a type that doesn't need any special *compiler* software. GIMP supports three scripting languages, *Script-Fu*, *Python*, and *Perl*, in varying degrees. (There are also experimental Ruby and C# add-ons you can download if you're a fan of either of those languages.) You'll learn more about the differences later in this chapter.

Scripts are especially easy to write and offer three benefits:

- They're easy for other people to write, so there's a good chance you can find a script already written to do what you need.

- They're easy to read, so if you can find a script similar to what you need, you might be able to modify it for your purposes.

- It's not very hard to write a script from scratch.

So let's take a look at what all this means. You'll learn how to find and install plug-ins, and how to find out which plug-ins you already have installed. You'll also learn how to find scripts, install them, read them, and modify them. And finally, you'll learn how to write a new script from scratch to automate some simple but useful operations. The chapter will cover the following topics:

- Plug-ins

- Writing GIMP scripts

- User interface options for scripts

- A Python script

- Finding out how to do things: the Procedure Browser

- A Perl script

- Writing a C plug-in

Plug-ins

Strictly speaking, anything that isn't built into GIMP's core libraries is a plug-in. You've probably already used lots of GIMP plug-ins: nearly everything in the *Filters* menu is a plug-in. About half of the *Colors* menu and most of the *Xtns* menu in the Toolbox are also plug-ins.

The Plug-in Browser

How do you know which plug-ins are already installed? With the Plug-in Browser (Figure 11-1), accessed through the Toolbox menu: *Xtns* ➤ *Plug-in Browser....*

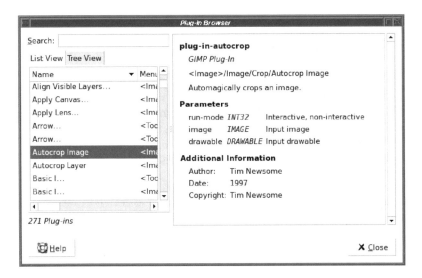

Figure 11-1. *The Plug-in Browser*

Yikes—there are a lot of plug-ins! Bet you didn't know you had that many installed.

The Plug-in Browser is a good way of finding functionality without searching through all the menus. If you're pretty sure that there's some sort of automatic crop function, try entering **crop** in the *Search* field. All plug-ins that include the name "crop" will come up in the list. You can get more information about each one by scrolling right: the browser will show you *Menu Path*, *Image Types*, and *Installation Date*. Or you can get a different overview of where each plug-in fits into GIMP's menus by clicking the Tree View tab, as shown in Figure 11-2.

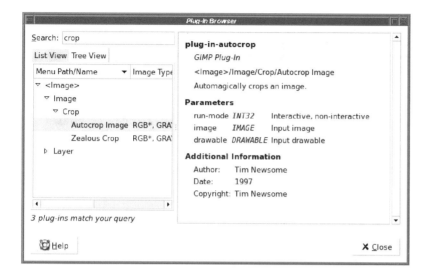

Figure 11-2. *The Tree View tab shows GIMP's menu structure; entering a term in the Search field limits the number of plug-ins shown.*

The *Image Type* field tells you which kinds of images the plug-in accepts. Some plug-ins will only work on RGB images, and will be grayed out if the current image is indexed or grayscale. Other plug-ins may work only on indexed, only on grayscale, or only on RGBA (RGB images with an alpha channel). "*" is a wildcard: "RGB*" means that both RGB and RGBA images will work, and "*" by itself means the plug-in will accept any type of image. A blank image type means the plug-in creates a new image (as with most plug-ins called from the Toolbox's *Xtns* menu) rather than working on an existing one.

When you click on a plug-in, the right half of the dialog gives you more information about that plug-in, including its location in the menus, a description of the plug-in, the parameters it takes (these are usually the same as the values you'll be able to change in the plug-in's dialog) in case you ever wanted to use it in another plug-in, and the name of the plug-in's author.

Finding External Plug-ins

What if you've searched the Plug-in Browser and there's nothing there? Might someone else have developed a plug-in to do what you need?

You have two options to find such a plug-in: GIMP's Plug-in Registry and a web search.

The Plug-in Registry

GIMP's official Plug-in Registry is located at *http://registry.gimp.org*. Anyone who develops a plug-in or script for GIMP can register it there.

The Plug-in Registry is theoretically a good resource. But it's a bit disorganized: a lot of plug-in writers don't register there, and even if they do, the registry's search isn't very flexible.

Try the Plug-in Registry first when you're looking for a way to do something in GIMP. But if you don't find anything there, don't despair: try a web search.

Finding Plug-ins on the Web

A web search often works much better for finding GIMP plug-ins. Lots of people develop plug-ins and never get around to listing them on the registry. Maybe they don't know about the registry, or they don't think their plug-in is quite polished enough to list there, even though it might be good enough for your purposes.

Use "gimp" as one of your search terms, along with the functionality you're looking for, such as "redeye." If you get too many hits (sometimes you'll get a lot of mailing list traffic discussing how to do things by hand), you could try adding "plug-in." If you use Google, searching for a hyphenated term like *plug-in*, without quotes, will match any of "plug-in," "plugin," or "plug in") or "script." For example, in the Google search box enter **gimp redeye plug-in OR script**.

Installing Scripts and Plug-ins

With any luck, the plug-in find will come with installation instructions. But some don't. Here's what you need to know about installing plug-ins.

You first need to know what type it is: whether it's a C plug-in or a script. Usually the page where you found the plug-in will tell you. In addition, a script will usually have an extension such as .scm (Script-Fu), .py (Python), or .pl (Perl), while a C file will end in .c.

If the file you downloaded has the extension .zip, .tar.gz, or .tar.bz2, that means it's part of a compressed archive. You must unpack the archive first (using a program such as *unzip* or *tar*) before you can proceed.

Installing a Script

Installing a script is easy: you just copy it to the right folder—either *scripts* or *plug-ins*—inside your GIMP profile.

If you don't remember where your GIMP profile folder is, check the *Folders* category in the *File ➤ Preferences* window (you may have to click on the triangle next to *Folders* to expand the category). There are separate entries for Scripts and Plug-ins. Clicking on either entry will normally list two different folders on your system: the location where GIMP's built-in scripts are stored (most likely a folder under wherever you installed GIMP) and the location of your personal scripts folder inside your profile.

In some cases, GIMP may not show both entries. If it doesn't show your personal folder, try clicking on one of the other entries in the *Folders* category: you can probably find your profile folder that way.

Once you've located your profile, to install a Script-Fu, just take the file.scm and copy it to the folder named "scripts." If you already have GIMP running, you can tell it to look for new Script-Fu scripts with the Toolbox menu: *Xtns ➤ Script-Fu ➤ Refresh Scripts...*.

For Python or Perl, copy the file to the "plug-ins" folder instead of "scripts." On Linux or Mac OS, you also need to make sure the file is executable (`chmod a+x file.py` or `file.pl`). There's no equivalent to *Refresh Scripts...* for Python or Perl, so you'll have to restart GIMP before it sees your new script.

Tip If you have the *gimptool* program installed, you can use it to install Script-Fu scripts. In a terminal window, type **gimptool --install-script file.scm** (that's two dashes before install, one after it). For Python or Perl plug-ins, use **gimptool --install-bin file** (two dashes before install, only one between install and bin).

This eliminates the need to find your GIMP profile, if you don't mind typing commands. You'll need gimptool for installing C plug-ins anyway (see the next section).

Installing a C Plug-in

Installing a C plug-in is no more complicated—*if* the plug-in has already been compiled for your platform. C is a *compiled language*, which means that in order to run anything written in C, it has to be translated (compiled) into machine language first. The compiled version is referred to as an *executable* or a *binary*.

Compiling makes a C plug-in run much faster than a script, since the compiler speaks the machine's native language. However, it also means there's an extra step in creating something that can run, and it has to be done separately for each platform.

If there's a binary available for your operating system, just take that file and move it to the plug-ins folder inside your GIMP profile. Alternately, if you have gimptool installed, you can use gimptool --install-bin. The next time you restart GIMP, the new plug-in should show up in the menus.

Tip Where did the new plug-in show up? A lot of plug-in developers forget to tell you where to look in the menus to find their plug-in once it's installed. Since GIMP has so many features already, searching for some-thing new could take quite a while! Fortunately, you can use the Plug-in Browser to figure out where it appears.

However, since many plug-in developers don't have C compilers for all three platforms, often they simply make the C source code available, and you have to build (compile) it your-self. You'll need some supporting programs to do that.

Installing a Gimp C Development Environment

On Mac and Linux systems, installing a C compiler is easy. The GNU C compiler (gcc) comes on the Mac OS X Development CD, and is included with most Linux distributions. If it's not installed, it can usually be installed easily using the software update tools provided with your system. You'll probably need a few additional packages, in particular the program gimptool. It's sometimes included with GIMP, but if not, look for a package called something like *gimp-dev* or *gimp-devel*.

You'll also need development packages for X11 and GTK. Most packaging systems should automatically include these when you install the GIMP development package, but if you get errors, these packages may be what you're lacking.

Windows is a bit harder since there's no built-in C compiler. If you don't already have a compiler installed, you're probably best off getting MinGW, the Minimalist GNU for Windows packages. Find them at *http://www.mingw.org*. You will need both MinGW and MSYS.

In addition, even if you already had a compiler, you'll need the development libraries for GTK+, glib, and other related features. You can get them by clicking on *GIMP for Windows* on the main *gimp.org* site. Look for packages with "-dev" in the name.

Building a C Plug-in

Once you have the compiler and libraries installed, it's time to build your plug-in. You'll need a terminal window open so you can type commands: the *Command Prompt* program should work on Windows systems, *Terminal* on Macs, or any terminal client on Linux. Then type

```
gimptool --build filename.c
```

where *filename.c* is the name of the plug-in file. Remember to use two dashes, not just one.

If this results in errors, it may be that you're missing libraries. Double-check that you have all the requirements installed.

Once the compile completes without errors, it's time to install it. Type

```
gimptool --install filename
```

where *filename* is the file you built in the previous step. (Some complex plug-ins may need to install more than one file, and use their own installers, usually run from a "Makefile," so the user need only type **make install**. Creation of Makefiles and installers is outside the scope of this book.)

Writing GIMP Scripts

Now it's time to take a closer look at what's inside GIMP scripts.

GIMP can be scripted in three languages: Script-Fu, Python, and Perl (plus Ruby and C# if you don't mind installing experimental packages). They each have their advantages and disadvantages.

Script-Fu (= Scheme (= Lisp))

Script-Fu (a pun on "kung-fu") is GIMP's built-in scripting language. Script-Fu has one big advantage: it is always available in every version of GIMP. If you want to write a script to distribute widely, Script-Fu is the best choice. You can be fairly sure everyone will be able to use it.

In addition, most scripts distributed with GIMP are written in Script-Fu. That means that you can find examples already installed on your system for all sorts of useful techniques. Since the easiest way to learn scripting is to copy an existing script (as you'll see in a moment), that's a big advantage.

The downside of Script-Fu is that its syntax is somewhat difficult for most people. Script-Fu is actually just GIMP's term for a language called Scheme, a dialect of Lisp. To be even more specific, GIMP 2.4 uses a dialect of Scheme called Tiny Scheme, and you can find some documentation on its syntax with a web search for "tiny scheme." Prior to 2.4, Script-Fu was based on a slightly different Scheme dialect called SIOD, and there's a migration guide on the GIMP website to help with translating old scripts.

Lisp is a language invented in 1960 for mathematics and artificial intelligence research. The name stands for "**list p**rocessing," because it's good at processing lists of items. But Lisp programmers joke that it actually stands for "Lots of Irritating Stupid Parentheses," a phrase that you will readily understand after looking at some Script-Fu examples.

Don't be too scared off by the parentheses. Often, you can copy bits and pieces from existing programs to make simple scripts without needing to understand much about Lisp. But if you really dislike the syntax, you may be better off with one of GIMP's other scripting languages.

Python

Python is a much more modern language, created in 1990. It has a clear, straightforward syntax and is a friendly introduction to general-purpose programming. It's also well integrated into GIMP, so it's fairly easy to write gimp-python scripts. It's much faster than Script-Fu, and can do most of the same low-level operations that C plug-ins can.

Sounds great—so what's the bad news? Well, Python didn't become part of the standard GIMP install until quite recently, and is even now a bit tricky to install on Windows. The Python situation is better than it used to be—gimp-python comes as part of GIMP 2.4—but in addition you need the Python language installed on your system. You can get it from *http://python.org* if you don't already have it. You may also need the PyGTK package, from *http://pygtk.org*.

You can easily tell whether you have gimp-python installed and working: check for a Python menu in the Toolbox under *Xtns*.

If you're just learning scripting and you have gimp-python installed, it's well worth trying it out.

Perl

Perl is a well-established and popular scripting language, commonly used on web servers and for system administration.

Perl used to come standard with GIMP, at least on UNIX systems. But somewhere along the line, it became less popular for GIMP scripting, and today it's not included as part of the standard GIMP package. You can see whether you have gimp-perl installed by looking for a *Perl* or *Perl-Fu* menu under *Xtns*.

It's still possible to install gimp-perl as a separate package, and there are still plenty of gimp-perl scripts in the Plug-in Registry and elsewhere on the web. If you're familiar with the Perl language and prefer it to Python or Scheme, then there's no reason not to use Perl as your introduction to GIMP scripting. If you're not already a Perl fan, though, you're probably better off sticking to Python or Script-Fu.

Reading and Modifying a Script-Fu Script

You don't have to be a programmer to write simple GIMP scripts, or to modify existing scripts, though of course programming experience will give you a head start.

It's easiest to begin with an existing script and modify it. A quick run through the process will show you how it's done.

Let's dig deeper by solving a problem that always frustrated me. GIMP has a useful little Sphere script, in the Toolbox *Xtns* menu under *Misc* (in earlier versions, look for *Misc* inside *Script-Fu*). It shows you the dialog in Figure 11-3, and produces a nice sphere like the one in Figure 11-4.

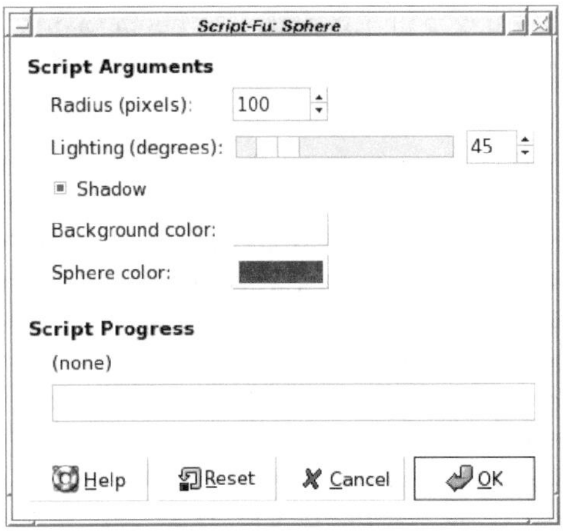

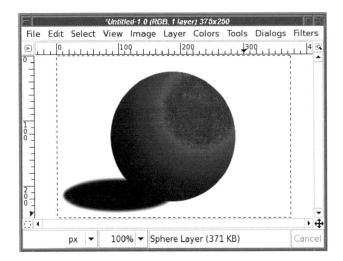

Figure 11-3. *The Sphere script's dialog*

Figure 11-4. *The sphere generated by the built-in Sphere script*

You might want to take one of these spheres and paste them into a drawing—wouldn't it make a nice Christmas tree ornament or poodle nose? But you can't! The sphere generated by the script always has a solid background.

If you want to paste the sphere into another image, you either have to use your selection skills to get rid of the background, or make your own sphere by hand (as you learned to do in Chapter 9). That's a lot of work. But GIMP is an open source program, and that means you aren't limited to the choices the developers made: you can take the Sphere script and do anything you want with it. Why not just make it do the right thing?

Find the Original Script

The first step is to locate the existing script. You can find where GIMP scripts are stored by looking in the Preferences window (*File* ➤ *Preferences* from the Toolbox): expand the *Folders* category and click on *Scripts*.

GIMP should show you at least two folders. One is the place where you can put personal copies of scripts; the other is in a system directory where GIMP has its own files installed.

Make a note of these two locations. You'll use them both.

Now find the script itself (in the system script directory). Usually it will have a .scm (short for "scheme") extension. You generally have to guess what the file name might be, but in this case it's not too hard: there's a file there called sphere.scm.

Edit a Copy of the Script

It's not a good idea to edit GIMP's existing scripts in place—what if something goes wrong but you don't have a copy of the original?—so be safe and copy sphere.scm to your personal scripts folder.

Caution There's a trick to copying the script on a Mac. Since it's inside an "Application," double-clicking the folder will launch Gimp.app! Instead, either right-click on the application icon, or use Ctrl-click if you have a one-button mouse. You'll be presented with a pop-up dialog, where you can select *Show Package Contents*. This will open a normal folder from which you can navigate to your scripts folder in the usual fashion. Alternately, for the adventurous, you can use the UNIX copy command cp from Terminal.app.

Give the script a new name, like *mysphere.scm*, and open it with a text editor. You need a program that handles plain text, not a word processor.

WHY A TEXT EDITOR?

Most word processors save to a format designed to preserve text fonts, styles, and layout information. The result may not be readable by *anything* other than the original word-processing program, and GIMP probably won't understand it at all.

It's better to just use something that naturally reads and writes plain text. A simple program like Windows WordPad is fine if you don't already have a favorite text editor. (Why not Notepad? It does handle text, but only the sort written in Windows. In particular, it's not very good at handling the various kinds of line breaks—what you get when you hit Enter—used on other computer systems.)

On Mac, TextEdit works perfectly. Normally, TextEdit is smart enough to open an .scm file as plain text, and save it the same way. But you should check anyway to make sure—if you can see *Make Plain Text* in the *Format* menu, use it!

On Linux, there are quite a variety of text editors available—such as joe, vim, emacs, ee, gedit, kedit—and you probably have a favorite already.

If you find yourself writing a lot of plug-ins, a good programmer's editor can make it easier by highlighting different parts of the program in different colors, handling indentation for you, matching parentheses, and other niceties.

Take a deep breath, open mysphere.scm in your text editor, and follow along on a tour through the script.

Make the Script Your Own

All GIMP scripts use a *registration procedure* to tell GIMP the name of the script and where to put it in the menus. The name of the file doesn't figure in.

Since you copied the script to a new place but haven't changed the name it uses when it registers, GIMP now has two scripts called Sphere, in exactly the same place in the menus. That's no good—this means that when you call one of them, you don't know which of the two scripts you'll get. To fix that, you need to change the name of the script—not just the file name, but the names it registers inside the file.

Skip to the end of the file and look for `script-fu-menu-register`:

```
(script-fu-register "script-fu-sphere"
                    _"_Sphere..."
                    "Simple sphere with a drop shadow"
                    "Spencer Kimball"
                    "Spencer Kimball"
                    "1996"
                    ""
                    SF-ADJUSTMENT _"Radius (pixels)"      '(100 5 500 1 10 0 1)
                    SF-ADJUSTMENT _"Lighting (degrees)"   '(45 0 360 1 10 0 0)
                    SF-TOGGLE     _"Shadow"               TRUE
                    SF-COLOR      _"Background color"     '(255 255 255)
                    SF-COLOR      _"Sphere color"         '(255 0 0))

(script-fu-menu-register "script-fu-sphere"
                    _"<Toolbox>/Xtns/Misc")
```

`script-fu-register` has several jobs. First, it sets the name of the routine that does the work. In this case, that's `script-fu-sphere`. You'll see how that's used in a moment.

Right after that is the name that GIMP will show the user: in this case, `_"_Sphere..."`. That's the name that shows up in the menus when you call the function. It's a good idea to change that now, so you can tell the difference between your version of the script and the one that's built-in.

What are those underscores? They're both optional; you may include them or not, as you choose.

The first one, outside the quotation marks, helps with translating the script into other languages. Someone translating the Sphere script will make a "catalog" of all the strings in the script and their translations. The underscore is an indication that this is a string that might need to get translated. Behind the scenes, it also helps implement the actual display of the translated strings so the user will see the right language. You can leave it off, but then it will be harder for speakers of other languages to adapt your script.

The second underscore has to do with menus: it's a way of accessing the function by using the keyboard. (If you have the *Misc* menu showing, and there's an underscore before the S in *Sphere*, then pressing S will run that function.) As a beginner script writer, you're fine leaving this underscore off (though it usually won't hurt anything if you leave it there).

So change `script-fu-sphere` to something like `script-fu-my-sphere`, and change `_"_Sphere..."` to `_"My Sphere..."` (notice that the underscore outside the quotes has been left in, so the script can be translated, but the one inside has been removed). Be sure to change the `script-fu-sphere` in `script-fu-menu-register` as well. So now they look like

```
(script-fu-register "script-fu-my-sphere"
                    _"My Sphere..."
                    "Simple sphere with a drop shadow"
```

and

```
 (script-fu-menu-register "script-fu-my-sphere"
                          "<Toolbox>/Xtns/Misc")
```

■**Caution** This two-part registration is new for GIMP 2.4. If you're using 2.2, or you want your script to work for 2.2 users as well as in 2.4, combine `script-fu-register` and `script-fu-menu-register` into one registration call, like this:

```
(script-fu-register "script-fu-my-sphere"
                    "<Toolbox>/Xtns/Misc/My Sphere..."
```

Since you've changed `script-fu-sphere` to `script-fu-my-sphere`, you also need to change it where that function is defined—in this case, at the beginning of the script:

```
(define (script-fu-my-sphere radius
                             light
                             shadow
                             bg-color
                             sphere-color)
```

You may want to try *Xtns ➤ Script-Fu ➤ Refresh Scripts* at this point (in GIMP 2.5, look in the *Filters* menu), to make sure your new My Sphere script appears in the *Xtns ➤ Misc* menu of the Toolbox.

Try Making a Change

To make minor changes, you don't need to know much about Script-Fu. You can usually guess where to start. In fact, learning *how* to guess is one of the more important skills!

In the sphere.scm case, the goal is to remove that background color. A reasonable first guess would be to start at the beginning and search for the word "background."

The first place you find that is

```
;   bg-color: background color
```

Anything that begins with a semicolon in Lisp is a *comment*. It's just a note the programmer added to explain aspects of the script. A comment can start in the middle of a line, too: anything from the semicolon to the end of the line is part of the comment. Adding comments is always a good idea when you do anything tricky that you might not remember six months from now, or which you think you might need to explain to someone else.

In this case, the whole line is a comment that's hinting that bg-color is associated with background color somehow. That's your clue that in addition to looking for "background," you should probably also be on the lookout for "bg-color" as you continue working through the script.

The next occurrence of either of those words comes in this block:

```
(gimp-context-set-foreground sphere-color)
(gimp-context-set-background bg-color)
(gimp-edit-fill drawable BACKGROUND-FILL)
```

Without knowing any Script-Fu, you can probably make a good guess at what this is doing. It's setting the foreground color to sphere-color (the color you set in the Sphere dialog) and the background color to bg-color (also set in the dialog). Then, it's filling the "drawable" (whatever that is) with the background color, using something similar to the *Fill with BG color* item in GIMP's *Edit* menu.

What's a *drawable*? In a GIMP plug-in, a drawable is anything you can draw on. Most often, it's a layer, but it can also be a layer mask or channel. In the Sphere script, if you search backwards for "drawable" (you'll have figured out by now that knowing how to search in your text editor is an important part of scripting!), you find this:

```
(drawable (car (gimp-layer-new img width height RGB-IMAGE
                               "Sphere Layer" 100 NORMAL-MODE)))
```

A long and somewhat complicated line! But if you scan over it, you'll notice a good clue: gimp-layer-new suggests that this is creating a new layer. In fact, drawable is the first and only layer used in the Sphere script. (What car means will be explained in a bit.)

So that gimp-edit-fill line is the first suspect. Try commenting it out by putting a semicolon in front of it:

```
;(gimp-edit-fill drawable BACKGROUND-FILL)
```

Try Your Fix

Now it's time to see if your fix worked. But first, you need to tell GIMP to reload scripts, so it will see your changes (*Xtns* ➤ *Script-Fu* ➤ *Refresh Scripts*, as you learned earlier).

If you changed the name of your script, GIMP should now find *My Sphere…* (or whatever you named it) in the *Misc* menu right next to *Sphere…*. Run it.

The dialog pops up. There's still a chooser for *Background color:*—that's okay: you didn't do anything to remove it. (You can worry about that later.) Go ahead and click *OK*.

Whoops! You probably see something like Figure 11-5. Obviously you have a little more work to do.

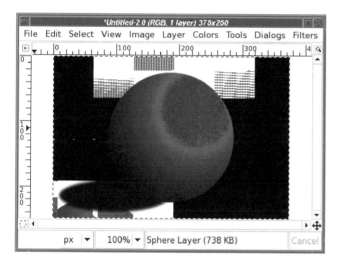

Figure 11-5. *Sphere taken over by cubists*

What Went Wrong? Some GIMP Peculiarities

There are two problems. First, the background was supposed to be transparent, but it's not. Second, what's all that stuff filling the space behind the sphere?

First things first. When you expect transparency but don't see it, your first question should be whether the image might be lacking an alpha channel. Unfortunately, GIMP doesn't provide a straightforward way to check. Try right-clicking on the layer in the Layers dialog: if *Add Alpha Channel* is enabled, then the layer doesn't already have an alpha channel (which indeed is the case for the sphere layer).

Tip Current versions of GIMP also show layers without alpha in boldface type in the Layers dialog, so you may be able to use that as a quick check.

How do you change the script to include an alpha channel in the drawable layer? Change RGB to RGBA (the A, of course, stands for *Alpha*) when creating the layer:

```
(drawable (car (gimp-layer-new img width height RGBA-IMAGE
                               "Sphere Layer" 100 NORMAL-MODE)))
```

Save the file, *Refresh Scripts*, and then run *My Sphere…* again.

Progress! Now the background is transparent. Well, mostly…but there's still a lot of random garbage there, as in Figure 11-6, different every time. What's going on?

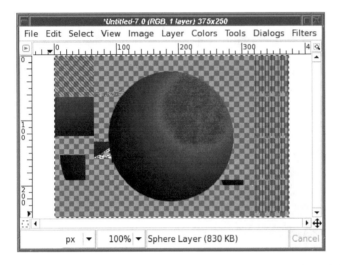

Figure 11-6. *Now the background is transparent, except that it's full of random garbage.*

One thing you need to know when writing GIMP scripts is that when GIMP creates new layers, it doesn't automatically clear them. GIMP doesn't know whether you're going to want a transparent layer or a filled layer, so it doesn't waste its time with one or the other. Consequently, the layer might end up being filled with whatever happened to be in that part of your computer's memory.

That sounds annoying, but all it means is that every time you create a layer, you should immediately either clear it, or fill it—do the equivalent of *Edit* ➤ *Clear* or *Edit* ➤ *Fill with…*. Since you commented out a call to `gimp-edit-fill` that filled with the background color, replace it now with a call to `gimp-edit-clear`:

```
(gimp-edit-clear drawable)
```

Another *Refresh Scripts* and you're ready to test it. Voilà! This time it works, and you see something like Figure 11-7.

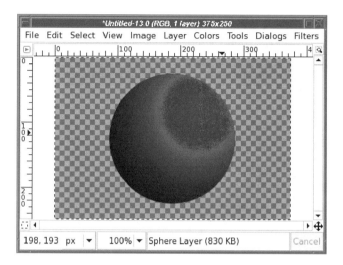

Figure 11-7. *Success! A sphere against a transparent background.*

Hooray! You now have a custom script to make a sphere that you can paste anywhere.

Bringing the Shadow Back

—yet it's gone. Why?

To find out, search for "shadow" in the script. You'll find a lot of operations involving shadow-x, shadow-y, shadow-w, and shadow-h: after you've read or written scripts for a while, seeing the combination x, y, w, and h will immediately make you think of *x* coordinate, *y* coordinate, *width*, and *height*. Read past those, and you get to the following:

```
(gimp-ellipse-select img shadow-x shadow-y shadow-w shadow-h
                      CHANNEL-OP-REPLACE TRUE TRUE 7.5)
(gimp-edit-bucket-fill drawable BG-BUCKET-FILL MULTIPLY-MODE
                       100 0 FALSE 0 0)))
```

The script selects an elliptical area, and then fills it—but it fills in Multiply mode. Multiply mode of a dark shadow against a white background makes sense, but it won't show anything against a transparent background.

Change MULTIPLY-MODE to NORMAL-MODE, rerun the script, and you get Figure 11-8.

If you intend to continue using your Sphere script, you'll probably want to make a few more changes. Since the background color isn't used anymore, remove it from the dialog, both in the script-fu-register command and in the parameters to the script-fu-sphere routine— or perhaps change the script to create a new layer with the background color, so you can turn it on or off as you choose. You can keep tweaking and adding as many new features as you like.

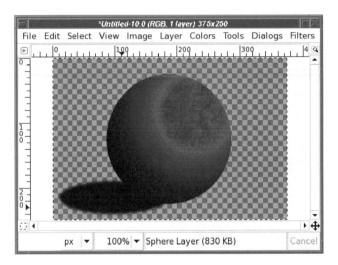

Figure 11-8. *The shadow in Normal, not Multiply, mode*

Anatomy of Script-Fu: A Stroll Through the Sphere Script

Let's go through the original Sphere script now, and try to understand what it's doing. It uses a lot of techniques you can borrow when writing your own scripts.

Lisp expressions are called *lists*, and they're always delimited by parentheses. Items inside the list are separated by spaces. These parenthetical expressions can be "nested" as deeply as necessary (you can have lists (inside lists (inside lists))).

A Lisp function is just another list. The function name is the first element of the list, and any parameters the function takes make up the rest of the list. Where some computer languages might say

```
gimp_image_new (width, height, RGB)
```

Lisp would say

```
(gimp-image-new width height RGB)
```

Arithmetic operations and conditional expressions such as "if" and "while" are just ordinary functions in Lisp, so they're expressed as lists too. For example, to add 3 to the multiple of 2 and 5 (in other words, to calculate 3 + (2 * 5)), you would say

```
(+ 3 (* 2 5))
```

That's called *prefix notation*. Read expressions like this from the inside out. In this case, first multiply 2 and 5, and then add 3 to that result.

If you have a text editor that lets you put the cursor on a parenthesis and find the one that matches it, that can be helpful when working on Lisp programs.

The script-fu-sphere Function

The Sphere script begins by defining the routine that does the work:

```
(define (script-fu-sphere radius
                          light
                          shadow
                          bg-color
                          sphere-color)
```

The values `radius`, `light`, `shadow`, `bg-color`, and `sphere-color` are called *parameters*. Nearly every script has parameters: they're values that control exactly what the script will do. In Script-Fu, they usually correspond to the items you can change in the script's dialog.

Often, they represent sizes (the radius of the sphere) or colors (of the sphere and the background). Sometimes they are true/false values (programmers call those *Booleans*, after mathematician George Boole): shadow is such a value, and corresponds to a checkbox in the Sphere dialog. *Light* is a number, and corresponds to the *Lighting (degrees)* slider in the dialog.

```
(let* ((width (* radius 3.75))
```

Here, `let*` is a way to set a list of variables in Script-Fu. Variables are quantities that you can calculate and store somewhere, so that you can use them later in the script. This line is setting a variable called *width* (which will be the width of the new image) to 3.75 times the radius chosen in the dialog.

Count the parentheses (counting parentheses is an important part of Script-Fu programming, as you've no doubt noticed by now). By the end of this line, there are two levels still open.

The inner level—the one right after the word `let*`—marks the list of variables to be set. There are going to be quite a few variables defined here, not just width, so this parenthesis level is not closed after the `width` line.

The outer level, the one before the word `let*`, defines the *scope* of the variables, or where you can use them. The variables you define inside a `let*` will be available until you close that parenthesis.

```
(img (car (gimp-image-new width height RGB)))
(drawable (car (gimp-layer-new img width height RGB-IMAGE
                          "Sphere Layer" 100 NORMAL-MODE)))
```

These lines set two more variables, *img* and *drawable*. In Lisp, you'll see the word "car" a lot. It has nothing to do with hot rods: it means "the first item in a list." So (car '(1 2 3 4)) gives you 1 (a single quote means "What follows is a list of constants, not a function call"). Why "car"? Way back in the early days of Lisp, someone thought that "Contents of Address Register" was a good way to express this concept, and now we're stuck with it.

Another term you'll see a lot is "cdr" (short for "Contents of Decrement Register" and pronounced "could-er"), which means "Everything except the first item." So (cdr '(1 2 3 4)) is (2 3 4). Sometimes these are combined together: *cadr* is short for the car of the cdr, so (cadr '(1 2 3 4)) is the same as (car (cdr '(1 2 3 4))), which is (try working this out on your own before reading the solution): 2.

Most Script-Fu routines return a list, but what you actually need to work with is the first element of the list. `gimp-image-new` and `gimp-layer-new` are two such routines, and you'll almost always take the first item, using `car`, and throw away the rest. If you get confused about whether a function needs you to take the car, just look at other scripts and copy what they do.

```
(gimp-context-push)
```

GIMP has a "context" that includes details like the foreground and background colors, the current brush, pattern, and gradient, and some other details such as font, opacity, paint mode, and palette. `gimp-context-push` saves all these values so that you can restore them easily when the script has finished its work. It's a good idea to do this early on if your script will change color, brush, or any similar value.

```
(gimp-image-undo-disable img)
```

This temporarily disables GIMP's Undo stack. As a result, when the script has finished running, a single Undo will undo the whole script, not each separate operation the script did. This is almost always a good idea for scripts and plug-ins.

```
(gimp-image-add-layer img drawable 0)
```

After a layer is created, it has to be added to the image before it can be used. The final `0` is the layer position, meaning add the layer at the bottom of the layer stack. `-1` can be used to add the layer at the top of the layer stack; any other number specifies a particular layer position.

```
(gimp-context-set-foreground sphere-color)
(gimp-context-set-background bg-color)
(gimp-edit-fill drawable BACKGROUND-FILL)
```

You've already seen what these do: set foreground and background colors, and then fill with the background color.

If you remove the `gimp-edit-fill` line and replace it with a `gimp-edit-clear` line, as in the last section, you can also remove the `gimp-context-set-background` line, since we're about to set the background color again. You could also remove the background color selector from the dialog; we'll get to that in a second.

```
(gimp-context-set-background '(20 20 20))
```

Colors in Script-Fu are represented as a list of the red, green, and blue values, ranging from 0 to 255. This line sets the background color to (20, 20, 20): a very dark gray. Remember, the single quote at the beginning of `'(20 20 20)` means "What follows is data, not a function call." Without the quote, Script-Fu would look for a function named 20 and try to run it with parameters 20 and 20.

```
(if (and
     (or (and (>= light 45) (<= light 75))
         (and (<= light 135) (>= light 105)))
     (= shadow TRUE))
```

This is a conditional—an "if" statement. Unfortunately, in Lisp they're a bit hard to read when you're getting started.

Think back to the way parenthetical expressions "nest" inside each other. Terms like "and" and "or" come first, followed by the two expressions being combined. (<= light 75) tests whether the light angle is less than or equal to 75, while (= shadow TRUE) tests whether shadow (the true/false parameter attached to the checkbox in the dialog) is true.

So this long *if* clause ends up saying: "If the light angle is greater than 45 degrees AND less than 75, OR if it's between 135 and 105 degrees, AND if we're supposed to draw a shadow, then…" and the next 11 lines are all part of that shadow-drawing clause.

```
(let ((shadow-w (* (* radius 2.5) (cos (+ *pi* radians))))
```

You may remember let* earlier in the script, which lets you set temporary variables that you'll use later. This is setting width, height, x, and y for the shadow.

The only difference between let* and let is that with let*, variables set later in the list can refer to earlier variables, while they can't in let. So in this case, if shadow-h was set to (shadow-w * 2), let would give an error, while let* would work.

If that confuses you, just use let* everywhere instead of let.

```
(if (< shadow-w 0)
```

If the shadow width is less than zero,

```
(begin (set! shadow-x (+ cx shadow-w))
       (set! shadow-w (- shadow-w))))
```

A Lisp "if" statement ordinarily takes a single clause after it, plus a second one, which is presumed to be an "else": (if (condition) (do-something) (do-something-else)) will *do-something* if *condition* is true, otherwise it will *do-something-else*.

begin lets you insert several expressions in an "if" statement (or other statements like it) where normally only one would be allowed. (begin (do_thing_1) (do_thing_2) (do_thing_3)) is treated as all one statement as far as "if" is concerned. In GIMP versions prior to 2.4, most scripts used the prog1 statement to do the same thing. But begin is considered better in Tiny Scheme (and will work in older GIMP versions as well), so GIMP's built-in scripts were all updated.

set! sets a variable; it's a little like let*, except that in let and let*, the value will only apply inside the let or let*. With set!, you can change a value and have it persist even outside the clause (such as the *if* here) that contains it. But in Tiny Scheme, set! will only work inside a let or let* where the variable was defined. (The older Script-Fu didn't make that restriction, and that's a common problem when using older scripts that haven't been updated for GIMP 2.4.)

So if the shadow width is negative, set shadow-x to be the width of the window minus the shadow, and set shadow-w to its absolute value. This will make the shadow go in the opposite direction.

```
(gimp-ellipse-select img shadow-x shadow-y shadow-w shadow-h
            CHANNEL-OP-REPLACE TRUE TRUE 7.5)
(gimp-edit-bucket-fill drawable BG-BUCKET-FILL
            MULTIPLY-MODE 100 0 FALSE 0 0)))
```

This actually draws the shadow, by making an elliptical selection of the right size, and then filling it in Multiply mode (Normal mode in your updated My Sphere script). CHANNEL_OP_REPLACE means "Replace the contents of the current selection," rather than adding, subtracting, or intersecting with it—equivalent to the Mode tabs in the tool options for Ellipse Select.

```
(gimp-ellipse-select img (- cx radius) (- cy radius)
                     (* 2 radius) (* 2 radius)
                     CHANNEL-OP-REPLACE TRUE FALSE 0)
```

Select the circle that will become the actual sphere.

We're back outside the shadow-drawing clause now, so this will be run every time, whether or not there's a shadow:

```
(gimp-edit-blend drawable FG-BG-RGB-MODE NORMAL-MODE
                 GRADIENT-RADIAL 100 offset REPEAT-NONE FALSE
                 FALSE 0 0 TRUE
                 light-x light-y light-end-x light-end-y)
```

This is the tricky line that actually makes the shading on the sphere. In fact, it's a simpler method than the one you used in Chapter 9. Rather than filling the whole circle with a color, shading it, and adding a highlight, you can do the whole operation using a single gradient. Most of the rest of the items are just settings in the Gradient tool options. So pull up a GIMP Toolbox, select the Gradient tool, and compare the tool options with the parameters in this call (or use the Procedure Browser, discussed later in this chapter):

- `gimp-edit-blend` is the command to draw a gradient, just like the Blend tool would do. (You may remember from Chapter 4 that the Gradient tool is also called the Blend tool.)

- `drawable` is the layer where the drawing will happen.

- `FG-BG-RGB-MODE` is the "blend mode" (not to be confused with drawing mode); this is usually the right setting.

- `NORMAL-MODE` is the drawing mode, corresponding to the *Mode* drop-down: `NORMAL` draws on top of anything that's already there.

- `GRADIENT-RADIAL` is the *Shape* option.

- `100` is the *Opacity*.

- `offset` corresponds to the *Offset* slider.

- `REPEAT-NONE` is the *Repeat* setting.

- `FALSE`, `FALSE`, `0`, `0`, and `TRUE` set some other values used by the Blend tool—reverse, supersample, max_depth, threshold, and dither—to reasonable default values. Not all of these are exposed in the tool options you see when you run the Blend tool, but don't worry—they won't make much difference most of the time.

The remaining four options are the coordinates to use for the blend: basically, they correspond to where you would drag if you were making the gradient interactively.

If you want to try this yourself, make a circular selection and set the foreground and background colors—remember the background color was set earlier to (20, 20, 20)? Then set all the Blend (Gradient) tool options to mimic what the script is doing, and drag from somewhere near the upper right of the circle, where the highlight should be, down and left to the edge of the circle. The Blend tool will do the rest, and should give you a nicely shaded sphere.

```
(gimp-selection-none img)
(gimp-image-undo-enable img)
```

To clean up, remove the circular selection, and re-enable Undo in the image. An Undo after running the script will undo everything back to the `gimp-image-undo-disable` call—in other words, it will undo the whole script.

```
(gimp-display-new img)
```

Display the image. If you don't include this in your script, the new image will never appear.

```
(gimp-context-pop)))
```

More cleanup: restore the context (particularly the foreground and background colors) from before the script was run. Notice the two extra close parentheses at the end: these close the first `let*` and the definition of the function `script-fu-sphere`.

Registering the Script

We're done with the routine that draws the script! All that's left is to register it so that it shows up in the menus, and to specify what options the dialog should have. (You've already seen a preview of script registration with the My Sphere script.)

```
(script-fu-register "script-fu-sphere"
```

`script-fu-register` takes several parameters. You have to get them in the right order. If you write a new script, it may be easiest to copy an existing one and just change all the names. The first parameter (in quotes in the previous code line) is the name of the function that will do the work for the script.

```
_"_Sphere..."
```

This is the name that will be shown to the user: it will appear in menus and in the dialog. The underscores have the functions discussed earlier: internationalization and menu mnemonics.

```
"Simple sphere with a drop shadow"
```

This is a description of what the routine does. This doesn't need an underscore, because it's not normally shown to the user (except in the Plug-in Browser window) and won't normally be translated.

```
"Spencer Kimball"
"Spencer Kimball"
"1996"
```

This is the script author and copyright holder (these two are almost always the same), and the date.

" "

This is where the list of valid image types would go for a script that runs from an image window, such as "*" or "RGB*". Since the Sphere script makes a new image rather than modifying an existing one, this is blank.

```
SF-ADJUSTMENT  _"Radius (pixels)"      '(100 5 500 1 10 0 1)
SF-ADJUSTMENT  _"Lighting (degrees)"   '(45 0 360 1 10 0 0)
SF-TOGGLE      _"Shadow"               TRUE
SF-COLOR       _"Background color"     '(255 255 255)
SF-COLOR       _"Sphere color"         '(255 0 0))
```

After the image type comes the list of options to be shown in the dialog. These must correspond to the parameters the function `script-fu-sphere` takes. You can use as many or as few as your script needs. See the next section for a list of all the possible user interface options and how to use them.

In your My Sphere script, you removed the call that used the background color. It would be a good idea to remove the `"Background color"` line from this registration routine too, so that the user doesn't get confused wondering why it's asking for a background color it never uses. If you do that, be sure to remove the `bg-color` parameter from the definition of `script-fu-sphere` at the beginning of the script, or GIMP will give you an error when you try to run the script.

```
(script-fu-menu-register "script-fu-sphere"
    "<Toolbox>/Xtns/Misc")
```

The Sphere script uses these lines to register its position in GIMP's menus. Many scripts do this as part of the normal `script-fu-register` call, and don't use `script-fu-menu-register` at all. If Sphere had done that, its register call would have started like this:

```
(script-fu-register "script-fu-sphere"
                "<Toolbox>/Xtns/Misc/Sphere..."
```

However, the GIMP developers recommend that you use the separate `script-fu-menu-register` for new scripts: it offers more flexibility, such as letting a script appear in two different menu locations. (The downside is that it's not backward compatible—it won't work in earlier GIMP versions.)

User Interface Options for Scripts

Scripts and plug-ins—in any language supported by GIMP—can choose from a variety of interface widgets to let the user choose values. In Script-Fu, these are names in all capital letters preceded by "SF-" (for "Script Fu"): for instance, `SF-TOGGLE`. All GIMP plug-in languages have the same set of options, but some use different prefixes instead of "SF-" (for instance, in Python or Perl a toggle button would be `PF_TOGGLE` instead of `SF-TOGGLE`).

For each element shown in the dialog, the first parameter is a label to be shown to the user: something like "Radius (pixels)" or "Background color."

TOGGLE

This is a toggle button representing a true or false value. It takes one parameter, either TRUE or FALSE. (Lisp programmers note: TRUE and FALSE are different from the Lisp values t and nil.)

STRING

This is a single-line string value, such as "Hello, world". A few scripts use VALUE as an alternate form of STRING.

ADJUSTMENT

This is a way of specifying a number—either an integer or a floating-point number. It can be a minimalist *spin box*, a text field with up and down arrows, like the radius parameter in the Sphere script. Or it can be a full-blown slider like the lighting parameter in the Sphere script.
The parameters are as follows:

- *value*: The initial value for the number.

- *lower*: The smallest value allowed.

- *upper*: The largest value allowed.

- *step_inc*: How much the number will change for each click of the arrow buttons, or when using the arrow keys.

- *page_inc*: How much the number will change when clicking in the slider's "trough" or using the Page Up/Page Down keys.

- *digits*: The number of places after the decimal point. Use 0 if you want an integer value.

- *type*: Either SF-SLIDER (0 will also set it to a slider) or SF-SPINNER (1 will work for a spinner).

In Python, you can also use PF_SLIDER and PF_SPINNER directly as types.

TEXT

This is a multiline text value. Initialize it with a string that includes newline characters.

OPTION

This is a way to show a "combobox" where the user can select from several values. The parameter is a list of string options: for instance, '("Horizontal", "Vertical").
This will be returned to the script as an integer, the number of the value chosen, starting at 0. So in the example given, if the user selects Horizontal, the script would see 0; if the user selects Vertical, the script would see 1. OPTION is available in Script-Fu but not in Python; in Python, use RADIO.

RADIO

This is a collection of values that are all tied together, like the station buttons on a car radio. Only one can be chosen at a time: when you press a button, whatever was previously selected becomes deselected. It's available in Python but not in Script-Fu; use `SF-OPTION` instead in scripts. Pass the default value (a string) followed by a list of all the options (one of which should match the default you passed) as a list of doubles, the name of the button followed by the type: for example, `(("Horizontal", 0), ("Vertical", 1))`.

COLOR

This is a color. GIMP will show a button with the default color you specify, and clicking on that button will pop up a color chooser. For the default, use an RGB triple like `'(255 255 255)`. In 2.6 and later, you'll also be able to use names, like "white."

FONT

This allows the user to choose a font. It takes one parameter, the initial font name, such as "Helvetica."

FILENAME

This is the name of a file (usually an absolute pathname on your system). It shows a button that lets users pop up a file chooser (to pick another file).

DIRNAME

This is the name of a directory or folder on your system.

ENUM

This is a way to let the user choose between some predefined values within GIMP. *Enum* stands for "enumerated," because the possible values are specified by number in a fixed list. It works in Script-Fu but not in Python. Its parameters are

- Enum name (e.g., "InterpolationType")

- Initial value (e.g., "linear")

BRUSH

This lets the user choose a brush. Its parameters are as follows:

- Brush name (e.g., "Circle (03)")

- Opacity

- Spacing

- Paint Mode (e.g., `Normal`)

PATTERN

This is the name of a pattern as it appears in the Patterns dialog—for example, "Pine."

GRADIENT

This is the name of a gradient as it appears in the Gradients dialog—for example, "FG to BG (RGB)."

PALETTE

This is the name of a palette for indexed colors—for example, "Web."

VECTORS

This is a path, specified by the name set in the Paths dialog.

IMAGE, LAYER, CHANNEL, DRAWABLE

These are used to pass in the image and drawable used by the plug-in, if any. They take two parameters: usually you'll pass in a name, and 0 (zero), as the erase-rows.scm script did. The system will take care of replacing that 0 with the currently active layer.

Usually, you'll see `image` and `drawable` as the first two parameters in any script that works on an existing image, like erase-rows. But by using `SF-IMAGE` or `SF-LAYER` you can let the user choose other images, layers, or drawables currently open in GIMP.

A Python Script

Conveniently, there's a Sphere script in Python, too, and it works exactly the same way as in Script-Fu. It's called *sphere.py*, and you'll find it in your GIMP system plug-ins folder if you have GIMP Python installed. If not, you can find it online with a web search for *GIMP sphere.py*. Comparing the two scripts is a great way to compare the two scripting languages. You'll probably find Python quite a bit easier to read than Script-Fu.

Pull up sphere.py in your favorite text editor. The structure should look very familiar once you've been through sphere.scm. There's a routine that actually creates the sphere, and then a routine that registers the script and inserts it into the menus. Let's walk through sphere.py to see the differences.

```
#!/usr/bin/env python
```

This line tells the operating system that the file is a Python script. This special character combination #! is called the *shebang*, because # is often pronounced "hash" and *!* "bang" by programmers. You'll see a similar line at the beginning of the Perl example later in this chapter.

```
#   Gimp-Python - allows the writing of Gimp plugins in Python.
#   Copyright (C) 1997  James Henstridge <james@daa.com.au>
```

In Python, the comment character is a hash (#), not a semicolon (;). (Yes, that means the "she-bang" line is technically a comment.)

```
import math
from gimpfu import *
```

The Python Sphere script imports Python's math library because it does some basic trigonometry and uses the value of pi. If you need any other specialized Python functions, you can import them here.

All Python GIMP scripts must include the second import line. That's what gives you access to all the GIMP functions. The special syntax of the import statement lets you use GIMP functions without inserting the sequence gimpfu. in front of each call.

```
def python_sphere(radius, light, shadow, bg_colour, sphere_colour):
```

def is how Python defines routines. Otherwise, this is much like Script-Fu.

```
    if radius < 1:
        radius = 1
```

Comparisons and variable assignments are much easier to read in Python than in Script-Fu.

In Python, indentation is important: it shows the structure of the program. A block of code inside an if clause must be indented more than the if itself; indentation is the only way to indicate that structure in Python, where other languages might use begin and end, braces ({and}), or parentheses. If you copy Python code, be sure to include all the spaces at the beginning of each line so you don't accidentally change indentation levels. And don't use tabs: they can confuse you (and Python) as to the exact indentation level. You're best off using a four-space indent for GIMP code, since that's what the standard GIMP plug-ins use.

```
    width = int(radius * 3.75)
    height = int(radius * 2.5)
```

Calculate the size of the canvas. int(value) converts a floating-point number to an integer.

```
    img = gimp.Image(width, height, RGB)
```

Python is object oriented. There's an object called gimp that contains all the important GIMP functions you'll be using. gimp.Image says to create an Image object from the object gimp. You can use the Image object (called img) later in your script.

```
    drawable = gimp.Layer(img, "Sphere Layer", width, height,
                    RGB_IMAGE, 100, NORMAL_MODE)
```

A Layer is also an object: this creates a new layer.

```
    old_fg = gimp.get_foreground()
    old_bg = gimp.get_background()
```

In addition to making new objects, the gimp object has routines like get_foreground() to fetch the current foreground color. This script saves the old colors here, so it can restore them at the end. This is the equivalent of the gimp-context-push call you saw in Script-Fu. Python can also push and pop the whole context; whether to do that, or simply save a couple of colors, is a matter of preference.

```
img.disable_undo()
img.add_layer(drawable, 0)

gimp.set_foreground(sphere_colour)

gimp.set_background(bg_colour)
```

Again, this has all the same operations the Script-Fu version did.

```
pdb.gimp_edit_fill(drawable, BACKGROUND_FILL)
```

Some functions, rather than being in the gimp object, are in another object called pdb, which stands for "Procedural DataBase." You can explore pdb functions with the Procedure Browser, described in the next section. Functions in the pdb object are generally named gimp_functionname.

Notice that Python uses underscores where Script-Fu used dashes. If Python sees a dash, it assumes you want to subtract something from something.

```
gimp.set_background(20, 20, 20)

if (light >= 45 and light <= 75 or light <= 135 and
    light >= 105) and shadow:
```

Python conditionals are much easier to read than the Lisp version. When there are this many options, though, you still have to stop and think about it.

The rest of the script is similar, so I'll skip ahead to the registration routine:

```
register(
    "python_fu_sphere",
```

Notice that unlike Script-Fu, this isn't the name of the routine that actually does the work. That routine is python_sphere. This is a name that will be made available externally in case another script wants to use the Python Sphere script.

```
    "Simple spheres with drop shadows",
    "Simple spheres with drop shadows (based on script-fu version)",
```

The description of the routine is repeated twice. The first is the short description; the second is a somewhat longer version to show up in online help.

```
    [
        (PF_INT, "radius", "Radius for sphere", 100),
        (PF_SLIDER, "light", "Light angle", 45, (0,360,1)),
        (PF_TOGGLE, "shadow", "Shadow?", 1),
        (PF_COLOR, "bg_colour", "Background", (255,255,255)),
        (PF_COLOR, "sphere_colour", "Sphere", (255,0,0))
    ],
```

Notice that Python uses square brackets ([ ]) to delimit the list of widgets to be shown in the dialog. Also, it precedes the names of the widgets with "PF_" instead of "SF-"—that stands for "Python Fu"—and note again how Python uses underscores instead of dashes.

```
[],
```

If the python-sphere routine returned useful values that could be used in calculations by other scripts, an indication of that would go here. Most interactive scripts just use empty brackets like this.

```
python_sphere)
```

Finally, at the very end of the register function comes the name of the routine that will do the work.

```
main()
```

You need to include this line at the end of any Python GIMP script: this is how GIMP actually runs the script.

Finding Out How to Do Things: The Procedure Browser

How do you find out the names of all those GIMP routines you can call? How did the author of the Python script know to call pdb.gimp_edit_fill in order to run the Bucket Fill tool?

First, you can look in other scripts. Often, that's the best way. If you know a script does something similar to your goal, simply read that script and find out how it works. If you're not sure, try searching for keywords such as "fill" in all the scripts GIMP has installed.

If a quick search through other scripts doesn't turn up what you need, you need the Procedure Browser. *Xtns* ➤ *Procedure Browser* brings up the window shown in Figure 11-9.

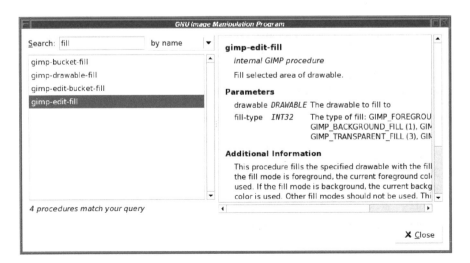

Figure 11-9. *The GIMP Procedure Browser*

It works a lot like the GIMP Plug-in Browser. You can type a search term, such as "fill," to search for only procedures that contain that term.

In this case, there turn out to be four different fill procedures. Click on each of them in turn and read the help in the right half of the window to find out what they do.

- *gimp-bucket-fill* says "This procedure is deprecated!" So you don't want to use that.

- *gimp-drawable-fill* fills a drawable (such as a layer) with the current foreground or background, white, transparent, or the current pattern.

- *gimp-edit-bucket-fill* works more like the Bucket Fill tool: it includes parameters for all the options that the tool offers, such as paint-mode, opacity, threshold, sample-merged, and so on.

- *gimp-edit-fill* fills a drawable using the same options as *gimp-drawable-fill*, but it also clarifies the difference: *gimp-edit-fill* will fill a selection if there is one, while *gimp-drawable-fill* will always fill the whole layer even if there's a selection present.

The Procedure Browser is an excellent way of finding details on all the useful functions GIMP makes available to scripts and plug-ins. Don't forget it's there.

A Perl Script

As mentioned earlier, Perl is no longer a supported part of GIMP. But some people still use it, and there are several useful Perl scripts available on the web. If you're a Perl programmer, you will probably want to install gimp-perl and try your hand at writing scripts.

GIMP-Perl doesn't come with a Perl version of the Sphere script. So instead, take a look at one of the simplest scripts it does have: *Mirrorsplit*, which splits an image in half and replaces one of the halves with a mirror image of the remaining half. If you have gimp-perl installed, you'll find this in your system plug-ins directory. Otherwise, you can get the source from GIMP's SVN: *http://svn.gnome.org/viewvc/gimp-perl/trunk/examples/mirrorsplit*.

Load it in your text editor. Let's take Mirrorsplit bit by bit:

```
#!/usr/bin/perl
```

This "shebang" line tells the operating system that this is a Perl script. Perl's comment character is a hash (#) just like Python's.

```
eval 'exec /usr/bin/perl  -S $0 ${1+"$@"}'
    if 0; # not running under some shell
```

Perl magic. Just copy it.

```
use Gimp qw(:auto __ N_);
use Gimp::Fu;
use Gimp::Util;
```

These lines tell Perl that it will be using GIMP routines. The odd first line has to do with reading text.

▮ **Tip** The command `perldoc Gimp` will give more information on what that first *use* line is doing, as well as other detailed information on GIMP-Perl. The capital "G" is important. `perldoc Gimp::Fu` gives a good general introduction to writing GIMP scripts in Perl.

```
use strict;
```

This makes Perl stricter about warning you on possible syntax errors. It's not necessary, but it's a good idea.

```
register        "mirror_split",
                "Splits and mirrors half of the image, according to settings.",
                "Just tick appropriate radio button.",
                "Claes G Lindblad <claesg\@algonet.se>",
                "Claes G Lindblad <claesg\@algonet.se>",
                "990530",
                N_"<Image>/Filters/Distorts/MirrorSplit...",
```

Like Python, Perl's `register` function lets you specify a string describing the function, and another one for help, followed by date, author, copyright owner, date, and location in the menus.

N_ in Perl performs much the same function that an underscore alone performed in Script-Fu and Python: it marks strings for translation into other languages.

```
                "*",
```

Unlike Sphere, the Mirrorsplit script modifies an existing image. So, instead of leaving the image type blank, the script specifies "*", a wildcard that means it can work on any type of image.

```
        [
        [PF_RADIO, "mirror", "Which half to mirror?", 0,
                [Upper => 0, Lower => 1, Left => 2, Right => 3]
        ]
        ],
```

The list of interface widgets to use begins with a single open bracket ([). Then each item—there's only one in this case—is delimited by its own set of brackets, and finally there's a close bracket. Notice that Perl uses a PF_ prefix, just like Python does (since Python and Perl both begin with a "P").

"mirror" is a radio box, a collection of values from which the user can select only one. Upper, Lower, Left, and Right are the possible values: the arrows (=>) tie each of these values to a number. GIMP will use the number when it runs the script.

```
        sub {
```

Instead of defining a named function like Script-Fu and Python do, Perl puts the important code in a subroutine inside `register`. If your Perl script is complicated, though, it's probably best to define another routine, and just call it from here.

```
my ($img, $layer, $mirror) = @_;
my $w = $layer->width();
```

my is the way Perl sets local variables, and Perl always puts a dollar sign ($) in front of variable names.

The rest of the script is straightforward. If you like Perl, and you've read through the Script-Fu and Python portions of this chapter, you'll probably have no problem following the Perl script. If you're not a Perl programmer already, it's probably safer to stick to a language that comes standard with GIMP.

Writing a C Plug-in

For most tasks, writing a script is easier than writing a C plug-in, and just as good.

But when you really need performance—especially when you need to loop over each pixel in the image—C is the best bet.

Writing a C plug-in is quite a bit more involved than writing a script, but the basics are the same. Programmers who know a little C—or a related language such as C++ or Java—should be able to create GIMP C plug-ins fairly easily.

To write a C plug-in, you need a development environment installed, including a compiler and the gimptool program, as discussed earlier in this chapter.

As with script-writing, it's usually best to learn by modifying an existing plug-in. As an example, I'll start with the *Zealous Crop* plug-in.

Zealous Crop examines the active layer and tries to crop away anything that seems to be background: anything that's transparent or a solid color. That's sometimes a useful function, but if you have multiple layers it probably won't crop the image to the right size. It also does strange things with transparency (Figure 11-10).

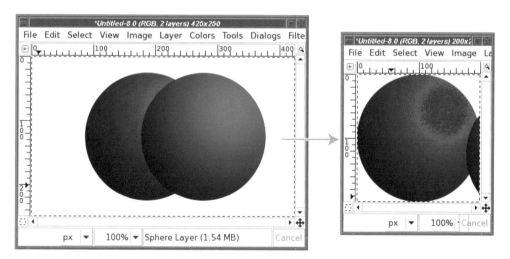

Figure 11-10. *Zealous Crop doesn't handle multiple layers very well.*

I often want something like Zealous Crop or Autocrop that examines all the layers, not just the active one. Then it would crop the whole image to a reasonable size, including the objects in all the layers. Why not make it happen?

Note Why start with Zealous Crop rather than Autocrop? Two reasons. First, Autocrop is longer than Zealous Crop, yet the code isn't any easier to read. Second, Zealous Crop illustrates some important principles of C plug-ins that Autocrop does not, so it's a better example for learning plug-in techniques. You could start from either one and come up with a perfectly good Autocrop All Layers plug-in.

Start by finding the source of Zealous Crop. If you've already downloaded the GIMP source, you can find it there, in plug-ins/common/zealouscrop.c. But if you don't have the GIMP source handy, try a web search for *gimp zealouscrop.c.*

A Tour Through Zealous Crop

The Zealous Crop plug-in begins with a comment.

```
* ZealousCrop plug-in version 1.00
* by Adam D. Moss <adam@foxbox.org>
[ ... ]
*/
```

In C, a comment begins with /* and can extend across multiple lines: the sequence */ ends the comment. The asterisks at the beginning of each line in between are simply for readability; C doesn't require them.

C plug-ins typically begin with a comment crediting their author and listing copyright and licensing information. Since GIMP is free software, licensed under the GNU General Public License, most people who write plug-ins use that license. That way, their plug-ins can be freely shared with other GIMP users (and perhaps, one day, included with GIMP itself, as this one is).

```
#include "config.h"
#include <libgimp/gimp.h>
#include "libgimp/stdplugins-intl.h"
```

#include is how C inserts interfaces for other libraries. The two that use quotation marks around the file name are specific to plug-ins built inside GIMP, and should be removed for external plug-ins. The one for gimp.h, with angle brackets, is needed for every C plug-in.

```
#define PLUG_IN_PROC "plug-in-zealouscrop"
```

The name of the plug-in is plug-in-zealouscrop, and this name will be used in several places. Rather than duplicate it each time, this lets you use a slightly shorter symbol to refer to it. If you ever change the name of the plug-in (as we're about to do), you only need to change it in one place.

```
GimpPlugInInfo PLUG_IN_INFO =
{
  NULL,  /* init_proc */
  NULL,  /* quit_proc */
  query, /* query_proc */
  run,   /* run_proc   */
};
```

The structure of a plug-in includes functions to initialize, quit, and query for information as well as run the plug-in. The scripting languages handle this for you, but in C you must include these lines.

```
static gint bytes;
```

bytes is a variable that contains an integer value. gint is the way the libraries used underneath GIMP refer to an integer. (The "g" ultimately derives from the GNU project, just like the G in GIMP.)

```
MAIN ()
```

This is a way to let GIMP call the plug-in, much like the similar call at the end of a Python script. Include this unchanged in each plug-in you write. Notice it's capitalized: it's a macro, not the usual C function called main(), so that each platform can use the plug-in code in whichever way works best.

```
static inline gint
colours_equal (const guchar *col1,
               const guchar *col2,
               gint          bytes)
```

Now we're getting into the actual programming. colours_equal is a C function that returns an integer (gint) and takes three parameters: col1, col2, and bytes. col1 and col2 are colors, and are specified as an array of guchar, unsigned characters (actually a pointer to a character, for those familiar with the C language). bytes specifies how many bytes each color includes; this might be 1 for grayscale images, 3 for color images, or 4 for color images with transparency.

```
  for (b = 0; b < bytes; b++)
    {
      if (col1[b] != col2[b])
        return FALSE;
    }
```

Loop over each byte in the two colors and compare them. If they're different at any point, return FALSE—the colors are not equal.

```
static GimpParamDef args[] =
{
  { GIMP_PDB_INT32,    "run-mode", "Interactive, non-interactive" },
  { GIMP_PDB_IMAGE,    "image",    "Input image"                  },
  { GIMP_PDB_DRAWABLE, "drawable", "Input drawable"               }
};
```

This describes the parameters the plug-in takes—args is short for "arguments," another word for "parameters."

For "run-mode" you'll almost always want to use Interactive (meaning it may pop up a dialog and take input from the user, and it shows a result). It's possible, though, to write non-interactive plug-ins that are primarily for use by other plug-ins, or a plug-in that needs no parameters passed to it.

This plug-in operates on an input image and drawable, but doesn't take any other parameters.

▪ **Note** Why all the emphasis on "drawables"? Why not just say "layer"? Because you can draw on things that are not layers, such as layer masks, channels, or even the QuickMask or a selection.

```
gimp_install_procedure (PLUG_IN_PROC,
                        "Automagically crops unused space from "
                        "the edges and middle of a picture.",
```

gimp_install_procedure and gimp_plugin_menu_register are similar to the register routine you've seen in the other languages, and take the same arguments.

The run Procedure

Finally, the run procedure. This is the routine GIMP calls when the user actually runs the plug-in.

```
static void
run (const gchar      *name,
     gint              n_params,
     const GimpParam  *param,
     gint              *nreturn_vals,
     GimpParam         **return_vals)
{
```

run procedures in GIMP C plug-ins always look longer and more complicated than you expect, especially if you're used to the more compact form of scripting languages. But a lot of this structure is very standardized, and you can just copy it directly from one plug-in to the next.

```
GimpPDBStatusType  status = GIMP_PDB_SUCCESS;
```

Notice that `status` is initialized to `GIMP_PDB_SUCCESS` here. Later on, that value will be returned, unless an error condition is encountered and `status` is changed to another value.

```
  INIT_I18N();
```

This is a GIMP internal function related to internationalization, and you will need to remove it in your own plug-ins.

```
  if (run_mode == GIMP_RUN_NONINTERACTIVE)
    {
      if (n_params != 3)
```

Check the number of parameters. The number must match the number of items in `GimpParamDef`, defined earlier.

This early code is pretty much the same for every plug-in, but after this point we go back to code that might need to be changed.

```
      /*  Get the specified drawable  */
      drawable = gimp_drawable_get(param[2].data.d_drawable);
      image_id = param[1].data.d_image;
```

C plug-ins need to access their parameters in the proper order before they can reference them by name. In this case, the image is the first parameter of the plug-in, while the drawable is the second parameter. (For some reason, the plug-in author has written the line to get the second parameter `param[2]` before the first parameter `param[1]`. What's important is the parameter numbers, `[2]` and `[1]`, not the order in which they're accessed in the C code.)

These two lines fetch the data part (`data`) of these two parameters, convert them to the right type (`d_image` or `d_drawable`), and then assign them to variables `drawable` and `image_id` so they can be used more easily.

```
      /*  Make sure that the drawable is gray or RGB or indexed  */
      if (gimp_drawable_is_rgb (drawable->drawable_id) ||
          gimp_drawable_is_gray (drawable->drawable_id) ||
          gimp_drawable_is_indexed (drawable->drawable_id))
```

Checking the image type is a good idea, especially if your plug-in can only work on certain types. In this case, though, it might be a bit excessive: what could the image be if not RGB, gray, or indexed? (Yes, these tests do work even if the drawable has an alpha channel.)

```
        gimp_progress_init (_("ZealousCropping(tm)..."));
```

You can display messages in GIMP's status bar during a plug-in, and display a progress bar to show how far along the plug-in is (you'll see that in a moment). Any type of plug-in can update GIMP's progress bar, including scripts, though the scripts shown earlier in this chapter have been fast-running, so they didn't need that.

```
        gimp_tile_cache_ntiles (1 +
          2 * (drawable->width > drawable->height ?
              (drawable->width / gimp_tile_width()) :
              (drawable->height / gimp_tile_height())));
```

C (and also Python) plug-ins have a speed secret compared to Script-Fu: they can use *tiling* to access pixels in the image. Tiles are a way of grabbing a batch of pixels into memory all at once. Plug-ins can then loop through the smaller batch instead of requesting the pixels at specifics x and y coordinates one after another. I'll explain more about tiling in a bit.

```
do_zcrop(drawable, image_id);
```

Call a function (defined here) that does the crop.

```
if (run_mode != GIMP_RUN_NONINTERACTIVE)
  gimp_displays_flush ();
```

The crop is finished (do_zcrop did all the rest of the work). This updates GIMP's display if it's been run in interactive mode.

```
gimp_drawable_detach (drawable);
```

When a C plug-in is finished working with a drawable, it should "detach" from it, which ensures that all tiles have been saved properly and all extra memory freed.

The Routine That Does the Work

Now the do_zcrop function, which does most of the work, begins.

```
static void
do_zcrop (GimpDrawable *drawable,
          gint32        image_id)
```

do_zcrop takes two parameters: a drawable and an image. The first few lines of the function merely declare local variables.

```
width  = drawable->width;
height = drawable->height;
```

Get the width and height of the drawable.

If you haven't forgotten the goal of modifying the plug-in to crop images with multiple layers, this may grab your attention. Getting the size of just the current layer won't be enough. Perhaps you'll have to modify this to be the size of the whole image, not the drawable. Or maybe this function should be called during a loop over all layers in the image. I'll examine those options shortly.

```
bytes  = drawable->bpp;
```

drawable->bpp is the "bits per pixel" of the drawable: probably 24 for an RGB image, 32 if it has an alpha channel.

```
killrows = g_new (gint8, height);
killcols = g_new (gint8, width);
buffer = g_malloc ((width > height ? width : height) * bytes);
```

g_new and g_malloc are two ways of allocating memory. killrows and killcols end up being arrays of integers big enough to hold one color channel (a gint8 is an 8-bit integer, just big enough for a single-color channel) in one row or one column. buffer is large enough to hold all three (or four, with alpha) color channels, and is big enough to hold either one row or one column—it takes the maximum of the two dimensions.

```
/*  initialize the pixel regions  */
gimp_pixel_rgn_init (&srcPR, drawable, 0, 0, width, height, FALSE, FALSE);
gimp_pixel_rgn_init (&destPR, drawable, 0, 0, width, height, TRUE, TRUE);

livingrows = 0;
for (y = 0; y < height; y++)
   {
     gimp_pixel_rgn_get_row (&srcPR, buffer, 0, y, width);
```

Loop over tiles (pixel regions) in order to read the individual pixels in the drawable.

Getting Pixels: Tiles and Pixel Regions

To speed up its operation, GIMP internally accesses drawables one small "tile" at a time. These are usually 64 × 64 pixels, but don't count on that being the case. Most access to pixels inside the tiles is done through *pixel regions*. (Python can also access pixel regions.)

Using Pixel Regions

A pixel region (type GimpPixelRgn in C) represents some area of an image that you want to access. It may be a row or column, a rectangle of any size, or a single pixel. Initialize it like this:

```
void
gimp_pixel_rgn_init (GimpPixelRgn *pr,
                     GimpDrawable *drawable,
                     int x, int y, int width, int height,
                     int dirty, int shadow);
```

Here, the parameters are

- pr: This is your local GimpPixelRgn variable.

- drawable: This is the drawable to be used.

- x, t, width, height: This is the area of the drawable you want to access.

- dirty: Set this to 1 if you're planning to write back to the drawable. If you're only reading it, you can set it to 0.

- shadow: If set to 1, GIMP will provide a place to write your new data. Set it to the same value as dirty.

Once the pixel region is initialized, you can fill it with pixels from the image by calling functions such as `gimp_pixel_rgn_get_pixel` (to get a single pixel), `gimp_pixel_rgn_get_row`, `gimp_pixel_rgn_get_col`, and `gimp_pixel_rgn_get_rect` (to get an arbitrary rectangle from the image, specified by x, y, width, and height). For each of these routines, you need to pass in a pointer to a region of allocated memory large enough to hold the data—in this case, where the plug-in reads one row or column at a time, that is

```
buffer = g_malloc ((width > height ? width : height) * bytes);
```

The memory buffer's size, in bytes, is the maximum of width and height (so it can hold either a row or a column) times the number of bytes per pixel (`drawable->bpp`).

Reading and Writing the Memory

How do you access the pixels after calling `gimp_pixel_rgn_get_row`?

The pixels in the buffer begin at the location you asked for. So in this case, `buffer` will contain a single (horizontal) row. Within that row, each pixel occupies as many bytes as there are color channels. So in the case of an RGBA image (4 bytes per pixel), the first pixel starts at the beginning of the buffer (location 0, since C always begins arrays at 0), the second starts at location 4, the third at 8, and so forth.

That's fairly straightforward for a single row spanning the width of the whole image. But it gets a bit more complicated when you're calling `gimp_pixel_rgn_get_rect` to get a rectangle from somewhere in the middle of the image. In this case, you have to keep track of the location where you got the rectangle, and its size.

You also need to know that the data in pixel regions is organized by row, not by column. Looping through a pixel region, you will see all the pixels for one row, and then immediately afterward you'll see the first pixel from the next row. In other words, x coordinates increase faster than y coordinates.

For instance, to get the pixel at x1, y1, with a bytes per pixel of bpp, you would read the bytes starting at `(y1 - y) * width * bpp + (x1 - x) * bpp`. Got that? The first part, `(y1 - y) * width * bpp`, gets you from the top (row y) down to row y1: each row takes up `width * bpp` bytes, and there are `(y1 - y)` rows since the beginning of this pixel region. The second part, `(x1 - x) * bpp`, is how far over in the row we need to be to get to x1. Whew!

Tiles and the Tile Cache

Using pixel regions, especially large rectangular regions, improves performance quite a lot vs. getting a single pixel at a time. But you can improve performance even more by working directly with the tiles GIMP uses. Normally, each tile is passed as a block of shared memory from the application to the plug-in. This can cause performance delays if the plug-in switches tiles often. In that case, you can keep a cache of tiles in the plug-in by specifying the number of tiles to be cached.

You can use this call in combination with pixel regions to make your plug-in faster. Say you're working primarily with rows or columns, as Zealous Crop does. Then it helps to cache enough tiles to span an entire row or column. If you'll be writing back to the drawable, cache twice as many tiles: you need one set for reading, and another set ("shadow" tiles) for writing.

You may remember from Zealous Crop's `run` procedure:

```
gimp_tile_cache_ntiles (1 +
        2 * (drawable->width > drawable->height ?
            (drawable->width / gimp_tile_width()) :
            (drawable->height / gimp_tile_height()))));
```

This is taking the maximum of the drawable's width and height, dividing by the width or height of GIMP's tiles (usually 64, but you shouldn't depend on it: always use `gimp_tile_width()` and `gimp_tile_height()`), and multiply by 2 to account for the shadow tiles.

Why add 1 to the result? Because integer math (like those divisions) rounds down to the nearest integer, so if you don't add 1, you may end up with a fraction of a tile less than you actually need.

SPEEDING THINGS UP BY TAKING PIXEL REGIONS DIRECTLY FROM TILES

Another way to use tiles to make your pixel-region code run faster is to use `gimp_pixel_rgns_process` to take pixel regions directly from GIMP's tiles. Used instead of routines like `gimp_pixel_rgn_get_row` or `gimp_pixel_rgn_get_rect`, this is a routine that automatically gets sequential chunks of data that are aligned to GIMP's own tiles. This avoids a lot of extra copying of pixels, and can be much faster.

If you're writing a plug-in that needs that kind of speed, be sure to check out the three-part "Writing a Plug-in" tutorial on *developer.gimp.org*, which includes examples of pixel-region processing code.

Searching the Image for Blank Rows and Columns

When we last left our hero (the Zealous Crop plug-in), it had just requested a pixel region row. Now you should have a better idea what that means. (Don't worry if it isn't completely clear. Working with pixel regions is confusing to most people, and it takes time to get used to thinking in those terms.)

```
livingrows = 0;
for (y = 0; y < height; y++)
  {
    gimp_pixel_rgn_get_row (&srcPR, buffer, 0, y, width);

    killrows[y] = TRUE;
```

We don't know yet what `livingrows` is, but we're about to find out. This loop will get each horizontal row of the image, starting at the top (y=0) and ending at the bottom. `killrows` is an array that has one entry for each row in the image; this row's entry is initialized to TRUE.

```
    for (x = 0; x < width * bytes; x += bytes)
```

Loop over each pixel in the row. Remember, `bytes` is the number of bytes per pixel, so each pixel spans `bytes` spaces in `buffer`.

```
if (!colours_equal (buffer, &buffer[x], bytes))
  {
    livingrows++;
    killrows[y] = FALSE;
    break;
  }
```

Aha! Remember the `colours_equal` routine from earlier? If the color of the current pixel is different from the color of the first pixel in the row, then increment `livingrows` and set `killrows[y]` to `FALSE`.

In other words, if this row isn't all the same color, then this row can't be just background and shouldn't be cropped away.

```
area += width;
if (y % 20 == 0)
  gimp_progress_update ((double) area / (double) total_area);
```

And now you see what `area` was for. It's for updating GIMP's progress bar. `gimp_progress_update` takes a floating-point number between 0 and 1. Since the plug-in loops over both rows and columns, it needs some measure of how far along it is in its task. Area is a good way of measuring that.

What's the `(y % 20 == 0)`? That's intended to ensure that GIMP won't waste too much time updating the progress bar instead of doing calculations. It only updates if y has no remainder when divided by 20.

In earlier GIMP versions, as printed in the first edition of this book, this line was slightly different: `if (y % 20)`. That seemed odd: it meant it would update 19 out of 20 times. In fact, that turned out to be a bug. If you see something like that and suspect a bug, try changing it and see what happens! If you find a change that makes a plug-in work better, such as adding `== 0` in this case, file it in the GIMP bug tracker (see the section on "Reporting Bugs" in Chapter 12) and maybe your fix will become part of the next GIMP release.

The next clause (omitted here) does exactly the same thing, but looping horizontally over each column in the image.

Writing to Pixel Regions

The next section performs the crop, removing rows and columns marked "killed." It illustrates how to write to an image using pixel regions.

```
destrow = 0;

for (y = 0; y < height; y++)
  {
    if (!killrows[y])
      {
```

```
        gimp_pixel_rgn_get_row (&srcPR, buffer, 0, y, width);
        gimp_pixel_rgn_set_row (&destPR, buffer, 0, destrow, width);
        destrow++;
    }
```

Looping vertically over rows starting from the top, if a row isn't on the kill list, the whole row is copied directly from the source pixel region into the destination. destrow is a count of the number of rows that were copied. Notice that this will happily just skip over any blank (killed) rows and continue on—so killed rows can be omitted from the middle of the image.

```
    destcol = 0;
    gimp_pixel_rgn_init(&srcPR, drawable, 0, 0, width, height,
                        FALSE, TRUE);
```

The source pixel region is initialized again. Why? Because we've just written those rows back to the image, so the image has changed since the last time we initialized.

With the new source region, we can loop over columns and write only the ones that aren't on the kill list, looping over x the same way we just looped over y.

Then we're done! The rest is just cleanup.

```
  g_free (buffer);
  g_free (killrows);
  g_free (killcols);
```

All the memory that had been allocated needs to be freed. Otherwise your plug-in will have a "memory leak" and will get bigger and bigger. For a GIMP plug-in, this usually isn't critical since a plug-in runs as a separate process, and the process exits (freeing whatever memory it used) as soon as the plug-in is finished running. But free your memory anyway.

```
  gimp_progress_update (1.00);

  gimp_image_undo_group_start (image_id);
```

Curiously, the plug-in doesn't start Undo until here. That's because the pixel region operations it's been doing don't affect GIMP's Undo system.

```
  gimp_drawable_flush (drawable);
  gimp_drawable_merge_shadow (drawable->drawable_id, TRUE);
```

These two lines make sure all the data from the destination pixel region are written back to the image.

```
  gimp_image_crop (image_id, livingcols, livingrows, 0, 0);
```

Since the image is probably smaller now, this gets rid of the excess.

```
  gimp_image_undo_group_end (image_id);
```

End the undo group.

Making a New Plug-in

Now that you're an expert on how the Zealous Crop plug-in works, it's time to adapt it to the new `Autocrop All Layers` function.

The first step is to make a copy of the source file (I'll call it autocropall.c).

Next, choose a name for your new function, and edit the C file to change the old name to your new name everywhere. Don't forget to change the author, year, and the name of the plug-in inside the `gimp_install_procedure`.

If you're starting with a plug-in from inside the GIMP source, like Zealous Crop, you'll also have to remove the internationalization routines. Those reference routines inside GIMP that aren't available to outside plug-ins. That means removing `_()`, `N_()`, and the `INIT_I18N` line. You'll also need to remove the internal `#include` lines. If you don't do that, gimptool won't be able to compile your plug-in.

Now you're ready to try compiling. `gimptool --build autocropall.c` (that's two dashes) builds the plug-in but doesn't install it. `gimptool --install autocropall.c` builds the plug-in and then installs it in your GIMP profile folder (assuming it built without errors, of course).The first time you compile and install your new plug-in, you'll have to restart GIMP before it will show up in the menus. Unfortunately, there's no equivalent to *Refresh Scripts* to make new C (or Python) plug-ins register themselves.

Fortunately, once the plug-in has registered, you won't need to restart GIMP again. You can rebuild the plug-in and rerun it, and your changes will take effect. You only need to restart GIMP for a plug-in when you've changed the registration routine somehow: if this is the first time you've built this particular plug-in, if you're changing its name, or if you're changing the parameters it takes.

After restarting GIMP, check your menus. The new plug-in name (such as *Image ➤ Autocrop All Layers*) should appear in the menus now. Try running it. You haven't changed anything related to its function, so it should still do a normal Zealous Crop.

Layer Coordinates vs. Image Coordinates

Now it's time to make the real changes: to make autocropall.c look through all the visible layers. The changes will all be in `do_acrop`.

One difference when working with layers, compared to a whole image, is that coordinates may change. Layers aren't always the size of the whole image, and sometimes they're offset compared to the image.

Take a look at the "two spheres" image in Figure 11-11. The layer containing the blue sphere is offset to the right and down compared to the image: the layer's upper-left edge is at image position (X_L, Y_L).

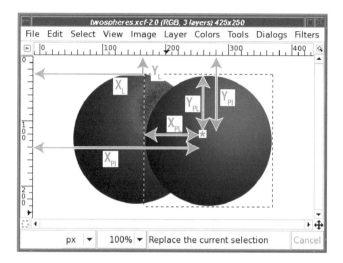

Figure 11-11. *Two spheres, three layers, three coordinate systems*

If a point in the blue sphere is at image coordinates (X_{PI}, Y_{PI}), the point's coordinates within the layer might be much smaller: (X_{PL}, Y_{PL}). These points are related by simple addition:

$$X_{PI} = X_L + X_{PL}$$

The coordinate of the point in the image is the coordinate of the layer plus the coordinate of the point in the layer, and likewise for the Y coordinates. If you get confused thinking about coordinate systems, always draw a picture—it helps.

Which coordinates did Zealous Crop use? It did everything relative to the drawable—the layer. So it was always using layer coordinates: the (X_{PL}, Y_{PL}) of Figure 11-11.

But wait! Could that be why it gets such strange results for images with several layers, as you saw back in Figure 11-10?

In fact, that's exactly the problem. Try Zealous Crop on your own multilayered image, and pay attention to where the layer boundaries begin and end. In the final image, the movement of the layers can be explained by where their layer boundaries start.

So for Autocrop All, in addition to looping over all layers, the coordinates of pixels will also need to be handled differently.

Setting Boundaries

Since Autocrop All doesn't need to crop in the middle of the image, it won't need the arrays `killrows` and `killcols`. All it needs is four integers representing the boundaries where the new crop will take place: call them `xmin`, `xmax`, `ymin`, and `ymax`. `xmax` is initialized to 1 (the left edge of the image) while `xmin` is initialized to `iwidth - 1` (the farthest right pixel), and similarly for `ymax` and `ymin`. So the `killrows` and `killcols` declarations can be replaced with

```
  gint          xmin, xmax, ymin, ymax;
```

`livingrows` and `livingcols` can go away too: we can figure out how many columns will "live" by subtracting `xmax - xmin`, and likewise for rows.

Right after buffer allocation, the plug-in will need to loop over the image layers. Get the number of layers in the image like this:

```
gint        *layers = NULL;
gint         numlayers;

layers = gimp_image_get_layers (image_id, &numlayers);
```

This will set `layers` to an array of all the layers in the image, and `numlayers` to the number of layers (the number of items in that array).

Tip How do you find out about calls like `gimp_image_get_layers`? Calls like that aren't in the Procedure Browser. Happily, *developer.gimp.org* has a very complete programmer's interface manual online, where you can find details of all the calls needed for plug-ins. See the "Additional Resources" section in Chapter 12 for more details.

`gimp_image_get_layers` allocates memory, so you should free it when you're finished with it, using `g_free(layers)`.

Instead of `width` and `height` of the drawable, you'll need the width and height of the image (which you can get with `gimp_image_width(image_id)` and `gimp_image_height(image_id)`). Inside the loop over the layers, you'll need the width and height of each drawable. To keep from getting confused about which is which, I've used `iwidth` and `iheight` for the image dimensions, and `dwidth` and `dheight` (declared inside the layers loop) for the drawable dimensions.

`layers` is an array of integers, which represent layer IDs. You can get the drawable for each of these layers with `gimp_drawable_get(layer_id)`. Then you can do all the operations that Zealous Crop did on its drawable, including the pixel-region operations.

Handling the Edges One at a Time

Once everything is set up, rather than looping over the whole width and height of each layer's drawable, you need only explore inward from each of the four image edges. Keep track of the maximum extent of the crop rectangle so far, in image coordinates, using `xmin`, `xmax`, `ymin`, and `ymax`. Since you aren't looping over the whole drawable, this is very fast; most of the time you'll only need to check a few lines before you find something that can't be cropped. Then you can move on to the next edge.

Since the plug-in will no longer loop over the entire image, there's no point in keeping track of area to update the progress bar. It should be sufficient to update the progress bar once after each layer. Update it to the current layer number divided by the total number of layers. That means you can remove `area` and `total_area` from the program.

Here is how to find `ymax`, the bottom edge from the current layer. The other three edges are similar:

```
    start = dheight - 1;
    if (layerOffsetY + dheight > iheight)
        start = iheight - layerOffsetY - 1;
```

Find the starting point for the loop. The loop should start at the bottom edge of the image, or the bottom edge of the layer, whichever is higher. (Remember, a layer can run off the edge of the image containing it.)

dheight is the height of the drawable (the current layer). Since coordinates start at 0, dheight - 1 is the coordinate of the bottommost pixels in the layer.

layerOffsetY + dheight represents the image coordinates of the bottom edge of the layer. If that is greater than the image height, the image's bottom edge lies off the bottom of the image, and start is adjusted accordingly, to the last *visible* pixel in the layer.

```
    for (y = start; y > 0 && layerOffsetY + y > ymax; y--)
```

Loop backwards (with y in layer coordinates) from the bottom visible pixel in the layer until we either reach the top of the image, or until the image coordinates of the current row (layerOffsetY + y) crosses the ymax we've already found from some other layer.

```
        gimp_pixel_rgn_get_row (&srcPR, buffer, 0, y, dwidth);
```

```
        for (x = 0; x < dwidth * bytes; x += bytes)
```

Get the row at this position, and loop horizontally over the pixels in it. Notice that this isn't checking to see if the pixels are really inside the image boundaries. That's something that should probably be added.

```
            if (!colours_equal (buffer, &buffer[x], bytes))
```

If the color is different from the color of the first pixel in the row,

```
                ymax = y + layerOffsetY + 1;
                break;
```

convert back to image coordinates and update ymax.

After checking all four edges like this, in each layer in the image, xmin, xmax, ymin, and ymax should hold the coordinates to pass to crop. Crop takes its parameters in a slightly unintuitive order: gimp_image_crop(image_id, new_width, new_height, offset_y, offset_x). xmax and ymax are coordinates, not dimensions, so you have to subtract:

```
  gimp_image_crop(image_id,
                  xmax - xmin, ymax - ymin,
                  xmin, ymin);
```

That saves a lot of work compared to writing to pixel regions and updating shadow tiles!

Note Since you're no longer writing to the image using pixel regions, you can eliminate destPR and every line that refers to it. But even better, you can change the gimp_tile_cache_ntiles call to remove the factor of two: you only need half the tile cache. That makes the plug-in use less memory.

All done! The new plug-in correctly crops multiple layers. Space doesn't permit a full listing here, but you can download the full source for the Autocrop All plug-in, autocropall.c, from *http://gimpbook.com* or in the Source Code/Download section of the Apress website (*http://www.apress.com*).

Summary

If you've made it this far, you're well on your way to becoming a GIMP plug-in writer—and, if you choose, perhaps a developer for GIMP itself.

You can develop your plug-in authoring skills by exploring the existing scripts and plug-ins, reading the documentation available on the GIMP website, and writing your own new plug-ins. Whether you're tweaking existing scripts, writing quick scripts for your own use, or developing polished plug-ins intended for distribution, don't be afraid to explore and try new things!

More than any other part of GIMP, plug-in writing benefits from good documentation. This book isn't intended to be a complete reference manual on GIMP programming; it only scratches the surface. You'll want to become very familiar with the online documentation and existing tutorials.

If you're wondering where to find all these web resources, keep reading. Chapter 12 will discuss the wealth of GIMP information on the web. You'll also learn about a few other topics such as GIMP's configuration files, screen shots, and printing.

CHAPTER 12

■ ■ ■

Additional Topics

By now, you're familiar with most of the basic techniques of image manipulation available in GIMP. In this chapter, I'll show you a few details that haven't been covered, explore ways of customizing GIMP, and describe some web resources that can help you learn even more. The chapter will cover the following:

- Printing

- Screen shots and scanners: the *Acquire* menu

- GIMP preferences

- GIMP configuration files

- Additional resources

Printing

Printing in GIMP isn't built-in; it's handled by a plug-in. That means printing may be different on various platforms. In addition, it changes with GIMP version. So the first step is to find out which printing system is available to you.

GIMP for Windows uses the standard Windows print dialogs. Any adjustment to the output will probably go through the dialogs supplied by your printer manufacturer. These may be different for each printer, so this book won't try to cover them.

On most Linux and Mac systems, there are two options for printing under GIMP 2.4. The older and more complex system is called Gutenprint. You may also see it called gimp-print. It comes from a separate development project and has been available ever since the GIMP 1.2 days (when it was called gimp-print). It's arguably still the best if you want high-quality prints with lots of control over the output. (The Gutenprint project is also the origin of many color printer drivers used by Linux and Mac OS X.)

The newer option uses the GTKPrint system from the GTK+ project. GTKPrint's dialog is simpler than Gutenprint's, with a more familiar interface. However, controlling details like brightness and color balance, or adjusting the position and size of the image printed on the page, is a lot more difficult.

These two systems can coexist. Generally, if you have both options installed, *File* ➤ *Print...* calls up GTKPrint, while *File* ➤ *Print with Gutenprint...* brings up the Gutenprint dialog. Most GIMP 2.4 installations will come with GTKPrint, but a few come with Gutenprint or even with both.

■**Caution** Printing should work fine on Mac OS X 10.4.*x* (Tiger) or later. But if you have installed GIMP 2.4 on 10.3.*x* (Panther) or any GIMP on an earlier version, printing may just flat out not work. Your easiest workaround is to save the image in some format another program—such as Preview—can read, then print from there.

Printing with GTKPrint

First is GTKPrint, the standard printing method in GIMP 2.4.

When you initiate a print with *File* ➤ *Print...*, you get the dialog in Figure 12-1, which lets you choose from a list of printers available to your system.

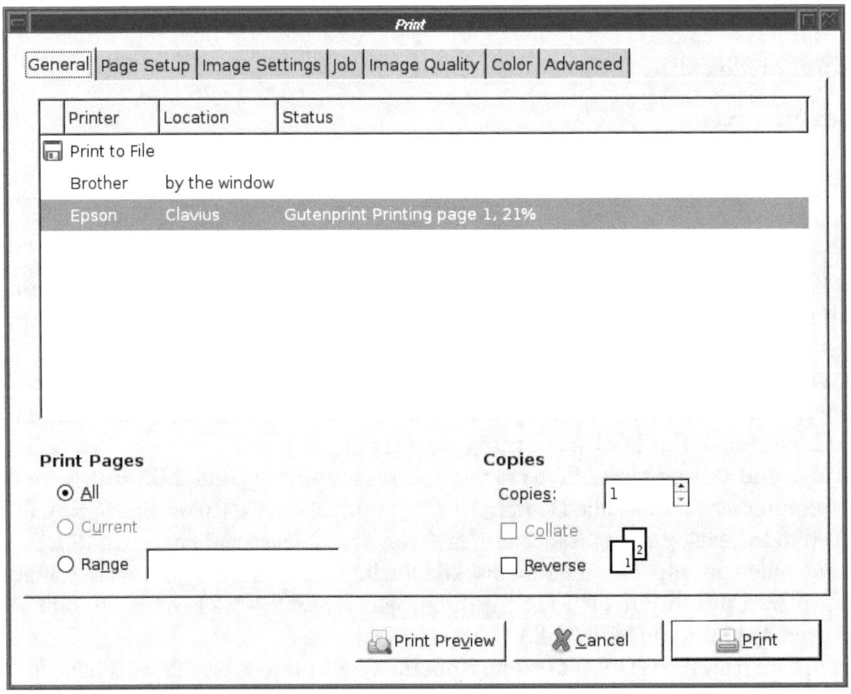

Figure 12-1. *The basic GTKPrint dialog*

Deceptively simple! But there are a lot of tabs there. The first one after General is Page Setup, which isn't as useful as you might expect—it's mainly there to let you change the paper type and duplex settings (whether you're printing two sides or one side).

Note Sharp-eyed readers may wonder why this dialog mentions Gutenprint when I've said this isn't the Gutenprint dialog. Did I mix up my screen shots and include the wrong figure here? No: the reason it says "Gutenprint" is that my Epson printer uses a driver that comes from the same Gutenprint project. So the dialog reflects using the GTKPrint dialog for a printer installed with Gutenprint drivers.

The next tab, *Image Settings*, is more useful. There you can see a preview of your image as it should be printed on the page. You can change the size and position on the page to some extent by changing the *Size* and *Position* numbers. If you want to change between portrait and landscape printing, click *Adjust Page Size and Orientation.*

The *Job* tab includes things like *Billing info* and *Add Cover Page*—stuff that most GIMP users won't care about.

The *Image Quality* tab has one item in it: *Resolution*, defaulting to Automatic. This is where you specify high resolution if your printer is capable of it.

The *Color* tab also contains only one item, *Color Model*. Usually you won't need to change this—the printing system should handle color conversions for you unless you need specific color controls.

Finally, the *Advanced* tab gives you a window into a list of features available for your specific printer's driver. This may include details like ink set, printing direction, interleave method, controls on brightness or saturation, corrections for each color of ink the printer uses, gamma adjustments, and much more.

At the bottom of the dialog (regardless of which tab is showing) are three buttons: *Print Preview, Cancel, and Print. Print Preview* sounds useful, but it can be jarring because choosing it dismisses the print dialog and substitutes a small PDF viewer window. You can print from there—the small arrow at the upper right displays a menu that includes *Print* as an option. However, you can't get back to the Print dialog from there (except by going back to the original image and choosing *File ➤ Print…* again). So don't click it if there's any chance you might want to go on adjusting values in the Print dialog. You're probably better off using the *Image Settings* tab for any previewing you need to do.

Printing with Gutenprint

If GTKPrint doesn't do what you need. GIMP's other print plug-in, Gutenprint, may fit the bill. It's much more flexible than GTKPrint, with only one drawback: it can't figure out on its own what type of printer you have, so you have to tell it.

Call up Gutenprint with the menu item *File ➤ Print with Gutenprint….* If your image has multiple layers or other GIMP-specific enhancements, GIMP will tell you it needs to "export" the image. Don't worry; it won't change your original image.

Then you'll see the dialog shown in Figure 12-2.

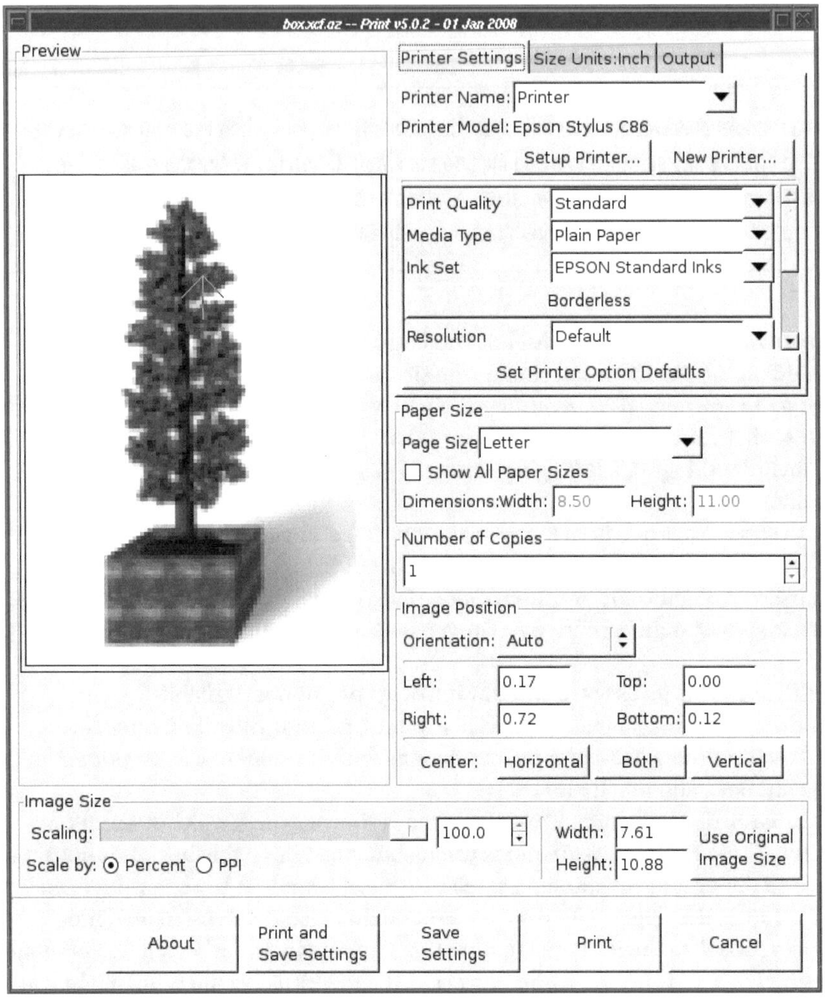

Figure 12-2. *The basic Gutenprint dialog*

On the left is a rough preview of your image and how it will look on the page. You can get a general idea of image brightness, but the preview's main use is to let you drag the image around to control its position on the page. Initially Gutenprint will try to make the image fill the whole page, but you can print it smaller by dragging the Scaling slider (under the preview) to less than 100%.

Go ahead and click the *Print* button if you want a fast full-page printout. For quick-and-dirty printing, you don't need any more than that. But if you want to print high-quality photos on fancy paper and have a printer that can handle it, read on. (If you got errors, or printed a page full of gibberish, try proceeding to the next step.)

Setting Your Printer Model

The single most common cause of Gutenprint problems is that it doesn't automatically set the *Printer Model* field (near the top right of the dialog), even if the printer is the default system printer. Don't be misled by the contents of Printer Name; what's important is what's listed next to Printer Model. By default it's usually set to "PostScript Level 2." To change it, click *Setup Printer...* (if there's no printer defined yet and *Setup Printer...* is grayed out, use *New Printer...*). Gutenprint will pop up a dialog containing a list of printer makes and models.

WHY POSTSCRIPT?

Why does Gutenprint default to PostScript? Because the printing system on Mac OS X, Linux, and most UNIX systems is based on Adobe's PostScript language (though that's changing as systems migrate to PDF). If GIMP creates PostScript, it can send it to the printing system, which will then translate it to whatever your specific printer needs.

Sounds nice and simple, right? And it usually works okay for basic printing (go ahead and click the *Print* button to try it, if you want). But the generic PostScript model used by the printing system doesn't do high-quality printing. It can't control any of the nifty special features most inkjet printers offer, such as high resolution or settings for special photo paper or inks.

Scroll down to find and select your printer make and model from the list in the dialog. If you don't find your exact printer model, something close may work (for instance, C84 works for an Epson C86).

If you don't find anything that's even close, go back to the *PostScript Level 2* setting (found under *Printer Make: Adobe.*)

▌Caution If you use the PostScript setting, you also need to look at the *Custom Command* field. If it includes "–oraw," delete that. It's a bug in some versions of Gutenprint that "–oraw" was included for PostScript printers: it's needed for all other printers, but should not be included for PostScript.

If you have a real PostScript printer, the *PPD File* field is a place where you can select a driver for that printer. PPD files apply only to PostScript printers. The field should not appear, or should be grayed out, for other printers.

Click *OK* and you're back in the Gutenprint dialog, with the correct *Printer Model*. It's a good idea to click *Save Settings* at the bottom of the dialog immediately after setting your printer, to ensure that GIMP remembers it. Otherwise, you'll have to do it all again next time you start GIMP.

Other Print Settings You Can Adjust

Once your printer is set correctly, Gutenprint's options should reflect the capabilities of your printer. Adjust *Print Quality*, *Media Type*, and *Resolution* to appropriate settings, depending on whether you're printing a quick draft on regular paper or a photograph on glossy photo paper. (With color inkjets, the type of paper will make a big difference in quality!) You generally shouldn't need to change *Ink Set*. Check to make sure *Page Size* is right (if you find you have to keep resetting it, use the *Save Settings* button to ensure GIMP remembers).

Then adjust the image's size and position on the page, starting with *Orientation* (Figure 12-3).

Landscape:

Portrait:

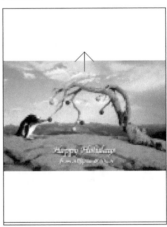

Figure 12-3. *Orientation options*

The choices are as follows:

- *Auto*: GIMP will use the orientation that best matches the image's own dimensions.

- *Portrait*: The image will be right-side-up when the paper is held like a normal page, taller than it is wide, even if the image is wider than it is high.

- *Landscape*: The image will be right-side-up when the paper is held, with its longer dimension horizontal.

- *Upside down*: Portrait, but with the image upside down. The bottom of the image will print first.

- *Seascape*: Landscape, but upside down.

Now skip down to the broad *Size* slider. Grab it and slide it to change the size of the image. The value 100% actually means "the largest size that will fit on the page," but you can scale the image down as small as you want. The preview will update as you adjust the slider, so you can see how the image compares to the paper size. The *Width* and *Height* of the image as it will be printed are displayed under the slider. After adjusting size, you can drag the preview image around to put it wherever you want on the page. Or use the *Center* buttons: *Horizontal, Vertical,* or *Both.*

Once you click on *Print* or *Print and Save Settings,* GIMP should begin sending data to the printer. At a high-resolution setting, this may take a while; watch the status bar at the bottom right of the GIMP image window for progress.

Fine-tuning: Image/Output Settings

If you want to make your prints look perfect, you may find you need to make some adjustments for your specific printer.

At the top right of the Gutenprint dialog, next to *Printer Settings,* are a couple of other tabs, including *Output.* Choosing that tab gives you a choice of *Color* or *Grayscale* (try a grayscale image both ways to see the difference), plus a big button to click, *Adjust Output…,* which brings up the dialog shown in Figure 12-4.

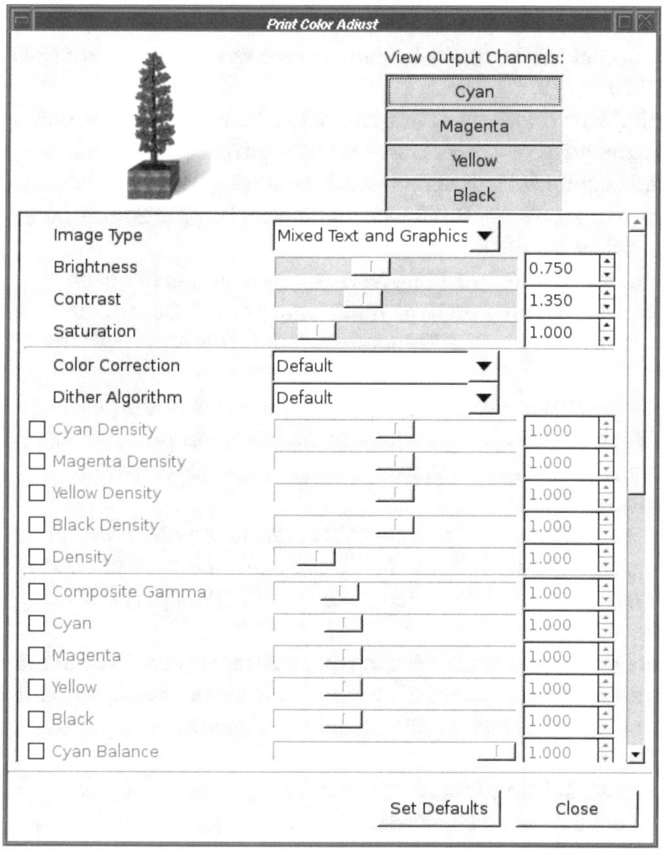

Figure 12-4. *The Print Color Adjust dialog*

The Print Color Adjust dialog gives you a lot of settings that let you fine-tune the brightness and color of the image, choosing from several presets. You can think of *Line art* as analogous to black-and-white drawings or text (2-bit color), *Solid colors* as analogous to indexed color (with areas over which the color is constant), and *Photograph* as 24-bit true color. If in doubt, leave it at the default setting, *Mixed Text and Graphics*.

You can also adjust the brightness, contrast, and saturation of your prints. Every printer model is a little different. Some may emphasize one color or another; others may print too light or too dark. This doesn't matter so much when you're printing out web maps and directions. But when you're printing glossy photos to hang on your wall or give to relatives, it matters.

To find out how your printer stacks up, you will probably have to experiment, printing several images and trying different settings. This can be somewhat costly since you can use up ink and expensive paper. Fortunately, you don't need to print full-page images to test a printer: you can print small images, feed the same page through multiple times, and use Gutenprint's position and size settings to place the image at a different location on the page each time. On a particularly tricky image, you might want to create a smaller test image that includes some of the "extremes" of the original.

If you need to adjust any of the colors individually (for instance, if your prints seem to come out with too much magenta), click on the toggle button next to any of the color controls to enable a slider that you can adjust.

Once you've found settings that look the way you want them (which usually means that the printed image looks similar to the image you see on screen), you can click *Save Settings* back in the Gutenprint dialog, and Gutenprint will remember these settings next time.

Each setting has a tooltip if you hover over it. But they're not always helpful. Some of the tricky ones are *Density*, *Gamma*, and *Dither Algorithm*.

Density controls the amount of ink used for printing. Normally, this should not need adjustment, but if your prints come out with so much ink that it smears or soaks into the paper, or so little that black areas aren't fully black or colors seem faded, this is the place to adjust it.

You met *Gamma* briefly in Chapter 2: it corresponds to the middle slider in the Levels dialog. Generally, gamma works like brightness: larger values mean a brighter print; smaller values mean a darker one. However, adjusting gamma won't change the levels of black or white in the image, only the middle tones in between.

Dither Algorithm controls how GIMP maps its internal RGB colors to the CMYK colors the printer understands. In addition, printing almost always involves some scaling: it's not likely that the number of pixels in your image will exactly match the number of dots your printer would use at the size you want the image to appear.

Fortunately, the print software does a good job of scaling and color mapping. Most of the time, the default methods it uses are fine, but if you ever want to fine-tune the result, you can choose from a variety of algorithms: *Adaptive Hybrid* (the default), *Ordered*, *Fast*, *Very Fast*, *Hybrid Floyd-Steinberg*, or *EvenTone*.

The Gutenprint project recommends using *Adaptive Hybrid* for highest quality. That should be the default, and most of the time you can leave it alone. If you want to experiment with other settings, *Ordered* can work just as well and is faster for images with mostly continuous tones (no text or line art). *Fast* is faster, but at the expense of quality (*Very Fast* is more so, but it sacrifices more quality than most people will tolerate). You can get details on some of the other algorithms on the Gutenprint website, *gimp-print.sourceforge.net* (yes, the website still uses the old name).

Screen Shots and Scanners: The Acquire Menu

Most of your work with GIMP will probably begin with existing images, such as photographs, or a blank canvas.

But there's another way to obtain images: the *File* ➤ *Acquire* menu. (In GIMP 2.6, these items will move to *File* ➤ *New*.)

Acquire offers two seemingly unrelated functions: screen shots, and communication with devices such as scanners. The *Acquire* menu also offers *Paste as New*, which you've probably already used in other contexts. It simply creates a new image out of whatever layer or selection has been most recently copied or cut.

Scanning from GIMP

If you don't have a scanner, only *Screenshot* will be available in the menu. If you have a scanner, you need two software packages to scan directly to GIMP:

- The driver for your scanner

- A scanning plug-in for the GIMP

Scanner drivers use one of two common protocols: TWAIN or SANE.

TWAIN is most commonly used on Windows systems, and is also popular on Mac. It's usually provided as part of the drivers shipped with a new scanner. The origin of the name is unclear: some say that it stands for "Technology Without An Important Name," but people on the TWAIN committee say it comes from Kipling's phrase "Never the twain shall meet," reflecting the previous difficulty of connecting scanners to computers.

SANE is an open source protocol. It stands for "Scanner Access Now Easy." It's commonly used on Linux and Mac systems, but it's available for Windows as an add-on. Its home page is *http://www.sane-project.org*.

Macs add one more menu entry, *Image Capture…*, which can grab images from a webcam, if you have one.

Whichever protocol you use for your scanner, you will need an appropriate plug-in for GIMP to find the scanner. For SANE, there's the xsane-gimp plug-in; for TWAIN, there's a Twain Acquire plug-in that should be part of the GIMP packages on Mac and Windows.

Either of these plug-ins will create a new submenu inside the *Acquire* menu, called *XSane* or *TWAIN Acquire*. With your scanner turned on, check the contents of this menu. It may list the scanner there already, in which case the menu item will bring up a scanning dialog. Alternately, it may simply give you the option to bring up a device dialog, which will attempt to identify your scanner.

Scanners are tricky beasts. Some scanners work perfectly out of the box, but others require help. You may have to fiddle with your scanner setup to make it show up as a TWAIN or SANE device. Possible issues with specific scanners are beyond the scope of this book.

Screen Shots

Screen shots are far less problematic than scanners, since there's no device driver to cause difficulties. *File* ➤ *Acquire* ➤ *Screenshot…* brings up the dialog shown in Figure 12-5.

Figure 12-5. *The Screenshot dialog*

The options are all straightforward. You can take a shot of a single window, with or without its borders: click *Grab*, and then click on the window you want to shoot. *Include window decoration* controls whether the screen shot will include the window's frame and title bar. Or you can take a shot of your whole desktop. You can also choose *Select a region* in order to drag out a region of the desktop with the mouse.

The *Wait [0] seconds before grabbing* option is particularly useful if you need to perform an action in the window while the screen shot is happening. For example, if you want a shot of a window with a menu showing, you can set a delay of five seconds, click *Grab*, move to the target window, and click to select it; then you have five seconds to pop up a menu. It's also useful if you need to switch to a different virtual desktop. You can set the delay as long or as short as you like, depending on the difficulty of the operation (and the speed of the system).

Screen shots have some limitations. For instance, on some systems, screen shots don't show the mouse cursor. If you need a screen shot showing a cursor, you'll have to cheat by getting a copy of the cursor image somewhere else and pasting it into your screen shot.

Tip If you ever need GIMP's special cursors for a screen shot, the GIMP source includes a file called gimp-tool-cursors.xcf that includes all the cursors used in GIMP. Each part of each cursor is a separate layer, so you can combine them as needed.

Screen shots of windows are usually limited to the window's own boundaries (Figure 12-6). If you need to shoot something like a menu that might go beyond the boundaries of the window, you're better off shooting the whole desktop, or a region of the desktop (you'll have to guess how far the menus will extend). You can always crop off any extra parts you don't need.

Certain types of windows, such as games that are using accelerated 3-D graphics, may not produce a screen shot that looks exactly like what you see.

Finally, GIMP will shoot the content of windows as it appears on the screen. If your window is slightly off the screen, or is partially covered by another window, the screen shot will show that.

Figure 12-6. *A screen shot of a window is limited to the window's boundaries, even if menus are showing that should extend beyond the boundaries.*

GIMP Preferences

Figure 12-7 shows GIMP's Preferences window (Toolbox window, *File* ➤ *Preferences* or image window, *Edit* ➤ *Preferences*).

Figure 12-7. *The Preferences window*

On the left side of the Preferences window is a list of categories. Selecting any category in the list shows the preferences associated with that category.

I'll go over each of the categories and some of the useful settings contained within each one.

Environment

The *Resource Consumption* preferences let you configure several factors affecting GIMP's memory usage. Most of these features are fairly self-explanatory: increasing them will give you better performance and more flexibility, but will cause GIMP to use more RAM. If you work with large images and have plenty of memory, increasing the size of the file cache can improve performance quite a bit, and, of course, having lots of undo levels is always nice if you have memory to spare.

Image thumbnails are stored in a common location so other applications can use the thumbnails GIMP generates. Of course, they do take up some disk space; you can control their size, or disable thumbnail generation entirely, with the thumbnail size preference.

Finally, GIMP normally asks about unsaved images, if there are any still open when you quit the application. You can disable this behavior here, which will cause any changes to be discarded without prompting. Be careful! Most people will want to leave this option enabled. You can double-click on an image in the dialog to call up that image's window, and you can leave the dialog up as you check the open images to make sure you haven't forgotten to save your work.

User Interface and Keyboard Shortcuts

The *User Interface* preference keyboard shortcuts category (Figure 12-8; the preference panel is headed *User Interface* though the category on the left says merely *Interface*) lets you configure the way GIMP's windows appear and behave.

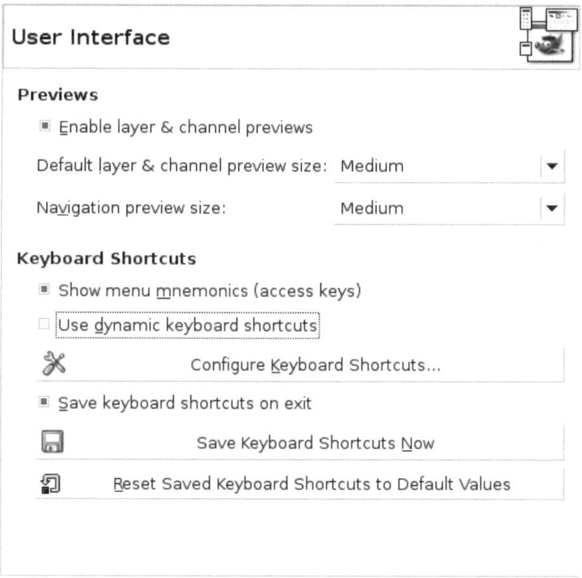

Figure 12-8. *Interface preferences*

The first group of options controls previews that will be shown in the Layers and Channels dialogs. If you find that you want a larger or smaller preview size, you can change them here.

The second group concerns keyboard shortcuts, and was already discussed in Chapter 1.

Theme

The *Theme* preference lets you apply a different look to the GIMP application.

GIMP comes with two themes: *Default* and *Small* (Figure 12-9). The *Small* theme makes the Toolbox and dialog windows smaller, so you have more screen space available to use for image windows.

You can also use this preference to install new themes—for instance, to use a different set of icons for each of the tools, or a less colorful set of icons to distract less from the image being edited. However, there don't seem to be many themes available for GIMP yet. Try a web search for *GIMP themes* if you want to see what is available.

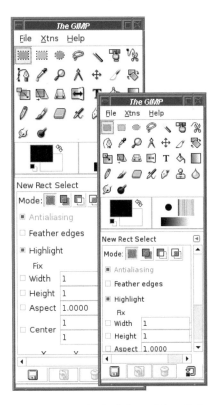

Figure 12-9. *Default (left) and Small themes*

Help System

The *Help System* preferences let you configure GIMP's online help. You can view the help in a browser of your choosing, or in a window of GIMP's making.

■**Caution** Some GIMP installations don't include a Help browser. If you have trouble viewing GIMP's built-in Help, check the place where you got your GIMP to see if it offers a separate GIMP Help package you can download. Windows and Linux GIMP installations often package the Help files separately.

GIMP will also show helpful tips when you start it, unless you deselect *Show tip next time GIMP starts*. You can see these tips at other times by choosing *Help* ➤ *Tip of the Day* from the Toolbox window.

Tool Options

Tool Options controls some common settings for a few of GIMP's tools (Figure 12-10).

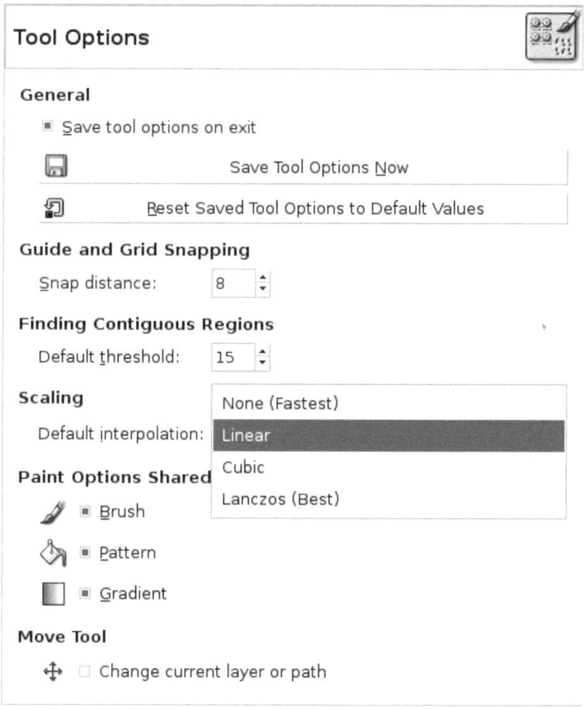

Figure 12-10. *Tool Options preferences, showing Scaling options*

First is a checkbox controlling whether GIMP saves tool options on exit. With this box checked, any changes you make in *Tool Options* dialogs will be remembered from one GIMP session to the next. Leave the box unchecked, and GIMP will reset all the tool options to default values the next time you start up. This is purely a matter of personal preference. If you don't save tool options on exit, there's a button to save the tool options once you get them just the way you want them.

The next option controls how strongly GIMP will "snap" to the grid (if you have it shown) or guides (if you have any in position). Snapping to the guides or grid can make it easier to put lines, squares, or rectangles in specific positions.

Finding Contiguous Regions controls the default value for the *Fuzzy Select* tool. See Chapter 5 for details.

The *Scaling* option was mentioned in Chapter 1. When you change the size of an image, it can be scaled larger or smaller in several ways, depending on whether you want the operation to happen more quickly, or whether you want the best quality in the final image. Either *Cubic* or *Lanczos* will give good results; the difference between them is fairly subtle. Even on a slow machine, you may still want to use one of these settings, and just be patient when scaling large images; but if it's too slow, try *Linear; None* will result in lower quality than most people can tolerate.

Paint Options Shared Between Tools enables the brush, pattern, and gradient to be set separately for each tool, or tools can all use the same settings. The default setting is probably fine for most people.

I discussed the *Move Tool* and its options in Chapter 3.

Toolbox

The three *Toolbox* options control which items are shown in the Toolbox window under the tool buttons. You can show or hide the color swatches, brush/pattern/gradient indicator, and current image thumbnail, individually or together, and get a smaller Toolbox window consisting only of the menu bar and the collection of tool buttons.

Default Image

The *Default Image* preferences (Figure 12-11) determine the default look of an image you create with GIMP's *File* ➤ *New* action.

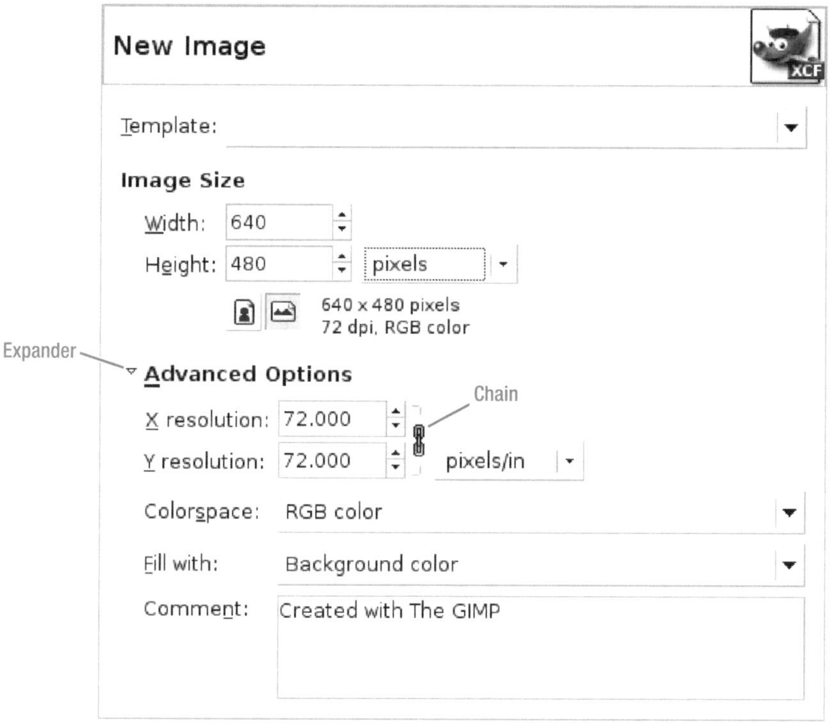

Figure 12-11. *Default Image preferences*

The first item is a list of templates. Most of the templates correspond to common pixel resolutions, such as 640 × 480, or fixed paper sizes, such as US Letter or CD Cover. You can create custom templates using the Templates dialog, accessed from *File* ➤ *Dialogs* ➤ *Templates* in the Toolbox window.

You can choose a template, then modify it—or simply use your own preferred image size and resolution. The *Image Size* group of options allows you to specify a preferred image's width and height. These can be specified in pixels, or in other units such as inches, millimeters, or points. You can edit the number in the text field directly, or use the up and down arrows next to each text field to make the number larger or smaller. Below the *Width* and *Height* fields are a couple of buttons that show whether the image will be *portrait* (taller than it is wide) or *landscape* (wider than it is tall). Switching between these modes will also swap the width and height values automatically.

The units menu, next to the *Height* field, lets you specify the image's width and height in any unit you prefer. You can work in inches, millimeters, or points if it feels more comfortable.

Since GIMP is an image-editing program, it always works in pixels, and converts other units into pixels using your current resolution setting. To change the resolution setting, open the *Advanced Options* section if it isn't already visible by clicking on the expander to the left of the words *Advanced Options*.

Resolution is normally specified in pixels per inch (also called dots per inch, or dpi), though you can change that with the units menu. Most often, you will probably want this to be the same as the resolution of your computer monitor (you can get this from the *Display* category in the Preferences window, which is discussed in the section "Display"), but you may want to set a higher resolution for images that are primarily intended for a printer.

Normally, the same resolution is used for both X (horizontal) and Y (vertical) dimensions, so when you change one, GIMP will change the other; they are "linked together." However, some printers may use different resolution settings for X and Y, and it might be important for some video and film setups. If you need to unlink two quantities that are chained together in GIMP, use the "chain link" button. When the link is closed (Figure 12-12), the two quantities are linked together: changing one quantity will cause the other to change. Click on the chain link, and it opens—now the two quantities are independent, and you can change them separately.

Closed
link

Open
link

Figure 12-12. *Chain link icons*

Below the resolution options is a *Colorspace* selector. New images can be in full color (RGB) or in grayscale. Most people will want to leave this option as RGB.

Fill with lets you control the page color of new images. You can use either GIMP's current background color, its foreground color, white, or transparent. Of course, you can change this for individual images from the New Image dialog.

Finally, images can have a comment associated with them. In some image formats, such as GIF, the comment will be saved along with the image. You can use this to attach copyright notices or signatures to your images. Or you can keep the default, *Created with GIMP*, to let people know which image-editing program you like best.

Default Grid

Moving on past the *New Image* category, we find *Default Grid*. You can make GIMP's grid visible from the *View* menu of an image window: *View* ➤ *Show Grid*. Grids can be helpful if you need to draw a lot of horizontal and vertical lines with well-defined intersections.

Image Windows

GIMP offers quite a few preferences that you can use to control the appearance and behavior of GIMP's image windows (Figure 12-13). *Use "Dot for dot" by default* controls how windows are zoomed; you probably won't want to change it unless you regularly work with very high-resolution images intended for a printer. *Marching ants speed* controls the way selections are shown.

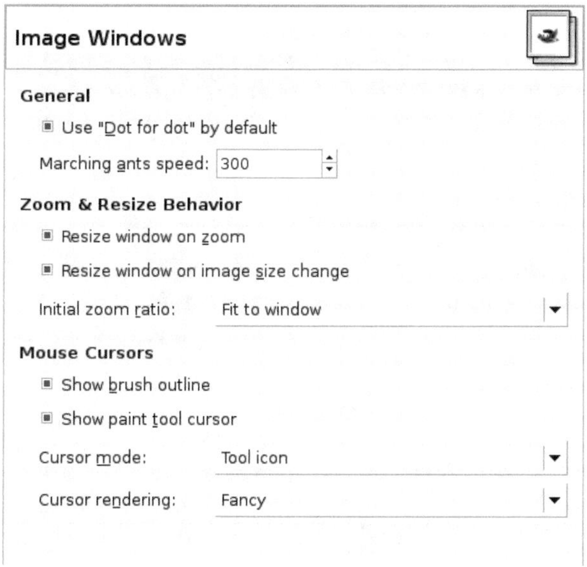

Figure 12-13. *Image Window preferences*

Zoom & Resize Behavior is a particularly useful group, already mentioned in Chapter 1. Enabling these two preferences makes windows resize themselves smaller or larger when you zoom in or out on the image. With the preferences disabled, the window will stay the same size when you zoom in or out, and will present scrollbars if needed. *Initial zoom ratio*, if set to 1:1, will always present images at full size when you first open them; otherwise, GIMP will scale the image up or down to make it a comfortable size to fit on the screen.

Mouse Cursors lets you change the appearance of the cursor as you move your mouse over different parts of an image. In particular, the cursor can show the size and shape of the current brush, and can reflect the current tool in use. Most people will want to leave these at their default settings, except perhaps on a very slow machine. However, some people may prefer the crosshair since it doesn't get in the way of the image as much as the regular cursor.

Image Windows: Appearance

This preferences panel lets you configure which elements are shown in each image window. The "padding" mentioned on this screen is the blank space shown to either side of the image in an image window if you resize the window to be larger than needed for the image. You can also add or remove many of these items using the *View* menu inside the image window.

Image Windows: Title and Status

This panel controls what information is shown in the title bar and status bar areas of image windows. You can use regular text, choose from a selection of useful samples, or design your own title or status string by selecting from special variables providing information about the current image.

■**Note** You can change these settings interactively and watch what they do in the image window. For a list of these variables and how to use them, see the gimprc manual, discussed elsewhere in this chapter.

Display

When GIMP displays an image that is partly transparent, the transparent parts are indicated with a light gray and dark gray checkerboard, so it's easy to see where they are. It may be easiest to think of this as GIMP keeping a gray checkerboard behind the image you're working on.

If the checkerboard annoys you, or if you're working on an image involving a gray checkerboard and can't tell it apart from GIMP's transparency indicator, you can change the way GIMP shows transparent areas here.

Also included in the *Display* preferences is GIMP's notion of your display's resolution (in dpi). Normally, GIMP can get this information from your windowing system, but if you need to change it check *Manually* and enter the resolution here. Notice that there's another chain link icon here linking the horizontal and vertical resolution values together, as discussed earlier in the *Advanced Options* section of the *Default Image* category. You can also choose *Calibrate*, which brings up a window with rulers that you can measure and compare to a real ruler to get your monitor's true resolution. You may be surprised at how far off your computer's idea of your monitor resolution is. Be careful not to scratch your screen with the ruler! (A cloth measuring tape or a piece of paper can work well here too.)

Color Management

The *Color Management* preferences let you specify color profiles matching particular monitors and printers. Most people should not need to change the color management preferences, but see Chapter 8 for more details on color management.

Input Devices

The *Input Devices* preferences control goodies such as graphics tablets, which you can use in addition to a regular mouse. If you have such a tablet, choose *Configure Extended Input Devices* to select which of your tablet's tools will be used by GIMP.

Tip The *Save Settings* button in this preferences pane is useful even if you don't have a graphics tablet. If you have a tool you use frequently in GIMP, you can make GIMP select that tool automatically whenever you start up by selecting the tool in the Toolbox and then clicking *Save Input Device Settings Now*.

Input Controllers

Here, you can configure GIMP's behavior in response to hardware such as a mouse wheel when used in a GIMP image window.

By default, the mouse wheel by itself scrolls up and down in the image window (assuming a scrollbar is present); holding the Shift key down while using the mouse wheel scrolls left and right. Holding the Ctrl key down makes the mouse wheel zoom the image larger and smaller. Other combinations of key modifiers cause other behaviors: in this preferences pane, you can view the current settings, delete current settings, or add your own by clicking on a setting, such as *Scroll Up* (Shift+Ctrl) then clicking the *Edit* button. This will bring up a dialog showing the actions you can trigger using the mouse wheel.

Clicking on the *Main Keyboard* tab shows functions that are bound to the arrow keys on the keyboard. By default, the arrow keys scroll by a small amount, unless a tool is selected (such as the *Move* tool) in which the arrow keys do something else. Again, you can customize the behaviors in response to the arrow keys using the *Edit* button, or *Delete* a behavior if it bothers you.

Window Management

This group of preferences, already mentioned briefly in Chapter 1, controls the behavior of some of GIMP's windows. If you have problems such as windows not staying on top when you think they should, or windows starting up in the wrong position, try changing these preferences.

Window Manager Hints controls whether the Toolbox and other docked dialogs such as the Layers dialog should be treated like dialogs and always kept above image windows, or treated like normal windows. Choosing *Utility Window* keeps the window always on top of every GIMP image window; *Keep Above* tries to keep it above windows from any program, not just GIMP's. Not every system supports all of these behaviors.

Activate the focused image makes an image window active as soon as it receives focus: in other words, as soon as you click on it, tab to it, or sometimes just move the mouse over it. Moving to a new active window changes the behavior of other open dialogs, such as the Layers dialog, which can be inconvenient, especially for Linux users who use "mouse focus." Disable this preference if you have this problem.

If you do disable *Activate the focused image*, you may find that you need a way to make a new image active without making any changes to it. An easy way to activate an image is to focus the image window, then press the spacebar or a modifier key such as Shift or Ctrl.

The remainder of the *Window Management* pane concerns GIMP remembering its window positions.

Folders

The Folders preference category lets you configure where GIMP stores its various preferences, plug-ins, brushes, and other information it needs. Normally, it's best to leave all of these at their default values. When you start adding collections of brushes and plug-ins, you can add folders to the lists here to make it easier to keep track of what's where.

GIMP Configuration Files

By now, you've probably referenced your GIMP profile folder for some reason or other—to install scripts or plug-ins, or to create new brushes or patterns. In addition, you've probably fiddled with your preference settings through GIMP's Preference dialog.

All these changes are saved inside your profile folder. But there's quite a bit more buried in there. Sometimes it's useful to examine your settings directly, or to change settings that aren't visible in the Preferences window. In addition, you can copy your profile folder from one machine to another if you want to make your GIMP settings available on a second machine.

Remember, you can find your GIMP profile folder by opening the Preferences window (*File* ➤ *Preferences* from the Toolbox window) and looking in the *Folders* category. Nearly every item in that category will have two entries: one for a system location, and one inside your personal profile folder. Take a look at your profile folder now as you go through its contents.

All of the configuration files in your GIMP profile folder are readable text files (though there are other types of files there as well, such as C plug-ins, brushes, patterns, and so on). You can copy your whole GIMP profile, or any part of it, to another machine (though compiled C plug-ins may not work if you move them to a different platform).

gimprc

Most of your saved preferences are stored in a file called gimprc. If you've changed any preferences from the default, the file might include lines like these:

```
# GIMP gimprc
#
# This is your personal gimprc file. Any variable defined in
# this file takes precedence over the value defined in the
# system-wide gimprc: /etc/gimp/2.0/gimprc
# Most values can be set within GIMP by changing some
# options in the Preferences dialog.

(interpolation-type lanczos)
(default-font "Helvetica Bold Italic")
(default-image
    (width 500)
    (height 400)
    (unit pixels)
    (xresolution 72.000000)
    (yresolution 72.000000)
    (resolution-unit inches)
```

```
       (image-type rgb)
       (fill-type background-fill)
       (comment "Created with The GIMP"))
(undo-levels 11)
(resize-windows-on-resize yes)
```

You'll probably recognize most of the options as preferences that are settable in the Preferences window. But what's that *default-font* line? Try as you might, you won't be able to find a default font setting in the Preferences window.

GIMP can understand preferences beyond those exposed in the Preferences window, and editing gimprc is the way to set them. As with editing scripts or plug-ins, you should use a plain text editor to edit gimprc (or any other file inside your GIMP profile), not a word processor (the sidebar "Why a Text Editor?" in Chapter 11 explains why).

First, you've probably already noticed that the syntax looks like Script-Fu: everything is delimited by parentheses. Options that take multiple values, such as the default-image settings, take a list of parenthesis-delimited lists.

You may wonder about that comment referencing /etc/gimp/2.0/gimprc: why is it 2.0, and not 2.2 or 2.4? GIMP sometimes confusingly uses "2.0" to refer to resources such as plug-ins or preferences that can be used by any GIMP version starting with 2.

Linux and UNIX users can get the latest on gimprc by typing **man gimprc** into a terminal window (it also works on Macs if you used MacPorts to install GIMP). This displays the manual page for gimprc, updated as of your current GIMP version, and should tell you all the latest options. On other platforms, or if you don't have the manual page installed, you can read it online at *http://www.gimp.org/man/gimprc.html*.

How do you find out which options you can set in gimprc? Here are some of the highlights that aren't already accessible through the Preferences window.

Stingy Memory Use

Any large program like GIMP needs to make trade-offs between speed and memory usage. By default, GIMP will assume there's plenty of memory, and will optimize for speed. On a low-memory system, you may see better performance by setting

```
(stingy-memory-use yes)
```

Default Brush, Pattern, Palette, Gradient, and Font

GIMP doesn't normally remember settings for these values (though some of them will be remembered if you chose *Save tool options now* from the *Tool Options* category of the Preferences window). But you can set them explicitly in gimprc, with lines such as these:

```
(default-brush "Circle (4)")
(default-pattern "Leopard")
(default-palette "Web")
(default-gradient "Full Saturation Spectrum CCW")
(default-font "Helvetica Bold Italic")
```

The names used in gimprc correspond to the names you see in the dialogs where you choose these items.

Share Palette

The *Tool Options* category of Preferences lets you share brushes, patterns, or gradients among all tools. But GIMP can also share fonts and palettes:

```
(global-font yes)
(global-palette yes)
```

"Perfect Mouse"

When you move the mouse quickly, computer systems may take a shortcut and pass only some of the positions to the application. This saves GIMP from needing to process every pixel that the mouse covers, and usually speeds up drawing.

Normally, GIMP doesn't take this shortcut: it processes every pixel the mouse crosses. If you notice lags while drawing lines quickly, it might be worth experimenting with the perfect-mouse setting by changing it to no:

```
(perfect-mouse no)
```

Imperfection may be faster on some systems.

Default Threshold

Tools such as Fuzzy Select and Bucket Fill have a threshold for what constitutes a "nearby" region, settable in *Tool Options*. Normally, this defaults to 15, but you can change that:

```
(default-threshold 10)
```

Saving Modified Images

Usually, when you tell GIMP to save, it will save even if it thinks the image hasn't been modified. You can prevent this behavior if you like:

```
(trust-dirty-flag yes)
```

Help Browser on F1

You can disable the Help browser (for instance, if you don't have one installed and want to use F1 for something else):

```
(use-help no)
```

Help Locales

Normally, GIMP should be able to figure out which language you use from your system's "locale" setting. If this doesn't work, though, you can specify it with help-locales. This is a colon-separated list. For instance, if you have US English plus a Great Britain locale that uses the UTF-8 character set, use the following:

```
(help-locales "en_US:en_GB.UTF-8")
```

Restoring Keyboard Shortcuts

GIMP has a preference in the *Interface* category to *Save keyboard shortcuts on exit* (assuming you've enabled dynamic keyboard shortcuts in the first place, of course). Naturally, GIMP will usually load your saved shortcuts whenever it starts. But if you don't want that to happen automatically, add this to your gimprc:

```
(restore-accels no)
```

In that case, GIMP will only load your customized key bindings when you go to the *Interface* category of the Preferences window and click on *Reset Saved Keyboard Shortcuts to Default Values*.

Tear-off Menus

If for some reason you don't like the tear-off menus, you can disable them:

```
(tearoff-menus no)
```

Plug-in Paths

You saw the Fractal Explorer, gfig, and GIMPressionist plug-ins in Chapter 7. You can set their data directories to something other than the default, or add additional directories:

```
(fractalexplorer-path
  "${gimp_dir}/fractalexplorer:${gimp_data_dir}/fractalexplorer")
(gfig-path "${gimp_dir}/gfig:${gimp_data_dir}/gfig")
(gflare-path "${gimp_dir}/gflare:${gimp_data_dir}/gflare")
(gimpressionist-path
  "${gimp_dir}/gimpressionist:${gimp_data_dir}/gimpressionist")
```

You can include multiple folders by using a colon between the names. ${gimp_dir} refers to your personal gimprc directory, and ${gimp_data_dir} to the GIMP system directory where these plug-ins are stored.

Changing Preview Sizes with gtkrc

You may remember from installing GIMP that it's built upon a user interface library called GTK, the GIMP ToolKit.

GTK's numerous configuration options can be set globally, but you can also set options for specific applications that take precedence over the global settings. GIMP's GTK settings reside in a file called *gtkrc* in your GIMP profile folder.

Most of the time, this file will be updated automatically to reflect changes you make in your GIMP user interface. But there are a few cases where it's helpful to view the file.

The most important use of gtkrc is to change the preview size in plug-in dialogs.

You may have puzzled over the two *Preview Size* options in the *Interfaces* category of Preferences. When you change the size, the previews in plug-in windows don't change. Why not?

The two options in Preferences affect different previews. The first, *Default layer & channel preview size,* controls the size of the preview thumbnails shown in each line of the Layers dialog. But they're tricky to use: GIMP doesn't actually honor them unless you close the tab, bring up the dialog again, and then re-dock it.

It's much faster to ignore the preferences and change the preview sizes from the dockable's menu. (You can also change them by editing the sessionrc file, as you'll see shortly.)

The second option, *Navigation preview size,* controls the size of the window that pops up when you click on the navigation panner button at the bottom right of an image window.

So what about those plug-in previews? The normal preview size is pretty small and it's sometimes hard to see much (Figure 12-14). You can resize the dialog, but you'd have to do that every time. You're probably wondering whether you can make the preview bigger by default.

Figure 12-14. *GIMP's default preview size is a bit small.*

Well, you can't do it using the Preferences window, but you can if you're willing to edit gtkrc. (If you don't already have a gtkrc file in your GIMP profile folder, you can create a new one with your text editor.)

Add some lines like this:

```
style "gimp-large-preview"
{
  GimpPreview::size = 350
}
class "GimpPreview" style "gimp-large-preview"
```

In place of 350, put whatever size you want your previews to be. The default is 200. You don't have to use the name `gimp-large-preview`; any name will do. As with most configuration file changes, you'll have to restart GIMP to see this change (Figure 12-15).

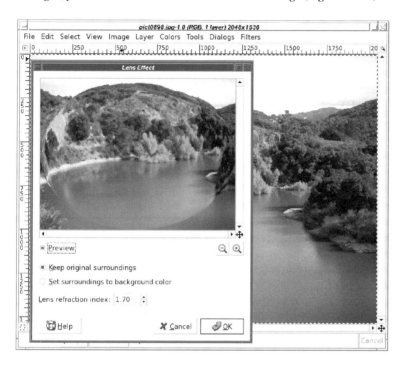

Figure 12-15. *Increase the preview size as much as you like.*

GIMP's Window Positions and Configuration: sessionrc

GIMP remembers the positions of its major windows (except image windows), so you can stow the Toolbox on one side of the screen and the Layers dialog on the other. It stores this information in the sessionrc file.

You will seldom need to touch this file. But this is the place to look if you have a problem with your window positions, or with the preview sizes in dockables like Layers. You can edit these values directly in sessionrc. Don't edit this file while GIMP is running, though, or GIMP will probably overwrite your changes.

Key Bindings for Menu Entries: menurc

The menurc file is the place where GIMP stores any key bindings you assign to menu items.

GIMP fills the file with key bindings corresponding to its menu entries—many hundreds of them—but most of them are commented out with a semicolon at the beginning of the line. A line that's commented out means that it hasn't changed from GIMP's default setting. Anything that's not commented is a key binding that you've added.

Key bindings look like this:

```
; (gtk_accel_path "<Actions>/file/file-save" "<Control>s")
; (gtk_accel_path "<Actions>/file/file-save-as" "<Shift><Control>s")
(gtk_accel_path "<Actions>/plug-in/plug_in_screenshot" "<Alt>s")
(gtk_accel_path "<Actions>/view/view-zoom-in" "equal")
; (gtk_accel_path "<Actions>/select/select-none" "<Shift><Control>a")
```

These lines say that Alt+S has been added as the key binding to do a screen shot, and the = (Equal) key will zoom in. Save, Save As, and Select None are at their default settings and haven't been changed.

Unfortunately, you can't use this file to set two different bindings for the same function (for instance, to make either = or + zoom in). Only the last binding you set will be used.

You shouldn't normally need to edit menurc. But it's a useful place to look if you're ever curious about which key bindings you've changed. GIMP's *Configure Keyboard Shortcuts* dialog (accessed from the *Interface Preferences* category) will let you change or remove individual bindings, but it doesn't offer a way to find out what you have changed from the default settings.

There's one other use for menurc: you can quickly install a whole collection of bindings. For instance, GIMP comes with a file called ps-menurc that makes GIMP's key bindings more like Photoshop's. Although it's usually a better idea to learn how to use GIMP with its native settings, people who are used to Photoshop may find the transition easier starting with a familiar set of bindings. To use a file like this, quit GIMP, copy ps-menurc as menurc in your GIMP profile, and restart GIMP, and you'll have the new bindings. You can also make your own custom key-binding set, and distribute it to other people.

Of course, if you've already made changes to your GIMP key bindings, it's a good idea to back up your menurc somewhere before you replace it with another file, just in case you want to go back. If you ever want to return to GIMP's default setup, just remove any menurc file in your profile. GIMP will regenerate it with default values (everything commented out) the next time you start up.

Other Files

Other files in your GIMP profile include

- *colorrc* is where GIMP stores the recently used colors that show up in the color chooser window.

- *controllerrc* has information about your mouse and keyboard—the items described in the *Input Controllers* category of Preferences.

- *devicerc* holds the information saved when you click *Save Input Device Settings Now* in the Preferences window's *Input Devices* category. It includes information about your graphics tablet if you have one; but in addition, it saves tool settings for the drawing tools.

- *documents* is the list of images you've edited recently—the same list you see in the *Open Recent* menu.

- *gimp-splash.png* is a way to set a custom "splash image" for GIMP to use when it starts up. This file isn't created automatically, but any PNG image you put here will become GIMP's new splash image. (See also the splashes folder, discussed in a moment.)

- *gtk-bookmarks.sav* holds the bookmarks you set in the *Open* and *Save As* dialogs.

- *parasiterc* holds global *parasites*. "Parasite" is a name GIMP gives to any sort of persistent data. Parasites can be attached to an image (EXIF information for a JPEG file is stored as a parasite) or can be global or application-wide. Plug-ins can use the global parasites defined in this file to store default values.

- *pluginrc* is a list of all your plug-ins and the parameters they take. Editing this file is almost always a bad idea, and GIMP regenerates it frequently (whenever it finds a new plug-in). The actual plug-ins are stored in the folder called plug-ins.

- *print-settings* are any stored settings for GIMP's GTKPrint plug-in.

- *printrc* is where the Gutenprint plug-in stores your printer settings.

- *templaterc* stores information about any templates you have created, as well as GIMP's standard ones. Templates are just combinations of the values you can set in the New Image dialog (size, resolution, image type, fill type, and comment) created with the *Save as Template…* command or through the *File* ➤ *Dialogs* ➤ *Templates* dialog. The actual templates, if you've created any, are stored in the templates folder.

- *themerc* stores information about the theme you're using, while themes you import should be stored in the themes folder.

- If you've customized your Toolbox (by reordering tools or changing which tools are visible from the Tools dialog), that information will be stored in *toolrc*. Even if you haven't, the standard Toolbox setup is stored in that file.

- *unitrc* contains a list of the units GIMP knows about. You shouldn't need to edit it.

Folders Inside the GIMP Profile

You'll also find a collection of subfolders inside your GIMP profile:

- *brushes, curves, gradients, levels, palettes, patterns, templates,* and *themes* all offer places to store tools you make in GIMP.

- *fractalexplorer, gfig, gflare,* and *gimpressionist* are used by these four plug-ins to store their options and data files.

- In *environ*, you can create files setting variables that you want plug-ins to be able to use. For instance, Python needs to know where the actual Python binary is on the system, which it finds in a variable called PYTHONPATH. So if Python is installed, you should have a file in the systemwide environ folder with a line like

```
: PYTHONPATH=/usr/lib/gimp/2.0/python
```

The colon tells GIMP to prepend the value to any existing PYTHONPATH that might already be defined on the system, using the colon as the separator character.

- The *fonts* folder is a place where you can install fonts that you only want to use in GIMP, not in other programs.

- *interpreters* is a place where you can store command interpreters other than Script-Fu. This is mostly for use in scripting. See your systemwide interpreters folder for examples of how these files look. It's not likely most people would try to add one: you'll only want to put files here if you're creating GIMP bindings in a new language.

- GIMP *modules* are loadable executables, somewhat like plug-ins, but at a lower level. The gimp-perl and gimp-python interpreters, which make it possible to write plug-ins in those languages, are modules, as are the external interpreters for Ruby and C#. The various color chooser tabs (like the watercolor chooser) are also modules. If you developed your own GIMP module, this is where you'd put it.

- The *plug-ins* and *scripts* folders are where you should install plug-ins (C, Perl, or Python) or scripts (Script-Fu).

- The *splashes* folder isn't created automatically. But if you create a folder by this name and put images in it, when GIMP starts up it will use one of your images (chosen at random) as its "splash" screen, rather than the built-in splash image. The images can be in any format except XCF.

- The *tool-options* folder is where the tool options for all of GIMP's tools are stored.

- *tmp* is simply a folder GIMP uses when it needs to create any sort of temporary file. If GIMP ever crashes, you may end up with some extra files here.

Additional Resources

You're nearly at the end of the book! Where do you go from here?

Fortunately, there's an extensive collection of GIMP information on the web, on the GIMP website, and elsewhere. If you want to learn more about GIMP, you won't run out of reading material any time soon!

Official GIMP Documentation

GIMP is one of the better-documented free software projects. To begin with, it has an extensive reference manual online: the GIMP User Manual. Point your browser at *gimp.org* and click on "Documentation" to see the 2.4 manual. It's available in English, Croatian, Dutch, French, German, Italian, Korean, Norwegian, Russian, Spanish, and Swedish. An older 2.2 manual is also available in Chinese and Czech, but they may be updated by the time you check in. Also, more translations may be added.

Whenever you're unsure about how to use a particular feature or what an option means, if you don't find the answer in this book, try the GIMP User Manual. It has a few gaps (remember, it's all written by volunteers), but it's amazingly thorough.

The manual begins with a "What's New?" section, which is a useful reference for finding out what has changed from one major version of GIMP (2.0, 2.2, 2.4) to the next.

WHY DO GIMP VERSIONS CHANGE BY .2 INSTEAD OF .1?

GIMP, like many free software projects, uses the convention that an odd version number after the decimal point is used for a *development version*, while an even number means a *stable version*.

After 2.2 was officially released, the developers began work on 2.3. That version number has been used for the unstable development version as new features are stabilized and important bugs fixed. When the developers decided it was stable, the version number was changed to 2.4, to indicate a new stable release.

While 2.3 was being developed, any important bugs found in 2.2 were also fixed, resulting in new GIMP stable versions such as 2.2.1, 2.2.2, and so on. Most users used one of the stable 2.2 releases, while people who wanted to help out with GIMP development could download the latest 2.3 and try it out, reporting bugs if they found any. Eventually it was released as GIMP 2.4, and the developers started work on 2.5.

Development releases are usually source releases. To try the very latest features or help with finding bugs, you may have to compile GIMP yourself.

Other Official GIMP User Documentation

Beyond the GIMP User Manual, the GIMP website has quite a collection of other documentation. This is the best place to find documents on GIMP configuration (how to install new fonts, tips for choosing your tile cache size to get the best performance, and so on).

GIMP's manual pages are also available online in the "Documentation" section of the GIMP website. If you're not on a UNIX-like machine and don't have the manual pages installed, but you want to read about the options you can set in gimprc, or about the details of building and installing plug-ins with gimptool, you can find all the information here. There's also documentation on the Script-Fu and Python modules.

But perhaps the most useful are the tutorials. The official *gimp.org* tutorials are divided into categories: mostly by experience level (Beginner, Intermediate, Expert), but also by category (Photo Editing, Web, Script Authoring).

Want to know how to make text that looks like it's made of shining gold? To find ways of making your photos look like sketches, beyond the simple layer-mode techniques of Chapter 10, or to turn a sketch into a colored cartoon-style figure? Want to see how a real artist uses GIMP techniques to draw a paintbrush with shading and a polished wood handle, starting from a blank canvas? Want to make a movie from a selection of images, or eliminate the noise from your camera's CCD chip? These techniques, and a lot more, are all on the GIMP tutorial site on pages that take you through the process, step by step.

Developer Documentation

Finally, there's documentation for developers at *developer.gimp.org*, which includes tutorials on writing scripts, articles about writing C plug-ins, and a fairly complete and very readable set of documentation on GIMP's API (*Application Program Interface*, the set of routines called by GIMP plug-ins and internal functions to do their work). This website is an indispensable resource for anyone writing GIMP plug-ins or contributing code to GIMP.

Equally important is the *Developer FAQ*, which lists guidelines for people interested in contributing code. Potential developers should also read the link labeled "Hacking," which gives you information on which packages you're likely to need in order to build the development releases and about some of the coding standards. (This is just a copy of the file HACKING that comes as part of the GIMP source.) And there's information about how to check out the very latest version of GIMP—the one the developers are working on *today*—from the "Subversion" (svn) repository (Subversion is a source code versioning system popular in the open source world).

A link labeled *Standards* gives an excellent discussion of the various image-format standards GIMP supports, as well as other standards covering such topics as color management, desktop icons, thumbnail management, and how drag-and-drop is implemented.

One of the fun entries on *developer.gimp.org* is the *ChangeLog*. This is a file in the GIMP source where every change made to GIMP is recorded. If you're curious about the pace of GIMP development, or about who works on which tasks, the ChangeLog can be interesting reading. Of course, the comments in it are usually deep in technical detail: you won't find a lot of high-level discussion of new features or plans.

News is a higher-level version of the same thing. Instead of showing every check-in by every developer, it summarizes the changes from one version to the next, much like the "What's New?" section of the User Manual, except that it covers the development "point releases" such as 2.3.3 and 2.3.4. Even if you're not a developer and not building GIMP from source, it's sometimes enlightening to check the developers' news and see what features you can look forward to in the next major version.

The Wiki

In addition to the official documentation, GIMP also has a wiki, located at *wiki.gimp.org*.

A *wiki* (the name comes from the Hawaiian term "wiki-wiki," meaning "quick") is a web application that allows users to contribute their own pages—or add to existing pages—to build a knowledge base. Wikipedia is the best-known example, but many projects like GIMP have their own wiki to let users contribute new documentation and hints.

The GIMP wiki currently contains a good list of tutorials (including many links to tutorials on other sites), some user FAQ documents, hints for printing and scanning, hints on building GIMP and on reading its internal source code, notes on navigating the GIMP website, and many more topics. It's worth a look.

Other Tutorial Sites

Of course, the GIMP information available on the web isn't limited to the official documentation on the GIMP website. GIMP is used by countless people worldwide, and many GIMP users enjoy sharing tips they've discovered or techniques they've learned.

You've probably already looked at the tutorials on *gimp.org*. But there are hundreds of tutorials on the web discussing how to use GIMP to accomplish various tasks.

If you're looking for a specific effect, try a web search. Suppose you want to add fire to a drawing you're making. Try searching for **gimp fire** or **gimp fire tutorial** and see what comes up. Often you'll get several different hits, so you'll end up with a choice of tutorials showing different ways of accomplishing the same effect. Choose the one you like best, or combine them.

You can usually adapt tutorials that were written for other programs, too. If you search for GIMP tutorials and don't find any, try searching for something like **fire image tutorial** or even **fire photoshop** or **fire "paintshop pro"**. There are lots of web tutorials written for other programs, and many of them work just fine in GIMP as long as you don't expect functions to be in the same places in the menus, use exactly the same settings, or have specific key bindings.

If you don't have a particular effect in mind and just want to learn something new or get ideas, try browsing tutorials. Once you've exhausted the ones on the GIMP site, there are many more sites for finding GIMP lessons.

Of course, the nature of the web being what it is, some of the tutorials will be old and written for older versions of the GIMP, as far back as GIMP 1.2. Don't let that scare you off, though. The techniques should all work in any version, so at worst, you might have to spend a little time searching through the menus or in the Plug-in Browser window (described in Chapter 11) to find a function mentioned in a tutorial.

Here are some good sources for GIMP tutorials:

The GIMP wiki's Tutorial page: *http://wiki.gimp.org/gimp/GimpTutorials*

Tigert Labs ("Tigert," you may remember from Chapter 1, is Tuomas Kuosmanen, a GIMP contributor and the artist who created the GIMP mascot Wilber): *http://tigert.gimp.org/gimp/tutorials/*

The GIMP User's Group, or GUG (which also has a discussion mailing list and a place for artists to upload their images, though unfortunately the website is often down): *http://gug.sunsite.dk/?page=tutorials*

The WinGIMP site (written for Windows users, but the tutorials apply to every platform): *http://www.wingimp.org/tutorial/*

GimpTalk: *http://www.gimptalk.com/*

In addition, there are some videos illustrating GIMP features at *http://jimmac.musichall.cz/gimp2demos.php*

Don't stop there, though. If you don't like any of those sites, try a web search for **gimp tutorials** or **gimp tutorial** and see how many other interesting sites come up. You may run out of time to read tutorials, but you probably won't run out of tutorials to read.

Mailing Lists

If you want to talk with other GIMP users and exchange tips, you can choose from quite a selection of mailing lists. Some of them aren't very active, but some are. Just go to *gimp.org* and click on "Mailing lists."

Your choices include the following:

- *GIMP User*: Discussions and questions related to using the GIMP.

- *GIMP Announce*: Announcements of new releases and other important GIMP news, without any discussion.

- *GIMPwin-Users*: Discussions for GIMP users on Windows. A great place to go if you need help with Windows-specific issues such as printing or building plug-ins.

- *GIMP Developer*: Discussions of the development of the next GIMP version.

- *GIMP Web*: Maintenance of the *gimp.org* website.

- *GIMP Docs*: Maintenance and development of GIMP documentation, especially the User Manual.

- *GIMP Images*: A place for people to exchange images created with GIMP.

- *GIMP Perl*: Use of the Perl module to develop plug-ins.

- *GIMP OS2*: Discussions related to using GIMP on IBM's OS/2 operating system.

The mailing list page includes tips on "netiquette." If you haven't spent a lot of time on technical mailing lists, it's a good idea to read the suggestions. It's often helpful to "lurk" for a while on a list before making your first posting, to become familiar with the culture of the list.

In addition to the official lists on the GIMP mailing list page, many of the GIMP user communities have forums or mailing lists. See the section "Art Sites and Imaging Contests" later in this chapter.

Reporting Bugs

What if you're pretty sure you've found a bug in GIMP?

GIMP's bug system is entirely open. Anyone can report a bug, or search for bugs already reported. The project uses a bug-tracking program known as Bugzilla, located at *http:// bugzilla.gimp.org.*

You can search the bug system and read bug reports all you want without creating an account, but to file a new bug or add comments to an existing one, you'll need to register. That's so that the Bugzilla system can notify you by email if the bug is fixed, if a developer needs more information from you, or if anyone else adds a comment regarding your bug.

It's a good idea to search Bugzilla before reporting a new bug. It may be that someone else has already discovered your bug and reported it. There's a search on the intro page, but it may not find what you want. If you decide you need a more flexible way to look for bugs, click on Search, then choose the Complicated Bug Search Form. *Don't panic!* The Complicated Search page looks scary, but if you ignore most of the page and use only a couple of the fields, it's actually quite simple, and it will often find bugs that the simple search won't.

First, you need some keywords for the bug you're looking for, just like you would for a web search. If you think you've found a bug in the Zealous Crop plug-in, then searching for "zealous crop" is a good start (you don't need to worry about capitalization—Bugzilla searches are case insensitive).

Then go to the *Product* field on the left side of the window and scroll down to find GIMP (Figure 12-16).

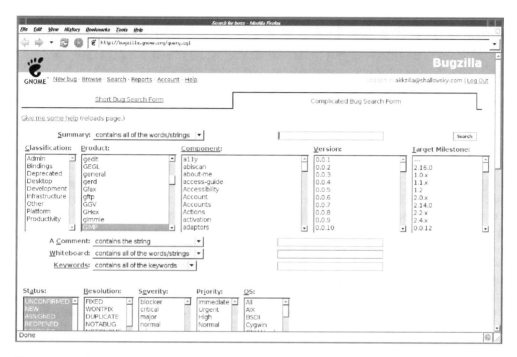

Figure 12-16. *The Bugzilla "complicated search" page*

You may be amazed by the long Products list. What are all those other products?

GIMP shares its Bugzilla system with a project called Gnome, which includes GTK (the toolkit GIMP uses) as well as many other applications. The total number of programs covered by the Gnome bug database is huge, which is why it's important to select the GIMP "Product" so you narrow the search to only GIMP bugs.

Once you've typed some keywords in the *Summary* and selected the GIMP product, you can click the *Search* button (to the right of the *Summary*; depending on your window size you may need to scroll right to see it). Or just press the Enter key. You'll be taken to a page showing a list of GIMP bugs related to your keywords. If there are no bugs associated with those keywords, Bugzilla will say "Zarro Boogs found." That was an overworked programmer's idea of a joke early in the development of Bugzilla, and unfortunately it stuck.

You can always use the *Back* button in your browser to return to the search page and try a different set of keywords. If you're surprised to find "Zarro Boogs," it might be worth clicking on the *Show Advanced Options* button and doing another search with all the *Status* options selected (Shift+click and Ctrl+click in these lists will let you highlight multiple values). By default, Bugzilla searches only for bugs that are still "Open." When a bug has been fixed in the current development version of GIMP, the bug is marked "Resolved" in Bugzilla, even though the version you're using may still have the bug.

If you find an existing bug that's similar to yours, read it. If you want to be notified when the bug is fixed or when someone makes a comment, add your email address (the one you registered with Bugzilla) in the *Add CC* field. If you have more details, you can add them: scroll down to *Additional Comments* and type in your information. When you've finished, click *Commit*.

Reporting a new bug is slightly more complicated. When you go to *bugzilla.gimp.org*, you're presented with the bug-reporting form. Otherwise, click New.

The most difficult part of bug reporting may be choosing the right *component*. GIMP has quite a few components, such as *Data, General, Help, Installer, Internationalization, Plug-ins*, and *User Interface*. If one of these categories seems relevant to your bug, choose it. If you're not sure, it's safe to choose *General*; someone who knows more about the structure of GIMP can change that later.

Be sure to specify the version of GIMP you're using. You can get that from *Help ➤ About*, or by typing `gimp --version` (that's two minus signs before "version") at the command prompt. Don't forget to mention which platform (Windows, Linux, Mac, etc.) you're using. You can use *Distribution/Version* to clarify that: for instance, if you choose *Windows* for *Operating System*, you might type something like **XP** or **2000** in the *Distribution/Version* field.

You can usually leave the *Severity* field set to *Normal*, unless you've found a way to make GIMP crash, in which case you can use *Critical*. Don't overstate the severity of your bug hoping to get the attention of developers.

Try to be specific about what you did, what you expected to see, and why it's a problem. Vague bugs saying things like "Crop is broken" will likely be closed or ignored. It's much better to create a specific bug like "The Zealous Crop plug-in ignores layer offsets," with a sample XCF image attached and a full description of what the plug-in does vs. what you think it should do. If an error message was involved, write down the exact text of the error message; don't just paraphrase it. (Some dialogs let you copy error message text while others don't; if there's too much to copy down accurately, try taking a screen shot or a picture with a digital camera.) Sometimes running GIMP from the command line will give you additional information about what's wrong, which you can then paste into a bug report. If you can't reproduce the bug in order to see the error message again—if it's something that only happened once and never again—the bug may not be worth reporting.

Gathering this information can take time, but remember the developers are all volunteers. Think about it this way: if you're hoping the developers will volunteer some of their free time to fix the bug, it can help a lot if you spend some of your own time making their jobs a little easier.

If the problem only happens with certain images, it's helpful if you can attach an image that the developers can use to reproduce the problem. (If they can't make it happen themselves, they won't be able to fix the bug.) If you can reduce your sample image to something relatively small and simple, that's ideal. To attach an image (or anything else besides text) to a GIMP bug, click on *Create a New Attachment*. If you're filing a new bug, you'll have to submit the basics of the bug first, and then go back to it and add the attachment.

Bugzilla can be intimidating the first few times you use it. But don't let it scare you. If you've found a GIMP bug, the developers want to hear about it so they can fix it.

Finding Source Code at svn.gnome.org

GIMP's source code is stored using the "Subversion" program, or svn, on a machine called svn.gnome.org.

If you have svn installed, you can check out the latest version of GIMP—the one the developers are working on—at any time. The GIMP website has instructions on how to do that.

But even if you don't have svn, and don't want to download the entire GIMP source code (about 15MB), you can view specific files and their revision histories using the web interface to svn: *http://svn.gnome.org/viewcvs/gimp/*. Click on *trunk* if you want to see the latest, or *branches* if you're looking for a specific version like *gimp-2-4*.

You can click on folder names to navigate to those folders, or on file names to view the revision history of the file (all the changes that have been made to it recently). If you want to see the current contents of a file, you can click on *View* to get a pretty colorized version, or *Download* to get a raw copy of the file that you can save to your local disk. This is an easy way to get copies of plug-in source to use as a basis for your own plug-ins.

Where to Find Freely Available Images

Sometimes you need a photo for a project, and you just can't find anything quite right in your own collection. Darn it, I wish I had my own photograph of an erupting volcano, or of the Sphinx—but my travel budget doesn't allow for either one.

What can a poor GIMP user do? Look on the web, of course!

The problem? Most images are copyrighted by the person who created them. It's not ethical—or legal—to use someone else's photographs in your own project without permission. If it's just for your own use, or for GIMP practice, you might be able to get away with it. But if it's an image you're planning to post on the web, distribute to other people, or especially if you're using it for any sort of money-making purpose, it's important to use images with copyrights that allow reuse.

Fortunately, there's a movement to make more forms of information freely available, and several projects have been created to help people share their images. In some cases, the images are free for noncommercial use, but if you intend to make money with the image, you must contact the person who owns the copyright. Other images are free even for commercial use.

In addition, quite a few US government agencies put their images in the "public domain," meaning they are free to use for any purpose because the images have already been paid for with taxpayer money. Government sites can offer excellent images on quite a range of subjects, and you may not need to look any further.

There's also the Creative Commons, a nonprofit organization launched by open source advocate Lawrence Lessig to enable the sharing of artistic works of all sorts, including images. You can read about the Creative Commons idea on their website, *http://creativecommons.org/*.

The website lets you search for images you can use in your own projects. Some images have restrictions; others are completely free for any use. You can specify what sort of license you need when you search for images.

If you use images from Creative Commons (or even if you don't), consider making your resulting art available for other people to use. The more people who contribute to the commons, the better it works for everyone.

Burning Well is a repository for public-domain images: images that can be used without any restriction. The website is *http://www.burningwell.org/*. You can search for images by keyword, or browse images by category. There are over a thousand images, and some of them are very good. They may have exactly what you need.

Stock.XCHNG is another free photo site. They have a large searchable collection of images organized by category, as well as forums for discussing photography at all levels of experience. The website is *http://www.sxc.hu/*.

US Government Sites

The US government is an excellent source of images you can use without copyright worries. It is considered good manners to give credit where it's due, and mention the folks who did the work. See the specific copyright information on each site for more details.

The National Aeronautics and Space Administration (NASA) has an excellent range of images of planets and other astronomical objects, as well as images of spacecraft. Some specific NASA image collections are found at the NSSDC Photo Gallery (a sort of "NASA's Greatest Hits" collection) at *http://nssdc.gsfc.nasa.gov/photo_gallery*, and the Jet Propulsion Laboratory (JPL) Planetary Photojournal at *http://photojournal.jpl.nasa.gov/index.html*.

And don't miss the NASA Image of the Day Gallery at *http://www.nasa.gov/multimedia/ imagegallery/*. Or search for images by keyword at NIX: *http://nix.nasa.gov/*. Finally, NASA has a website devoted to 70mm Hasselblad camera images taken by astronauts on lunar missions at *http://www.lpi.usra.edu/resources/apollo/catalog/70mm/*.

The US Fish and Wildlife Service offers photos of wildlife and related scenery at *http:// images.fws.gov/*.

The US National Oceanic and Atmospheric Administration (NOAA) has lots of good images at *http://www.photolib.noaa.gov/*. In addition to photographs of storms, coastlines, ships, and corals, they have collections for marine animals, space (atmospheric satellites), and other interesting topics.

The National Park Service has huge collections of stunning scenic shots, as well as wildlife and cultural events related to the parks. The website is currently at *http://photo.itc.nps.gov/ storage/images/index.html*. If that changes, start at *http://nps.gov* and poke around. You'll find it.

Art Sites and Imaging Contests

You're armed to the teeth with GIMP techniques, and itching for an excuse to use them. Even more, you'd like an audience to appreciate some of the funny images you're making. Where can you look for a community of like-minded people?

There are quite a few GIMP community sites for sharing artwork, tips, tutorials and other bits of GIMPery. They include the GIMP User Group (GUG), *gug.sunsite.dk*; *gimptalk.com*; *gimpgallery.net*; *gimpstuff.org*; *gimpusers.com*; and a "GIMP guru" group on *flickr.com*. deviantArt is a community of digital artists. It's not all GIMP users, but a number of GIMP artists hang out there. There's an enormous sampling of digital art to browse, discussion forums, and it's even possible to sell art. The website can be found at *http://www.deviantart.com*.

Then there are the "Photoshop contests." Don't let the name put you off: you can use GIMP or any other program to enter. Photoshop contests are websites where participants create digital images according to a set of guidelines, and then everyone votes for the winners. Most often, the images are very entertaining. Even if you're not interested in entering a contest, it can be addictive to browse Photoshop contest sites. And entering the contests can be a great incentive to practice your GIMP skills.

Some sites use a theme, like "Extreme sports," and participants are free to create any image that illustrates the theme, such as someone juggling live tigers, or waterskiing on the back of a great white shark.

Other sites provide an image, and the goal is to modify the image in some (usually humorous) way.

Some contest sites are free to enter while others charge a small fee; some give prizes to the winners, others don't.

A web search for "photoshop contest" should turn up several likely candidates.

Summary and Conclusion

That's it! You're on your own now. But you should have enough information to accomplish anything you want in GIMP.

You can print your GIMP creations (assuming you have a suitable printer) and make screen shots of your GIMP windows for writing your own tutorials. You know where to find and set the various GIMP preferences. You can read and understand your GIMP configuration files, and edit them when you need to make changes. If you find a bug, you can track down the details and report it.

If the skills you need for making an image aren't in this book, maybe they're covered in the GIMP User Manual on the GIMP website. Or maybe there's a tutorial to show you exactly what you need, either one of the official ones on *gimp.org* or somewhere else on the web.

Finally, you know some sources to look for raw images for your creations, images with appropriate licenses so that you can distribute your derived art. You've explored some art sites that can give you inspiration, and you have places you can post your art when you have something to show off.

The rest is just practice. The more you work with GIMP, the easier it gets. Tasks that seemed impossibly confusing the first time you tried them (like making a selection with Bezier Paths) become second nature. You may have stayed away from plug-ins because you're not a programmer—but eventually you may change your mind and decide to try writing or modifying one. You may have joined a mailing list or two in order to ask for help…and before long, you're the one helping other people. You may even decide some day to become a GIMP contributor, writing code or documentation or web pages.

Proceed at your own pace, and work with the kinds of images that interest you most.

The only rule is: be sure to have fun!

APPENDIX A

■ ■ ■

Getting and Installing GIMP

You've decided to learn to edit images with GIMP! But if it's not already on your computer, first you have to install it.

You may have Windows, Linux, a Mac, or another UNIX system such as FreeBSD. All of them can run GIMP, but each has a different installation method. Of course, if you can, you'd certainly prefer to run the most recent 2.4 version. Most computers can, but some OS variants are too old. If that's the case, you may have to run an older version. We'll explain those options in Appendix B. If you wish, you can also build GIMP from source, which is covered in Appendix C.

Here, you'll learn

- Requirements

- Where to find GIMP

Then skip to the appropriate section:

- Installing on Windows

- Installing on Mac

- Installing on Linux or UNIX

Requirements

GIMP doesn't require an especially fast machine. However, if you want to work with large images, you'll find that more memory will help a lot. A faster processor won't hurt, of course.

On Windows, GIMP 2.4 should work on NT4, Windows 2000, XP, or Vista. If you have an older version of Windows, skip to Appendix B.

You can download GIMP 2.4 for Mac OS X Tiger (10.4) or Leopard (10.5). The more adventurous Panther (10.3) users can also build GIMP 2.4 using the MacPorts system, but it's probably easier to just download GIMP 2.2 as *Gimp.app* from *http://gimp-app.sourceforge.net*. OS X systems older than Panther face other problems (see Appendix B). If you have OS 9.2 or earlier, you cannot run GIMP at all; it was never supported and never will be.

Recent Linux and other UNIX-based systems will have GIMP 2.4 in their packaging system, and it may very well have been part of your initial installation; you probably already have it.

On UNIX-based systems (including Mac OS X and Linux), GIMP is also an "X" application: it's built on top of a toolkit called GTK+ that uses the X Window System (sometimes called X11 since most systems use version 11) for drawing to the screen, creating windows, and other low-level operations. X doesn't stand for anything except "the next letter after W." (Seriously! X was the successor to a window system called W, which was in use at MIT in 1984 when X was being designed.)

So you'll need X in order to run GIMP. This is only likely to be an issue on Macs, since most Linux and UNIX systems are already running X. (There's a version of GTK+ in the works that will run on OS X without requiring X, but it's still experimental. If you want to try a GIMP built on the Mac-native GTK, you may be able to find builds at *http://gimp-app.sourceforge.net*.)

One thing you shouldn't need is money. GIMP is free software: free because you can get it without paying, and also because you're free to redistribute it or modify it.

You *can* buy GIMP from various sources, and sometimes these versions include extra goodies like an installer or a collection of cool brushes. But most of the time, you'll do just as well starting with the free version.

IF GIMP IS FREE SOFTWARE, IS IT LEGAL FOR PEOPLE TO SELL IT?

Yes. GIMP is licensed under the *GNU General Public License* (GPL), which allows anyone to distribute the software, and even to charge money for it.

However, the GPL does insist that further redistribution be allowed (the seller can't prevent you from making copies and giving them out to your friends). Also, the source code for the program (the human-readable programming instructions that make the program work) must be included, or at least be made available.

The GPL also requires that you receive a copy of the license itself along with the program, so you can learn about your rights to share the program, modify it, or contribute to the project.

Where to Find GIMP

The GIMP project lives at *http://gimp.org*. There, you can find links to downloadable versions for several operating systems along with instructions on how to get GIMP for even *more* systems. You can also find out how to build it yourself if you want to try the latest cutting-edge version.

At *gimp.org*, you'll also find a substantial collection of documentation. There's a complete user's manual, a large collection of tutorials, and information on GIMP's programming interfaces for anyone interested in writing scripts or plug-ins. You can sample a collection of mailing lists and IRC channels where you can ask questions, volunteer to help, or just trade tips.

Please remember that any URLs listed here may change. The web is beyond our control!

Installing on Windows

Unlike previous versions, installing GIMP 2.4 on Windows is very much like installing any other software (except you don't have to pay for it). The only tricky part is Python. If you want GIMP to be able to run Python scripts, you'll need PyGTK (from *http://pygtk.org*) plus all its dependencies. Getting them all to work can be somewhat challenging on Windows (it might be easier to install Linux!).

The Quick Start Version

1. First, point your browser to *http://gimp.org* and download GIMP.

2. Unzip and run the installation program.

The (Slightly) Longer Version

First, navigate your browser to *http://gimp.org*. The opening page will have a Download button right in the title bar. Click that and you'll probably be taken to the Windows Download Page automatically (*gimp.org* tries to figure out what system you're using). The first link should be the Installer, which you download.

When the download is finished, double-click the EXE file to expand it and get to the installation window. First you'll see a typical Welcome screen. Click *Next* to get going. You'll then be given an opportunity to read the GNU General Public License—the GPL you may have heard about. When you've had enough, just click *Next* again and you're at the Install page.

Your options are *Install now* (which is fine) or *Customize*. If you choose the latter, you can indicate an installation folder that's different from the default, choose which components to install, indicate which file types should launch GIMP, choose your Start Menu folder, and indicate if you should have a desktop icon and/or a Quick Launch icon. Generally, you won't want to change any of this, but if you do, then *Customize* is your best option.

Either way, you'll end up clicking an *Install* button and eventually get a screen that tells you the installation is complete and offers the option to launch GIMP (the default has a checkmark beside it).

You can delete the installation EXE now if you wish. You're done!

Installing on Macintosh

Before downloading GIMP 2.4, make sure you have X11 installed (or optionally XQuartz on 10.5 Leopard). If it's already on your system, it should be in the Utilities subdirectory of your Applications folder. If it's not already there, you can install it from your System Install disc. Can't find your old discs? Download the appropriate version from Apple using your *Mac OS X Software…* finder menu option. X11 will be in the Unix & Open Source section. (Leopard users may be able to get GIMP 2.4 there too!)

The Quick Start Version

1. Point your browser to *http://gimp.org*, click on *Mac OS X* to go to the Wilber Loves Apple site, and get the proper version for your machine.

2. Double-click the DMG to mount it, then copy GIMP 2.4 to your Applications folder. Start it as you would any other application (it will automagically start X11 for you if it's not already running).

The (Slightly) Longer Version

The GIMP project doesn't provide Mac builds (or, indeed, builds for any system), but works with another organization: the Wilber Loves Apple community. If you start at *gimp.org* and click on *Mac OS X*, it takes you to their site: *http://darwingimp.sourceforge.net*.

You'll be faced with four possibilities: OS X 10.5 (Leopard) or OS X 10.4 (Tiger), Intel, or PowerPC? Surely you know! But if you don't, both questions are easily answered by going to the first item in your Apple menu, *About This Mac*. The *Version* line will say 10.4.something (Tiger) or 10.5.something (Leopard). The *Processor* line will list either a PowerPC or an Intel chip.

Note If About This Mac says 10.3.something (that's Panther) or earlier, you're out of luck in this section and should proceed to Appendix B. Or you can upgrade your system. Your call.

Download the correct version. Go to your usual download destination and double-click the *Gimp2.4.blah.blah.dmg* as you normally would. This will mount a virtual disk and open a window with the GIMP application in it…and one other thing: the GNU Public License. What you do with the latter is up to you, but the former should be copied to your Applications folder. This may take some time since it's a fairly big file.

Once that's complete, you can double-click the Gimp (not all caps!) icon to start the application. It has some housekeeping to do on first startup, so it might take a while. Subsequent starts will be much faster.

If all went well, you can unmount the Gimp virtual disk and trash the DMG file. That's all there is to it!

Installing on Linux (and Other UNIXy Systems)

Of course, you'll need to be running X to use GIMP, but you probably are. If you're running any programs that involve a mouse, you probably have X. Also, most distributions will have already installed GIMP for you. Type `which gimp` at the command line, and if you don't see something like `gimp: command not found`, then you already have it.

What if you don't have it? Don't bother with *gimp.org* in that event—they'll just tell you to install the packages supplied by your distribution. Really, that's the best idea.

The Quick Start Version

1. Using the package management system of your distribution, install GIMP.

2. There is no #2.

The (Slightly) Longer Version

If you haven't yet used your package management system to install software, here are some common ways to go about it on various systems. Most systems have more than one way to install packages, including user-friendly *Install new software* entries in the system menus; but failing that, here are some popular command-line methods that are known to work.

You'll have to gain root access to use these commands either by using sudo or su.

If your distribution is older and includes a previous version of GIMP, there are two reasonable options: either install and use the older version or upgrade your system with a newer version of your distribution. While it is possible to build GIMP 2.4 for some older systems (see Appendix C), it's almost always better just to keep the system and software in sync.

Suggested Installation Commands for Various Systems

- Fedora and Red Hat users, type: `yum install gimp`

- Debian, Ubuntu, and other Debian derivatives, type: `apt-get install gimp`

- OpenSUSE users, type: `yast -i gimp`

- Mandriva users, type: `urpmi gimp`

- Gentoo users, type: `emerge -va gimp`

- FreeBSD users, type: `pkg_add -r gimp`

While you're at it, check to see whether there are any other GIMP-related packages you might want to install. Many distributions offer packages for some of the more popular plug-ins, like xsane (for scanning), gap (for animations), ufraw (for reading raw images), and so on. GIMP's online help files are also often packaged separately. You might also want the "development" package, named something like gimp-devel or libgimp2.0-dev, if you want to install more plug-ins or write your own. Ubuntu or Debian users, type `aptitude search gimp`; Fedora users, type: `yum list available | grep gimp`; SUSE users, type `zypper search gimp`; and Gentoo users, type `emerge -spv gimp`.

That's all there is to it. Your system should take care of everything else for you.

Of course, there are far more Linux and UNIX variants than can be listed here. The rest of you are on your own!

APPENDIX B

■ ■ ■

Installing GIMP on Older Systems

On Linux or other UNIX-like systems, the process is the same as in Appendix A: just use your package manager and install whatever system was available from either disc or online repositories. You may have to dig through a dusty pile of CDs or ask around, but in almost every case you'll succeed. Or, if you're adventurous, you can attempt to install from source (see Appendix C).

For those with older Windows systems, it's not unreasonable to install GIMP on Windows 98 SR2 or ME. GIMP 2.2, though unsupported, ran just fine. However, earlier versions of Windows may prove to be a challenge.

Macintosh systems prior to OS X generally cannot run GIMP. OS X 10.4 and 10.5 have already been discussed. The easiest approach for any earlier OS X version will boil down to getting GIMP 2.2 rather than 2.4 (though there is a special case: see the expanded section on Mac later in this appendix).

Here you'll learn the details of

- GIMP on older Linux/UNIX systems

- Installing GIMP on Windows systems older than Windows 2000

- Installing GIMP on Mac OS X versions prior to 10.4 (Tiger)

Please remember: any URLs listed here may change or just go away. We cannot control the World Wide Web!

Older Linux or UNIX Versions

If you can't just install from your original discs or use a package manager that can download from remote repositories, you can still build from source. This may be a bit complicated because there will be GTK and other dependencies that may not be new enough on your system. For further information, see Appendix C.

You may also be able to locate older binary installation packages for your specific system (which again may have dependencies that need to be satisfied). Here, your favorite search engine will be your best friend. The number of possibilities is simply too enormous to address in a book this size.

Good luck!

Older Windows Versions

Overall, this will be pretty simple for Windows 98 SR2 or ME users.

1. First, point your browser to *http://gimp-win.sourceforge.net/old.html*.

2. Download "GIMP for Windows" (this is normally the first download link).

3. While you're there, download "GTK+ 2 for Windows 98/ME and NT4" (usually the third link).

4. Navigate to your download folder and double-click gtk+[version]setup.zip. This will launch an installer. Follow the directions.

5. Double-click "gimp*[version]*setup.zip" and follow the directions again. It's probably best to let it install a desktop shortcut.

6. Double-click on the GIMP icon to start it. Click the *Continue* button whenever you see it until GIMP finally opens. Don't worry; you can change any of those settings later.

If you have a version of Windows older than 98 SR2, you're into something of a crapshoot. Earlier versions of Windows 98 *might* successfully install GIMP 2.2, or they may just mysteriously fail. Windows 95 users cannot install GIMP 2.2.

Should that be the case, you may want to try GIMP 2.0, which will be similar to 2.2 and 2.4. It should work fine on any Windows 98 system, but may run into trouble on some versions of Windows 95.

If it does hit a snag, or you have an even *older* version of Windows, your best bet is to skip lower on the page (past GIMP 2.0) to GIMP 1.2 in the little box at the bottom of the page. You'll also need the version of GTK+ just above it.

Older OS X Versions

If you're running OS X 10.3 (Panther), you're in pretty good shape.

But first you should make sure you have Apple's implementation of X11. If it's present on your system, you should see it in the Utilities directory of your Applications folder.

If you don't yet have X11, you'll need to install it. It came on your install discs, so if you have them you can install from there. If not, it should still be available from Apple at *http://www.apple.com/support/downloads/x11formacosx.html*...but as always, URLs are apt to change without notice.

Panther users have two reasonable options for running GIMP. The easy approach is to download GIMP 2.2 as *gimp.app* from *http://gimp-app.sourceforge.net*. It installs just like any other OS X program, supplies a Dock icon, and mostly works just like any other application. GIMP 2.2 was not quite as nice as 2.4, but it was pretty close in most ways, and you shouldn't have any problem using it to work through this book.

But if you want to try 2.4, you do have an option: MacPorts. It's a system that lets you download and automatically build software from source. You won't need to be a computer whiz to use it, but you will need to type on the command line a little bit.

You can get MacPorts from *http://www.macports.org*. There are thorough instructions for installing the system. After that, type the simple command `sudo port -d install gimp` into your terminal. Don't let that simple brevity fool you, though; it will build and install dozens of packages, probably taking several hours.

However, the resultant GIMP 2.4 will not seem quite so much like a typical OS X program. It won't have a Dock icon, so you'll have to launch it either from the command line or the X11 menu. Also, it may not be able to print (you can always save your work as a file type some other program can read and print from there—*Preview* will work for most file types).

What about systems older than OS X 10.3 (Panther)?

You can run GIMP, but you're in for a fight. Apple does not supply a version of X11 for any system prior to 10.3. You can't run MacPorts (they don't have a version for anything prior to Panther). About your only real hope is *Fink*, available at *http://www.finkproject.org/* (click on the downloads link after you read about the project). They have systems to support OS X versions 10.1 through 10.5.

You'll need to get their version of X11 and the most recent available GIMP package for your OS X version. That's always a moving target! Follow the instructions on the Fink site…and keep your fingers crossed.

APPENDIX C

■■■

Building from Source

For really uncommon platforms, the only answer may be to build GIMP yourself. And there are other good reasons to build your own GIMP.

Perhaps you want the absolute latest and greatest version, to check out the hot new features. Maybe you want to have several versions installed at once. What if you're running an older OS, and the only GIMP available for it is too old? You might want to contribute to the GIMP project, or just read the code and play with it a bit to understand how it works. These are all good reasons.

In this appendix, you'll find

- Getting the source

- Notes on assembling dependencies

- The three stages of building: configure, make, and make install

Getting the Source

GIMP source usually comes packaged as a "tarball," a compressed file named gimp-x.y.z.tar.gz or gimp-x.y.z.tar.bz2. Unpack this with the tar program: `tar xzvf gimp-x.y.z.tar.gz` or if it ends in "bz2", `tar xjvf gimp-x.y.z.tar.bz2`.

If you want a recent version of GIMP, you may be better off checking out a copy from svn, the source code repository the GIMP developers use themselves. Follow the svn instructions at *developer.gimp.org* to check out a copy of the source.

Once the source has been unpacked, it's a good idea to peruse the files README and INSTALL. The latter is especially important, as it contains advice on how to build GIMP.

ASSEMBLING DEPENDENCIES

Building GIMP is easy. However, assembling the *requirements* to build it can be difficult. GTK+, the main underpinning of GIMP, needs a lot of additional libraries to work properly. The library list includes names such as GLib, Pango, ATK, FreeType2, Fontconfig, and libart2.

The *gimp.org* site doesn't keep a current list of dependencies, and it can take time to gather all the requirements. Some Linux distributions can help with that: for example, on Debian Linux systems (and Debian derivatives such as Ubuntu and Xandros) you may be able to use `apt-get build-dep gimp`.

If you do find prebuilt versions of the required libraries, make sure you install the "development" components of the libraries as well as the runtime.

On Linux, the development components are usually packaged separately. Typically, they're named something like *[package name]*-dev or *[package name]*-devel. For instance, on Debian, in addition to installing libgtk2.0-0 you should install libgtk2.0-dev.

You will also need a C compiler, since GIMP is written in the C programming language. On Linux or UNIX, this is usually just a matter of installing the gcc package to get the GNU C compiler. On Mac, gcc is on the Development Tools CD that came with your copy of OS X. Windows users can download gcc from *www.cygwin.com*, but if you don't expect to be doing heavy software development, you may be better off with a smaller package containing the minimum you need to compile software: the Minimalist GNU for Windows, available at *www.mingw.org* (you will need both MinGW and MSYS).

Finally, during the build process you may find that you need other packages too (see the section "Configure"). Try not to get discouraged; it can take a while to assemble all the dependencies, but once you get them all together, you're done and you'll be able to build the GIMP and lots of other interesting software as well.

Once you have a compiler and all the required libraries, it's time to start the build. You will need a terminal open in order to build GIMP. All commands in this section are typed at your terminal prompt. It's not important what terminal window you use; on Mac you can use either Apple's Terminal program or the xterm program that comes with X11; on Windows, use either the DOS shell or one of the terminal programs available from Cygwin; on Linux, any terminal program will work.

Most open source software, including GIMP, is built by typing three commands, one after the other:

```
./configure
make
make install
```

Configure

The *configure* step of the build is usually the hardest. This is where GIMP's build system searches your computer for the dependencies it needs. If it fails to find something, it will stop with an error message. Interpreting these messages can sometimes be challenging.

Caution If you're trying to build a cutting-edge GIMP from svn, type ./autogen.sh instead of ./configure. You'll probably also need recent versions of the autoconf and automake packages.

Sometimes the messages are straightforward: it wants version 2.8.4 of something; you only have version 2.6, so the solution is to upgrade.

Other times it's not so easy. If configure says it needs a library and you're fairly sure you have it, check where the library is installed. Perhaps it's not in a standard location, or you need to update the system to notice the newly installed library. Or maybe you have the "runtime" part of the library installed, but you don't have the "development" part (usually this consists mostly of C header files, small text files ending in an .h extension).

You can customize some aspects of GIMP by running configure with arguments: ./configure option1 option2.... Type ./configure -h (that's h for "help") to get a list of options. The default—no extra options—should produce a usable GIMP on most platforms.

If you need to install more than one version of GIMP on the same system, use a different --prefix (that's two minuses) each time so that each GIMP will look in a different place for its files. For instance:

./configure --prefix=/usr/local/gimp-2.4.2

The configure program will also build extensions to GIMP if you have the appropriate libraries. For instance, support for many different image formats requires additional libraries. If you don't have libjpeg installed, you may end up with a GIMP that works fine but can't read or write JPEG files. Watch the messages printed by configure when it finishes: it will tell you if there are components it doesn't find. If they are components you care about, you can look for the appropriate libraries, install them, and then run configure again.

If you hit a wall trying to interpret configure's messages, try looking at the file named *config.log*. It contains all of configure's output, starting with the arguments you passed to configure. The useful information, about what configure was looking for and how it failed, will usually be near the end of the file. Configure does some fairly esoteric things, so it may be difficult to interpret the log, but sometimes it's fairly clear what's wrong. If all else fails, you can provide the errors at the end of config.log to a guru on the mailing lists or IRC channel to get help. (Please don't paste long error messages into an IRC channel without asking first, though!)

Make

Once you've configured, the *make* stage is time consuming but easy. Simply type make. If all goes well, you will see a huge amount of output scrolling down your terminal window. Unless you have a very fast machine, this will probably take quite a while (half an hour or more). Find something else to do while GIMP is compiling, or go have a snack.

When the output stops scrolling and you get your prompt back, it's done. If there's no error message, you've successfully built GIMP, and you're ready to install it.

Make Install

The *make install* phase is how you install GIMP after you've built it. If you're installing to a system directory, as is usually the case (though you can override that with `configure --prefix`, as discussed previously), you'll probably need "root" or administrator privileges for this stage.

Then type `make install` and watch the messages scroll past. This will produce nearly as much output as the make phase did, but it will take a lot less time.

When make install finishes, you're ready to try out your new GIMP!

■ **Note** On some Linux systems, you may see error messages about libraries not found when you first run GIMP compiled from source. If that happens, try running the command `ldconfig` as root.

■ ■ ■

A Preview of GIMP 2.6

This book is based on GIMP 2.4. But software projects don't stand still, and as the second edition goes to press, GIMP 2.5 is being built into what will eventually become the GIMP 2.6 release.

Although there's no telling what else might change, here is a preview of some of the important differences you're likely to see in GIMP 2.6. You can get a look at them yourself by downloading one of the experimental 2.5 builds (but be warned: not all the bugs have been squashed yet). Among the important differences are

- No more Toolbox menus (and the new "no image" window)

- The improved Free/Polygonal Select (Lasso Select) tool

- GEGL (the Generic Graphics Library)

- Color tool improvements

- "Brush Dynamics" for painting

- Text tool wrapping

No More Toolbox Menus

The first difference you'll notice when you start GIMP 2.5: the Toolbox menus are gone. There's no more *Xtns* menu.

So what about all those plug-ins that you're used to calling up from the *Xtns* menu—the Script-Fu and Python menus, the Plug-in and Procedure Browsers, the Logo scripts, the Patterns and Web Page Themes, and the Sphere? Where should you look for them?

The Script-Fu and Python menus, including *Refresh Scripts*, have moved to the *Filters* menu. The Plug-in and Procedure Browsers are in *Help*. Most of the rest of the Toolbox menus—the operations that create new image windows—have moved to the *File* ➤ *New* submenu of the image window.

Wait a minute—what if you've just started GIMP and there isn't an image window yet?

That's the other difference you'll notice: GIMP 2.5 *always* has an image window. If you start it without specifying any images, GIMP will display the "no image" window, basically an image window with no image (and with many of the menu items grayed out).

You can drag images into the no image window to open them, or you can use *File* ➤ *New…*, which works as it always has. But the *File* ➤ *New* submenu (Figure D-1) offers all the scripts and plug-ins you're used to seeing in the Toolbox's *Xtns* menu, plus some items from the Toolbox's *File* menu, such as *Screenshot…* and an *Acquire* menu for scanners, if you have one. (You may be wondering about the two different items marked *File* ➤ *New* in GIMP 2.5. With any luck, one of them will get a new name by the time 2.6 is released.)

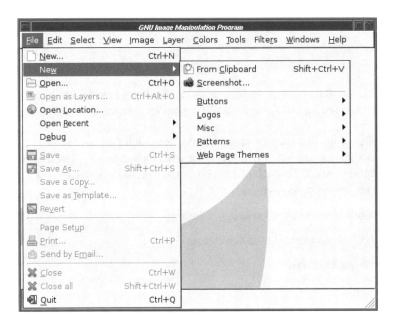

Figure D-1. *The File* ➤ *New submenu*

The *Dialogs* menu has moved to *Windows* ➤ *Dockable Dialogs*. But *Windows* has some other very useful entries, like an entry for each image window you currently have open. It also has entries for the Toolbox and for any open dialog docks, so you can hide those windows and only call them up when you need them. And don't miss *Windows* ➤ *Recently Closed Docks*. Remember I mentioned in Chapter 1 that once you close a set of docked dialogs (like the one that opens automatically the very first time you start GIMP), there's no way to get it back? Now there is.

The Improved Free/Polygonal Select Tool

One of 2.5's best improvements is the new Lasso Select tool. It still offers the same free selection as the old Lasso tool—drag anywhere in the image to draw arbitrary shapes. But it also offers a *polygonal* selection mode: click at points in the image to connect the dots, just as you would with the Paths tool. Best of all, there's no mode selector in its tool options; it draws free selections or straight lines based entirely on whether you're dragging or clicking. You can mix the two modes as much as you like, using free select for parts of your selection and straight lines for other parts (Figure D-2).

Figure D-2. *The new Lasso Select tool lets you combine free and polygonal segments in the same selection.*

You can even go back and move polygonal points to other places. When you've finished, click on the point where you started to end your selection. You're done!

GEGL

One of the biggest changes in 2.5 isn't visible in the user interface: it's GEGL.

What's GEGL? It's the Generic Graphics Library (*http://gegl.org*), the long-awaited new back-end library for GIMP. Instead of the 32-bit color used in GIMP 2.4 and earlier, GEGL does its calculations in floating point, so it can handle the high color depths that come from high-end scanners or raw format images from digital cameras.

That doesn't mean GIMP 2.5 fully handles high color depth operations—at least not yet. It just means that for some GIMP operations, users who want to experiment with GEGL can do so. More GEGL support will be added as GIMP moves toward 2.8.

You can also use the GEGL tool—*Tools* ➤ *GEGL Operation...*—to experiment with some of the fancy operations GEGL offers.

Color Tool Improvements

Aside from GEGL on the back end, there are a few user-visible changes in the color tools. Ever wondered how Brightness-Contrast, Levels, and Curves (Chapter 2) relate to one another? The Brightness-Contrast tool now sports a button that lets you *Edit these Settings as Levels*. Click the button and you're taken to the Levels dialog, preloaded with settings equivalent to what you had set in Brightness-Contrast. Even better, the Levels dialog gives you the chance to *Edit these Settings as Curves*. You can't go back the other way, though: Levels is more complicated than Brightness-Contrast, so you can't take a Levels setting and show it in terms of just brightness and contrast, and likewise, Curves is more complicated than Levels.

Brush Dynamics

GIMP's drawing tools (the pencil, paintbrush, and so forth) get some new flexibility in 2.5 with *Brush Dynamics* (Figure D-3). You can vary four aspects of the line—*Opacity*, *Hardness* (of the brush's edge), *Size* (the width of the stroke), and *Color* (currently, that jumps between the foreground and background color)—according to *Pressure* (if you have a drawing tablet), *Velocity* (how fast you make your stroke), or at *Random*. The triangles to the right of each collection of checkboxes pop up a slider to let you adjust the strength of each effect.

Figure D-3. *The Brush Dynamics options*

There's also a related option of interest: when you choose *Stroke Path* or *Stroke Selection* using one of the paint tools, you can enable an option called *Emulate brush dynamics.* This helps you achieve a number of useful effects: for example, if you stroke a path with the Paintbrush tool, enable *Emulate brush dynamics,* and set the Paintbrush tool's *Brush dynamics* options to vary *Size* with *Pressure,* you'll get a line that's thick in the middle and tapers to a point on either end. Very nice, and there's no other easy way to get this effect in GIMP.

Text Tool Wrapping

GIMP's Text tool is being revised. The big changes probably won't appear until GIMP 2.8, but in 2.6 you'll see one very useful change: wrapping.

As you type in your text, the tool will draw a rectangle with resize handles around it. You can drag those resize handles—just like those in the Rectangle Select tool—to define the size of the text box. GIMP will then wrap your text to fit in the box. You can change the box size at any time and the text will rewrap to fit the dimensions of your new box.

Other Changes

A few other useful changes coming in GIMP 2.5 include

- More space around the canvas in the image window—it's now possible to make a selection that extends off the edges of the current image boundaries (this will be especially helpful with the Perspective and Perspective Clone tools).

- Transparency for the transform tools (Rotate, Scale, Perspective, and so on)—now you can make a layer partially transparent and see what's under it while you rotate it or change its perspective.

- Better control of rulers and guides.

- If you accidentally close a set of docked dialogs, you can get them back with *Recently Closed Docks.*

- Better quality when scaling.

- Better "remote" functionality on all platforms—if you use GIMP to open an image when you already have GIMP running, you won't get a second instance any more.

- Integration with the online user manual.

- Improved Python APIs.

GIMP 2.5's changes may be mostly "under the hood," like the GEGL library, but there are still plenty of user-visible changes we can look forward to in 2.6.

Index

You Need the Companion eBook

Your purchase of this book entitles you to buy the companion PDF-version eBook for only $10. Take the weightless companion with you anywhere.

We believe this Apress title will prove so indispensable that you'll want to carry it with you everywhere, which is why we are offering the companion eBook (in PDF format) for $10 to customers who purchase this book now. Convenient and fully searchable, the PDF version of any content-rich, page-heavy Apress book makes a valuable addition to your programming library. You can easily find and copy code—or perform examples by quickly toggling between instructions and the application. Even simultaneously tackling a donut, diet soda, and complex code becomes simplified with hands-free eBooks!

Once you purchase your book, getting the $10 companion eBook is simple:

❶ Visit **www.apress.com/promo/tendollars/**.

❷ Complete a basic registration form to receive a randomly generated question about this title.

❸ Answer the question correctly in 60 seconds, and you will receive a promotional code to redeem for the $10.00 eBook.

THE EXPERT'S VOICE™

2855 TELEGRAPH AVENUE | SUITE 600 | BERKELEY, CA 94705

Offer valid through 06/09.

Printed in the United States
by Baker & Taylor Publisher Services